Globalization and Survival
in the
Black Diaspora

SUNY Series in
Afro-American Studies

John Howard and Robert C. Smith, editors

**Edited by
Charles Green**

Globalization and Survival
in the
Black Diaspora

The New Urban Challenge

STATE UNIVERSITY OF NEW YORK PRESS

Production by Ruth Fisher
Marketing by Nancy Farrell

Published by
State University of New York Press, Albany

© 1997 State University of New York

For information, address the State University of New York Press, State University Plaza, Albany, NY 12246

Library of Congress Cataloging-in-Publication Data
Green, Charles (Charles St. Clair)
    Globalization and survival in the Black diaspora : the new urban challenge / Charles Green.
        p.   cm. — (SUNY series in Afro-American studies)
    Includes bibliographical references and index.
    ISBN 0-7914-3415-X (alk. paper). — ISBN 0-7914-3416-8 (pbk. : alk. paper)
    1. Blacks—Social conditions.   2. Blacks—Economic conditions.
    3. Poverty.   4. Urbanization.   I. Title.   II. Series.
    HT1581.G694   1997
    305.8'96—dc20   96-41495
                                                               CIP

10 9 8 7 6 5 4 3 2 1

In memory of
Dr. Wilfred G. Cartey
a son of Trinidad and Tobago, a scholar, a dear friend

Contents

Preface

In the spring of 1989, while preparing my syllabus for a course on social change in developing societies at Hunter College, several prospective students (who happened to be African-American and from inner-city New York) approached me with their concern to have comparative data on the plight of urban Blacks outside of the United States integrated in the syllabus under the section on Urbanization and the Third World. At once I began a review of the literature and was startled that I could not identify a single work that analyzed and compared the Black urban condition across the diaspora.

The following year I left for Tanzania on a Fulbright, where I lectured in the Department of Sociology at the University of Dar es Salaam. Through my active participation on the Urban Project which was housed in the Department of Sociology and the opportunity to work with a number of gifted scholars, I learned of the brewing urban crisis in that relatively stable East African state and the similarities between that crisis and the problems afflicting the inner cities all across the United States. In time I made contact with scholars and activists from other African states, from which arose the opportunity to observe and compare the urban condition in Lusaka, Zambia, Harare, Zimbabwe, Nairobi and Mombasa, Kenya, and Mbabne, Swaziland.

The event that solidified my decision to edit this volume occurred in May 1993, when I was invited by the Caribbean Students Association at York College (CUNY) to assist with planning a forum on

"Urbanism and the Black Diaspora: Facing the Challenge" and to serve as one of the panelists. The event was successful, with many of the participants expressing the need for further dialogue and scholarly activity around this important topic.

An extraordinary interdisciplinary group of scholars was assembled for this volume. They are specialists in their respective disciplines and the societies they cover. All of the essays, with the exception of Carolyn Somerville's "Reaction and Resistance: Confronting Economic Crisis, Structural Adjustment, and Devaluation in Dakar, Senegal" and Loïc J.D. Wacquant's "Urban Outcasts: Stigma and Division in the Black American Ghetto and the French Urban Periphery," were originally prepared for this volume.

The authors were given a free hand to develop their ideas and positions with one condition, that they not compromise objectivity. Thus, in reading this collection of essays the reader will observe the authors' ability to strike a balance between their identification with the victims and their plight on the one hand and their commitment to accurately present the facts on the other. In adopting the structural approach to the problem of urban poverty, the authors maintain a critical eye on the economic and political forces that persist in subjugating the poor and working classes. It is because of this approach and their confidence in the urban poor and their leaders to struggle for a better life that feelings of optimism and hope for the future permeate the volume.

At this juncture of rapid global economic and social transformation, identifying long-term solutions for the victims at the bottom, in this case Black urban sufferers, is a major challenge for all of us. It is our hope that this work will be envisaged as an advocate for change and to the extent that it can levitate its readers in that direction, it will give us all a reason to celebrate the dawn of a new millennium.

Acknowledgments

Without the support and encouragement of a number of people this project, which began in the summer of 1993, might not have been completed. At the earliest stage I consulted several scholars and activists about prospective contributors to the volume and its organization. Among them were Rod Thurton, Selwyn McLean, Ewart Bertete, Ivelaw Griffith (Florida International University), Juan Flores (The Center For Puerto Rican Studies, CUNY), Elena Cervallos (Hofstra University), Rhoda Reddock (University of the West Indies, St. Augustine Campus), George Priestley (Queens College), Carl James (York University), and Basil Wilson (John Jay College of Criminal Justice). I am grateful to Roberta Kilkenny, Trevor Grant, Calvin Holder (The College of Staten Island), and Robert Knox (New College of USF), who read and commented on various sections of this manuscript.

I am indebted to The PSC-CUNY Research Award Program and New College of the University of South Florida Foundation for assistance with travel expenses, manuscript preparation, and the services of my principal research assistant, Sebastian Canon. A bundle of thanks goes out to Neil Israel, Jenny Smitha, and Charlene Seaman for their technical assistance in the initial manuscript preparation.

Last but not least, I am grateful to my family for their patience during the many hours I spent away from home working late at the office to ensure the timely completion of this book.

ACKNOWLEDGMENTS

The editor is grateful to the following publishers and organizations for permission to reprint material from their works:

Greenwood Publishing Group, for permission to reprint Carolyn Somerville, "The Impact of the Reforms on the Urban Population of Senegal: How the Dakarois View the Crisis," from *The Political Economy of Structural Adjustment in Senegal*, ed. Chris Delgado and Sidi Jammeh (New York: Praeger, 1991), pp. 151–171, as Chapter 1 in this book. Praeger is an imprint of the Greenwood Publishing Group, Inc., Westport, Conn.

Blackwell Publishers Ltd., for permission to reprint Loïc J. D. Wacquant, "Urban Outcasts: Stigma and Division in the Black American Ghetto and the French Urban Periphery," *International Journal of Urban and Regional Research* 17 (1993): 366–383, as Chapter 15 in this book.

Nota Publishing, Inc., for permission to reprint lyrics from the song "Me levanto los domingos" (*Sin Parar*, 1994), by Wisco G., in Chapter 5 of this book.

Prime Entertainment for permission to reprint portions of the songs "Pal Cruse" (*Prime Underground*, 1994), by Falo; "Yo quiero" (*Rub-a-Dub Style*, 1992), by Brewley M.C.; and "El filósofo" (*Misión: La Cima*, 1990), by Vico C, in Chapter 5 of this book.

Charles Green

Introduction

Globalization, Challenge, and the Black Diaspora

This book is about the processes of globalization and urbanization and their impact on persons of African descent on the African continent and beyond. Economic globalization, which refers to trade and commerce between nations, is rooted in history. Current globalization trends differ from the past mainly in terms of scale and the negative impact upon significant sectors of the world's population (Mander and Goldsmith 1996). A leading argument that is developed is that as globalization accelerates, the definition of urban space and, too, the nature of the response by urban masses to their present challenge are consequently being altered.

The idea of the urban challenge and the need to address it is not a recent theme. The early industrial cities of Europe and the United States were mean streets that presented a host of challenges to factory workers and their families. Issues of inadequate housing, hazardous work conditions, and labor exploitation were prevalent. For the vast majority of European immigrants who constituted the bulk of the American proletariat at that time, it was all of these combined with the difficulties of adapting to a strange environment and learning a new language. Karl Marx, one of the most prolific social philosophers to emerge in the nineteenth century, devoted a good portion of his life to unravelling these conditions and to restructuring society on behalf of the laboring proletariat. In the midst of that great social and economic transition,

1

sociology was born. Sociology's special contribution would be to advocate for social change through the systematic analysis of society that emphasized the study of those forces that held societies together and those that triggered change.

During the nineteenth century, the socio-cultural and political landscape of the cities and towns in regions we now refer to as "The Third World" was quite different. The people who inhabited these societies were still very much bound to the land and their ethnic cultures. Politically, a number of these societies were still colonized, with their cities serving the immediate interests of their colonial protectors in having major ports, retail outlets, and administrative centers. However, political independence for the peoples of the Caribbean, Africa, and Latin America[1] did little to change the subordinate status of their cities in the world system. Activist historian Walter Rodney understood the new role of the former colonial powers in the succeeding phase of neo-colonialism. He did not fail to overlook the puppet role adopted by many heads of state in the former colonies, which has contributed to their persistent dependency and underdevelopment. With a focus on Africa, but with implications for the rest of the developing world, Rodney observed:

> The importance of this group [political puppets] cannot be underestimated. The presence of a group of African sellouts is part of the definition of underdevelopment. Any diagnosis of underdevelopment in Africa will reveal not just low per capita income and protein deficiencies but also the gentlemen who dance in Abijan, Accra, and Kinshasa when music is played in Paris, London, and New York. (1982:27)

In the advanced societies, rapid industrialization, mechanization, and modernization were accompanied by the downsizing of their agrarian labor sectors and, hence, the rise of more towns, cities, and urban masses. In the contemporary United States, less than five percent of the labor force is engaged in farming and related activities. This is also true for other advanced industrial countries.

 The majority of the world's population today is urbanized, residing in mega cities, mid-size cities, and suburban areas. The United Nations Population Growth projections indicate that the level of urbanization for the world as a whole is expected to increase to 51 percent by the year 2000 and 65 percent by the year 2025. But it is in the less developed regions of the world that the growth factor has had the greatest impact. While the projected growth rate for the advanced regions for the year 2000 and 2025 is 45 percent and 61 percent respectively, for the less developed regions the projection is 75 percent by the year 2000 and 83 percent by the year 2025 (U.N. 1990:7–16). Moreover, by the year 2000 seventeen of the world's twenty largest cities will be in less developed countries and of the seven mega cities with a population of fifteen million or more, five will be in developing countries. Two of these are expected to be in Latin America, Mexico City and São Paulo (Gugler 1988; Gilbert and Gugler 1993).

For a significant portion of the developing world, increased urbanization has been the end product of foreign capital expansion that has taken the form of offshore assembly operations and manufacturing in those regions. Low-wage jobs have served as the catalyst for rural folk from the countryside, who were already experiencing land displacement and losses due to food importation and substitution policies, to venture into the urban areas.

A late-twentieth-century social and economic transformation is in progress. Urbanization was an outgrowth of the Industrial Revolution. It is not surprising therefore to find urban areas in the eye of this late-twentieth-century storm. In the present era, commonly referred to by such phrases as "the new information age," "the information superhighway," and the "the age of cyberspace," knowledge is the key resource. Some manual skills are required, but an abundance of theory and education are quintessential (Toffler 1980; Reich 1991a, 1991b; Kennedy 1993; Drucker 1994). In the introduction to their controversial new book, *The Bell Curve*, authors Richard Herrnstein and Charles Murray state:

> In our time, the ability to use and manipulate information has become the single most important element of success, no matter how you measure it: financial security, power, or status. Those who work by manipulating ideas and abstractions are the leaders and beneficiaries of our society. In such an era, high intelligence is an increasingly precious raw material for success. (1994:1)

It should be pointed out that what is controversial about Herrnstein and Murray's study is not their observation that a cognitive elite is rapidly emerging as the hegemonic class in American society, but their inference that those who lack intellectual savvy, whatever the reasons, suffer a misfortune of life whose amelioration should not be the preoccupation of government or its policies.

This knowledge-based cultural transformation is a major source of the contemporary urban crisis in the developed regions. The Industrial Revolution shifted the rural peasantry from the land and forced them to adapt to a new way of life in urban areas. There was ample work for those with limited skills who were willing to adjust and work hard. In nineteenth-century United States, unprecedented numbers of Europeans were admitted into the country to fill the demand for industrial jobs that required mostly entry-level skills. There was, however, a ready supply of Black labor that lay idle in the southern region; but due to naked racism, they were bypassed in favor of immigrant whites. Their turn to occupy industrial jobs and real wages would not come until World War I when the U.S. industrial complex was threatened by the temporary halt to European workers.

At this historical juncture, the broad industrial and manufacturing base that attracted low-skilled labor is in decline in the developed world. Replacing that base are newer service sector positions that range from very low to mid to highly skilled technical jobs (Aronowitz and DiFazio 1994). One visible consequence of this for the United States is the increasing number of predominantly Black residents who are presently isolated in the once-productive industrial centers (Bluestone and Harrison 1982; Wilson 1987; Wacquant 1989). Racism and classism, requisites of the American capitalist state, have eclipsed their chances of meeting the latest labor requirements of adequate educational preparation, technical skills, and a positive work ethic. The situation has given rise to a stream of frustrated, rebellious young people who in their struggle to survive oppression are defining new coping strategies—not uncommonly perceived as threatening by the wider society. The term "urban underclass,"[2] an invention of social scientists, journalists, and legislators, was specifically developed to describe this entrapped population.

The less developed regions whose stability is inextricably linked to the policies of the "G–7" nations[3] are directly affected by the current upheaval. The plight of their urban poor and working classes in many respects parallels the turbulence now observed in the more advanced regions. Human redundancy and unemployment, the influence of informal sector activities, the menace of a drug subculture, street crime, restlessness among youths, and the severing of traditional cultural values are manifestations of the global urban crisis. Across the regions the crisis is exacerbated either by the state's reluctance to respond or the bankrupt nature of implemented state policies. In Brazil, for example, death squads have assumed an official role in containing that country's street children crisis. In the United States, the prevailing response is to hire more police and build more prisons. In the wake of an outbreak of serious crime in Trinidad and Tobago, a bill was recently introduced to limit bail release for that nation's most serious criminal offenders.

Manuel Castells's critique of the urban crisis is instructive at this point. In his examination of the "urban question" (formulated as the urban crisis), specifically as it relates to developed societies such as the United States and Britain, he stresses the need to distinguish ideology from reality. For Castells, the notion of urban crisis is an ideological construct of the dominant classes in society that requires demystification (Castells 1980: 1–8; 379–429).

Urban Blacks in the diaspora provide a compelling case study. In the Anglo, Dutch, and Franco Caribbean and in certain Latin American countries, Black people and mixtures of African, European, and native Indian—mestizo and mulatto people—constitute a majority of the population. In developed societies such as the United States, Canada, the United Kingdom, and France, where Black people constitute a critical mass, they tend to be concentrated in the inner cities. Their migration to the cities and towns in the United States was the result of internal capital exploitation. That commenced at the point of World War I when scores of African Americans were encouraged to abandon their agrarian life style in the South and head mainly to northern cities where industrial jobs were in great supply.[4] In Britain and France, it was the case of colonial and, in the post-independence period, former colonial subjects immigrating to the mainland with the hope of finding a better life for themselves and their families. In the developing regions, Black urbanization was largely the effect of foreign capital expansion.

It is important to keep in mind that the contemporary Black urban plight is a historical reality that is linked to their history of racial subjugation and exploitation throughout the world, which has been exacerbated by the present global economic transformation. Race, therefore, is an important factor in explaining the Black urban condition in the diaspora with observed differences based on such aspects as the colonial legacy, and the existing ethno-racial mix. For example, whereas in the United States a classificatory system of race prevails (i.e., racial shading among minority Blacks is not recognized, instead white and black phenotypes are recognized), in the anglophone Caribbean and Latin America, race is a more complicated matter. In the Caribbean and Latin America, a system of racial shading is recognized, but it is one's class (i.e., social background, education, economic position) that determines one's mobility in the social structure. Patterson (1972) has described the system for the Caribbean as continuous denotative in which majority Blacks and the minority whites are included alongside each other. The system in Latin America resembles the United States in that although racial shading exists, the white descendants of Europeans are ascribed a status of privilege above and beyond the other racial categories. He describes that as a discontinuous denotative system.

This book is a collection of essays that examines the specific ways in which the present global urban crisis has impacted and continues to impact Blacks cross-culturally. Most importantly, it examines the different strategies they have adopted to cope with the present challenge. The contributors analyze an array of problems that confront urban poor and working-class people in select societies. Their analyses are accompanied by thought-provoking recommendations for change.

The investigation covers five regions of the world where there is a significant Black presence. These include the developing regions of the anglophone Caribbean, Latin America, and sub-Saharan Africa. They are considered alongside the developed regions of North America and Europe. Up to now, the tendency has been to focus on the problems of urban Blacks either regionally or country by country.[5] Consequently, there is an absence of studies that have examined, in a single volume, the common and distinct aspects of the urban crisis across the Black diaspora. Not only will this approach strengthen the case for the global Black plight and the need to address it, it will contribute to the ongoing discourse concerning the immediate and long-term solutions. Needless to say, an important void will be filled in the literature on development and urbanism.

Two important methodological footnotes are necessary at this point. The first concerns the inclusion of sub-Saharan Africa. Recognizing Africa at the center of the Black diaspora, it is possible that its inclusion here may appear misleading or even superfluous. To the contrary, the inclusion of Africa is viewed as critical to the overall analysis. The immiseration and powerlessness of Blacks on the continent lends support to the argument that their crisis is entrenched. Another way of expressing this is to say that whether the analysis begins from Africa outward or from outside Africa, the precarious situation of Black people is a daunting reality. As well, questions may loom about the inclusion of two East African states, namely Tanzania and Kenya. Briefly, these neighboring states followed opposite political paths in the immediate post-independence period. Tanzania chose to walk the nationalist-socialist path while Kenya pursued closer ties to the West, chiefly the United States and Britain. Not only does their inclusion here provide compelling comparative data on the declining urban condition in East Africa— a region that is not adequately addressed compared to western and southern Africa—it calls to question the thesis put forth by modernization theorists that close linkages with advanced economies is a prerequisite for Third World development.

The second footnote concerns the conceptualization of commonalities and differences of the urban crisis across the diaspora. In the present global economy, societies have become more interlinked than ever before. Technology and new age communications systems have dramatically affected the pace of cultural diffusion or homogenization. Consequently, the perception of the world as a small place surfaces as life styles, dress codes, patterns of behavior, and the social problems people experience across continents seem to converge. In this atmosphere Black inner-city areas such as New York City, Kingston, Jamaica, or Liverpool, England, appear indiscriminable. This was a profound observation during my

recent visit to Leyou, St. Vincent, a small village located just outside the central city of Kingstown. Without incident, one evening
my companion, a retired Vincentian man, and I came face to face
with five teenage males whose demeanor was menacing. Their
dress style including large gold necklaces, hair styles, and body
language led me to doubt for that brief moment that I was actually
on the small eastern Caribbean island and not in one of New York
City's Black urban districts. But one must be reminded, as Gilbert
and Gugler (1993) point out in their comparison of urban cities
across continents, that despite stark similarities, economic and cultural differences exist between and among societies that temper
the cultural homogenization thesis.

Our analysis begins in Africa, the center of the diaspora. Essays
by Carolyn Somerville on urban reforms in Dakar, Senegal; Joe
L. P. Lugalla on Tanzania's changing urbanism; and Kinuthia Macharia on Nairobi's informal economy provide us the opportunity to
examine and compare the challenge confronting urban Blacks on
the West and East corridors of Africa. Moreover, they make us
aware that Senegal, Tanzania, and Kenya are only the tip of the
iceberg and that the crisis is pervasive across the continent.

Where racism is implied throughout the essays on Latin America and the Caribbean, the effects of political and economic instability on the urban masses in these regions are explicit. In his
analysis of the crisis of Black Panamanians, George Priestley
underscores a history of military and political intervention in the
internal affairs of Panama—most recently the U.S. invasion on December 20, 1989. The interventionist argument is encountered as
well in Raquel Z. Rivera's analysis of "rap" music among poor urban youth in San Juan and other cities of Puerto Rico. Rivera
forces us to look squarely at United States colonial policy and to
ask why after years of occupation by the world's wealthiest and
most ardent proponent of democracy, Puerto Rico's urban masses
remain poor and marignalized. Focusing more on domestic political
affairs, Esther I. Madriz uncovers some of the contradictions of
state neo-liberal policies and the impact on the continued suffering
of the Black and mestizo urban masses of Caracas, Venezuela.
Vânia Penha-Lopes' essay targets state neglect and racism as co-
conspirers in the violence and abuse being waged against mainly
Black and mixed-race children in Brazil's major cities.

Drawing attention to the urban dislocation in Trinidad and Tobago, my essay links the regional crisis to the larger issue of cultural and economic strangulation by dominant foreign powers and
calls for a new analytical approach. Obika Gray and Joyce Toney
continue the critique of the impact of external political and economic policies on the poor in their analyses of politically motivated
gang violence in Kingston, Jamaica, and the crisis confronting urban women and their households in St. Vincent, respectively.

Considered next are the industrial, developed regions of North
America and Europe. Although the problems associated with youth
are reflected throughout the volume, this issue is singularly addressed in North America where inner-city youth are felt to be out
of control. Gerald Horne's lead essay, "The Political Economy of the
Black Urban Future: A History," with the city of Los Angeles, California, serving as a backdrop, gives us a historical overview and
analysis of the Black condition across the United States. Essays by
Kevin Arlyck and Kwando M. Kinshasa examine the matter of
youth violence and rebelliousness and the rap genre as responses
to racial and class oppression in the urban trenches.

Due to the dominant role played by the United States in the
geopolitics of the region, the perception of Canada for many Americans is that of a stepchild of the United States or a geographic
extension of the United States. The truth is that Americans know
very little about their neighbors to the north. The fact that Canada's population of approximately twenty-eight million includes a
sizable urban Black population whose struggle against racism and
other destabilizing conditions has a long history, is a well-kept secret. Carl E. James's essay, "The Distorted Images of African-Ca-
nadians: Impact, Implications and Responses," is an important addition to this section as it provides a comparative glance at the
state of Black civil society in the racially divided city of Toronto.

Finally, turning to Europe, Stephen Small carefully analyzes the
history and the future of the Black condition in Britain's most troubled
cities. By juxtaposing the French urban periphery and the Black
American ghetto, Loïc J. D. Wacquant offers us critical insight into
the unique structuring of the French capital. Taken together,
Small and Wacquant draw our attention to the persistence of race
and class marginalization among Afro-Europeans.

We hope that this volume will assist its readers in dispelling the myth of African Americans as "privileged" Blacks by virtue of their residence in the world's wealthiest nation. As these essays inform us, in a rapidly changing global landscape where race and class prevail, people of African descent in every corner of the diaspora remain perpheralized. The challenge, therefore, for activists, progressive leaders, heads of state, and policy engineers for the next century whose resolve it is to uplift the race, will be to find common ground. That will demand that they identify those positive forces that presently unite and strengthen Black people and more urgently, those forces that threaten to keep them subjugated and divided as a people.

Appreciating the fact of societal and cultural differences, no attempt has been made here to advance a generic formula that would neatly satisfy the needs of every country. We do, however, present in the conclusion some of our ideas about how to work together for the common good.

Experience has taught us that policy recommendations for change are beneficial insofar as they are seriously considered and can be implemented. Experience has also taught us that the task of organizing for change should not be monopolized by scholars and other assumed experts. We recognize that creating an atmosphere that would encourage participation by the urban poor in the ongoing debate is the only way to move forward. It is our hope that the recommendations that emerge from this volume will ignite a new and broadly participated debate on how to bring about constructive change for diasporic Blacks and all people living at the edge in the urban trenches around the world.

NOTES

1. Most Latin American societies gained their independence by 1830. See: Gilbert, Alan and Gugler, Josef, *Cities, Poverty and Development: Urbanization in the Third World.* New York: Oxford University Press, 1993, p.19.

2. A number of scholars disagree with this term. They see it as just another victim blaming ploy invented by the elite class. See for example: Herbert Gans, "The Dangers of the Underclass: Its Harmfulness as a Planning Concept" (a marvelous essay by Gans taken from a collection of his greatest essays entitled, *People, Plans and Policies.* New York: Columbia

University Press); Stephen Steinberg, "The Underclass: A Case of Color-
blindness," *New Politics*. Vol. 2 (Summer 1988); Michael B. Katz (ed.), *The
Underclass Debate: A View From History*. Princeton: Princeton University
Press, 1993.

3. The "G-7" refers to the seven wealthiest industrial countries in the
world: United States, Canada, Japan, Germany, Britain, France, and Italy.
For a clear description of this group and their relationship to the global
economy see Noam Chomsky, *The Prosperous Few And The Restless Many*.
Berkeley: Odonian Press, 1985.

4. This was the start of the greatest internal migration of people in
history. For an expanded discussion of this historical experience, see for
example: Nicholas Lemann, *The Promised Land*. New York: Vintage, 1991;
Jacqueline Jones, "Southern Diaspora: The Origins of the Northern Underclass," in Michael Katz (ed.), *The Underclass Debate: Views From History*.
Princeton: Princeton University Press, 1993.

5. So many studies can be cited that focus on the crisis either regionally
or from the perspective of single nations. Recent among them are: Richard
Stren, *African Cities in Crisis*. Boulder: Westview Press, 1989; Joe Lugalla,
*Crisis, Urbanization And Urban Poverty In Tanzania: A Study of Urban
Poverty and Survival Politics*. Lanham, Maryland: University Press of
America, 1995; Ambursley and Cohen (eds.), *Crisis in the Caribbean*. New
York: Monthly Review Press, 1983; Charles Green and Basil Wilson, *The
Struggle For Black Empowerment In New York City*. New York: Praeger,
1989; William J. Wilson, *The Truly Disadvantaged*. Chicago: University of
Chicago Press, 1987; Elijah Anderson, *Street Wise: Race, Class and Change
in an Urban Community*. Chicago: University of Chicago Press, 1990.

——————————— REFERENCES ———————————

Aronowitz, Stanley and William DiFazio. 1994. *The Jobless Future: Sci-
    Tech and the Dogma of Work*. Minneapolis: University of Minne-
    sota Press.

Bluestone, Barry and Bennett Harrison. 1982. *The Deindustrialization of
    America*. New York: Basic Books.

Castells, Manuel. 1980. *The Urban Question: A Marxist Approach*. Cam-
    bridge, Mass.: MIT.

Drucker, Peter F. 1994. "The Age of Social Transformation." *The Atlantic
    Monthly* (November).

Gans, Herbert. 1991. *People, Plans And Policies*. New York: Columbia Uni-
    versity Press.

Gilbert, Alan, and Josef Gugler. 1993. *Cities, Poverty And Development:*

Urbanization in the Third World. New York: Oxford University Press.

Gugler, Josef (ed.). 1988. The Urbanization of The Third World. New York: Oxford University Press.

Herrnstein, Richard J. and Charles Murray. 1994. *The Bell Curve*. New York: Free Press.

Kennedy, Paul. 1993. *Preparing for the Twenty-first Century*. New York: Random House.

Mander, Jerry and Edward Goldsmith (eds.). 1996. *The Case Against the Global Economy: And For A Turn Toward The Local*. San Francisco, CA.: Sierra Club Books.

Patterson, Orlando. 1972. "Toward a Future that Has No Past: Reflections on the fate of Blacks in the Americas." *Public Interest* (27).

Reich, Robert B. 1991. *The Work of Nations: Preparing Ourselves for 21st Century Capitalism*. New York: Knopf.

———. 1991b. "Secession of the Successful". *New York Times Magazine* (January 20).

Rodney, Walter. 1982. *How Europe Underdeveloped Africa*. Washington, D.C.: Howard University Press.

Steinberg, Stephen. 1988. "The Underclass: A Case of Colorblindness." *New Politics* Vol. 2 (Summer).

Toffler, Alvin. 1980. *The Third Wave*. New York: Morrow.

United Nations Population Newsletter. December 1990. No. 50.

Wacquant, Loic J.D. 1993. "The Return of the Repressed: Urban Violence, Race, And Dualization In Three Advanced Societies." (Russell Sage Foundation).

Wilson, William J. 1987. *The Truly Disadvantaged*. Chicago: University of Chicago Press.

Part One

AFRICA

Carolyn Somerville

1

Reaction and Resistance

Confronting Economic Crisis, Structural Adjustment, and Devaluation in Dakar, Senegal

On many of New York City's major streets and avenues are rows of men (and an increasing number of women) selling items ranging from music to musk oil and from socks to sweat shirts. A good number of New York's illegal sidewalk hawkers are from the small West African nation of Senegal. Officially, 2,500 Senegalese make their home in New York City.[1] In the past, Senegalese looking for opportunities would migrate to the former metropolis, France. But, now, due to the fever pitch of anti-immigrant sentiment among the French and the limited economic and job opportunities available in Europe, the United States has become the country of preference for Senegalese. What brings the Senegalese to the United States? In part, the economic crisis in Senegal created by years of drought, economic mismanagement, official corruption, falling revenues and declining demand for the principle export crop (groundnuts), and the social and economic consequences of painful structural adjust-

Previously published as Carolyn M. Somerville, "The Impact of the Reforms on the Urban Population of Senegal: How the Dakarois View the Crisis," from *The Political Economy of Structural Adjustment in Senegal*, ed. Chris Delgado and Sidi Jammeh (New York: Praeger, 1991), pp. 151–71. Praeger is an imprint of the Greenwood Publishing Group, Inc., Westport, CT.

ment policies have made life in the capital city of Dakar and other urban areas unbearable and, increasingly, unsustainable.

This chapter examines how years of International Monetary Fund (IMF) imposed structural adjustment policies implemented to overcome a profound economic crisis have impacted on the urban population of Dakar and surrounding suburbs. Through survey analysis, I examine how the citizens of Dakar cope with the social and economic consequences of adjustment. As to be expected, reactions to the crisis and strategies to rise above the current economic malaise vary depending upon individual assessment of the problem and personal resources. But sensing that their government has abandoned them with a public policy of "every one for himself," the Senegalese are devising their own methods for coping with the crisis, including the growing trend of migration to the United States.

The Crisis and the Reform Policies

At the dawn of independence, the Senegalese economy was characterized by openness to the outside world and a lack of internal integration. Moreover, it was an economy little diversified—peanuts accounted for seventy-eight percent of total export receipts and took up more than fifty percent of all cultivated land. Peanuts, which played a predominant position in the well-being of the economy, made up at least twenty-five percent of the Gross Domestic Product (GDP) (Parti Socialisté du Sénégal 1985:18–19). This heavy dependence on a monocultural economy would haunt Senegal by 1968, with the beginning of recurrent droughts that lasted for the next sixteen years. During the first big drought (1968–1974), crop yields declined from 904 kilograms per hectare to 620 kilograms per hectare, resulting in the fall of export receipts to about 35 billion CFA in 1971 (*Ibid.*:16). As the economy went into a decline, peanuts—as a percentage of total exports—dropped from eighty to forty percent (*Ibid.*:17). A vicious circle ensued; as production dropped, so too did the prices paid to peasants, which fuelled declines in production.

Gradually, agriculture became a less viable means of productive activity. A strong rural exodus began, swelling the slums of Dakar and its environs. The decline in primary sector activity could not be overcome by any substantial growth in the secondary sector. For one thing, the majority of Senegalese industries were foreign owned. Independence had brought an end to economic integration under the Federation of French West African states. Before independence, French West Africa was a regionally integrated economic unit. Labor and capital could travel more freely across fluid borders. But with independence, other countries in the former French West Africa zone were keen on supporting their own indigenous business class through protectionist economic policies. The closing of West African markets to Senegalese businessmen contributed to a decline in private investment—from 13.6 percent of the GDP in the 1960s to a paltry 3.8 percent in the 1980s (*Ibid.*:14). No appeals could be made, in the name of national well-being or patriotism, to exert these foreign enterprises to expand operations and hire more Senegalese. For one thing, to the extent that there was industry, it was heavily protected; it was highly noncompetitive and costly. By the late 1970s, Senegalese industry was in no shape to pick up the economic slack left by the crisis in the primary sector.[2]

Senegal also encountered difficulties in savings and investment in the two decades following independence. After 1971, Senegal's investment ratio, a measurement of domestic investment as a percentage of GDP, stagnated. Simultaneously, GDP growth rates declined, and they were lower in the 1976–1981 period than ten years prior. The result was that investment effectiveness dropped. While the need for resources grew, domestic savings dropped from eight percent of the GDP in 1965 to three percent in 1983 (Club du Sahel 1986: 9). For the most part, what savings and investment did occur in the two decades after independence went into nonproductive activities. Little of it found its way to the rural sector.

At the same time, a number of government actions on behalf of the population only intensified and exacerbated the decline in the rural sector. To maintain urban peace, the government raised the minimum salaries of urban workers and subsidized the cost of basic necessities. Wheat and rice imports were sold at costs below that of locally produced cereals. Senegalese consumers soon preferred to purchase the imports, and the demand for local cereals dropped. Simultaneously, the prices paid to producers declined. As production fell throughout the latter half of the 1960s, urban and rural unrest increased. The government took steps to provide relief through the creation of public and parapublic investments. Aside from the creation of public enterprises, the government also became a major employer. By 1982, 61,000 people worked in the government and wages accounted for fifty percent of the state budget (West Africa 1983:1810).

The growth in government involvement in the economy through the creation of public and parapublic companies rose throughout the 1970s. By the 1980s, the government was the sole or majority owner of eighty-six of these entities and had minority participation in over 100 enterprises. These government-owned companies represented twenty percent of the modern sector GDP and employed 35,000 workers.

Initially, the parapublic enterprises delivered in terms of economic performance. The surpluses generated, however, soon turned into operation deficits with the decline in commodity prices and the return of drought in the late 1960s. Needless to say, the creation of these parastatals did not stem economic decline, but actually accentuated the problems. In addition, the public and parapublic enterprises themselves were plagued by a host of internal problems: mismanagement, inefficiency, and ill-defined objectives, to name a few. Rather than generate resources, they contributed to devouring scarce resources. In the end, the government was forced continually to bail out these non-performing enterprises. While the most notorious case is that of the Office National de Coopération et d'Assistance pour le Développement, known by its acronym ONCAD (with its total debt of $267 million U.S. dollars at the time of its dissolution in 1980), it was by no means the only non-performing enterprise. Between 1978 and 1983 roughly, thirty parapublic enterprises operated with deficits.

In addition to these internal factors, external factors contributed to Senegal's economic woes. Prices for Senegal's exports fluctuated heavily, while the price for its imports rose steadily. In 1974 and 1979, Senegal was hit by the oil price hikes. In 1977, oil imports took up 6.5 percent of export revenues, and by 1981 they accounted for thirty-one percent. Oil was not the only import to become more expensive. The taste transfer from locally-grown to imported foodstuffs, including wheat and rice, continued throughout the 1970s despite the fact that prices for these imports also rose. In 1972, one ton of wheat cost 22,000 CFA, and two years later the same ton cost 33,500 CFA, an increase of fifty percent (Parti Socialist du Sénégal 1985:21).

The combination of an over-bloated bureaucracy, growing wage bills, poorly performing enterprises, and a stagnating rural sector put the economy as a whole into a state of disequilibrium and chaos. The substantial and growing resource deficit was made up by borrowing externally. Taking advantage of the huge number of petrodollars in circulation during the mid-1970s, Senegal borrowed from private banks. Between 1974 and 1979, forty percent of its borrowing came from private banks at market rates (*Ibid.*:26). Senegal increased its dependence on foreign financial institutions and creditors. Unfortunately, the cost of borrowing grew onerous as interest rates increased and repayment terms stiffened. (See Table 1.1)

By 1978, Senegal found itself in a profound economic crisis that could no longer be ignored or dealt with in a business as usual manner. Clearly, continued foreign borrowing could not help Senegal overcome its growing resource gap, since the funds could not continue to pay for the deficits on the government's current and capital accounts. Basically, Senegal was not using this external capital to invest in the most productive endeavors.

Without a fundamental change in policy, Senegal's debt crisis would only continue to grow. With each increasing round of loans, resources available for productive investments shrank as more and

Table 1.1 Senegal's External Outstanding Debt and Debt Service (in millions of dollars)

	1980	1991
Total Outstanding External Debt	1,473	3,522
As a percentage of GNP	50.5	63.1
External Debt Service as a percentage of exports	28.7	19.9

Source: World Bank, *World Development Report 1993*. New York: Oxford University Press, 1993, pp. 278, 284.

more capital was needed to pay off the old accumulated debts. Eventually, the economy would have collapsed, causing tremendous political and social upheavals.

In 1979, Senegal signed the Medium-Term Economic and Financial Recovery Plan (PREF) with the IMF, and a structural adjustment loan (SAL) with the World Bank, to restore economic balance. These accords had two major objectives: first, to reduce the balance-of-payments and budgetary deficits; and second, to decrease the state's role in the economy through the reduction of the public and parapublic sectors (West Africa 1983:1809).

Soon it was evident Senegal could not meet the objectives of these programs, and a cancellation of the structural adjustment loans took place. Following their cancellation, other adjustment measures began. In 1981, 1982, and 1983, Senegal conducted debt rescheduling with the Paris Club. In 1984, debt rescheduling with the London Club was also concluded. Between 1980 and 1984, Senegal received a total of US$437.6 million in emergency financial resources to help ease the liquidity squeeze (Club du Sahel 1986:38). This amount included IMF standby agreements, Paris Club rescheduling, structural adjustment loans, cancellations of old loans and interest rate subsidies from the Fonds d'Aide et de Coopération de la République Française (FAC).

Some policy changes occurred under the 1980–1983 Extended Fund Facility agreement: current account expenditures slowed down, prices were raised on some basic foodstuffs, duties on imports rose, and taxes were raised on alcohol and kola nuts. Still, there remained more profound structural reforms to implement. A study of the 1980–1983 period showed that as external borrowing increased, so did consumption. For every dollar borrowed, national product grew by only twenty percent, while total consumption increased by more than seventy percent (Parti Socialiste du Sénégal 1985:73). As the drought returned in the early 1980s, the economic imbalances grew steadily worse. In 1983, the current account deficit still stood at US$354 million. The ratio of debt service to exports went from 2.9 percent in 1970 to 28.7 percent in 1980. Had conditions been allowed to continue, it is estimated that Senegal's outstanding debt as a percentage of GDP would have reached one hundred percent by 1995 (République du Sénégal 1984:61).

With the Senegalese presidential elections out of the way in the early part of 1983, the government undertook serious reform measures. A number of standby agreements were signed with the IMF, beginning in 1983, and more austere terms were imposed. The new medium-term structural adjustment plan implemented consisted of two parts—one covering the period 1985–1989 and the other 1989–1992.

The reforms called for far-reaching and wide-ranging changes in the way government and society had operated since independence. The social contract between the government and the population, established during the Senghor era was to be quickly dismantled. The reforms consisted of several elements: (1) the reduction of government expenditures; (2) the improvement of public sector management; (3) the development of the growth sectors; and (4) the mobilization of the domestic savings for investment. These reforms were elaborated by the New Agricultural Policy (NAP) and the New Industrial Policy (NIP) (Ministére du Développement Rural 1984).

To reduce government expenditures, the government was obligated to remove subsidies on food items. As a result, prices for staple food items rose dramatically with the implementation of the reforms.[3] Overall, the government moved to raise prices on previously subsidized items. Between 1980 and 1984, Senegalese consumers paid more for gasoline, imported vegetable oil, wheat flour, utilities, and transportation. These measures, referred to as a "policy of true pricing," aimed to synchronize domestic prices in line with world market costs. The purpose was to promote the production and consumption of local food products. The assumption is that if food imports become too expensive relative to local products, consumers will switch to locally grown foods.

A second measure undertaken to reduce government expenditures was to limit the growth of the civil service. Traditionally, the government guaranteed civil service jobs to all university graduates. Between 1975 and 1982, the civil service growth rate averaged six percent yearly. In agreement with the IMF, the government acquiesced to a growth rate of the civil service of 2.5 percent per annum. The government was to rein in the expansion of the civil service through a variety of measures: (1) making it more difficult to enroll in civil service schools; (2) imposing severe controls over recruitment into the civil service; (3) reducing the fringe benefits (e.g., housing and automobile entitlements); and (4) slowing down advancements and promotions. The government announced that it would cut the civil service from 67,000 to 45,000 employees over the course of the medium-term recovery plans through a combination of retrenchment and retirement.

The process of retrenchment began in 1980 with the demise of ONCAD, as its 5,000 employees were put out of work. Only 1,200 of these employees were hired to work for the Société Nationale d'Approvisionnement du Monde Rural (SONAR), a parapublic enterprise set up to perform ONCAD's role of distributing agricultural supplies and implements. SONAR and another rural development agency, Société des Terres Neuves (STN), were to have a short existence and were to have been phased out by 1985. Contrary to government pronouncements, they were still operating after the scheduled target date. Other agreements worked out with the IMF included government divestiture of nonessential enterprises in banking, tourism, and other commercial businesses. The government had hoped to divest two or three of these enterprises by the end of 1986. However, discussions over the process of negotiations and the terms of sale with prospective buyers entailed delays.

Although divestment was slow in materializing, cutbacks in staffing occurred more rapidly. Between 1981 and 1985, reliable figures on the number of employees laid off in both the public and private sectors were hard to come by. Estimates ranged from 5,000 to 20,000. A study of employment retrenchment for those years, carried out by the Direction of Employment, found that the majority of cutbacks occurred in manufacturing, building and public works, mechanical industries, and agribusiness (Ministére Fonction Publique de l'Emploi et du Travail, Direction de l'Emploi 1985: 3).

Another area of reforms was the passage of more liberal labor regulations and policies. Past labor policies limited employers' freedom to lay off workers. Employers were required by law to file papers requesting permission to do so. The requests were reviewed and then either approved or rejected by the government. Needless to say, the process, resented by employers, was burdensome, inefficient, and costly. With changes in labor laws leaning far more to the side of employers, the dictates of the market have begun to operate more freely. Now, employers have the flexibility to remove excess (or uncooperative) workers. The assumption is that more liberal measures will increase worker productivity. Combined with changes in the tax code designed to favor capital relative to labor, unemployment grows as businesses find it easier and more profitable to reduce labor costs through the introduction of machinery whenever possible.[4]

In sum, the recovery program aimed to liberalize and open up the Senegalese economy. The government hoped to re-dynamize and expand those sectors in which Senegal was thought to have a comparative advantage—agriculture, tourism, and fishing. Manufacturing industries that have little, if any, comparative advantage are losing their government subsidies and compensations. Local industry is being forced to compete with more efficient global industries through the elimination of export subsidies.

The government, too, is being forced by its international creditors to clean up its act. By 1983, all arrears owed to external creditors were paid off, after which the government began to turn its attention to paying off its internal arrears (amounting to thirty-six billion CFA in 1986).[5] In changing the way in which business was to be conducted, the government of Senegal accepted (in principle) being restricted to carrying out what the international financial institutions and creditors considered "legitimate government activities." Senegal's creditors pushed the government to cease activities considered redundant of private enterprise. This was to be accomplished with the sale of public enterprises as well as other measures outlined in the recovery program.

Evaluating Structural Adjustment in Senegal

According to World Bank assessments, Senegal's economic difficulties have abated somewhat since Senegal began adjusting its fiscal and monetary policies in line with the international donors' policy prescriptions. According to the Bank's report analyzing the turnaround in macroeconomic policies of twenty-six African countries, Senegal ranked fair in terms of having achieved "small improvement" in its macroeconomic policies (World Bank 1994:58).

Other authors have documented the positive effects of structural adjustment policies.[6] Adjustment policies have improved conditions in the rural areas, as peasants receive higher official producer prices for crops, which have spurred an increase in agricultural production and income (Weissman 1990:1627). Youm argues that after the adoption of the adjustment program in 1984, Senegal experienced a reduction in deficit trends which improved the budget and foreign exchange constraints. As a result, the savings rate increased to 7.4 percent in 1986 compared to 1.2 percent in 1985 (Youm 29).

On the other hand, this economic housecleaning is not without substantial pain for the Senegalese population. Unemployment has increased as public (and private) enterprises have closed down or reduced activities. Private businesses are also affected as the credit squeeze makes it difficult for smaller firms to expand and hire more workers. Structural adjustment policies liberalized the importation sector; consequently, 6,000 out of 120,000 employees in the private sector have lost their jobs (Weissman 1990:1628). As the Senegalese economy moved toward liberalization and opened itself up to the world market, local industries suffered as a result. The Senegalese milk, car assembly, poultry, and textile industries have struggled to survive against the onslaught of cheaper imported products.[7]

For those who have lost jobs in the private sector, no longer can the unemployed turn to government as an employer of last resort. Structural adjustment affects public sector employment as well. In the public sector, about 4,000 people have been removed over the course of the 1984 adjustment program. This represents about one-seventh of public sector employees (Weissman 1990:1628).

The costs of basic foodstuffs have risen tremendously since the government began lifting subsidies on food items; wages have not kept up. Purchasing power continues to decline. Estimates indicate a drop in the average worker's purchasing power of more than thirty percent since 1985 (*Ibid.*). To compensate for the loss in the male head of household income, more and more women are entering the informal economy to make ends meet. Mothers engage in informal work that may force them to be away from home for most of the day. In addition, families find they cannot afford the rising cost of education for all of their children. As a result, unsupervised street children is a growing phenomenon, especially in popular neighborhoods.

Moreover, even social services formerly provided by the government must now be paid for by users. For example, user fees have been instituted for health care services. Structural adjustment policies exacerbate the deteriorating health services and infrastructure. Per capita spending on health fell by twenty percent between 1981 and 1988 (Weissman 1990:1629). But even the implementation of users' fees has not stemmed the deterioration in health care. Public clinics and hospitals remain empty of basic medical supplies critical for the provision of decent basic health care. Those who can afford to have turned to the private health clinics that dot the cities; people without funds turn to traditional healers to be cured.

Health care is not the only victim of structural adjustment. Education, long considered a birthright of the population, has also undergone reforms. To reduce educational expenditures the government introduced double-shift and multi-grade classes and the recruitment of more assistant teachers and monitors. Other measures introduced through the structural adjustment policies include the postponement of the beginning age of school from six to seven years, the reduction of compulsory schooling to only four years, and the elimination of teaching staff (Bathily: 132). Although parents pay higher school fees for their children, the quality of education has declined (*Ibid.*).

The impact of structural adjustment policies has hurt the educational system. Between 1980 and 1990, gross enrollment rates rose from twenty-four percent of school age population to thirty percent. Yet, as enrollment rates increased, educational spending declined from thirty-three percent of the national budget to twenty-six percent (Noonan 1993:23). As educational attainment is placed out of the reach of many children, growing economic and social inequalities will be marked by those whose parents pay for education and those whose parents cannot. Without formal education and skills, many will not be able to compete in the modern economy, reducing their life chances to escape from the poverty of the informal market.

How the Dakarois View the Crisis and the Recovery Programs

A survey of Senegalese attitudes toward the crisis and its impact was conducted from September to November 1986. Interviews were conducted of 137 Dakarois. Efforts were made to randomly select the interviewees in order to capture, as thoroughly as possible, the demographic diversity of Dakar and its environs. Of the sampled population, 47 percent were female and 53 percent were made; 50 were under the age of 35 and 49 were over; 54 percent lived in Dakar and 45 percent lived in the surrounding area—Pikine, Gué-diawaye. Salaried or civil service employees made up 39 percent of the same; 7 percent were part-time or day laborers, 23 percent were self-employed, 24 were unemployed, and nearly 8 percent were students. Household size varied from one to thirty, with the average holding eleven persons.

The questionnaire used in the study consisted of both closed and open-ended questions. Interviewees were asked a series of questions concerning their perceptions of the crisis: when it began, the population's reaction, the impact on daily life, and whether they thought it could be resolved. In addition, the subjects were asked about their attitudes toward the government.

The Beginning of the Crisis

When asked to specify the date when the economic crisis began in Senegal, answers varied between 1960 and 1982. When asked, "What are the events that in your opinion mark the beginning of the crisis?" responses clustered around four basic issues: agriculture (drought, the decline in agriculture, and the rural exodus), the economy (rising prices, unemployment, terms of trade), social problems (population pressures, the young, problems of the mentally ill, and mendicancy), and political issues (political rights and the resignation of President Senghor). (See Table 1.2) Economic issues were cited by 65 percent of the respondents. This was followed by agricultural issues (18 percent), social problems (10 percent), and political issues (6 percent). Many respondents (46 percent) defined the nature of the crisis as comprehensive, comprising economic, political, and/or cultural factors.

When asked whether the crisis had changed over the past several years, 86 percent thought that the crisis had worsened. Only 3 percent of the respondents believed the crisis had become less severe, and 11 percent were of the opinion that the crisis had stayed the same. For many Dakarois, the economic stagnation and the

Table 1.2 The Nature of the Crisis

	N	Percent
Economic	33	25.0
Political	7	5.3
Cultural	2	1.5
Social	1	0.8
All of the above	61	46.2
Some of the above	28	21.6

structural adjustment program are not theoretical issues to be debated, but involve a harsh economic reality. It becomes clear by the population's perceptions that the Senegalese are being hard hit by the economic crisis and the economic reforms that are in effect. Ask any Senegalese on the street about the *jafé jafé koom koom* (meaning economic crisis in indigenous Wolof language), and one will be told about the painful impact of the crisis on individuals, families, communities, and the nation.

Reactions to the Crisis

The second set of questions asked respondents to indicate their perceptions of how the population is dealing with the crisis. In general, the Senegalese felt that their compatriots' reaction to the crisis was negative, but that their own behavior was positive. A majority, 60 percent, felt that most Senegalese were reacting badly to the crisis; the rest, 40 percent, felt that the reaction of the population was good.

As one would expect, the majority of the Senegalese judged their own behavior positively, in spite of whatever hardships they may have endured. When the respondents were asked how they and their families dealt with the crisis, 67 percent answered positively: "Cut down on spending," "We adapt," "We do the best we can," while only 32 percent responded negatively: "Life is difficult," "We can't make ends meet," "We have problems eating." Many respon-

dents perceived a decline in morality as part of this negative behavior pattern. Quite a few cited the behavior of women as an example. One woman stated, "Life is hard and women are taking up
bad habits [prostitution]. It's a question of survival."

Impact of the Crisis

Another set of questions asked respondents to evaluate the impact
of the crisis on (1) social relations, (2) daily life, (3) places of habita-
tion, and (4) traditional ceremonies. The first question elicited the
following response categories: (a) "Relations are now based on material self-interest and money"; (b) "People are more individualistic
and opportunistic"; (c) "There has been a degradation of relations
with family and friends"; (d) "There have been more misunder-
standings between individuals," or "There have been difficulties in
getting along with others"; (e) "There has been a decline of tradition and solidarity"; and (f) "Solidarity has not changed." The three
most frequently cited effects were that there had been a degradation of family and friendship ties (28 percent), greater exhibition of
individualistic and opportunistic behavior (20 percent), and a decline in tradition and solidarity (17 percent). Only 11 percent were
of the opinion that social relations had been unchanged by the
crisis. (See Table 1.3.) Men were twice as likely as women to state
that solidarity and tradition continued in spite of the crisis. Also,
respondents under the age of thirty-four were more likely than

Table 1.3 Evaluation of the Effects of the Crisis on Social Relations

	N	Percent
More materialism	26	14.1
Individualism, opportunism	37	20.1
Social ties are breaking	52	28.3
Difficulties in getting along	17	9.2
Culture is changing	32	17.4
There is no change, no impact	20	10.9

older respondents to state that the crisis had weakened relations with family and friends.

Some differences among interviewees were found with respect to household size. For those in households with more than 21 persons, 44 percent stated that the crisis entailed no change in social relations, while 33 percent replied that the major impact was a weakening of family and friendship ties. Among those in small and medium-sized households, the most common response mentioned by respondents was the fracturing of family and friendship ties (mentioned by 30 percent).

A difference in perception of the impact of the crisis on social relations emerged when occupational status was examined. Students, the unemployed, civil servants, and salaried workers all suggested that the major impact of the crisis was the decline in ties to family and friends (46, 35, and 29 percent respectively). Part-time and day laborers were most likely to indicate the rise in material self-interest and concern over money as the major by-products of the crisis (33 percent). The self-employed, on the other hand, disagreed with all of the other employment categories. Half of the self-employed felt that there had been no change in social relations.

Next, respondents were asked to indicate how the consequences of the crisis impacted on their daily lives. Comments to this question elicited five classifications of responses: *General comments* (people are tired, we're doing the best we can, life is difficult, the misery is increasing); *Economic Issues* (unemployment, declines in purchasing power, lack of money, not enough to eat); *Anomie* (mendicancy, delinquency, prostitution, mental illness, drugs and alcohol, violence and theft); *Customs and Relations* (individualism, crisis in values, solidarity declining, rejection by my family/friends, impact on children); *Political /Cultural* (decline in cultural activities, decline in political activities).

The most frequently cited grouping was that of economic problems, followed by social and anomic problems, and general comments. For residents of Dakar, the effects of the crisis have often been multiple, as indicated by the large number of respondents who offered more than one answer to the question.

The size of the household made some difference. Respondents from households with fewer than 10 people were more likely to suggest that economic problems were the most common conse-

quences on daily life (mentioned by 32 percent). The same sentiment was expressed by 27 percent of those whose household size
consisted of 11 to 20 people, and by only 20 percent of the respondents from very large households. For households of more than 21
members, anomic issues seemed to be more troublesome (43 percent cited this set of issues). In smaller and medium-size households, anomic issues were mentioned by 35 percent and 31 percent,
respectively. When divided by occupational groupings, all categories (with the exception of salaried workers and civil servants)
listed the anomic effects most often. Civil servants and salaried
workers, however, were more likely to mention economic issues as
having an important effect on daily living.

Perhaps this indicates that much of the economic burden has
been placed on those with steady employment. As more Senegalese
lose their jobs, as a result of the economic stagnation, they rely
increasingly on employed relatives and friends. As one respondent
indicated, "It used to be that when a man married, perhaps a
bride's sister would come to stay with the newlyweds. Now when a
young man thinks of marriage he wonders if her whole family will
come to live with them." This survey found that the extended family living under one roof has grown as employed family members
are obligated to support more relatives. It was not unusual to come
across a household of ten to fifteen relatives of which only one or
two members are gainfully employed.

Finally, the consequences of the crisis on daily lives were viewed
differently depending on where the respondents lived. Residents of
Dakar mentioned economic issues as the greatest consequence (38
percent), while residents of the outlying areas of Dakar (42 percent) believed that social problems were the most important consequence of the crisis.

For many Dakarois, the impact of the crisis was felt keenly in
the domicile. Housing shortages and the high cost of lodging have
forced people to delay the purchase of a home, to move in with
friends or relatives, or even to move into the streets. Respondents
were asked if they thought the crisis had an impact on their habitats. The most frequently expressed difficulties were the high cost
of housing, the lack of housing and/or the smallness of available
housing, and problems in living. Problems in living include: "People forced to live off others," "The difficulty in maintaining relationships under such conditions," "The rise in promiscuity and alcohol-

ism as a result of the stress due to the crisis," and "Unsanitary living conditions."

Differences were found according to education and residence. Better-educated respondents were more likely to comment that the crisis created problems of living. Perhaps, with modernization, the most educated chose to opt out of a traditional Senegalese life style with many family members sharing one roof. The other difference that emerged was that the most frequently registered complaint of Dakar residents was the high cost of housing (37.6 percent), while suburban residents complained most about the shortage of housing (31.4 percent).

Finally, respondents were asked to indicate whether traditional ceremonies had been changed by the crisis. In the Senegalese culture, ritual celebrations for births, deaths, and marriages are important occasions that serve to strengthen social cohesion within the community (Diop 1984:143). The major impact of the crisis has been to simplify (cited by 48.1 percent) or even eliminate (mentioned by 33 percent) family ceremonies.

Respondents perceived that ceremonies have become less ostentatious affairs due to the lack of financial resources. Only one group, part-time and day workers, were more inclined to say the number of ceremonies has been reduced as a result of the crisis (44 percent). It appears no matter how tough times get, the Senegalese remain attached to the rituals of tradition. Cutting down, but not eliminating, ceremonies allows tradition to continue despite the economic difficulties.

In general, the results show that both the relatively privileged and the thoroughly underprivileged have witnessed their lifestyles change. For the middle class, the crisis entails the cutting back or elimination of the extras: cinema, restaurants, and extravagant parties. While this group finds that it can still eat three meals a day, the quantity of ingredients is reduced. Moreover, each meal is now shared with more family and friends. For the working class and the poor, life, while always precarious, has become even more so.

Resolution of the Crisis

The Senegalese were clear and articulate when discussing their views on the resolution of crisis. Two-thirds of the respondents answered "no" to the question, "Is the government in power capable of resolving the problems engendered by the crisis?" The only groups with confidence in the government's ability to handle the crisis are the self-employed and the least educated.

A variety of responses were offered when interviewees were asked to clarify their statements. For those who felt the government could solve the problems, most believed that it would need help in doing so. For the majority of the interviewees who believed that the government could not solve the problems brought on by the crisis, many thought the government to be either incapable or unwilling to solve these problems. Typically, women, the most educated, respondents from large households, the unemployed, and Dakar residents were most pessimistic about the government's ability or willingness to solve the country's problems. (Table 1.4.)

When asked to predict whether the quality of life for the Senegalese would improve over the next several years, 49 percent expected that it would improve, 48 percent believed the opposite, and 3 percent sensed that life would both improve and worsen. Again, predictions varied by gender, educational attainment, household size, and place of residence. According to the survey results, the optimists included the self-employed and unemployed, and the least educated. On the other hand, pessimism about the future was most pronounced among students and those with more than primary education. This group strongly believed life would get worse

Table 1.4 Evaluation of the Government's Ability to Resolve the Crisis

	N	Percent
Yes, with internal and external help	29	23.4
Yes, if the government implements SAP	10	8.1
Yes, because it is obligated to; has no other choice	10	8.1
No, because government is incapable, unwilling	31	25.0
No, problems too great; we need a miracle	23	18.5
No, because government needs help	21	16.7

Table 1.5   Best Partners to Help Senegal Improve Its Economic
Situation

Partners	N	Percent
Industrialized nations	126	62.7
Third World nations	43	21.4
Anyone willing to help	16	8.0
Socialist nations	10	5.0
Senegal alone	5	2.5
God	1	0.5

over the short term. Diametrically opposed views were found to be held by Dakar and suburban residents. While about two-thirds of suburban residents were optimistic about the future, two-thirds of those living in Dakar expressed pessimism about the future.

To ascertain how respondents envisioned an improvement in the economic situation, they were asked to mention which countries could best serve as Senegal's partners. The vast majority commented that the industrialized countries would be the best partners to help Senegal overcome its economic difficulties. (See Table 1.5) Besides the industrialized nations, Senegalese view the Third World as a potential source of help. Very few respondents felt that the Socialist world or even Senegal itself would improve the economic situation. Clearly, the overwhelming majority look to outsiders to turn around a very dire economic, social, and political situation.

The results of this survey taken in 1986 and reconfirmed by subsequent trips to Senegal in 1990 and 1993 reveal a population devastated by economic crisis and the structural adjustment program imposed on the government and the population to redress Senegal's severe economic problems. The structural adjustment program may have benefited some Senegalese, but for the vast majority it has torn apart families; wounded a generation of youth devoid of any hope for the future; exacerbated existing poverty; contributed to growing social ills such as drug and alcohol use and abuse, juvenile delinquency, and prostitution; led to growing insecurity due to the rise in violence; accelerated rural-urban migration; turned traditional values upside down; and increased political apathy, as many feel that the government does not care about them. Already shocked by ten years of structural adjustment, the Senegalese received another economic thunderbolt in early 1994.

Devaluation

As if Senegal did not feel enough pain from the structural adjustment program in effect, the devaluation of the CFA[8] currency introduced more economic bad news for the population. Since 1948, the CFA had been fixed at 50 CFA to 1 French franc. But on January 12, 1994, it was unilaterally adjusted by France to 100 CFA to 1 French franc. Overnight, the value of the CFA dropped by half. Although the devaluation had long been predicted, it was a profound shock to the population, who saw the prices of such basic items as rice, flour, sugar, cooking oil, electricity, gas, and transport prices rise between 20 and 33 percent (bentsi-Enchill 1993–1994:3,42). To alleviate the hardship resulting from the rise in essential commodity prices, the Diouf government instituted a price freeze and reduced the price of certain main commodity items. But devaluation, despite these short-term balms, has hit the average Senegalese hard.

Within a month of the announcement of the devaluation, on February 16, 1994, rioting broke out in Dakar and six policemen were lynched by angry mobs. This was the first time in Senegal's history that mob violence against police officers was carried out. Following on the heels of these events, the university closed due to a teachers' strike strongly supported by students. While student strikes are nothing new to Senegal and have occurred frequently since the 1980s, what is new is the growth in resistance of a more violent nature. Sporadic, random violence continues to hit areas in and around Dakar as groups of young people have mounted a campaign to destroy property. These events have shaken the Senegalese and have heightened their worries about personal security.

Surviving the Crisis

For many Senegalese the solution to Senegal's crisis lies beyond the capacity or the willingness of the government. Pressed to survive to fulfill the needs and demands of their families, many are opting not to depend on the world economy or the national economy to turn around. The way out of the impasse is to take matters into their own hands. The desparate daily struggle to make ends meet affects all classes. Women of all classes now involve themselves in trading on a scale never seen before. While middle-class women voyage to neighboring and far flung destinations to pick up goods to trade; working-class and poor women trade food they have grown or processed themselves for sale on the streets. The educated elite try to parlay their expertise into a contract with international non-governmental or governmental organizations. Even bureaucrats, who formerly had enviable and secure positions within the Senegalese bureaucracy, moonlight to make ends meet. Others survive by begging or engaging in illicit or quasi-illegal activities. According to police and judicial data, crime and delinquency rates have accelerated as people survive by engaging in unlawful actions including stealing, drug abuse, and prostitution (Bathily 1989:130).

But many have given up hope of making ends meet while remaining in the country. Hence, the growing number of Senegalese who choose to leave the rural areas for Dakar, and finding no opportunities in the capital, decide to leave for the United States. Setting up stalls along the streets and avenues of New York's busiest boroughs, Senegalese merchants can earn enough money to finance an entire household's needs back home. Many Senegalese families survive solely from the remittances sent by these brothers, fathers, and husbands as well as sisters, mothers, and wives.[9]

For the wealthiest Senegalese traders in New York, annual income levels reach as high as $50,000 to $60,000.[10] But for most Senegalese men, a more modest income can be earned driving taxis, working in gas stations, in stores, or restaurants. For women, income is earned by hair braiding, and preparing and selling African dishes. In addition, Senegalese women find menial work in supermarkets, restaurants, and retail stores. Senegalese men and women, even those whose incomes are quite modest by American standards can send home monthly remittances of more than $100.[11]

Such sums go a long way in a country whose GNP per capita income registers $780.

Besides devising schemes to turn their own economic difficulties around, the crisis has forced Senegalese to alter traditional customs and practices. Wedding, birth, and other life events have, in the past, been spectacular and extravagant affairs for which no expense was spared. Quite a few Senegalese question the amount of money spent to clothe and feed family and friends and to pay griots to sing the family's praises during such events. Respondents of this survey indicated a new approach to traditional ceremonies. Unable to eliminate them all together, families are searching for ways to cut down on expenses. For example, nowadays the birth of the first child might require the expenditure of considerable sums of money, but the births of children born subsequently are celebrated with less fanfare, if they are celebrated at all.

The tradition of solidarity in the face of adversity has also been marked by the current crisis. The Senegalese are known for their hospitality and a complex of social and religious practices that reinforce and praise those who give to the needy. Economic adversity severely tests the culture of solidarity. Although solidarity is far from being a relic of the past and still continues in vigorous practice today, many wonder about the extent to which solidarity is possible given the pressure being placed on the few income earners in a family. The Senegalese still feel an obligation toward immediate and extended family members as well as friends, but question whether it extends to far-flung and extended relatives of questionable kinship. In the past, when the cousin of your grandfather's wife's brother came calling, the tendency was to give without asking. Nowadays, Senegalese with the means to give might put off giving or give while grumbling about traditional ties. Such demands on individual resources test the traditional social policy of communalism. More and more, individualism and self-interested politics guide personal decisions.

Apart from individual choices to confront the crisis, some Senegalese see a solution in politics. Senegalese, disenchanted with thirty years of Parti Socialiste rule, look to like-minded political groups or communities to provide a political alternative. Currently, there is a multitude of oppositional parties, eighteen political parties all together. Though the political opposition (the most prominent leaders being Abdoulaye Wade of the Parti Démocratique Sénégalais (PDS) and Landing Savané of And-Jëf/Mouvement Révolutionaire pour la Démocratie Nouvelle) has consistently challenged the PS to have a more open and fair democracy, it has failed to seize power by beating the PS at the ballot box.[12] The urban battle cry of "*Sopi*" which means "change" in the Wolof language and is claimed as the party slogan of the PDS has not translated into enough votes in either the 1988 or the 1993 presidential elections. Despite very deep opposition throughout society, the PS time and time again is able to outmaneuver the opposition parties and capitalize on its reputation and incumbency to remain in power. Nevertheless, Diouf's margin of victory has consistently declined since he first stood for elections in 1983, perhaps in part due to the fact that more and more people have become cynical over an outcome they perceive to be predetermined. Why bother to vote when the PS is surely going to win? As a result of the voters' lack of confidence in or cynicism about democratic elections, the percentages of registered voters who refuse to vote have also increased since 1983. In the last presidential elections, held in February 1993, only 51.5 percent of the registered voters bothered to turn out and vote. Sensing that involvement in politics cannot alter the situation, a number of Senegalese look to other social and political symbols and authorities for comfort.

Feeling abandoned by the state and unable to convert discontent into a change in regime, some Senegalese now look to religion for the answers to their problems. Islamic associations as well as a newly emerging band of charismatic Islamic leaders who are in opposition to the state are mushrooming.[13] For the most part, their expressions of opposition to the current situation take a spiritual, and not a political, form. This Islamic revivalism is especially appealing to those who maintain distance and wariness of both the government and the opposition political parties. A number of fundamentalist leaders advocate a return to a strict Islamic practice and a more modest life style, both of which resonate strongly among a population growing more socially divided, politically disempowered, and economically impoverished each day by the "*jafé jafé koom koom.*" The challenge posed by Islam can be seen in the presence of the "Baye Fall" who regularly circulate throughout Dakar begging aggressively for money and refusing to look for

work. In addition, religious opposition to the current regime includes more overt political expressions. The Moustarchidina movement explicitly vocalized its opposition to Diouf during the 1993
elections, one of the few Islamic brotherhoods to do so. Accused of
inciting violence and transgressing state security during the February 1994 riots, the government's treatment of the Moustarchi-
dines has been vigorous and harsh. Its leaders and members have
been arrested or picked up for questioning. Already one Moustar-
chidine leader, Lamin Samb, has died in prison, in February 1994
from injuries due to torture at the hands of the Senegalese police
(Peter Da Costa 1994:58–60). For decades, stability and democracy
"Senegalese-style" have been possible because of the interdepen-
dence between the government and the traditional religious leadership. It is not clear whether harmonious relations between the regime and the religious community will continue as a younger and
more politicized generation of religious leaders takes over.

Conclusion

Beyond the breathtaking sights of Senegal's beaches along the Cor-
niche, the appeal of the beautiful and haunting Gorée Island, and
the regal grace of the Senegalese people themselves, lies a harsh
reality found in the poorer urban neighborhoods of Médina, Grand
Dakar, Pikine, and Guédiawaye. There, behind the tourist sites,
lives a population struggling to survive structural adjustment policies and devaluation. Urban life in Dakar has become more difficult as rural dwellers migrate to Dakar in search for a better life
after finding that the government's New Agricultural Policy (the
rural component of the structural adjustment package) has forced
many farmers to compete with cheaper imported European and
American products. Even college educated youth discover after
completion of tertiary studies that there are no jobs to be found.
The economic and social problems intensified by structural adjustment and devaluation have contributed to the increasing decay of
the quality of life in urban Senegal and fuels the rage and frustration of Dakar's poorer and younger denizens. How long will the
government, with the help of its external allies and internal supporters (the religious leadership within the Muslim brotherhoods

and the political and economic elite), keep the country from erupting in a paroxysm of violence? The question begs to be answered: how much longer?

———————————— NOTES ————————————

1. These are the figures of the New York City Department of Planning. Other sources within the Senegalese community believe the numbers of Senegalese residents in New York to be much higher.

2. For an excellent article that documents the problems faced by Senegalese industries see Catherine Boone, "The Making of a Rentier Class: Wealth Accumulation and Political Control in Senegal." *The Journal of Development Studies* 26:3 (1990): pp. 425–449.

3. For example, according to an article published in 1986 in the newspaper *Le Soleil*, the cost of rice and sugar per kilogram in 1960 was 30 and 70 CFA, respectively. In 1982, rice cost 105 CFA, and jumped to 160 in 1985. One kilogram of sugar cost 260 in 1980 and 375 in 1983. Peanut oil, an essential ingredient in Senegalese dishes, rose from 198 CFA per liter in 1975 to 568 CFA by 1984.

4. Boone argues that in the case of the textile industry the predicted outcome of a shift to capital-intensive inputs has not materialized for political reasons.

5. République du Sénégal, Ministére de l'Economie et des Finances (MEF), *Programme d'Ajustement Economique et Financier à Moyen et Long-Terme*. Dakar: MEF, 1984, pp. 94–95.

6. See: Prosper Youm, "The Economy Since Independence," in Christopher L. Delgado and Sidi Jammeh (eds.), New York and Westport: Praeger Publishers, 1991, pp. 21–30; and Stephen R. Weissman, "Structural Adjustment in Africa: Insights from the Experiences of Ghana and Senegal," *World Development* 18:12 (1990): pp. 1621–1634.

7. This is the assessment of Abdoulaye Bathily in the article, "Senegal's Structural Adjustment Programme and its Economic and Social Effects: the Political Economy of Regression," in Bade Onimode (ed.), *The IMF, The World Bank and the African Debt Volume 2: The Social and Political Impact*. London and New Jersey: Zed Books Ltd. and the Institute for African Alternatives, 1989, pp. 125–139.

8. The CFA, the currency of the Commuauté Financiére Africaine, is used in thirteen former French-American colonies—Benin, Burkina Faso, Cameroon, Central African Republic, Chad, Comoros, Congo, Côte d'Ivoire, Gabon, Mali, Niger, Senegal, and Togo. The Franc zone countries enjoyed

the stability that came with the fixed parity and the attractions of investments made possible by the franc's easy convertibility.

9. While the majority of Senegalese immigrants are men (about four-fifths), increasingly women both single and married are immigrating to the United States.

10. According to a Senegalese journalist and businessman living in New York, interviewed on June 21, 1994.

11. This figure is based on research done by Michael L. Fleisher, "Visions of Dallas: A Study of Senegalese Immigration to the United States," Master's Thesis, Columbia University, 1991, p. 43.

12. For two analyses of the 1988 and 1989 elections, see Crawford Young and Babacar Kanté, "Governance Democracy, and the 1988 Senegalese Elections," in Goran Hyden and Michael Bratton (eds.), *Governance and Politics in Africa*, Boulder: Lynne Rienner, 1992; and Leonardo A. Villalón, "Democratizing a (Quasi) Democracy: The Senegalese Elections of 1993," *African Affairs* 93, (1994): pp. 164–193.

13. One such group, the Moustarchidinia wal Moustarchidate ("Men and Women Who Fight for the Truth" in Arabic), led by Moustapha Sy, has been the object of severe government repression.

REFERENCES

Bathily, Abdoulaye. 1989. "Senegal's Structural Adjustment Programme and its Economic and Social Effects: The Political Economy of Regression." In Bade Onimode (ed.), *The World Bank and The African Debt Volume 2: The Social and Political Impact.* London and New Jersey: Zed Press.

bentsi-Enchill, Nii K. 1993–1994. "Devaluation hits the African franc zone." *Africa Recovery* 7:3–4 (December-March).

Boone, Catherine. 1990. "The Making of a Rentier Class: Wealth Accumulation and Political Control in Senegal." *The Journal of Development Studies* 26:3.

Club du Sahel. 1986. "Foreign Aid and Financial Crisis in the CILSS Member States." *Sahel D.* (86) 296. Paris: OECD.

Ministère du Développement Rural. 1984. La Nouvelle Politique Agricole. Dakar: MDR.

Ministère de la Fonction Publique de l'Emploi et du Travail, Direction de l'Emploi. 1985. Les Compressions de Personnel dans le Secteur Moderne Dans la Region de Dakar de Janvier 1981 à Decembre 1985. Dakar: MFPET.

Noonan, Patricia. 1994. "Continuing Crisis in African Education." *Africa Recovery* 7:3–4 (December 1993–March 1994).

Diop, Abdoulaye. 1985. *La Famile Wolof*. Paris: Editions Karthala.

Parti Socialiste du Sénégal. 1985. *Politique d'ajustement économique et financier*. Dakar: Conseil National du Parti Socialist.

The World Bank. 1994. *Adjustment in Africa: Reforms, Results and the Road Ahead*. Washington, D.C.

Weissman, Stephen. 1990. "Structural Adjustment in Africa: Insights from the Experiences of Ghana and Senegal." *World Development* 18:12.

West Africa. 1983. "The bankers move in." (August 8).

Youm, Prosper. 1991. "The Economy Since Independence." In Christopher L. Delgado and Sidi Jammeh (eds.), *Political Economy of Senegal Under Structural Adjustment*. New York and Westport: Praeger.

Kinuthia Macharia

2

Meeting the Challenge in an African City

Nairobi's Informal Economy in the 1980s and 1990s

This chapter focuses on the nature of the challenge facing the majority of Africans who live in the city of Nairobi and over the last thirty years have learned to adapt to city life and to think of it as an alternative home. This is in contrast to the situation before Independence in 1963, when the city was predominantly a "White man's place" and the African was considered a sojourner and a misfit in the city (Soja 1970). I argue that despite the many years that Kenya has had close ties with the West[1] (mainly the United Kingdom and the United States) compared with its neighbor Tanzania, whose leader Julius Nyerere chose the path to socialism and maintained ties with the East, especially China, Kenya cannot boast of a better urban life. Working and living conditions have worsened for the majority in the low income strata. Close ties with the West have accelerated class formation in the last thirty years, producing many unemployed persons and squatter settlements where people engage in various informal economic activities, most of which produce very little income.

In the city of Nairobi, with its current estimated population of 2.5 million people, at least fifty percent of its population is struggling in what has been popularly called "Jua Kali." The term Jua

Kali comes from the Swahili language and means "hot sun," in reference to the open locations (usually under no roof) where various
self-employed business activities like metal working, welding, and
hawking of various commercial goods take place. Jua Kali is the
equivalent of the informal economy described in urban literature.
The concept, informal sector, was first used by Keith Hart in his
study of Ghana in 1971 and then popularized by the International
Labor Organization (ILO) in its study of Kenya in 1972. Others
such as Portes *et al.* (1989) and De Soto (1987) have applied the
concept to similar work situations in both developed and developing countries. De Soto's work in particular has shown in detail how
informal workers operated in Latin America, exposing the bureaucratic hurdles that those in the informal economy have been able to
avoid by going informal—mainly a labyrinth of government licensing procedures. While the bureaucratic hurdles are also notable in
Nairobi, failure by the government authorities to allocate certain
locations for the Jua Kali operation has been a major concern and
one that has confined the two sides to constantly playing "a game
of hide and seek." This game is expensive for the Jua Kali operators, who risk the confiscation of their merchandise and tools and
the demolition of their temporary homes, and face having to start
all over again.

The proliferation of informal social structures, that is, the informal economy and informal political structures in the city of Nairobi, is emphasized in this chapter. I argue that such informal
structures have given informal loans to thousands of families, who
have migrated to Nairobi with disadvantages such as little or no
education, to assist them in acquiring formal "white collar jobs"
and forging limited social networks in the new city. This explains
why the new city dwellers have continued to rely on their rural ties
as the basis for their social connections in the city. In a study of
social networks for those operating in the informal sector, ethnicity, rural places of origin, and kinship ties were the major bases for
the network ties (Macharia 1989). The relationship between the
rural areas and those who have migrated from them to Nairobi and
engage in the Jua Kali sector has continued to be one that provides
both economic and social remittances. Once in the city, the new
migrants seek out people from their rural home who have migrated
to Nairobi earlier, for support and assistance. The social connec-

tions they had in the rural areas are reproduced in Nairobi in at least three key ways.

First, the newly arrived gets shelter for the initial days or months in the city; second, the same rural contact starts to introduce the newly arrived to his friends in the city who may become the source of temporary employment or at least of information as to where to start looking for a job or which corner of the street will be lucrative and safe to start an informal sector business activity; and third, the rural networks now fully reproduced in the city become almost always the first source of income (Ksh 500 to Ksh. 1000).

Furthermore, my findings from a 1989 study of the role of social networks in the informal sector in Nairobi show how such networks enable the sector to continue financing itself without capital from the formal banks. The social capital formed through those networks, which in turn establishes the sense of trust, becomes a source of non-interest loans that are the main source of the start-up capital for most of the respondents (Macharia 1989).

The economic recession in Kenya, where growth fell from seven percent annual growth in the 1970s to about three percent in the 1980s, was exacerbated by the structural adjustment programs of the International Monetary Fund and the World Bank (Republic of Kenya 1990). That has harshly impacted members of the informal economy, whose incomes of about Ksh 500 (roughly US$12) per month could not keep up with price hikes for both food and shelter, as well as the raw materials for their operations. Overcrowding and living in constant environmental risk have therefore become the order of the day for the African masses in Nairobi. The state's harassment and demolition of the homes of those working in the Jua Kali sector has only worsened the situation.

Nairobi was developed as the white man's colonial city. It was never intended to be a home for Africans, and all policies for housing and other services were minimal for Africans. Before getting to the contemporary crisis, a brief historical overview of the development of the city of Nairobi is relevant. This will both highlight and support the argument that a large proportion of the economic, social, and political ills that derail policy implementation and hence produce weak programs can be traced from a colonial past that was unsympathetic to the African and therefore never prepared the city as a future home for the indigenous people.

In discussing the historical situation I do not put total blame on the colonial past, mainly because it is my contention that the independent African government has not done as much as it ought to have done for the urban working class and the urban poor. I will show how the economic environment, especially for small-scale entrepreneurs, continues to be as difficult as it was during the colonial era if not more severe. Harassment of traders on Nairobi's streets and the demolition of their "Kiosks"[2] by the authorities continues. It is my thesis that harassment orchestrated by both the central and local government, in which the city police have been ordered to make early raids and confiscate all material goods and ensure that the targeted sites are wiped clean, kills the entrepreneurial spirit of individuals and families. Furthermore, it is my contention that these families have been actually quite awake and ready to face the urban challenges they found themselves in and, left at peace, they could have made a difference in their lives. This has been especially the case for the majority that did not have the skills for white collar jobs and have had no proper housing amenities—some indeed living in worse squalor than they previously had in the rural areas.

Industries and manufacturing jobs have not been part of Third World urbanization yet it is in such Third World cities that migration to the city and natural population increase have been highest. Exacerbating the situation is the mismanagement of the few resources by corrupt central and local governments, who have mismanaged land allocations in the cities, causing demolition of numerous squatter settlements, some of which are the initial homes of new (as well as some old) migrants (Macharia 1992). This has also led to what Stren *et al.* (1989) have referred to as a management crisis in African cities.

Given the poor living conditions in most of the rural areas, especially with decreasing prices for cash and cultivated food crops, and the effects of intensive and commercialized agriculture, the city has continued to be the rational choice for most rural people. The urban bias hypothesis first advanced by Lipton (1977) has continued in the 1990s, hence the non-reversal of the rural migration to the major cities like Nairobi. It is not so much the bright lights that attract people to the city but the conceived and rationalized ideas that life could be better in the city where the possibility of cash employment is said to be higher. Obviously, many of the migrants have been frustrated by not getting the "hoped-for job." The effects of relative deprivation are felt more by the new migrants, who have to bear seeing for the first time the affluence of the wealthy city dwellers juxtaposed against their own poverty. The conspicuous nature of city poverty and its level of concentration in sprawling slum areas make life in the city for many of the new (and also older) migrants more miserable than they had expected. The search for opportunities, especially in the informal sector, has been a step in the right direction for the new "city dweller," who has to try every trade possible in order to make ends meet given the hard fact that "where they came from" is usually worse than "where they are currently."

Historical Overview of the City of Nairobi

During the colonial period in Kenya, and specifically in the city of Nairobi, public housing for Africans was not officially supported. The few houses that were built in the 1940s and 1950s were one-room houses for single men, who were not expected to bring their families. This led to overcrowding in those same one-room houses when the Africans were finally permitted to bring in their families.[3] The colonial laws restricting Africans without jobs to the rural areas as labor reserves for their plantations did more harm than good, especially because the rural areas were becoming overcultivated and poor.

In 1948, in the first official census for Kenya, the country had only seventeen urban centers, with an aggregate of 285,000 people. While this populace comprised only 5.2 percent of the total population they were disproportionately distributed in the two main cities of Nairobi and Mombasa. The former would continue to take this lead in the 1990s. By 1962, the number of urban centers in Kenya had doubled to thirty-four and the urban population had increased to 671,000, with Nairobi absorbing the lion's share of this increase. Without legal and administrative restrictions on rural-urban migration after 1963, the urban population grew from 671,000 in 1962 to 1,082,000 in 1969, growing at the rate of 7.1 percent per annum (Republic of Kenya 1974). Besides rural-urban migration, natural increase has continued to swell the city population. Over-crowding and mass poverty have become the most notable features of the "African city of Nairobi" as a consequence of both this influx of people into the city and the fact that the colonial rulers had not developed the city in such a way that it could meet the challenge that ensued after 1963.

In many respects Nairobi was a "European city" like Harare in Zimbabwe and Johannesburg in South Africa. It is contrasted with what may be referred to as a true "African city" like Ibadan in Nigeria, where the Yoruba established settlement around 1820 and developed their own city without any European influence. But what we are finding today is that there is a convergence of the two formerly contrasted cities. The African city (Ibadan) is becoming more modern, with skyscrapers and a motorway system similar to a European city, while the formerly European city (Nairobi) is becoming African, especially with the growth of Jua Kali activities flourishing all over the city where they dared not step during the colonial period and during the early years of independence.

The city of Nairobi is an excellent example of the converging city in Africa which exposes both Western and African influence in its development. Hardships associated with the sheer poverty in the city have caused some areas to become extensions of rural life, where urban agriculture thrives and forms of traditional tinsmithing have become the core of the Jua Kali trade, as it was in some of the rural areas (Freeman 1991).

The rich have to live in constant fear of attack as the inequality between them and the poor has grown in recent years. High-rise barbed wire fences enclose the mansions of the rich and at least two twenty-four-hour armed guards are hired to provide additional security. Such fear has led to Nairobi being declared "Category B" by the United Nations, removing it from "Category A," which had suggested that the city was as safe and secure as Geneva, New York, or Paris, cities that house other United Nations Agencies (Weekly Review, January 1994). Carjacking and residential robberies have become a major concern in Nairobi and constitute the major forms of urban violence in the 1990s.

Nairobi became a city in 1950, when the population was estimated at 200,000 people. In 1962, the city had 500,000 people, and by 1979 this number had risen to 1.2 million, doubling in less than twenty years. Currently the population is estimated at 2.5 million (Republic of Kenya 1994). It is clear that due to the process of rapid urbanization and natural population growth in the city of Nairobi, what was a small city in the 1950s has joined the ranks of what Castells (1977) referred to as megalopolis. The population is predominantly African, with a substantially smaller population of European descent but a sizable Asian population (about 250,000, mainly of Indian descent), who despite their minority position dominate most of the economic institutions and commerce in Nairobi and Kenya in general.

The Asians' advantaged economic position has a historical origin. They were mainly involved in commerce during the colonial period. Unlike most of the European administrators and missionaries who went back to Europe or America when Kenya became independent, almost ninty-five percent of the Asians stayed on in the country and took a leading business position in the major towns. They literally became the new economic masters, employing the skilled and unskilled newly migrating Africans and forming deep and strong alliances with the new African elite who took over the government positions. The competition in business among the Asians and a few African entrepreneurs has continued to date, with Asians outwitting the African entrepreneurs due to their longevity in business and their ability to secure more established positions through networks they have formed with the African leaders in the government, and by pursuing joint ventures and outcompeting the African small-scale entrepreneurs. They also have capital and they help each other out through bank or family loans.

The Growth of the Informal City: Economic Activities

The city operates as an official or formal economy inasmuch as every economic activity is expected to be licensed and a direct form of taxing is exercised. Also in place are certain codes and standards to cover various operations. But Nairobi has become an "African informal city," in which many innovative small-scale entrepreneurs, with technical and/or entrepreneurial skills or simply business awareness, have started selling goods on the street sides and keeping up a "cat and mouse chase" with the city officials and police authorities. In this environment, codes are not adhered to and taxes are not collected.

Informality as an analytical concept encompasses a way of life of the people who have come together in the city and have defied classical modernization theories, which predicted a melting away of traditional folkways and an adaptation of institutional ways of life molded by modern city institutions. In the case of Nairobi, some rural (folk) ways of doing things have persisted and the city has in many ways become a reflection of ethnic and rural origins, noticeable in neighborhood settings in the city. People have migrated to Nairobi and settled along ethnic lines, thus reinforcing and giving new significance to strong social ties originally formed in the rural areas. Such strong ties from the rural areas have become the social capital that those in the informal sector in particular have utilized not only for entry into the various trades they are involved in but also in acquiring financial loans and start-up capital from friends, co-ethnics as well as relatives. The informal sector operators who are unable to borrow from formal banks due to lack of collateral rely more on the social networks when they encounter financial difficulties.

The social organization of the informal sector or Jua Kali is very important, as it explains its economic success. The social basis of the economy involves relying on various social networks (mainly friendship, ethnic, kinship) for information, financial support, court bails in case one is arrested for selling in what may be officially an illegal zone, as well as emotional support. While unemployment has been rising in the last ten years in Kenya (it is currently estimated to be twenty percent), especially among school dropouts, the development of small-scale enterprises has become a major alternative to employment in government offices and the established private companies (Republic of Kenya 1994).

I distinguish between the popular and technical usages of the term Jua Kali. Popularly, the term refers to the informal sector, mainly those small-scale businesses on the streets, like the drum sellers in Nairobi, that operate without having proper licenses and avoid paying taxes. The technical usage of the term refers to the small-scale enterprises, but specifically those using some technical skills or acquired technical knowledge to either fabricate or repair items. What is also important to sort out is the state's selective response to these related activities.

The state has tended to give more support to the technology-based Jua Kali activities, which have been legitimized through a cabinet position created in 1989 with the name, Ministry of Technical Training and Technology, popularly referred to as the Jua Kali Ministry. Such favoritism by the state has caused confusion and concern to other entrepreneurs, mainly retailers and street vendors, who happen to be the majority, numbering 62 percent nationwide and 55 percent in Nairobi (Macharia 1993). Those using technical skills have been known to employ more persons by a rate of two to one compared with the food sellers, and the street vendors and retailers, who rarely employ help due to the small size of their operations.

Some of the chief business activities that I would list as Jua Kali (technical usage) include tailoring, carpentry, welding, and tinsmithing. Open-air garages, where most Nairobi drivers take their cars for repairs to avoid the high costs of established company-operated garages, are common in all Kenyan towns, but more so in Nairobi, which has the highest number of automobiles. In Nairobi, main areas of concentration of the metal artisan work, welding, and tinsmithing are located along Jogoo Road, a highway built to open up Nairobi's Eastlands (Shauri Moyo, Bahati, Uhuru, and Kamukunji), an area that was planned for Africans.

Historically, most of the informal sector activities that have been run by Africans were started less than a mile away from the city center, toward the Eastlands of Nairobi. That trend has continued to date and is evidence of the continuation of inherited urban-biased policies—a bias that lasted until the late 1980s, when the government seemed to accept the significance of the Jua Kali activities in the general economy of the country and of the city of Nairobi in particular (Republic of Kenya 1992).

The Growth of Informal City: Housing

Nairobi has not only witnessed the emergence of informal business activities but also an upsurge of informal settlements, which I esti-

mate to house about sixty per cent of Nairobi's city dwellers.
Squatter settlements continue to thrive in various parts of the city.
Those that develop too close to the Central Business District are
eventually targeted for demolition. This was the case in Muoroto
(Macharia 1992) and other settlements in the Eastlands of Nairobi,
past the already-occupied residential areas, and still others in the
traditional squatter areas of Mathare Valley and Kibera. I refer to
these as "informal settlements" mainly because they do not meet
the standards set by law for a city dwelling, which in Nairobi (for a
family living quarters) is a two-bedroom with a kitchen and a bath,
constructed of permanent material such as stone or concrete. A
later post-independence modification has allowed for semi-permanent material like bricks and timber, although the latter is seen as
a major fire hazard and is therefore discouraged. The informal sector economic activities and the informal settlements are interre-
lated mainly because those operating informal economic activities
during the day are the ones occupying the informal housing during
the night. It is unfortunate that the two are treated separately.
When squatter settlements are targeted for demolition, the government that is supporting the growth of the Jua Kali on the one hand
is inadvertently destroying it on the other by declaring war on the
their residential quarters. The informal settlement has usually occurred on vacant private and public land alike. It is on the private
land that forceful evacuations are more likely to occur.

The houses in the squatter settlement may not meet city bylaws
but they are the homes where the family units of the Jua Kali
operators live and where important economic decisions for these
families or single persons are made. They may be makeshift cardboard houses, or mud houses, but they are nonetheless home to the
urban poor and no less significant than the homes that shelter the
rich in the suburbs west of Nairobi.

Improvement by upgrading such makeshift informal settlements,
as well as making them permanent where the land is public,
should be encouraged by those who actively support Jua Kali development as contributing to the economy of the country and that
of Nairobi. To avoid a situation of homeless unemployed people
roaming the streets of Nairobi, a more sensible policy would be to
allow those who are economically active to live in their makeshift
houses in the squatter settlements, even if they do not meet city

standards, until they can afford better housing. This has actually happened in some parts of Nairobi, where, through subsidized programs, those who used to live in squatter settlements have moved into better permanent structures. This has occurred in Dandora, where, through soft loans from some non-governmental organizations like the Roman Catholic Church, former squatters have been able to live in one room and rent at least two others, which has allowed them to repay their soft loans and to have a little income (Macharia 1994).

The formal government, both in city hall and in the central government, should be pressured to recognize informal housing as a necessary starting point for a majority of poor urbanites who cannot afford housing in the private sector but are economically active and contributing to their families and to the city—which in any case has no budget for welfare. The genuineness of the central government or the city government that elects to demolish shanty towns and squatter settlements is left open to question. Amidst allegations of corruption by state officials who manipulate housing meant for low income groups, doubts about government commitment to the urban poor are reinforced.

The Effects of the Global Economy

The world system theorists, beginning with Wallerstein's work in the 1970s and Chase-Dunn (1989) and others in 1980s, have argued that the world is influenced by one capitalistic economy and therefore the economic woes of one region or country will be economic gain for another. Without going into the details of world system theory, suffice it to say that Kenya, and specifically Nairobi, has been part of the world economy, having been incorporated, albeit as an unequal player, early in the twentieth century. At that juncture the colonial economy established Nairobi mainly as a central railway hub which would be used to extract cash crops like tea and coffee from the former white Highlands in readiness for export to the core countries, mainly Europe and later on the United States. In the 1960s and 1970s, Nairobi became a center for light manufacturing following the import substitution policy, a situation that generally did not benefit the newly arrived Africans from the

impoverished rural areas. Some of the import substitution industries like the East African Industries, British American Tobacco,
East African Breweries (later Kenya Breweries), Firestone, and
Coca Cola Bottling became the hope of many who migrated to
Nairobi in search of factory jobs. The search for jobs was usually
disappointing for many. The formal Western education that a lucky
few rural Kenyans had received in the 1950s and 1960s prepared
them for white collar jobs which were few, both in the private
sector as well as the civil service. With the impoverishment of
the rural areas and overpopulation in some regions like Western
Kenya, Lake Region, and the Central Region, the lure of the city
was an ever-tempting one, in which hope for a better life was fore-
seen. The low wages in the multinational companies like Firestone
and East African Industries did not help the situation of those few
lucky ones who got jobs there (Leys 1975; Langdon 1978; Kaplinsky, 1978).

Indeed, during my study of the informal sector operators in
Nairobi, I came across ten out of a sample of 200 persons who had
left their jobs with East African Industries to start on their own.
They reported making more income than the salary in their former
jobs (Macharia 1989, 1992). Thus the multinational companies in
Nairobi have been known not to benefit the many facing the urban
challenge in Nairobi. Instead, they have enriched a few government leaders, who cut deals with these multinational companies
assuring them of protection for their goods—leading to inferior
quality that costs the average Kenyan more money. This has been
the case especially with the American tire company, Firestone
(Bates 1984). The government has also indirectly supported the
low wages of the factory workers by ensuring inactive trade unions
and declaring strikes illegal. This has continued to weaken the bargaining position of the Nairobi workers who have had to cope with
high inflation rates in the 1980s and 1990s while earning the salaries of 1960s and 1970s.

In the 1980s, the structural adjustment programs have weakened the buying power of most Nairobians in general, the worst hit
being the low income earners and in particular women, who had
been disadvantaged even beforehand due to their lack of education
and competitive job skills versus men. The relative deprivation
among lower income groups and women has increased. The infor-

mal economy, while acting as a safety net at present, faces problems, especially if it has to move from the survival stages to an income-generating and eventually employment-creating venture. A few of the informal sector occupations such as welding, auto repair, and carpentry are creating employment, but the income levels of about Ksh.1000 (approximately US$20) per month is still very meager given that at least half of these earnings will go toward housing in "indecent" places like the squatter settlements where informal landlords charge rent for the dwellings despite their temporary nature. Most squatter settlement dwellers pay rent to informal landlords who claim the cardboard or mud houses on the basis that they put them up. The difference between these houses and those in the formal private market is that the informal landlord cannot guarantee duration of stay in the same house as they are as vulnerable to demolitions as the tenants. The tenants suffer more in such an eventuality because they lose their rent as well as their belongings, not to mention that they are in the lowest income group to begin with.

Conclusions

The peripheralization of Nairobi's workers both in the formal and the informal sector has continued and the country's huge national debt, brought about by the tightening measures imposed by the International Monetary Fund, has not helped the situation at all. The hardship appears continue without much hope for Nairobi's urban masses. What is clear is that Kenya's close ties to the advanced industrial giants of the West has had little if any positive impact on the lives of the poorest Nairobians.

The solution for the future will rely on a number of factors all aimed at improving the current impoverished situation of most of those migrating and being born in the city. The lessons from the informal economy (Jua Kali) certainly give some hope for the future. It is very clear that those involved in these activities have a strong will to survive and are very innovative. This is so despite the lack of support from the government. With support, logistical planning, a sense of security, an infrastructure to reach their otherwise unreachable locations, and a generally favorable enabling

environment with a positive attitude that sees these Jua Kali operators as contributors rather than a nuisance, it is possible that
these hard working people may finally be able to turn their lives
around.

Allocation by the authorities of plots from which to operate will
give confidence both to the Jua Kali operators and also to their
customers, who will be sure to find the artisan or the carpenter in
the same location in subsequent visits. The customers will feel free
to leave a deposit for an item to be made if there is an assurance of
permanence of location. This is why the question of land tenure in
the city should be revised and allocations performed appropriately
and in recognition of the informal entrepreneurs. Eventually, the
centrality of the location would also be profitable to the City Council, who might charge the Jua Kali operators for services and amenities provided with the hope that by that time they will have
started making some profits from their businesses.

The already established social networks have created a social
capital among the Jua Kali operators and this could be tapped in
the future by formal financial institutions to facilitate granting
loans. The social capital created here is mainly trust that has been
built up as a result various social networks, relatives or friends
who not only provided shelter those first days in Nairobi but in
some cases also gave an interest-free loan for start-up capital.
Given that trust may be the only "collateral" most of these people
might have, the extent to which this could be used in the future by
a modern financial system like a bank could significantly improve
the lives of those in the informal economy. Thus the existing social
capital should be seen as a starting point for translating it through
various modifications to conventional capital, and there is ample
potential here.

The informal squatter settlements should also be supported and
not condemned, given that the city of Nairobi cannot possibly provide the housing stock for the many looking for houses every year.
Similar to the informal business economy, informal housing is a
brilliant idea for people who do not want to sleep in the open
streets and for those who still cherish the idea of the home as a
place to raise their children and to make economic decisions as a
family unit. Demolitions and constant threats will only undermine
the efforts of those in the informal housing. Instead, the central

government and city officials should devise ways to encourage
them, by upgrading the physical infrastructure, sanitation facilities, and at least giving the people a sense of permanence in their
residential areas. They would be more productive knowing that
they did not have to move to another area and lose their belong-
ings. As in the case of commercial plots, the land tenure issue
should be revisited here to assure that public land is distributed to
the needy and not to powerful politicians who will use their power
to manipulate the forceful evacuation of squatter settlers.

Advocating a bottom-up approach for those in the informal economy and in the informal settlements encourages hope for the future because these people are themselves very dynamic and innovative. Their efforts have usually been undermined from the top,
which is why I advocate direct support especially from those in the
West who have usually given grants or loans to the government.
This support has rarely reached the Nairobi masses. It is clear that
their own efforts have sustained them, and it is with them that the
future should begin.

NOTES

1. As partial evidence of this, we must consider the fact that many multinational companies and international organizations have selected Nairobi, Kenya, for their African headquarters. Among these organizations
are the United Nations Environmental Programme (UNEP), Habitat, The
World Bank Regional Headquarters for East and Central Africa, and international non-government organizations like The Environment Liaison
Center.

2. Kiosks are temporary cardboard or wooden structures that house
quick stop-over retail stores and eateries.

3. Traditionally, an African family is usually larger than the average
Western family, as it includes both the nuclear family of husband, wife,
and at least five children as well as members of the extended family and
even neighbors from one's rural place of origin.

REFERENCES

Bates, R.H. 1984. *Markets and States in Tropical Africa*. Berkeley: University of California Press.

58 AFRICA

Castells, M. 1977. *The Urban Question*. London: Edward Arnold.

Chase-Dunn, C.K. 1989. *Global Formation: Structures of the World Economy*. Oxford: Basil Blackwell.

De Soto, H. 1987. *The Other Path: The Invisible Revolution in The Third World*. New York: Harper and Row.

Freeman, D.B. 1991. *A City of Farmers*. Montreal: McGill-Queens University Press.

Hart, K. 1973. "Income Opportunities and Urban Employment in Ghana." *Journal of Modern African Studies* 11: 61–89.

International Labor Organization (ILO). 1972. *Employment, Incomes and Equality: A Strategy for Increasing Productive Employment in Kenya*. Geneva: ILO.

Kaplinsky, R. 1978. *Readings on the Multinational Corporation in Kenya*. Nairobi: Oxford University Press.

Langdon, S. 1978. "The Multinational Corporation in the Kenya Political Economy." In Kaplinsky, R. (ed.), *Readings on the Multinational Corporations In Kenya*. Oxford: Oxford University Press.

Leys, C. 1975. *Underdevelopment in Kenya*. London: Heinemann.

Lipton, M. 1977. *Why Poor People Stay Poor: Urban Bias in World Development*. Cambridge, Mass.: Harvard University Press.

Macharia, K. 1989. "The Role Of Social Networks and the State in the Urban Informal Sector: The case of Nairobi, Kenya." Unpublished Ph.D. dissertation, Department of Sociology, Berkeley, University of California.

———. 1992. "Slum Clearance and The Informal Economy in Nairobi." *Journal of Modern African Studies* 30:2: 221–236.

———. 1993. "Informal Sector Data Analysis." Commissioned Paper by the World Bank for the Ministry of Technical Training and Technology in Kenya.

———. 1994. "Small Scale Enterprises and Alleviation of Poverty in Kenya." Research Paper for the United Nations Development Unit (UNDP), oNairobi Regional Office.

"Nairobi's Insecurity and the Future of the United Nations Mission." *Weekly Review* (January 14 1994). Nairobi: Stellascope Publishers.

National Housing Cooperative Union (NACHU). 1990. "A Survey of Informal Settlements in Nairobi." Nairobi: NACHU Publications.

O'Connor, A. 1983. *The African City*. New York: Africana Publishing Company.

Portes, A., Castells, M., and Benton, L.A. 1989. *The Informal Economy: Studies in Advanced and Less Developed Countries*. Baltimore: The Johns Hopkins University Press.

Republic of Kenya. 1974. *Five Year Development Plan: 1969–1974*. Nairobi: Government Printer.

———. 1989. *Five year Development Plan: 1984–1989*. Nairobi: Government Printer.

———. 1992. Sessional paper No. 2 of 1992 On "Small Scale Enterprises and Jua kali Development In Kenya." Nairobi: Government Printer.

———. 1994. Annual Economic Review. Central Bureau Of Statistics. Nairobi: Government Printer.

Soja, E. 1970. "The African Experience." In John N. Paden and Edward Soja (eds.), *The African Experience*. Evanston: Northwestern University.

Stren, R. and White, R.R. (1989) *African Cities in Crisis: Managing Rapid Urban Growth*. Boulder: Westview.

Wallerstein, I. 1974. *The Modern World System*. New York: Academic Press.

Joe L. P. Lugalla

3

Where Do the Majority Live in Urban Tanzania

Why and How?

Tanzania is one of the countries in Africa that has been experiencing rapid urbanization. Since colonialism, the urban population has been increasing at the rate of nine percent. Because rapid urban growth is taking place without a corresponding economic growth, the government is experiencing severe financial difficulties. Hence, most of the urban areas lack essential facilities and the majority of urban residents live in poor conditions.

The aim of this chapter is to describe the housing conditions in urban Tanzania, for the purpose of exposing the living conditions of the majority urban poor. In doing this, I attempt to adopt a political-economic approach in which I shall implicitly present two arguments that confirm specific trends. First is the argument that a specific pattern of social, political, and economic organization within Tanzanian society, which has evolved over a long period of time, has created an evident social and economic structure. Secondly, that this social structure has divided urban dwellers into different social classes and that this process has been responsible for determining the struggle of different classes to survive and shape their living in urban areas.

In order to understand how the urban social structure determines the social pattern of urban housing, a historical account of urbanization as a social process in Tanzania is important.

61

The Politics of Urbanization During Colonialism

The history of urbanization in Tanzania owes a lot to the politics of colonialism. Most of the towns in Tanzania emerged as political administration centers of the colonial state. Dar es Salaam and other towns with regional headquarters developed as a result of this process. Some of the towns emerged at railways and crossroads, like Morogoro, Dodoma, and Tabora. Others developed as important ports for export and import trade. As years passed, commercial functions came to dominate the economic life of these towns. Although these towns were not industrial, all functions that took place in urban Tanzania were in line with the interests of the colonial economy and therefore had a direct relationship to the surrounding countryside.

Due to the close relationship between these towns and the colonial economy, all institutions for supervising and monitoring the colonial economy were set in them. Since these towns were nonindustrial, their relationship with rural Tanzania was exploitative and parasitic rather than generative. For years this has acted as an impetus to rural-urban migration rather than a hinderance.

Colonialism created a unique social structure in both urban and rural areas. While the domain of urban areas was in administration and commerce, the countryside's economic domain was in cash crop production and mining. Land alienation took place in certain areas in order to pave the way for settler plantation farming. Some areas were earmarked and reserved for providing migrant labor. In these areas cash crop production was deliberately discouraged by the colonial government in order to force the natives to depend on selling labor as a means of survival. In order to force the natives to participate effectively in the colonial economy, money economy and taxes to be paid in money form were introduced. Colonial policies aimed at enhancing colonial economic activities led to the development of regional inequality on the one hand and social class differentiation on the other.

A similar process of class differentiation took place in urban areas. A nascent working class comprised of Africans was formed. Some few Europeans who worked as administrators in the colonial state and others who worked for foreign companies became urban based. Merchant capitalism, which was also urban based, was mainly dominated by Asians. This exchange merchant capitalism was not independent but was rather incorporated into and subordinated to metropolitan capitalist economies. While Europeans occupied jobs of higher status followed by Asians, the Africans occupied jobs of lower cadre. In general, there was a very close relationship between race and class, and occupation and income.

Towns were designed in such a way that their physical layout reflected the social distances of hierarchical colonial social organization (Brain 1979:271). Racial and class segregation was dominant in these towns. Europeans lived in essentially attractive suburbs. Their houses were large and well built and set in expensive spacious gardens. Streets in these areas were maintained and had lights. Houses were supplied with water, electricity, and modern sewage connections. Golf courses, social clubs, and other recreational facilities surrounded these luxurious residential areas of the whites. The best examples of these areas are: Oyster Bay in Dar es Salaam, Kijengi in Arusha, Isamilo and Capri-Point in Mwanza, Mlimani in Dodoma, Loleza in Mbeya, and Gangilonga in Iringa. During colonialism these areas were called "Uzunguni," a Swahili word that means a European area. Most of the houses in these areas were built in low-density plots. Next to the "Uzunguni" area was the "Uhindini" area, an area of residence for people of Asian origin, which in several towns housed shops and was the central area for trade, business, and commerce. This was the next favored area in terms of provision of urban social services, and the majority of the houses were built on medium-density housing plots. Africans were left to reside in high-density areas, sometimes in unplanned residential settlements of poor quality without piped water, electricity, street lights, or modern sewage systems. Residential segregation was also accompanied by segregation in the provision of social services like hospitals and schools.

In summary, the facilities and living areas of the towns were different for each of what were seen as three racial communities— African, Asian, and European. Each of these had its own schools, churches, clubs, hospitals, bars, and so on (Brain 1979:17). This was considered to be equality from the point of view of colonialism.

From the above analysis, it should be clear that descriptions of high-, medium-, and low-density residential areas were mere technical terms used in colonial urban planning in order to camouflage or conceal the terms "African," "Asian," and "European" housing, whose application would seem to be more racist.

In his analysis of Dar es Salaam, Iliffe has argued that in order to prevent intermingling, the Germans began in 1912 to divide the town into three racial building zones. The British completed the scheme after 1918, and located the African zone west of the commercial center of Kariakoo which used to be a camping site for their carrier corps (Iliffe 1979:385). It is in this area that Africans leased plots and built their own houses for rental and owner-occupier purposes.

As the city continued to grow, typical settlements for Africans became located far away from the city center. Ilala, which became a new African settlement next to Kariakoo, grew under this principle. The conditions of the African residential areas were appalling, since most of the Africans who lived in them were either unemployed or received very low incomes. (An investigation carried out in 1939 showed that sixty percent of the employed Africans earned less than Tsh.15 a month [*Ibid.*:386].)

Iliffe has described the forms of social organization in these settlements as follows. They ranged from one that was purely political in nature to one more ethnic in form and content. There emerged tribal associations, which performed several functions, such as assisting new migrants in securing employment, and accommodating and assisting fellow tribesmen in matters concerning funeral and marriage ceremonies. Earlier on, the Germans had established a regulation that forced tribes to bury their tribal mates who had died in hospitals (Iliffe 1979:389). This laid down the foundation for the urban social networks of affiliation and assistance that are now dominant in urban areas in Tanzania.

It is this kind of complexity and composition which the postcolonial state inherited during the eve of independence on December 9, 1961, in the case of Dar es Salaam. Other urban areas experienced a similar kind of "development" trend. These trends have continued to surface to date.

In brief, it is now clear how colonialism distorted the self-sustaining pre-colonial social and economic structure. The colonial economy not only distorted the traditional African social and economic structure, but also introduced rural and urban capitalism, an economic system that was based on commodity production and was outwardly oriented. Africans came to adhere to the laws of motion of the colonial economy. Some joined cash-crop production, and others wage-paying employment. In some areas this involved rural-rural migration, and in others, rural-urban migration. In both patterns of migration, the main reason was economic.

It is also clear now how the colonial economy created new settlements called towns. The role of these settlements was to service, monitor, and administer or supervise the colonial economy, and their major functions remained thus administrative and commercial. Since the employment structure of these towns was almost wholly in the tertiary sector, the towns did not themselves directly produce economic surplus. Their survival depended on the performance of the agricultural sector. It is this situation that independent Tanzania inherited.

What major changes were brought by independence? Did independence alter the already established colonial social and economic structure? What was the impact of the post-colonial state's policies on the process of urbanization? Some of these questions are answered in the sections that follow.

The Post-Colonial State Policies and Urban Development

Until late 1960, Tanzania, like many other post-colonial African countries, did little to define its urban development policy. The development of towns and cities was to continue more or less along the path already laid down by the colonial state. No attempts were made at the beginning to question the ideological background and content of the urban policies of the colonial state. Thus, urban plans were to continue along the lines suggested and recommended by colonial planners.

Immediately after independence, the post-colonial state abolished all colonial laws and regulations that restricted the flow of Africans into urban areas. Hence the African population in urban areas grew very fast. In Dar es Salaam there had been an average rate of increase of nine percent per annum between 1948 and 1957, but this shot up to fourteen percent between the 1948 and 1967 population censuses. High rates of growth for the Africans and predominantly low-income population were also notable in other, smaller towns (Stren 1979:189).

The first major post-colonial government's approach to urban development throughout the sixties was the control and allocation of land by the state. All land was declared a national property, and under a series of acts and regulations beginning in 1963, all freehold land was converted to government leasehold, and the previous owners were obliged to pay land rent (*Ibid.*:189). Conditions for development were laid down for all urban land, with the details agreed upon by the Town Planning Division and the Lands Division (*Ibid*:190). The zoning policy of the colonial government that had divided residential urban land into low-, medium-, and high-density areas continued to operate.

Residential segregation in terms of race was also abolished. At the beginning, emphasis on plot allocation and the provision of services was shifted from the former European areas to the high-density and low-income African areas (*Ibid.*:190). There were efforts also to construct low-cost housing.

However, the announcement on February 5, 1967, of the Arusha Declaration as a blueprint for socialist construction brought a new emphasis to Tanzanian urban policies. By virtue of the fact that the post-colonial state via the Arusha Declaration had vowed to abolish inequality exploitation and was aiming at building a country based on principles of socialism or "Ujamaa," it became necessary for the state to devise strategies to arrive at such objectives. At the level of urban development, the state was confronted with the problem of rapid urban growth and its concomitant effects. Amidst this was also the problem of rural-urban inequality and the fear that urban areas were exploiting the rural areas.

In order to avoid and solve these problems, the post-colonial state identified one major policy on urban development. This was introduced in 1969, and its main objective was to decentralize urban growth via the dispersion of industrial investments in designated "Growth Pole Centers." The other, minor approach adopted, and in fact related to the above one, was the enactment of bylaws and regulations aimed either at restricting rural-urban exodus or at repatriating to their home areas all those considered as loiterers in urban areas. The other major post-independence policy on urban development was the 1973 decision to relocate the capital from Dar es Salaam to Dodoma.

Although a variety of urban planning policies have been adopted since independence, these plans have not been able to change the social class structure that was a legacy of colonial policies. In essence, post-colonial policies have enhanced the process of class differentiation. In the following section, an analysis of the present social structure evident in urban Tanzania is presented.

The Urban Social Class Structure

Tanzania's urban population can roughly be divided into five social classes of distinct consumption patterns. I shall describe these classes mainly in terms of their consumption behavior. But this has to be seen as a product of the position these classes occupy in the urban social system and in relation to production.

At the bottom are the unemployed, domestic servants, hawkers, street vendors, and the like, whose earning and survival depend on luck and the vagaries of the urban system. In most cases their survival is sporadic and very uncertain. Most of them operate in the informal sector as employees and not as masters or owners. They live under very poor conditions without adequate food and shelter. In urban areas they can easily be seen scattered around the streets operating in petty trades; some work as parking boys, others as quick-service cheap prostitutes.

The second group of consumers consists of the very low level of the middle class. These include the unskilled and semi-skilled employed minimum wage earners. Some may be janitors, messengers, clerks, or small craftsmen. In light of the present fiscal crisis, their consumption pattern and behavior is more likely to resemble that of the first group. The only difference is that these people are officially employed. In reality, they cannot afford to buy new clothes or eat well and live luxuriously. My research findings reveal that most of these people have also joined in the activities of the informal sector and frequently use the labor of their children or relatives to supplement their incomes. The ones who do not have the capital and ability to operate small economic projects live by borrowing and shuffling debts.

The third group comprises the middle income earners. Most of them are employed in the formal sector as teachers, lecturers, doctors, administrators, and all those whose incomes range between twice as much as the official minimum pay and the lower level of the starting point of the high income earners' level. These people have officially stipulated social benefits, job security, and some have access to official transport. Due to their official position, most of them have attractive fringe benefits like official housing and free medical treatment. Their consumption pattern varies, but it is far better than the first two groups.

The fourth, and conspicuously visible, class of consumers consists of all those senior government, party, and parastatal organizations' officials and other upper echelons of the formal sector. Senior civil servants like principal secretaries, directors, very senior military officers, Directors General, General Managers, some politicians, and some Professors in institutes of higher learning like the University of Dar es Salaam belong to this group. For them, as one can see, things like food, clothes, and housing have been available in abundance. Since independence they have acquired new needs. These people are not hidden. One can identify them by the nature of their residential areas or the number plates of the official cars they use.

Closely related to this group, especially in terms of consumption patterns, are the very rich private individuals—contractors, industrialists, merchants, and other commercial bourgeoisie. Most of the Asians, Arabs, and semi-Arabs with business contacts abroad belong to this group. The majority own luxurious cars and villas. The politics of trade liberalization have helped them a lot. Again, like their counterparts above, this group of people has acquired new needs since independence. Trips abroad are common. Most of them own luxurious houses which are fitted with satellite dishes, television and video sets, cars. Whatever new products sweep the West, these people are never far behind in adopting them. Imitative Westernism is the hallmark of the majority of this class, and the glitter of their life styles stands in sharp contrast with the abysmal living conditions of the masses.

The consumption pattern of these affluent classes has had a very negative impact on the majority. Given a limited production capacity, overconsumption by a few segments of the urban population is bound to put other people at a disadvantage, in the following way. Luxury public-owned cars that are fuelled and repaired at the expense of the government, free treatment in private hospitals at home and abroad, the creation of duplicates of parastatals, (some dealing just with distribution) have cost the government a lot of money in recurrent expenditures. The economic crisis the government is currently experiencing is indeed a product of this extravagance.

The emergence of small but economically dominant groups of conspicuous consumers characterizes and shapes the mode of urban dynamics in Tanzania. Formal sector activities tend to dominate and, in some cases, ruin the activities in the informal sector. As a result of this, social disparities are widened, enabling the process of class polarization to take its course.

If this is the situation, where do the majority poor live? How do they live? What do the majority urban poor do to survive in such an urban system? The following sections attempt to answer these questions.

Class, Status, and Urban Housing

The relationship between housing, class, and status reveals directly how the government establishes policies that favor some sections of the urban community. Existing studies of urban housing in Tanzania reveal that the majority of the urban dwellers are low income earners, and most of them (more than seventy percent) live in settlements of squatter type (Ndjovu 1980: 35; Lugalla 1995: 47). The present government policy of dividing residential areas in urban areas in terms of standards based on income and status at least acknowledges the fact that there are divisions of people in terms of class or status. The best and the worst housing tends to be clustered in enclaves, with luxury housing catering to the privileged sections of the urban population and the spontaneous housing serving the very poor. These extremes are etched into the urban landscape by being visually and geographically separate from what is otherwise a more heterogeneous residential pattern. The residential areas of the highly learned elites, highly salaried civil servants, executives of commercial and industrial firms, and diplomats and foreign expatriates are usually located within the city boundaries, and in the case of Dar es Salaam, near the Indian Ocean, where there are cool sea breezes. They are clearly isolated from the residential areas of the ordinary people. Oyster-Bay, Msasani, Masaki, and Mbezi beach areas in Dar es Salaam are a case in point. Most of the elite housing and luxury flats are publicly or employer-owned, and most of them are provided with all amenities, like running water, electricity, indoor bathing and kitchen facilities. Other houses have separate servants' quarters and car parking spaces and garages. These belong to what are commonly referred to as the "low-density-residential areas."

The "medium-density-residential areas" constitute all those enclaves of the middle income people and are distinctive with the above ones in the sense that most of them have been built privately, some by the National Housing Corporation or the Registrar of Buildings, and are located sometimes right at the central part of the urban area. The areas have been well planned, and the housing units enjoy the protection of the state.

The "high-density-residential areas" are areas that accommodate low-cost-income housing. These houses are crowded in relation to the space provided, and the density of population is usually high. In some houses, water and electricity are available, and in others they are not. Most of the houses are privately owned and built on surveyed and well-planned plots.

The fourth type of residential pattern is *spontaneous housing*. While the first three types of residential patterns are officially planned and accepted by the government, this fourth type is illegal, and is associated with squatter settlements. In comparison with the above types, it is at the opposite extreme, usually found beyond city boundaries in suburban or peri-urban areas. The government continues to use technical planning concepts such as *high-*, *medium-*, and *low-density* areas. In reality, these planning concepts are class based and stand for the differentiation of residential areas of the *poor*, *middle-class*, and *rich* people.

In late 1972, the cabinet decided that all government and parastatal employees occupying public housing would pay rent on a sliding scale system of 7.5 percent, 10 percent and 12.5 percent of their income. Originally, as Stren (1979) has argued, it was felt that the upper income earners, who would pay more rent under the new system, would in effect be subsidizing the lower income earners, who would generally be paying less than before (Stren 1979: 191). In practice, this has not been the case, because most low income earners are legally not entitled to be provided accommodation by their employers, and even where the employer has several vacant housing units, the sliding scale rent system influences the employer to house only those employees of high income category, even if they are not his employees, in order to get a reasonable amount of money as rent contribution. The minimum wage earners have to depend on housing in the private sector, where they are always at the mercy of their landlords. The Rent Restriction Act of 1984, which was created by the government in order to regulate and control the landlord-tenant relationship, has a lot of loopholes and has not been able to operate in favor of tenants.

Urban Poverty and Housing Quality

Data from the 1967 census show that the residential areas for the affluent social class—for example, Oyster Bay and Regent Estate—maintained their low-density status, as suggested by Gibb, with 6.3 persons per acre. Europeans constituted seventy-five percent of the population in Oyster Bay and sixty-three percent in Regent Estate. Hardly any African people resided in these areas during this period (Schmetzer 1982). Eighty-two percent of the people living in the medium-density areas were Africans, with the exception of the Eastern Kinondoni area, where twenty-nine percent of the residents were European. The high-density residential areas had an African population of more than ninty-five percent.

The data provided by the 1978 population census shows that the situation had worsened instead of improving, especially for the majority of African people living in high-density and overcrowded areas. While the average density per acre increased from 6 to 8 persons in low-density areas, and held at 42 persons in medium-density areas, the average density in high-density and overcrowded areas increased from 86 to 106 persons and from 138 to 158 persons respectively. This information provides only the quantitative side of the problem and does not tell us anything in depth about the conditions of the housing units or residential areas occupied by different social groups.

In order to know what kind of housing is used by different social groups, it is important to examine the conditions of these residential areas and their housing units, and the way they are integrated into the urban service system. In their analysis of the 1967 census report, Egero and Henin (1973) revealed that only 34.8 percent out of a total 83,431 households available in Dar es Salaam were considered to be living in permanent structures. They showed that 57.4 percent were in semi-permanent structures, and 5.7 percent were in other structures, and 2.1 percent were undefined (Egero and Henin 1982: 28).

The surveys that provide the basic information about the housing conditions in Tanzania are the Household Budget Surveys (HBS). Only three such surveys have been carried out in Tanzania since independence. The first one was in 1969, the second in 1977, and the most recent one was carried out in 1991 and 1992. I have borrowed some data from these HBS in order to examine the conditions of housing in Tanzania. Improvements took place in the use of corrugated metal sheets for roofing, in foundations, and in concrete-cement or stone flooring between 1969 and 1977. In case of walls, the use of poles, branches, and grass declined while that of poles and mud and of mud blocks increased. A very significant improvement took place in the use of toilet systems. The percentage of pit latrines increased from 23 percent to 56 percent while the number of houses without toilet facilities declined from 50 percent to 22 percent (ILO 1982: 122).

The 1991 and 1992 HBS shows that in the rural areas, about 84 percent of the households had poor floors; in Dar es Salaam it was about 10 percent. Thirty-four percent of the households in Dar es Salaam had no electricity and about 40 percent of the urban population in the whole of Tanzania lived in overcrowded houses. Only 41 percent of the population of Dar es Salaam had water piped into housing units, and 83.1 percent of the population in the whole country used pit latrines. The situation is expecially appalling in squatter settlements and other high-density residential areas.

These data show that urban housing conditions still leave much to be desired. Bearing in mind the fact that the majority of the urban population (70 percent) live in squatter settlements, it remains self-evident that most of these settlements are of low quality and reflect, in a way, conditions of abject poverty and squalor. In order to understand how the poor survive, one needs to examine the nature of the informal sector.

The Informal Sector and the Urban Poor

There is plentiful evidence that the majority of the urban poor in Tanzania derive their incomes from informal activities, such as through the sale of informal products or earning informal wages (ILO 1982).

Bagachwa, in his study of the informal manufacturing sector in Tanzania, operationalized a survey covering seventy-one informal establishments engaged in basic needs activities that employed an average of fewer than ten persons, in Dar es Salaam (Bagachwa 1983). The survey covered only established units with some fixed capital investment, a premise, and a significant degree of value added. Areas covered included Kariakoo, Gerezani, Manzese, Tandika, and Kinondoni.

According to the survey, the establishments employed a total of 322 persons. Four-fifths (81 percent) were regular employees, while almost one-fifth (19 percent) were employed on casual terms (*Ibid.*: 6). Bagachwa noted that individual ownership was dominant (70 percent) (ibid.:12). Informal artisans preferred not to work on cooperative arrangements because of fear of being registered and hence subjected to income and sales tax and price control (*Ibid.*:12) The workers used mainly hand tools and performed manual labor, a fact that entails that most of these informal activities are less demanding in terms of operational and management skills, and that most of the skills can easily be acquired locally. The monthly wages for the regular employees ranged from Tshs. 480 to Tshs. 980. Bagachwa calculated that the mean monthly pay for regular laborers was Tshs.538. The official minimum wage during the period of this survey was Tshs.600 (*Ibid.*:23). Since wages were the major principal source of income (at least during those days), Bagachwa argued that the majority of the employees in this sector were within the poor, low income category (*Ibid.*:23).

Bagachwa's study dealt mainly with informal sector activities that had permanent fixed premises and needed some form of fixed capital investment. My 1987–1988 field survey of the informal sector looked at activities that had no fixed premises, such as hawking, street vending, car-washing, peddling, illegal foreign currency dealing, prostitution, and others.

Any new visitor to Dar es Salaam may be surprised by the pres-

ence of a vast market, which is distributed all over the city: behind
bus stations, along both the main and lesser streets, at crossroads,
outside principal formal institutions like post offices, churches,
mosques, and other places. Hawkers or street vendors selling different types of items, from cigarettes, stationeries, chewing gums,
to cooked and uncooked food, ply these areas in search of customers. The "Mishikaki-Nyama Choma"(roasted meat) boys are
visible in large numbers and are strategically located. These petty
trade activities have developed rapidly recently without technical
prescription or foreign assistance. They continue to grow and flour-
ish progressively despite various legal obstacles. Rossett (1987) has
argued that Peru's informal artisians rely not on government pa-
ternalism and planning, but rather on their own wits, energy, and
ambition in order to survive and prosper. The same is valid for
Tanzania (Rossett 1987:4).

In order to understand the mode of operation of these activities
in Dar es Salaam in terms of income, ownership, and the problems
encountered, a survey was administered to 200 hawkers, peddlers,
and street vendors (Lugalla 1995: 132). One-half of the respondents operated in the Manzese area, in the Kinondoni District,
while the remaining half operated in the Tandika area, in the Tem-
eke District. Those interviewed dealt with petty trade activities.

Three-quarters of the respondents were engaged in petty trading
of raw and cooked food items. The majority of the petty traders
were youths (boys and girls aged between fifteen and twenty-four
years), most of them had undergone primary school education, and
some were still attending schools. While most of the boys tended to
be mobile in their operations and specialize in various items, the
selling of cooked items like fried chicken, "vitumbua," "maandazi,"
dried and smoked fish, which requires immobility, was the occupation of women. This reflects the Tanzanian traditional family culture of the dominance of women in home economics and kitchen
work. Most of the hawkers and street vendors were males (74 percent).

The majority of the respondents (93 percent) stated that the
business in which they worked did not belong to them, but to their
parents or relatives or guardians with whom they stayed. The majority did not have a permanent income, but got non-monetary benefits like free food, accommodation, money for transport, clothing,

and security from the people whom they assisted in the business. This in a way means that most of these petty trading activities are family based, with heavy use of unpaid and, most likely, family labor. Regular wage employment in petty trading informal business is uncommon. Sometimes the sellers do sell a commodity at a higher price (than that agreed by the owner) and pocket the difference in order to pay themselves. Petty traders in Dar es Salaam and other urban areas in Tanzania work from early in the morning until sunset. Certain items like cooked food take a lot of time to prepare. Although it is the male youths or adults hawking cooked food items in the streets, such businesses belong and are in most cases controlled or dominated by women. Only thirteen out the 200 respondents owned their own business. All of them were adults, and twelve of them sold jewelry articles, women's rings ("Pete, vibanio na Urembo"), empty bottles (for recycling), cigarettes, and traditional medicines (herbs).

My findings reveal that during periods of economic crisis, informal sector activities do not remain the domain of the unemployed urban poor alone. The majority of the employed section of the urban population tend to join these activities in order to supplement their official incomes. They do so by investing part of their wages in these economic activities. More than four-fifths of the petty traders I interviewed stated that the owners of the business were employees in the formal sector. This means that many employed persons have become street hawkers and vendors (via family labor) as a temporary response to poverty. The conventional argument that informal sector activities are purely a domain of the unemployed urban poor is no longer valid in the case of Tanzania. What does this mean to the real urban poor? Generally it means that they have to compete with those who have an assured official income. To most of them, this situation has meant total marginalization and impoverishment.

Hawkers and street vendors do not reinvest all the money they get in expanding their businesses, partly because it may not be enough to keep them surviving, partly because of various constraints. Expansion of their activities may require more paid labor and fixed premises. Operating a business in a fixed location may subject them to the government arm(regulations). Licenses may be required. Health regulations have to be fulfilled, lest they end up

violating the bylaws that govern such activities and thus be subject
to penalization. It is also difficult to evade taxation if one operates
in fixed premises. That is why most of the petty traders prefer to
operate small manageable projects that permit mobility. Being mobile, the hawkers and vendors can easily pick up their commodities
and evade the police, as well as the health and tax officers. Un-
licensed or illegal traders balance carefully the tradeoffs between
the scale of operation and their ability to evade arrest and mini-
mize losses in fines and confiscations (Smart 1987:13). It is easier
to run with fewer articles that are small rather than many big and
heavy articles. Hence, some operators retain a small-scale operation for strategic reasons rather than as a result of insufficient capital accumulation (ibid.:13).

Social and economic hardships in families have a severe impact
on the living conditions of children. Some children find life in their
families difficult, so they move into the streets as beggars, scavengers for food scraps from hotels and the cafeterias of institutions of
higher learning, like the University in Dar es Salaam. Other children enter into illicit activities of black-marketing goods like cigarettes, where they are hired and used by people with urban connections and influence to procure huge amounts of cigarettes from the
official channels. Others enter into the business of pickpocketing,
and others end up as "parking boys," who earn their living through
odd jobs. In trying to escape their misery, they start smoking
"Widi," "Majani," and "Misokoto" (Bhang and Marijuana). Others
sniff petrol in order, Ishumi (1984) has argued, to get high and
withstand the scorn of passers by. Some of them "smoke" glue to
shut out feelings of poverty, loneliness, and hunger.

Young girls are forced into prostitution at a very tender age.
They become aware that one of the means of making quick money
is through prostitution. In their struggle for survival, the girls go
to bed with men who are as old as their fathers, apparently closing
their eyes to the haunting moments of struggling to survive.

Many of these youths are truants or school dropouts. Boys and
girls of this caliber can easily be spotted on what have come to be
known as "jobless corners" (Ishumi 1984). Girls loiter outside famous hotels and guest houses and provide a smiling gesture whenever their eyes meet those of the men. They frequent famous disco
clubs at night in search of entertainment and money via commer-

cialized sex. The majority of these youths (especially boys) are homeless. An interview with a few scavengers in Dar es Salaam reveals that it is hardship at home, matrimonial problems of their parents, and poverty which have led these youths to experience such situations.

The plight of the street children is hard to imagine. Since most of the street children hover on the periphery of other people's lives, most of the people in urban areas tend to look at them in an unseeing way. They are given bad names like "Wadokozi" or "Wachomoaji" (pickpockets) or "Wahuni" (hooligans). But the street children themselves are more down to earth. They normally label themselves as "Watemi," "Magangwe" (which means tough, carefree people who are used to problems), and some call themselves "Born-Town" or "Born-Here-Here," indicating that they were born in the city and are products of the urban areas. In reality, these children face severe threats but cannot report them to the police because, according to law, they are considered as criminals themselves. The problems these children confront in the urban areas, and how they surmount them, shows in concrete terms that to survive on the streets requires exceptional fortitude, a creative mind, and an astute knowledge of human nature. Contrary to the conventional belief, these children are not necessarily dropouts from society, nor are the streets where they live and operate "schools of crime." Hence, the belief that street children are or will inevitably become criminals is more of a popular belief than a reality.

Problems Encountered by Informal Sector Operators

Operating in the informal sector is not easy. There are risks and constant harassment from government precisely because, according to law, most of these activities are operated illegally. Following procedures means that one has to apply for a license, which calls for fixed premises, payment of taxes, and the government's influence over prices. The red tape involved is tangled and expensive. On the other side, there are disadvantages to operating a business outside the country's legal framework. One has to function in the business under the psychological stress of uncertainty. One has to work with several eyes in order to spot the direction where the authorities might appear. My findings reveal that most of the hawkers, street vendors, and other informal sector operators keep money in their pockets to bribe the authorities to look the other way. However, bribing one officer does not save one from being harassed by another officer. Some unlucky ones end up paying out all their daily income as bribes to different officials. The money paid as a bribe buys them nothing beyond the freedom to try to earn a living (Rossett 1987:6). Although President Mwinyi's 1989 directive admonished officials to stop harassing vendors, in practice it has not eased the level of hardship for the operators.

This was the second time that President Mwinyi issued such an order on the question of petty traders. However, the problem recurs precisely because the president's directives have not forcefully encouraged the City Council to repeal its bylaws and health regulations. It must be clear that it is these coercive, unrealistic bylaws that focus the negative attitude of the city fathers on the informal sector operators. As long as such laws continue to exist, the harassment of these urban poor will continue. For example, after waiting a long time to round up all the street vendors and hawkers popularly known as "machingas"[1] in the famous "Congo Street" in the Kariakoo area, by the Dar es Salaam City Council finally implemented its decision in early August 1993. The City Council ordered the Field Force Unit of the police to round up the vendors, beat them, and confiscate their property under the pretext of "Putting the City Clean." The vendors reacted violently by beating the police, looting the nearby shops, and vandalizing both public and private property.

While the Central Government saw vending and hawking as a survival tactic of the poor, the City Council held a very negative attitude towards vendors and hawkers. The City Council's view is well summarized by the words of the City Director Mr. Mukhandi, who argued that, "The City Council will continue discharging its duties including ensuring that the city environment is clean and hygienically safe. Most of these vendors are criminals operating illegally and this can be proved if they are rounded up" (*Daily News* 1993). The most recent confrontation along Congo Street occurred on February 16, 1995, when policemen clashed with the "machingas" whom they tried to evict. The clash was violent and one of the "machingas" who was injured and sent to the hospital said, "We have never been allocated any place for our business. We came here because there are no jobs in the rural areas" (Newsreel IPS: 1995).

Besides the problems associated with harassment, some petty traders complain about the scarcity of customers. Not every day is a good day for petty traders, and on bad days, when customers are few, traders who deal in perishable articles like meat or fruits suffer. Their supplies rot. If the demand goes down, it is the petty traders who lose, and if the police, tax, and health officers come and confiscate their items or demand bribes it is again the petty traders who lose.

While some people within the urban system eat well, informal sector operators work hard for long hours for little money. The street boys sleep on street pavements. They are never sure of the source of their next meal, and risk their lives by scavenging and having to run from the police. The street girls experience bodily humiliation at a tender age. They are sexually exploited, abused, and misused. They surrender their bodies to men in exchange for money, drinks, clothes, food, and accommodation in a good hotel or house. Like the prostitutes, they sleep with men whom they do not know. Some are beaten, raped by several men, left unpaid for the services they have provided, and they are vulnerable to sexually transmitted diseases.

Conclusion

The overall conclusion emanating from the above analysis reveals concretely that the majority of the urban poor live in poor housing. The conditions is these areas are appalling and lack the necessary services like water, electricity, drainage, and sanitation. Due to these unhygienic conditions, these people tend to be vulnerable to water-borne diseases like cholera, typhoid, and diarrhea, as well as tuberculosis and respiratory infections. It is the situation of poverty that has relegated the majority of urban people to this situation. Due to poverty, these people depend on marginal jobs or economic activities in the informal sector, where they are not only confronted with marginal, unreliable incomes but are also subject to police harassment.

The analysis of the urban social class structure shows that poverty coexists with wealth. This is evident in urban housing in which luxurious houses stand in contrast to unreliable, miserable-looking houses in squatter settlements. These two opposed developments, which in fact reflect the class position of dwellers and therefore determine their ways of life, are not isolated trends. They are two sides of the same coin. Both colonial and post-colonial development policies have been responsible for creating these trends. It is these policies that finally determine who lives where and how and gets what in an urban system. Unless these policies are transformed to take into consideration the needs and problems of the majority of urban dwellers, the situation is likely to remain the same.

NOTE

1. The "machingas" ("marching guys" in the Swahili language) are mostly teenage boys from the rural southern border of the country who are poor school dropouts that migrate to the city to peddle various items for mainly Indian wholesalers and merchants.

REFERENCES

Bagachwa, M.S.D. 1983. "Structure and Policy Problems of the Informal Manufacturing Sector in Tanzania." *Economic Research Bureau Paper*. No. 1. University of Dar es Salaam.

Brain, A. 1979. *The Political Economy of Urbanization in Tanzania*. Unpublished Ph.D. Thesis, University of British Columbia.

Daily News Paper. 1985. Dar es Salaam (Sunday 22).

Directive On Housing Allowance. 1967. Standing Committee on Para-statal Organizations (SCOPO). No. 2. Government Documents, Dar es Salaam.

Egero and Henin (eds.). "Analysis of the 1967 Population Census," quoted in Chachage, S.L.C. *The Housing Problem and the Policy of Socialism in Dar es Salaam*. Unpublished B.A. Degree Dissertation, University of Dar es Salaam.

Ilife, J. 1979. *A Modern History of Tanganyika*. Cambridge, Mass: Cambridge University Press.

International Labour Office (ILO). 1982. *Basic Needs in Danger: A Basic Needs Oriented Development Strategy for Tanzania, Jobs and Skills Program for Africa.* Addis, Ababa.

International Press Service (IPS). Harare. (February 17, 1995).

Ishumi, A.G.M. 1984. *The Urban Jobless in Eastern Africa.* Scandinavian Institute of African Studies, Uppsala.

Lugalla, Joe L.P. 1995. *Crisis, Urbanization, And Poverty In Tanzania: A Study of Urban Poverty and Survival Politics.* Lanham, Md.: University Press of America.

Ndjovu, C.E.K. 1980. *The Housing Market in Dar es Salaam.* Ardhi Institute: Dar es Salaam.

Rossett, C. 1987. "Peru's New Economic Order in The Informal Economy." *CUSO Journal.* (December).

Schmetzer, H. 1982. "Housing in Dar es Salaam." *In Habitat International,* Vol. 1, No. 4.

Smart, J. 1987. "Street Hawking in Hong Kong." *CUSO Journal.*

Stren, Richard E. 1979. "Urban Policy." in Barkan, J.D., and Okumu, J.J. (eds.). *Politics and Public Policy in Kenya and Tanzania.* Nairobi, Kenya: Heineman Educational Books.

Part Two

LATIN AMERICA

George Priestley

4

Post-Invasion Panama

Urban Crisis and Social Protests

On December 20, 1989, the United States sent 26,000 troops into Panama, ravaging El Chorrillo, San Miguelito, and Colon, working-class communities of mostly brown and Black people. The U.S. economic sanctions, the invasion, and neoliberal economic policies have worsened the lives of the inhabitants of these urban communities.[1]

Colon City, on the Atlantic coast of the Panama Canal, and El Chorrillo, on the Pacific entrance to the Canal, are communities whose histories are intimately linked to the U.S.-controlled waterway. San Miguelito, on the other hand, seventeen kilometers northeast of Panama City, is a postwar phenomenon. Serving as a receptacle for rural migrants from all nine provinces, it grew from fewer than 12,000 inhabitants in 1960 to nearly 300,000 in 1994.

Panama's geographical position, the narrowest link between the Atlantic and the Pacific Oceans, has shaped the country's external economic and social relations. While these matters will not be detailed in this chapter, it is important, nevertheless, to point out that commerce, real estate, and services dominate Panama's economy and are mostly concentrated in the Metropolitan area.[2] That is one of the reasons that urban property was and continues to be a source of conflict amongst various parties—the U.S. government, the Panamanian urban commercial elite, and organized city dwellers.

Two factors have limited rational allocation of land use in Panama's metropolitan area. First, the presence of the 500 square mile U.S.-controlled Canal Zone enclave at either side of the Panama Canal. This enclave, part of the metropolitan area, has been under Washington's control since 1903, and for most of this century it has claimed a treaty right to use any and all lands it deemed necessary for the construction, maintenance, and defense of the Canal. Second, the control of urban property by the country's dominant commercial and real estate elite. Being so close to the Panama Canal, the dominant economic activity in the country, urban land has always been expensive and out of reach of the impoverished majority.

While the urban crisis is not limited to El Chorrillo, San Miguelito, or Colon City, this chapter will underscore the urban history and experiences of these similar yet different communities in the wake of the invasion. Policy recommendations, short- and long-term, are offered that might begin to address the plight of the Panamanian urban masses.

Early Urbanization and Racial Segregation in Panama

Prior to the building of the Panama Canal, Panama City was really two cities: an enclosed city occupied by well-to-do white Panamanians, and the *arrabal*, occupied by mostly Black or mulatto Panamanians, outside of the walled city. The U.S. Canal Zone, a parallel garden-like city created during the construction of the Panama Canal, was also two communities: one white and the other Black. When West Indians came to build the Panama Canal, they were housed in both Colon and Panama cities and in segregated communities in the then-recently created Canal Zone. Housing and social segregation in the Zone were sanctioned by U.S. laws, and in Panama City de facto segregation prevailed.[3] Following Canal construction, the lighter-skinned economic elite moved out of the walled city to more fashionable high-rent communities like La Exposicion, La Cresta, El Cangrejo, Altos del Golf, and, in the 1970s, Punta Paitilla, an area off Panama Bay that was under U.S. control until after World War II.

During the first four decades of the twentieth century, when the core of the city did not go beyond Perejil, one could identify well-defined communities that were either Black and mulatto, mestizo, or white. San Felipe, occupied by the commercial elite prior to the Canal, became mestizo and mulatto; Santana remained primarily mestizo and mulatto; El Chorrillo, Calidonia, Maranon, and Guachapalí, housing workers escaping from legal segregation in the Canal Zone, were mostly Black and brown, and La Exposicion, with its imitation of U.S. colonial structures, was mostly white.[4]

While these socio-racial patterns are still visible fifty years later, housing segregation is now a function of both class and race. The U.S. Canal Zone, which practiced apartheid until the 1950s, expelled most of its Black population in the late 1950s, preferring to depopulate rather than desegregate. Hence, many of the sons and daughters of the Canal "diggers" began the long trek to the United States, particularly to Brooklyn, New York. On the other hand, rural-to-urban migration and economic modernization, both postwar phenomena, brought about significant population growth, expansion of the city, and an increase of the mestizo group; there was also important economic and social mobilization, permitting an expansion of the middle sectors and enabling some middle class Blacks and mulattos to integrate white and mestizo communities (Uribe 1989:60–68).

Modernization, Migration, and Urban Change: 1950–1980

Between 1950 and 1975, Panama's economy grew at an annual rate of eight percent. Industries flourished, new roads crisscrossed the countryside, and commerce thrived as never before. During the same period, industry grew at a rate of eleven percent per year, increasing its contribution to the GNP from less than five percent directly after World War II to almost twenty percent in 1980. Meanwhile, agricultural modernization accelerated and production increased, putting tremendous pressure on rural structural changes in Panama's social organization. Rural economies were transformed; a new and fast-growing industrial workforce appeared; and the professional middle class increased in numbers, expanding its influence (Priestley 1990).

These new social forces began to demand greater participation in the country's politics, but the oligarchic regime refused to democratize political affairs, leading eventually to its ouster from power and the advent of a populist/nationalist military regime led by General Omar Torrijos, which overthrew President Arnulfo Arias on October 11, 1968 (Priestley 1986).

Migration and urban growth responded to huge capital investments made by the United States in the context of World War II and by the import-substitution industrialization process spawned by the government of Jose Remon Cantera in the 1950s. Panama City increased its population from 216,600 in 1950 to 794,300 in 1990, and by 1990 that district of Panama was 83.1 percent urban (Mendez 1992:491–492). In this period, many new communities emerged. But not every one could afford the expensive urban rents, and so rural migrants and urban poor began to invade private and state properties.

San Miguelito: A Profile of the Urban Crisis in the 1970s

In the 1950s, when the rural poor and landless began to arrive in Panama City, they settled on several privately owned lands in what was to become San Miguelito. By the 1970s, as a result of public-sponsored housing programs, the Special District of San Miguelito had begun to transform itself from essentially a shantytown to a mixed community of poor and middle class Panamanians of various racial types (Uribe 1989; Velàsquez 1993). What follows is a synthesis of the military's response to the social and urban crisis, particularly in San Miguelito (Priestley 1987).

Unlike earlier governments controlled by the Panamanian oligarchy, the military government that came to power in 1968 sought to implement a number of reforms to deal with the symptoms of the urban crisis. General Omar Torrijos, leader of the so-called "October Revolution," designed and implemented rural colonization projects to stem the tide of rural migrants; organized state-owned companies to provide rural and urban jobs; introduced educational reforms to provide basic agricultural training for rural-based students; reformed the nation's labor code to modernize labor-management relations; and instituted housing reforms to provide affordable state-financed housing for urban wage owners and lower-middle income groups. These economic and social reforms were part of a larger populist/nationalist strategy that the military government designed in order to forge a large anti-oligarchical and anti-colonial coalition.

While these 1970s reforms benefitted some urban groups, they were insufficient to meet the needs of the ever-expanding urban population, most of whom lived in San Miguelito, swelling the ranks of the informal economy. In any case, the success of Torrijos's reform strategy depended on external financing and on the ability of the military to mediate class and group conflict. By the mid 1970s, external finances began to dry up, debilitating the ability of the Torrijos regime to continue to finance the reforms, which also came under political fire from the economic elite from the late 1970s onwards. After the signing of the Torrijos-Carter treaty, the populist coalition unraveled, crumbling in 1981 after the general died in a mysterious plane crash. The years that followed have been especially difficult for the urban poor as economic growth has declined and the state has reduced social spending to meet the requirements set by the IMF and U.S. government agencies (Velàsquez *op.cit.*) One community that was particularly affected by these changes in economic and social policies was San Miguelito.

San Miguelito is 51.3 sq.km. and lies northeast of Panama City. While in 1960 its population was 12,975, today it is more than 243,025, constituting a little less than one-third of urban Panama. (Censos Nacionales 1990:12). Like much of urban Panama, San Miguelito's population is relatively young, an average of twenty-two years (*Ibid.*).

Most of San Miguelito's residents are the rural and urban poor who migrate to metropolitan Panama in search of jobs, housing, health, and education. They come from every district of the nine provinces of the Republic. They also come from other districts within the metropolitan region, primarily from the older Black and brown communities of Maranon, Calidonia, Chorrillo, etc. San Miguelito has no significant economic base, its residents are mostly underemployed low wage earners who work in Panama City. Its unemployment rate has been consistently higher than that of metropolitan Panama. From 27 percent in 1960, the unemployment rate dropped to 13.6 percent in 1980, but has since increased to 17 percent in 1990 (*Ibid.*). Following the 1978 Torrijos-Carter treaty and the demise of Torrijos, urban Panama and particularly San Miguelito suffered from increased military corruption and IMF-imposed structural agreements.

Unlike 1968, when San Miguelito's residents took to the streets to demonstrate and protest against the military coup, in 1984 in the first direct and popular elections, they voted for the political opposition. The Nicolas Ardito Barletta ticket (Democratic Revolutionary Party-PRD), supported by General Manuel Antonio Noriega, lost by 10,000 votes.[5] Furthermore, the Democratic Opposition Alliance (ADO), a coalition of conservative parties, obtained two of the five legislative seats.

Balbina Herrera, a maverick within the PRD, was elected mayor of San Miguelito, winning without the support of Noriega or the PRD party machine. Balbina Herrera belonged to a splinter group of the *Tendencia*, the left wing of the PRD. During her mayoral years, she survived the challenges of the *Tendencia* by putting together an impressive team of young community organizers who worked with dozens of community groups seeking solutions to housing, light, water, and unemployment (Priestley 1987). In the crisis period 1988–1989, she adopted a staunch nationalist position and opposed the U.S. invasion of December 20, 1989.

In May 1989, the PRD lost the national elections by a 3 to 1 margin and Noriega annulled the elections, claiming U.S. interference. Seven months later, the United States invaded Panama and the U.S.-supported Democratic Civilian Opposition Alliance (ADOC) took office. PRD elected fewer than ten legislators to the 68 member legislative body; Balbina Herrera of San Miguelito was one.

In 1994, Ms. Herrera was reelected to the National Assembly, and became the first woman to occupy the presidency of Panama's legislative body. As a member of the legislature during the 1990–1994 Endara government, she became the principal spokesperson for the PRD, a party whose reputation was badly damaged for being associated with the Noriega regime.

Balbina Herrera's success is due to the political maturity of San

Miguelito's electorate. While electing and reelecting Ms. Herrera to various offices over the years, the residents of San Miguelito voted against Noriega and the PRD in 1984 and 1989. In 1989, the Endera coalition won in San Miguelito, but because of its austerity policies it was repudiated in November 1992, when more than fifty percent of eligible voters abstained from participating in the constitutional reforms sponsored by the Endara government, while the other fifty percent voted 5–1 against the reforms. This was indicative of how the population felt about a government that turned its back on their everyday needs while disbursing hundreds of millions to pay the national debt.

San Miguelito is very different from what it was in 1960 or even the 1970s. The district not only increased its population from 12,000 (1960) to nearly 243,025 (1990) inhabitants, but many of its communities have a considerable number of middle income residents. This new demographic and economic development makes it difficult to duplicate the successful mobilization of the 1950s and 1960s. Furthermore, the military governments and the Catholic and Evangelical churches have coopted some of the most effective leaders, while many of the potential young leaders have been lost to drugs and violence. Nevertheless, San Miguelito has become a major electoral force in the 1990s. In 1994, 115,493 of the 164,073 eligible voters participated in the national elections, voting overwhelmingly for the PRD candidates, including President Ernesto Perez Balladares, who has promised to pay more attention to the social debt than the public debt.[6] The people of San Miguelito wait to see whether the PRD and Balbina as president of the National Assembly will create adequate housing and employment programs to meet their needs or whether they will continue the IMF recommendations of the 1980s and early 1990s.

Structural Adjustments, Sanctions, and Labor Protest in the 1980s

During the decade of the 1980s, especially after Omar Torrijos's death in a mysterious air crash in July 1981, the military lost much of its bargaining power to the Panamanian economic elite and the U. S. government. The urban masses were the first to feel the impact of this new correlation of forces as they confronted the International Monetary Fund's imposed structural adjustment agreements of the 1980s and the U.S. economic sanctions of 1987–1989, which were followed by the invasion of December 20, 1989.

Unencumbered by the clientele relations of the Torrijos years, the urban popular movement mobilized against the International Monetary Fund (IMF) structural adjustments in 1984 through 1986. In March 1986, Noriega's Panamanian Defense Force (PDF) broke the back of a national strike called by the National Confederation of Workers (CONATO), repressing workers of the National Oil Refinery in Colon. Despite Noriega's repression of the labor and popular movement, he continued to command partial support from labor and popular leaders during the 1987–1989 confrontation with the United States (Gomez and Hughes 1985). In that difficult period when the United States all but dismissed Panamanian sovereignty, many popular-sector leaders chose what they perceived as national loyalty over class solidarity, and in the face of economic sanctions and threats of invasion, some even joined civil defense groups called "Dignity Battalions." Many of the recruits were from El Chorrillo and San Miguelito.

Economic sanctions imposed by the United States on Panama during the months of 1987 through 1989 had their most devastating impact on those who depended on public sector and construction jobs, the urban poor. Undoubtedly, Panama's economy was in bad shape before the U.S.-imposed economic aggression against it in 1987. According to official sources, the production of goods and services in 1988 declined by twenty percent compared to 1987; collection of tax revenue declined by fifty percent; and unemployment increased by fifty percent in the same period. Social services and other public services also dwindled; investment in and maintenance of health and educational facilities dropped significantly, while water, light, garbage collection, and public transportation suffered massive budget cuts.

The sectors most severely affected by U.S.-imposed sanctions were those connected to productive activities. On the other hand, the least affected were involved in export-oriented activities—the Panama Canal, U.S. military bases, banana companies, the Colon Free Zone, and the petroleum refinery and oleoduct—associated with U.S. capital. Notwithstanding the differential impact of the sanctions, the salaried population, manual (workers) and non-manual (middle strata) suffered an average salary reduction of more than forty percent. Those who work in the informal sector of the economy (sub-proletarian) delivering personal services also experienced significant decline in income.

While salaried groups faced increasing economic instability and poverty, the size of the informal sector grew and those in it faded ever deeper into the penumbra of economic impoverishment (D'Avila 1992:461). On the other hand, the sanctions strengthened other sectors. For example, services associated with export activities had, in relative terms, maintained their levels of production; national private banks opened new branches abroad; and the National Defense Forces (FDP) seemed to gain new strength. As the confrontation with the United States continued throughout 1988, the urban population grew disenchanted with the PDF and the Partido Revolucionario Democratico (PRD) which it controlled, and began to look more favorably on the U.S.-backed Alianza Democratica de Oposicion (ADOC).

The true test occurred on 7 May 1989 when the Noriega backed electoral coalition, National Liberation Coalition (COLINA, led by the PRD), lost the presidential and legislative elections to the anti-military coalition, Alianza Democratica de Oposicion Civilista (ADOC), led by Guillermo Endara (President), Guillermo "Billy" Ford (First Vice President), and Ricardo Arias Calderon (Second Vice President).

Having supported the invasion, calling it a "liberation," the Endara government gave priority to economic reactivation and debt payment, turning its back on the mounting urban crisis and repressing the victims of that crisis—the urban poor.

The U.S. Invasion of Panama: Epilogue of a National Project

On December 20, 1989, the United States invaded Panama, violating the country's rights of self-determination, national sovereignty, and territorial integrity. The invasion was regarded by many as necessary to remove Noriega and achieve a transition to democracy, which they said could not have been accomplished by electoral or other peaceful means. President Guillermo Endara, the ADOC political leadership, and Monseignor Marcos McGrath referred to the invasion as a "liberation." Others argued that the invasion was the final product of a Low Intensity Conflict strategy designed to oust General Noriega from power and dismantle his power base, the PDF.

I maintain that the invasion of December 20 was an epilogue and final defeat of a national project, which had reached its zenith in the 1970s under General Omar Torrijos. Torrijos's populist alliance began to unravel soon after the ratification of the Torrijos-Carter treaty in 1978. By the early 1980s, political liberalism had replaced Torrijos's experiment in popular participation under military rule, and neoliberal economic policies and IMF structural adjustments had replaced the redistributive policies of the populist state, which under Noriega became a repressive authoritarian state. Under Noriega, nationalist rhetoric became an empty shell unable to mobilize the popular sectors which had once supported the Torrijos regime and were now unable to resist U.S. intervention.

Popular sector neighborhoods, Black and brown, were the prime target of "Operation Just Cause." Thousands of Chorrillo, San Miguelito, and Colon residents lost their lives, their limbs, and their homes, while President Guillermo Endara's daughter posed with U.S. military personnel in celebration of what the priveleged groups in Panama refer to as liberation from Noriega. The world still does not know exactly how many died in the invasion of December 20. U.S. official figures released shortly after Noriega was captured indicated that twenty-three U.S. soldiers and three civilians had perished, while only 323 Americans were reported wounded. The same report indicated that 314 PDF soldiers and 220 Panamanian civilians had died and 124 PDF wounded. Although several important U.S.-based human rights groups have supported these conservative estimates, Ramsey Clark, a former U.S. Attorney General, claims that several thousand Panamanians died as a result of the invasion. His figures are supported by CODEHUCA and COPODEHUPA in Costa Rica and Panama, respectively.

Most of the dead, the wounded, and the traumatized were urban dwellers from El Chorrillo, Colon, and San Miguelito, and the little resistance there was to the invasion also came from these areas.

For example, the Dignity Battalions were comprised mostly of young urban dwellers who resisted the invaders. In the U.S. press they were demonized as thugs; whatever their politics, they died defending the nation against an illegal and unnecessary invasion.

Neoliberalism and Its Impact on the Urban Community

What does neoliberalism mean in the Panamanian context? It means ridding the country of the last vestiges of the economic and social reforms of the 1970s and replacing them with the market reforms of the 1990s; it means dismissing public sector workers; privatizing state run enterprises; and removing all barriers to imports. It also means promoting the export capacity of an already oversized tertiary dependent economy, which has proven capable of simultaneously generating relatively high economic growth rates and increased poverty. But most of all, it means privatization and a flexible labor code to replace the already modified 1972 Labor Code (Cabrera 1992). Endara, Ford, and the international financial institutions have been unable to privatize major state-owned firms, reform the labor code, or downsize the public sector (Abrego 1993).

Besides intractable economic problems made worse by U.S. sanctions and invasion in the late 1980s, Panama was beset by many other long standing problems that the Endara government either ignored or was incapable of solving. These include but are not limited to unemployment and poverty; urban crime and personal insecurity; drug-trafficking and an ineffective police force; and a decline in educational and health services.

In the 1990s, unemployment and poverty continued to rise despite impressive growth rates in GDP. For example, the nation's economy grew at rates above five percent during 1990–1993 (the service sector—banking, finances, commerce—and construction experienced high growths, while agriculture and manufacturing declined), while unemployment remained close to fifteen percent and poverty rose from forty-four percent to fifty-four percent in less than five years.

Public sector workers were among the most affected by the sanctions, the invasion, and the neoliberal policies that motivated them to lead the struggle against the Endara government. Besides the many marches and protests, public sector employees and the urban masses were instrumental in defeating the 1992 constitutional referendum sponsored by the government as well as preventing the government from privatizing major government-owned industries.[7] What made matters intolerable for the urban masses, many of whom were incorporated into the informal economy during the 1985–1989 period, was government indifference to their plight (Adames 1990:13). For example, on February 2, 1990, Ruben Dario Carles, Comptroller General, announced that the treasury had less money than was generally believed. He warned that monies forthcoming from the United States were earmarked primarily for private enterprise affected by the invasion and for stimulating export production to the United States. Juan Jovane, a progressive Panamanian economist, analyzed the 1990 budget and its effect on social spending. He pointed out that while $400.8 million was allocated to international financial institutions to pay the public debt, health services received $148.7 million and education $233.7 million. (Opinion Publica 199010–12). Another study points out that government spending on health and social services declined from 12.4 percent of the national budget in 1970 to 5.1 percent in 1987.

Urban Protest Movements: Chorrillo and Colon

Protests against the invasion and Endara's neoliberal policies were widespread, continuing throughout the period 1990–1993. For purposes of this chapter, however, we will concentrate on protest in El Chorrillo and in the city of Colon. Both communities, predominantly Black and brown, continue to struggle against major odds to improve their economic and social conditions. Both communities have been in the forefront of protest against the invasion and the IMF/Endara neoliberal policies. Both communities also have a history of struggle.

El Chorrillo was mainly populated by working-class immigrants from Antillean countries who came to work on the Panama Canal; the presence of these foreigners was welcomed by landlords interested in high urban rents, but resented by many Panamanian elites who saw them as "strange and foreign." Prior to the settlement by Antilleans in the early part of the twentieth century, El Chorrillo was home to working-class Panamanians, who were not allowed to live within the "walled" city of the white and rich.[8] Because of increased population, El Chorrillo was officially designated a *corregimiento*[9] in 1915.

Wooden tenements with outdoor bath and toilet facilities were built in 1913 to accommodate canal workers. The buildings, destroyed during the invasion, had been in disrepair since the 1920s, when unemployment on the Canal Zone skyrocketed following the end of the construction of the Canal.[10] Tenants were nevertheless faced with rent increases in 1925. Chorrilleros joined the Liga de Inquilinos (The Tenants League) and organized a rent strike in protest of the unfair rent hikes. The Liga was attacked by the government of Rodolfo Chiari as anarchist and communist, leading the United States to send troops into Panama to put down the Tenant Strike of 1925.

With the exception of public housing such as Renta "1" in 1944 and Barraza in the 1970s, neither public nor private enterprise renewed or repaired El Chorrillo's housing stock, which over the years was depleted by several fires and then by the invasion of December 20, 1989 (Davis 1990:26).

At the moment of the invasion, El Chorrillo had approximately 26,000 inhabitants, and nearly half were left without housing. Subsequent to the invasion, much of the protesting by Chorrilleros and their supporters centered around obtaining decent housing from Panamanian or U.S. authorities; adequate reimbursement for furniture lost in the invasion; and compensation for bodily injuries and loss of life.

The U.S. government has so far denied responsibility for bodily injury or loss of life, but in March 1990 the Congress allocated $42 million to finance new housing; rebuild damaged infrastructure; and provide credit and financial support to merchants who were affected as a result of U.S. action during the invasion. Nevertheless, for more than a year, more than 2,300 Chorrillero refugees spent their days and nights in very uncomfortable makeshift quarters in a U.S. facility at Albrook.[11]

The package known as "El Plan Chorrillo" was for 1,800 residential units funded by AID and administered by the Ministry of Housing (MIVI) and other agencies, whose business it was to decide who qualified for the $6,500 "donation." Once that was done, the person was given a choice: either wait for housing in El Chorrillo built by MIVI or select a unit farther away from the city. Not only did most Chorrilleros want to return to El Chorrillo, but the majority earned less than $200 a month and were not creditworthy to obtain bank mortgages. So fewer than 500 of those eligible for the program returned to very small, inadequate, and windowless cement apartments in El Chorrillo, while the vast majority settled for equally poor housing fifteen or more kilometers outside of the city (Arias 1990).

While delays in housing delivery, inadequate reimbursement for furniture lost in the invasion, and government indifference fuelled the protests in El Chorrillo, these acquired national significance because they were joined by groups and individuals who rejected the invasion and who sought to rescue Panama's right to self-determination and sovereignty.

On March 13, 1990, a group of Chorrilleros staged a massive demonstration on the strategically located Puente de las Americas (Bridge of the Americas), which links Panama City with the Central and Western provinces of the country. After paralyzing movement on the bridge for several hours, the protesters marched to the Legislative Assembly where they presented a five point demand: (1) speeding up of their housing under construction; (2) the restitution of all furniture and personal property lost in the invasion; (3) government help in securing employment; (4) reimbursement for merchants who lost businesses during the invasion; and (5) pensions or subsidies for families that lost members on 20 December. Three months later, on June 20, Chorrilleros marched to the Presidential Palace where they restated their demands. Other popular groups that joined the march condemned the invasion; requested the immediate departure of U.S. troops from Panamanian soil; and demanded indemnization from the United States. Although he set up a High Level Commission to deal with the problms of El Chorrillo, President Endara failed to meet the most important demands made by the Refugee Committee.[12]

Government failure to meet demands of the Chorrilleros eventually caused schisms within the movement as more radical leadership emerged. Rafael Olivardia, a long-time community activist, was replaced by Isabel Corro who led the high-profile Association of the Families of the Dead. Corro, who had participated in the 1988–1989 National Civilian Crusade against General Manuel Noriega, emerged as a leading voice against the invasion, demanding U.S. accountability for the dead and indemnization for their living relatives. Isabel Corro also gained notoriety for leading several campaigns to locate mass graves and exhume the bodies. After several years, when it became clear that the United States would not honor any monetary claims from the relatives of the dead, Corro's hegemony over the movement was challenged by Hector Avila, a former professional soccer player.

Hector Avila resumed the tactics of mass civil disobedience, organizing demonstrations at the Puente de las Americas, the only passageway to the interior of the country. Throughout 1992 Avila led several of these confrontations with the government, which responded by arresting and jailing him on several occasions. As a result of these jailings, Avila's popularity increased, causing the government to launch an attack on his character. Alma Guillermoprieto in an August 1992 *New Yorker* article, "Letter From Panama," joined the attack on Avila, depicting him as a mad opportunist and linking him to the Dignity Battalions, which she insists were responsible for arson in Chorrillo on the night of December 20, 1989 (Guillermoprieto 1992:60–71).

Eyewitnesses to the invasion contradict Guillermoprieto's account of Dignity Battalion activities on the night of the invasion. In a September 1990 article written by Francisco Goldman for *Harper's Magazine*, Chorrillo dwellers denied that Dignity Battalion members had burned buildings; on the other hand, they depicted what they said was wanton killing of Panamanian civilians by U.S. soldiers on the night of December 20 (Goldman 1990).

As the 1994 election drew closer, the politics of protest gave way to party politics as political parties swamped the area, seeking clients including Hector Avila and four-time world boxing champion Roberto "Manos de Piedra" Duran both of whom accepted legislative nominations, from the Solidarity Party and the Arnulfista Party, respectively.

As is the case in many Latin American countries, political parties in Panama are primarily electoral machines controlled by the monied class, which use their resources to buy influence and win over the leadership of the popular movements. In the case of Chorrillo this is exactly what happened. Both Avila and Isabel Corro abandoned the leadership of their movement to accept nominations from political parties. On the other hand, the Refugee Committee of El Chorrillo remains active but weakened in the 1994 post-election period.

Unlike El Chorrillo, leaders of the Movement of the Unemployed of Colon (MODESCO) did not accept nominations for electoral office, but their movement suffered from some of the same weaknesses of the popular movement in the rest of the country: lack of resources; relatively inexperienced leadership; government repression; and a clientele network that persistently seduces and coopts its members.

Colon: An Island of Riches in a Sea of Poverty

Colon City is in the Province Colon, one of nine provinces of the Republic of Panama. The City is 2.9 sq.km with a population density of 18,846 peopleper sq.km. It has 16 streets, 10 avenues, 15,471 houses, and 54,654 inhabitants. The City is part of the metropolitan region of Colon which is comprised of the City, Cristobal, the urban parts of Sabanitas and Cativa. Metropolitan Colon is dedicated mostly to commerce and services. Its main activities are in the Colon Free Zone, operating since 1948 and doing upward of $7 billion worth of export and re-export per year.

The inhabitants of the city and the city itself benefit very little from the presence of the Free Zone in Colon. The Free Zone pays no municipal taxes or fees to the city; however, of the 15,000 employed there, Colonenses comprise about 10,000, mostly in low-paying jobs.[13] Jorge Luis Macias, the representative of the corregimiento of Cristobal, put the unemployment rate in Colon at about 71 percent (La Prensa 1993). High unemployment, old dilapidated housing stock, crime, delinquency, and drugs are some of Colon's gravest social problems.[14] But this declining city of just over 50,000 was once prosperous.

Eduardo Galeano, in his *Open Veins of Latin America* captures the boom and bust character of economies like Colon's. With the advent of the Panama Railroad in the 1850s, Colon's economy first prospered and then declined when the railroad was no longer competitive. In the twentieth century, employment soared during

Canal construction and again during World War II, but ever since the end of the war Colon's economy has been in the doldrums in spite of the creation of the Free Zone in 1948.

In 1979, the military government commissioned a Plan to deal with unemployment and housing in Colon. Known as the "Plan de Desarrollo Integral de Colon (1979–1984)," the plan was financed by the national government, the World Bank, and Japanese enterprises. The plan modernized the Colon Free Zone, the Cativa-Colon highway, and the Center for Professional and Technical Training of Colon. Unfortunately, it failed to solve Colon's chronic unemployment and dilapidated housing stock.

Racism and Resistance in Colon

The city, like most cities in urban Panama, has known racial separation. According to historian Ernesto de Jesus Castillero Reyes, Colon after the construction of the railroad was really two cities: one occupied by white railroad administrators and functionaries living in clean, nice-looking houses, and the other occupied by Blacks and poor workers living in barracks-like houses made of zinc and wood and situated near swamps in the vicinity of the railroad.

For most of the twentieth century, except during canal construction and two World Wars, Colon has languished, losing significant numbers of its inhabitants, who continue to migrate to other parts of the province, to Panama City, and to the United States, namely Brooklyn, New York (IDEN 1992:63–67).

Colon also has a history of resistance. In 1885, Pedro Prestan was accused of burning down part of the city; in 1959, Colonenses organized the famous Hunger March, which mobilized tens of thousands to fight for the country's first minimum wage; and in 1990, they organized a similar march from Colon to Panama to protest the post-invasion neoliberal policies.

MODESCO'S Struggle for Employment in Post-Invasion Panama

Building on lessons learned from these many struggles, a number of unemployed and educated youth organized the Movement of the

Unemployed of Colon in 1992. MODESCO's leadership was mostly Black and mestizo. They were advised by Father Nicolas Delgado, a mulatto priest in his mid-30s, from whose offices hung paintings with Black motifs from Haiti, Brazil, Africa, and Panama. At the height of MODESCO's struggle for jobs and housing in the summer of 1992, Father Delgado received notice from the church hierarchy that he was being transferred to Brazil or to Africa.

In an interview, Father Delgado, mentor to MODESCO, asserted that in spite of the economic reactivation talked about by governmental authorities, "the GNP does not reach the masses."[15] In part this is due to the fact that the Endara government's priority is to pay the foreign debt almost to the exclusion of the social debt.

In a 1992 human rights document, *Panama, en el camino de la impunidad,* the authors claim that Panama owed $540 million, to international financial institutions and paid them $645 million, an excess of more than $100 million. The same study reports that the level of poverty increased from forty-four to fifty-four percent between 1988 and 1992, documenting increases in cholera and AIDS, teenage prostitution, and handgun-related violence.

These are some of the conditions that gave rise to the social protests by MODESCO in 1992. The first demonstrations were met with government indifference and selective repression, but after they grew in intensity and frequency and were supported wholeheartedly by Monseignor Ariz of Colon, the Endara government appointed a high-level commission to look into and find a solution to MODESCO's complaints. The Commission, comprised of political and business elites and members of MODESCO, studied a proposal presented by Monseignor Ariz.

The proposal, which led to what is known as Agreement No.1 of March 1992, called for the government to raise $500,000 in taxes per month from Transit, S.A. Transit is a government-owned Colon Free Zone company. The money was to be administered by members of the Association of Panamanian Executives (APEDE), the Fund for Emergency Services (FES, an agency originally funded by AID to deal with post-invasion social problems but which now receives funds from the United Nations), and members of MODESCO. The monies were to be used for urban beautification, drainage projects, and job training.

On July 7, 1992, MODESCO, dissatisfied with the implementation of the agreement, mobilized twenty thousand Colonenses to bloc the main highway leading to the Colon Free Zone. MODESCO's leadership made several demands: cut the red tape and release funds already approved; indemnify Anibal Ponce, a MODESCO militant who had lost an eye in an earlier protest; free Hector Avila, the leader of El Chorrillo; provide better working conditions for Maquiladora workers; stop the eviction of tenants occupying houses reverted by the U.S. government to Panamanian authorities and legalize their housing status; appoint health promoters; and utilize the $500,000 per month that the government allocated to Colon (Herrera 1992).

One year later, MODESCO was still not satisfied with the government's implementation of agreements. Its last significant demonstration was staged on August 6, 1993, when it mobilized 400 of its members to bloc the entrance to the Yacht Club. On that day, the rich and famous of Panama were enjoying an air show by the Brazilian Air Force when the demonstrators demanded that the government keep its end of a prior agreement to secure the jobs of 2,800 Colonenses. Needless to say, MODESCO's leaders were again arrested. Like El Chorrillo, the MODESCO movement was weakened by cooptation, repression, and the return of electoral politics in 1994.

Conclusion

Colon continues to be an island of riches in a sea of poverty; El Chorrillo is still a shadow of what it was prior to the invasion of December 20, 1989, and San Miguelito remains a powderkeg despite progress in some of its communities. The plight of these Black and brown people will go unattended despite their heroic resistance and unless a number of conditions are met. First, their oppression has to be seen as a product of the interplay of race, ethnicity, color, and class. Progressive and conservative intellectuals are too quick to point out to Black leaders that indigenous areas are the poorest in the country. While there is truth to this observation, it is equally true that Black and brown people, as well as Black and brown areas (Provinces of Darien, Bocas del Toro, and

Colon, and Black communities in Panama and Colon), are among the most depressed in the society. Second, there is a need for the revitalization of the Black Movement, which played a significant role in the 1970s during the Torrijos period (Priestley 1989). Third, this movement must join with women's groups, human rights organizations, indigenous groups, and labor organizations in the building of a strong popular movement. Fourth, given the ouster of the Endara government, which took office on a U.S. military base the night of the invasion and which throughout its four years was completely insensitive to popular demands, the popular movement should seek new working relations with the new centrist government led by Dr. Ernesto Perez Balladares.

Urban problems and protests can only be solved when major economic and political restructuring occurs in Panama. The country's service-oriented economy must be restructured to provide for a meaningful manufacturing and agricultural component capable of providing sufficient decent paying jobs in areas and provinces other than Panama's overcrowded metropolitan centers. The Perez Balladares government must not only begin to build new infrastructure, it must design, organize, and implement an urban development program, one that is decentralized and participatory. Given the level of urban deterioration and the threat that this poses to economic growth and human progress, urban planning is an urgent priority for the new government. Besides jobs, the government and private enterprise must undertake an aggressive low income housing program; build the North and South Corridor in Panama City, two major highways long postponed; reorganize the Public Force into an effective non-politicized police force; and reintroduce the integral health care system created by Omar Torrijos in the 1970s. Once these reforms are in place, life for Black and brown urban dwellers will become more tolerable.

NOTES

1. Panama's economy is highly dependent on the export of goods and services, particularly to the United States.

2. The Metropolitan area includes Panama City, Colon City, San Miguelito, and Arraijan.

3. In 1913, Panama's population was about 300,000; the province of Panama contained 70,000, and Canal workers numbered 56,000. The pres-

ence of these workers made Panama City predominantly Black. See Alvaro Uribe, *La Ciudad Fragmentada*. Panama: Centro de Estudios Latinamericanos (1989), p. 16.

4. In the 1930s, ninety or ninety-five percent of the population in the Black and brown communities of Panama City and Colon City were tenants rather than homeowners.

5. The Revolutionary Democratic Party (PRD) was created by the late General Omar Torrijos in 1978; in the 1980s, the party became a tool of the Noriega regime and many of its members were jailed and persecuted after the U.S. invasion of December 20, 1989. However, the party won the 1994 elections, managing to regroup and renew itself during 1990–1994.

6. Figures compiled from data provided by the National Electoral Tribunal of Panama.

7. As a result of the U.S. sanctions, Panama's economy had a negative growth of 20 percent in 1988; its urban informal sector grew rapidly as a result of the debt crisis, structural adjustments, sanctions, invasion, and neoliberal policies. In 1982, the informal sector accounted for 25 percent of the urban economy, jumping to 32 percent in 1989. See Lionel Mendez D'Avila, in Eduardo Stein *et al.* (eds.). 1992.

8. As early as 1905, the United States had taken over the delivery of public services, including water, sewage, light, etc.

9. A *corregimiento* is the smallest local political administrative unit of the Panamanian government. El Chorrillo is one of 511 corregimientos in the country.

10. Technically speaking, the Canal Zone never had unemployment. Workers dismissed from the Zone automatically lost living quarters and were compelled to move to working-class neighborhoods like El Chorrillo and Colon.

11. Barbara Trent's award-winning film *The Panama Deception* reveals the subhuman conditions of these refugees and documents their frustration, discontent, and protests.

12. In the summer of 1994, I interviewed several members of the Refugee Committee at their headquarters in Chorrillo. The main complaint was that the invasion destroyed Chorrillo as a socioeconomic and cultural entity.

13. Ricardo Stevens, *Colon: Vocacion de Cargabultos?*. Colon (October 1981), p.19.

14. In 1991, the White Cross conducted a study of drug use in Panama. The study found that in the city of Colon, 18 percent used cocaine, while 15 percent used marijuana and 3 percent used crack. See, "La delincuencia asalta a Colon," *La Prensa* (19 November 1993); p. 6A. In 1980, 77 percent of the crimes in Colon Province occurred in Colon city, and by 1990 that figure was 88 percent. See IDEN y Misionera de Colon Report (May 1992).

15. Interview with Father Delgado, Summer 1993. Panama averaged 5 percent growth in GNP between 1990 and 1993.

REFERENCES

Abrego, Jose Eulogio Torres. 1993. *Los contrastes del programa de privatizacion en Panama: La celada del proyecto de ley 72.* Published by the author in Panama City.

Arias, Magela Cabrera. 1990. "El Chorrillo: Anàlisis de la Situaciòn Social." In *El Chorrillo: Situaciòn y Alternativas.* Panama: Instituto de Estudios Nacionales, Universidad de Panama.

Cabrera, Edgar Jiménez. 1992. *El Modelo Neoliberal en America Central: El Caso de Panamà.* Costa Rica: CEDAL (Fundacion Fredrich Ebert).

Censos Nacionales de Poblacion y Vivienda. 1990. Direccion de Estadistica y Censo, contraloria General de la Republica, Republica de Panama (May 13).

Central American Update. 1990. Vol. XI, No. 1 (Jan/Feb).

D'Avila, Lionel Mendez. 1992. "Visión, términos y perspectives de la informalidad en el Istmo Centroamericano." In Eduardo Stein (ed.), *Democracia Sin Pobreza.* Costa Rica: Editorial Dei.

Davis, Eduardo Tejeira. 1990. "El Chorrillo: Su historia y su arquitectura." In *El Chorrillo: Situacion y Alternativas* Cuadernos No. 5 (Octubre). Panama: Instituto de Estudios Nacionales Universidad de Panama.

Goldman, Francisco. 1990. "What Price Panama." *Harper's.* (September).

Gomez, Jose Antonio and William Hughes. 1985. *Desarrollo, Crisis, Deuda y Politica Economica en Panama.* Panama: Universidad de Panama.

Guillermoprieto, Alma. 1992. "Letter from Panama." *The New Yorker* (August 17).

Herrera, Claudio. 1992. "Testigos afirman que joven muerta en Colon recibio disparo de la policia." *La Prensa* (July 8).

IDEN and Diocesis Misionera de Colon. 1992. *Colon y Kuna Yala Desafio para la Iglesia y el Gobierno.* (May).

La Prensa. 1993. "El desempleo castiga a Colon." (November).

Opinion Publica. 1990. No.28 (June). Panama.

Priestley, George. 1987. "Squatters, Oligarchs and Soldiers in San Miguelito, Panama." Bildner Center for Western Heisphere Studies, Urban Policy Paper Series No. 8 (July).

———. 1986. *Military Government and Popular Participation in Panama.* Boulder, Col.: Westview.

————. (ed.). 1989a. *Ethnicity, Class, and the State in Central America.* (special issue) *Cimarron* Vol.II, No.1–2 (Spring/Summer).

————. 1989b. "Obstacles to Democracy and Sovereignty." *Radical History* No.40 (Fall).

Quintero, Jose. 1992. "No habra mas detenciones ni protestas violentas en Colon." *La Prensa* (July 29).

Uribe, Alvaro. 1989. *La Ciudad Fragmentada.* Panama: Centro de Estudios Latinamericanos.

Velasquez, Giovanni B. 1993. *Crisis Economica, Ajuste Estructural y Politicas de Vivienda del Estado Panameno 1980–1987.* Masters Thesis, Universidad de Costa Rica.

Raquel Z. Rivera

5

Rap in Puerto Rico

Reflections from the Margins[1]

For a little over ten years now, there has been a lively rap scene in Puerto Rico. After remaining an underground but widespread form of youthful artistic expression throughout most of the 1980s, it became a great success in the local music market after 1989. Rap is today not only one of the most popular music genres among young people, but it is also tightly bound to the construction of their self-identities.

Although as a media phenomenon it has a wide audience, it is an art form primarily developed by and identified with youth from poor urban communities. The northern Metropolitan Area, which encompasses the towns of San Juan, Río Piedras, Bayamón, Carolina, and Guaynabo, is where most clubs, concerts, and presentations, as well as the majority of home and commercial studios, are concentrated. Given the social construction of fear—much like those prevalent in other parts of the world—that regards poor young people with the utmost suspicion, it is no surprise that rap is frequently viewed as the musical expression of delinquency. Intensifying the matter is rap's lyrical commitment to historicizing what the artists perceive as everyday reality. Due to their position as the socio-economically underprivileged targets of repressive state rhetoric and policies, their account of daily life is explosive and, for many, too much to take.

There are two other major issues that fuel the distrust and

sometimes outright hostility with which this genre is predominantly received. First, given that social class and race are intricately bound in Puerto Rican society, rap artists and audiences are not only primarily poor but also primarily black (if we are to understand "black" as a tendency towards the darker shades of the phenotypical spectrum in a racially mixed society). Besides questioning class-based power structures, rappers also espouse a racial discourse that clashes with the dominant ideas on race. Whereas the dominant racial discourse is built around the myth of racial democracy, rappers acknowledge and explore racial inequalities and proclaim rap as an Afro-Puerto Rican musical form. The other factor that fosters the marginalization of rap is the fact that it is a cultural expression that arose outside the island's borders and was not predominantly informed by what are considered traditional Puerto Rican musical forms. This is a particularly sensitive issue, for Puerto Rico is still a colony of the United States, nearly one hundred years after Spain ceded her as booty in the Spanish-American War. For the nationalistic cultural purists, rap is merely another product of cultural imperialism; if left to its own devices, rap can cause irreparable damages to the "true" Puerto Rican culture.

Rappers and their audiences, particularly those who identify as *raperos and raperas*, are indeed very conscious of the social odds they are up against. Their music is an act of construction and reflection. Oftentimes they represent a defiance to dominant social structures; in other cases, they are in communion with the predominant discourses. This chaper will explore some of the histories and matters involved.

Raíces/Roots

New York ghettos were the cradle of what we know today as rap. Its first examples date approximately from the early 1970s (Hebdige 1987:137). It is a music strongly rooted in Afro-North American musical traditions, and therefore informed by Black spirituals, blues, and jazz. Its particular oral style makes reference to older verbal games such as signifying and the dozens, and is directly linked to the work of the Last Poets and of Gil Scott-Heron (Toop 1991:119). In spite of being firmly situated in an Afro-North American musical tradition, rap is not an artistic expression exclusive to the United States. This genre is also a testimony to the cultural interaction between U.S. Blacks, Puerto Ricans, and other Caribbean immigrants in New York City (Hebdige 1987:146; Flores 1988:35).

Caribbean music has consistently influenced Afro-North American music since the first decades of the twentieth century. In the 1940s, Cuban pioneers of Latin jazz, such as Machito and Mario Bauza, played side by side with musicians like Dizzy Gillespie. The rhythm and blues of the 1950s was marked by mambo and other Caribbean musical expressions. During the 1950s and1960s, Afro-North Americans and Caribbeans sang doo-wop along the same New York streets and parks. Furthermore, the urban musical culture of the late 60s and early 70s which gave rise to rap was deeply informed by reggae music.

Keeping to this tradition of cultural fusion, Puerto Ricans have also participated in the urban hip-hop culture of the United States. Felipe Luciano, a leader of the Young Lords Party,[2] was also a member of the Last Poets, the group that greatly influenced the development of rap. Two Afro-North American pioneers of rap music, Afrika Bambaata and Grandmaster Flash, incorporated salsa rhythms into their songs (Hebdige, *op.cit.*:144). Charlie Chase, the Cold Crush Brothers' D.J. and the only Puerto Rican member of the group, remembers:

> I would sneak in Spanish records. Beats only, and if the baseline was funky enough, I would do that too. Bobby Valentín stuff. He played bass with the Fania All-Stars, and he would do some funky stuff. (Flores 1992:1020)

The presence of salsa in U.S. rap is not limited to Bambaata, Flash, and Chase. Later male and female rappers, such as Queen Latifah and Nice 'n' Smooth, have mixed salsa rhythms and song fragments into their music. Many others, like the Fantastic Five, the Fearless Four, the Fat Boys, K–7, Latin Empire, the Beatnuts, and Funkdoobiest have or have had Puerto Rican group members. Popular rap artists like Fat Joe Da Gangsta, The Real Roxanne,

Frankie Cutlass, Hurricane Gee, and Kurious Jorge are also Puerto Rican.

The Emergence of Rap in Puerto Rico

The strong hold that rap exhibits among certain youth sectors responds in part to the migratory reality of many young Puerto Ricans. Rap, as an expression shared among Caribbeans and Afro-North Americans in U.S. ghettos, is part of the cultural baggage of the young Puerto Ricans who return (or arrive) to Puerto Rico. Since rap is an integral part of the cultural life of migrant youth, it cannot, therefore, be considered simply as a foreign import. Although it is true that large commercial interests have promoted the consumption of rap on the island, migration has operated as an alternate route for distribution.

Puerto Rico's continued colonial status explains the close economic and demographic[3] ties that bind the island to the United State. Thus, unlike other countries where the diffusion of rap has depended mostly on mass media, the development of this genre in Puerto Rico is tightly linked to U.S. rap through a distinct and immediate human connection.

The emergence of rap in Puerto Rico was directly related to the rise of breaking (i.e., "breakdancing" [sic]) and to the proliferation of graffiti. The coexistence of these artistic expressions in Puerto Rico is not surprising, given that all three are intrinsically related within urban hip-hop culture in the United States (Rose 1994:34). Young immigrants were a key factor in their development on the island (Adorno 1994).

Rap, graffiti, and breaking became most deeply entrenched among youth from poorer classes. This is due in part to the fact that the migrant population that has lived the culture of hip hop in U.S. ghettos is, predictably, composed of Puerto Ricans of lesser economic resources. On the other hand, the experience of poor Afro-North American youth has much in common with the reality of impoverished youth in Puerto Rico. Rap, graffiti, and breaking reflect an experience shared by both groups: social marginalization.

There is another issue that has bearing on the question of why these three art forms became more popularized among young people from poor communities. That issue is race, which will be taken up later.

In the early 1980s, U.S. rap had already been commercialized in Puerto Rico. But rap was by no means a phenomenon exclusive to mass media. Many young people began to rap at their meeting places, such as parks, street corners, schoolyards, and parties (Ortiz 1991:20). Some, like Vico C., Piro J.M., E.Z.D., M.C. Base, and Jacob D. made home recordings for distribution and sale among friends and acquaintances (D. J. K-Kemit 1994; D.J. Scratch 1994). Rap was first disseminated through informal means and before reaching the air waves had become popular as an underground music outside the scope of mass media.

Vico C., born in Brooklyn, New York, and raised in Puerta de Tierra, was one of the rappers whose underground recordings were able to transcend the borders of his neighborhood. Vico C. started to compose and rap around 1983, while in seventh grade. The home recordings that Vico C. made during those years travelled from hand to hand all over Puerto Rico. The rage that followed the release of "En Coma"/"In Coma" at the end of 1987 was felt in many neighborhoods and high schools. Vico C. was most certainly a legend. He recounts having received news that his raps had reached New York (Osorio 1993:2).

Vico C.'s "De la calle"/"From the Street,"[4] was another popular underground rap. It is representative of the initial stages of rap in Puerto Rico. Daily life was the narrative thread, and the text emulated the richness and aggressiveness of everyday speech.

As expressed by the young poet José Raúl González, the objective of rap produced in those days was to affirm "that the street has flavor and history, that being from the street has magic" (González 1994). The street represents the spaces where youth from lower classes live and hang out; it begins to be identified in rap as a symbol of marginalization. But to be from the street is not, in fact, a source of shame. Rappers proudly inscribe upon their language, style, and dress the signs of their marginality.

This first stage of Puerto Rican rap was therefore characterized by its being a dialogue regarding marginalization. However, as time passed, and rap was eventually commercialized, the listening public of this genre became more diversified. Furthermore, market norms and restrictions began having an impact on the music being produced. These pressures encouraged a change in the language, perspectives, and styles of rap.

From the Barrio to the Radio and Beyond

It soon became clear that rap had a great potential in the underground economy. Negro, Vico C.'s d.j., was one of the first businessmen that ventured in this area.

In spite of the rising popularity of local rap toward the end of the 1980s, it continued to be an underground phenomenon; the media and record labels had not yet identified its commercial potential. The initial efforts of many rappers to find agents and to get radio exposure were unsuccessful.

It was only after the explosive radio success of Brewley M.C.'s, "Sida Rap" in 1989 that radio programmers, recording studio owners, producers, and others involved in the music industry became interested in this genre. Those that had previously ignored the efforts made by Brewley M.C. and other rappers like him, started to compete to sign them on. Rap, until then an underground cultural expression, suddenly became a mass media phenomenon.

The first songs to become popular on the radio were about crime, violence, drugs, and urban deterioration. They had clear didactic intentions to advise the public regarding these social problems and to provide a good example for their contemporaries and for younger generations.

In contrast to the underground rap that had become popular at the margins of mass media, a new style of rap known as "positive rap" appeared. It also spoke of marginalization, but from the dominant perspective. The spontaneity and crudeness that characterized the themes and the language of underground rap were transformed in order to be effectively packaged and sold according to market stipulations. A large portion of positive rap spoke of urban deterioration, but from a more simplistic and detached position, losing in many ways its previous sense of immediacy and urgency.

Rubén D.J.'s "Puerto Rico" is an example of this kind of approach. He reduces unemployment to a lack of motivation at an individual level without addressing the structural conditions that make unemployment such a widespread phenomenon. Rubén D. J. hence falls in line with the dominant ideology, which blames poor communities for their own problems.

During the first stages of rap's commercialization, many lyrics also made reference to the rapper's dexterity, and to his or her superiority over other exponents of this genre. Sexual relationships were also a recurring theme during this period. These songs usually called for a reflection on sexuality, emphasizing the possibility of negative consequences such as sexually transmitted diseases, unwanted pregnancies, and interpersonal conflicts.

Social problems, artistic superiority, and sexuality became the three most prominent themes in positive rap. But by 1991, a new trend within commercial rap had settled in; the pointed use of Caribbean rhythms. As mentioned above, rap in the United States was partially nourished by Caribbean musical traditions, particularly reggae. However, musical forms from the Hispanic Caribbean have been principally used in U.S. rap to "spice up" the mix, but not as the predominant musical component. The deep fusion between the music most commonly sampled in rap (like funk, soul, rock, and jazz) and such genres as salsa, merengue, and mambo is an insular Puerto Rican innovation.

The third stage in the development of rap in Puerto Rico can therefore be characterized by the strong influence of Caribbean musical forms. It is important to note that not only did the musical base vary to incorporate Caribbean rhythms, but that the themes evolved as well. The two predominant themes became sexuality and the pleasure of dancing. The way in which sex was treated at this time, however, was quite different from the way it was elaborated earlier in positive rap. The emphasis shifted from reflection, self-control, and restraint toward a relatively carefree celebration of human sexuality.

The fourth and final stage in the development of rap in Puerto Rico has been characterized by a renewed vindication of the street as a space for the construction of identities and alliances. In the realm of mainstream media, this trend emerged in 1993 with Vico C.'s *Xplosión* and Big Boy's *Mr. Big*. Contrary to the tone that predominated in both positive and Caribbean influenced rap, everyday life and a personal approach to the problems of the ghetto arise once again as central themes. The laws, violence, and magic of the street begin once more to gain visibility; this is evident in both underground and commercial rap.

It is worth pointing out that the international commercialization of the U.S. hardcore and "gangsta" rap has allowed and encouraged the mass distribution of the "return to the street and to our roots" message now present in Puerto Rican rap. Also, in this fourth stage, the fusion of rap with reggae becomes intensified. In actuality, the boundaries between both genres are uncertain.

In conclusion, rap in Puerto Rico has undergone four general stages in its development: underground rap, positive rap, Caribbean influenced rap, and "return to the street" rap. Rap became commercialized with the emergence of positive rap. Rubén D.J.'s *La escuela / School* was one of the most successful rap recordings of that time, selling more than one hundred thousand copies and competing favorably with the most successful salsa, merengue, and pop-ballad productions (Merced 1994). Vico C.'s *La recta final / The Final Stretch* was yet another commercially successful rap production, selling sixty thousand copies.[5]

Nearly four years later, rap was still a powerful commercial success. The "Fortnightly Hit Parade" published by *The Sales Report*, states that Jerry Rivera's, *Cara de niño / Baby Face* reached number one, followed by Vico C.'s, *Xplosión*. The number three hit was Gilberto Santa Rosa's, *Nace aquí / Born Here*, followed at number eight by Big Boy's, *Mr. Big*.[6]

Rap has not only had wide underground and commercial popularity, but its influence has extended to other musical genres and other aspects of cultural life. The Pleneros de la 23 Abajo have fused rap and *plena*[7] in some of their songs. Gilberto Santa Rosa in his song, "Imán Jala-Jala," incorporates rap cuts into salsa. Within merengue, Jossie Esteban and La Patrulla 15 recorded a song in 1993 that included the chorus from Big Boy's rap, "¿Dónde están?"/ "Where are They?" Furthermore, groups such as Fobia Estatal and Los Inconformes combine rap, rock, ska, and punk.

Rap has also become an integral part of musical presentations within diverse cultural activities. Conscience, a rap group from Carolina, and Vico C. played at a dinner-concert given by the Pentecostal Church of Puerta de Tierra.[8] The *a cappella* group Seven to Heaven, also present at the dinner, included rap in their repertoire. It has become quite common in small town festivals to have rap groups share the stage with *tríos*,[9] plena, and salsa groups. The 1994 Festival del Pescao (Fish Festival) in Cabo Rojo included appearances by Nova and Chachi D.J. Rap, the Trio Los Caborrojeños, the Pleneros del Quinto Olivo, and Andy Montañez and his Orquestra. Also, radio and television commercials have used rap jingles for promoting pharmacies, liquor stores, drinks, anti-drug campaigns, to mention only a few examples.

As is evidenced in this brief history, rap has had quite an impact on contemporary Puerto Rican culture. Not only is it highly popularized and profitable on the music market, it has become a standard item in cultural activities such as festivals and concerts. It is also an integral part of day-to-day action in streetcorners, schoolyards, parties, parks, and churches. Rap has, in fact, become one of the most powerful vehicles of expression for Puerto Rican youth.

From the Street: Philosophers With No Degree

Rap, as a cultural discourse, is rooted in the daily experience of urban youth at the end of the twentieth century. The social panorama that this generation has faced has been characterized not only by an economic recession, but also by an official discourse that points its accusatory finger toward the poorest strata. In Puerto Rico, Governor Pedro Roselló's anti-crime policy is directly informed by an international phenomenon that proposes a restriction in civil rights as the government's answer for controlling crime (Candela 1993:8; Lipsitz 1992:11). Examples of this include the recent efforts to enforce curfews for youth and restrict the right to bail.

The population most affected by these repressive policies are youth from the lower economic strata. Their guilt is inscribed in the state's narrow definition of violence, which indicts the lower classes while overlooking crime and violence perpetrated by the elite (Silvestrini 1980:5; Messerchmidt 1986:52).

In light of such a partialized definition of crime, it is not surprising that the average inmate in Puerto Rico is nineteen years old or less (de Ríos 1994:15). The fact that living conditions within penitentiaries are abominable becomes an aggravating element creating an environment entirely inadequate for rehabilitation (Borges

1994:16). The social prospects out on the streets are not promising either, considering that unemployment among youth is up to forty percent. Ironically, the highest degree of financial independence among young people is enjoyed by those whose main source of income is revenue from the sale of drugs (Roche 1994:9).

The bleak social opportunities available to young people are merely a reflection of the dire general state of the Puerto Rican economy. According to the 1990 federal census, 2.1 million of the island's inhabitants (59 percent of the population) live below the poverty line. In 1993, official figures indicated that 18.1 percent of the working population was unemployed (Candela *op.cit.*:20). Unemployment figures for 1996 reveal continued stagnation.

It is within this context that rap music has developed. A dynamic and innovative form of expression, rap evolved not only in spite of, but also because of the social inequalities lived by a large percentage of youth. Although by no means homogenous, most rap constitutes part of a counter-hegemonic project that contests diverse social structures through the subversion of the dominant discourse regarding violence and social inequality.

Vico C. explains that rap is a "music of the ghetto, and both here [in Puerto Rico] and out there, those of us who perform it are from the 'hood" (Ortíz *op.cit.*:20). By participating in rap, marginalized youth counterposition their vision of reality against the dominant discourses. It is for this reason that many rappers explain that their music is a continuation of the social function of the plena as the poor's newspaper. Chuck D., member of Public Enemy, has noted that something similar takes place in the context of the United States, where he defines rap as the Afro-North American version of CNN (Havelock and González 1991:180).

By proclaiming themselves narrators and critics of the histories of their own communities, rappers challenge a society that only recognizes academic historicism. This narrow concept of intellectualism is constantly questioned in rap through the re-vindication of street knowledge and invention. Puerto Rock declares: "Being a teenager on the streets of the Bronx in the late 70s, that was college for me."[10] Likewise, Vico C. asserts himself a "philosopher without a degree" and a "master of the arts"; the members of Fat Pocke's describe themselves as the "teachers"; Prince Komazshi considers himself "admirable"; and Wiso G. defines himself as "the genius."

The historical approach undertaken in rap is usually very personal. Rappers take on the role of contemporary historians through the anecdotal reconstruction of their everyday life. Most of these stories focus on el gufeo (goofing off) and el jangueo (hanging out). Fun, leisure, and desire are the aspects of daily life most frequently stressed. This discourse of pleasure is part of what has been termed the "conquest of the present." María Milagros López explains that "this conquest entails abandoning self-sacrifice as the mediation necessary to achieve pleasure" (López 1994:124).

Forsaking the ethic of hard work and self-sacrifice can be interpreted as a reflexive response to the dismal socioeconomic prospects facing the majority of Puerto Rican youth. With unemployment at steadily high levels, police repression and attempts to curtail civil rights on the rise, and the public education system in a dismal state, self-sacrifice seems like wasted effort. Many rappers, like Wiso G. in "Me levanto los domingos" (I Get Up on Sundays),[11] thus concentrate on savoring and poeticizing the pleasure derived from leisure.

Like "Me levanto los domingos," Falo's "Pa'l Cruce" (1994)[12] is also a narration of everyday life. "Pa'l Cruce" is particularly interesting because it offers an alternative account of daily events in poor communities. The drug dealing puntos (spots), mostly found in these communities, are constant objects of news coverage. For the media, the youth that occupy such spaces (whether they be working or hanging out) are criminal or potentially criminal. Falo challenges the dominant discourse by reconstructing the facts from a very different perspective, namely the inside. What is simply a drug dealing spot for the mainstream media is for Falo a communal space for sharing and passing time, for making histories, and for constructing identities.

Through personal experience, Falo describes police violence as well as their hypocrisy when it comes to the use of drugs. The aggressiveness with which Falo reacts is both comical and ironic, and differs from being simply a frustrated hood's unthinking response by presenting itself as a legitimate answer to State violence. "Pa'l Cruce" is part of the testimony of the generation hardest hit by the Mano Dura (Hard Hand) anti-crime government policy.

Violence in rap is sometimes a cathartic fantasy, sometimes a metaphor, and other times represents daily reality. It responds to concrete living conditions and functions as an answer to the violence of the surroundings. As Tricia Rose has explained," the ghetto badman posture-performance is a protective shell against real unyielding and harsh social policies and physical environments" (Rose *op.cit.*:12). Faced with a hostile environment, being a "motherfucker"[13] is as much a mechanism of defense as it is a way of finding self-validation and demanding respect.

Puerto Rican rap has developed in a context of violence, social inequalities, and police aggression. Just as, in the 1980s, young "cocolos" were identified as gold chain-stealing hoods,[14] in the 1990s, it is *raperos* who are the symbol of delinquent youth. The weight allocated to the term *"rapero"*—in reference to the artists as well as to their audience—as a social category is notably visible in the following El Vocero headline: RAPPER KILLED,[15] MOB DISMEMBERS RAPPER'S BODY.[16]

Prejudiced media attitudes toward rappers are blatant in journalistic coverage of events such as the following assassination of four youth:

> It must have been eleven at night when the four youth, singing to rapper Vico C.'s lyrics, according to the only eyewitness, were driving towards Simón Madera Avenue . . . (Acevedo 1993:8).

Although it is typical for tabloids to sensationalize their coverage of news events by going into minute details, it is worth asking if the journalist would have mentioned the songs that the youths were singing had they been salsa or merengue. Considering the violent circumstances of their death and its possible connection to drug business, the act of mentioning that they were listening to rap denotes the writer's intention to prove their closeness to criminality.

"Rapper" is a term whose use is not limited to defining those who actually perform or listen to rap, but is intricately bound to a style of dress and a particular way of projecting oneself through verbal and body language. *Claridad* columnist Fernando Clemente asks:

> For whom is the "rapper look" convenient, and worse yet, the "rapper conduct"? For Puerto Rican culture? Definitely not! (Clemente 1994:10)

For Clemente, as for many others like him, the rapper dress style is irremediably tied to delinquent behavior.

Rappers carry the inscriptions of their social marginality: their dress and self-projection denounce their class status. They understand, as articulated in their art, that this is part of the reason for their criminalization. An unidentified rapper in a 1994 underground recording bitterly points out how the police equate dressing like a rapper with commiting a crime; thus, "the cops mess with me just because I'm from the street." Ivy Queen holds a similar view, for "rappers are discriminated against and even thrown in jail, just for being rappers."[17]

Unlike previous generations that had to validate themselves before society as "humilde pero decente" (humble but decent), rappers proclaim themselves—as stated in a graffiti on Domenech Avenue, San Juan—"humilde pero no pendejo" (humble but not stupid). "Humble but decent" implies working hard for a minimum wage; "humble but not stupid" allows for the possibility of finding respect and sustenance within marginality. The previous generation's hope for a better material life and for social ascent through "honest" work has been lost for many youths. They, instead, have opted for the conquest of the present, claiming their entitlement to pleasure and re-vindicating their marginality.

The fundamental importance of the street as a symbol of social marginalization resides in the discourse of rap pointing to a class-based identification and solidarity. In rap, the Nation and the State are far from being the primary sources of cohesion and identity; instead, the street and the immediate community have come to signify the primary spaces for rappers, their actual "sense and foundation."[18] But social class, in Puerto Rico, is inextricably linked to racial matters. Clearly aware of this relationship, rappers address both class and racial subordination.

"Race" and Identity Poetry

Rap in the United States has been characterized since its early years for questioning the racial and socio-economic power structure. Just as in the United States, rap in Puerto Rico is a class-conscious form of cultural expression, where "class" is as tightly bound to the economic realm as to the racial. This genre, born out of the urban ghettos, seeks to vindicate through its discourse the most evident markings of marginality in these communities, poverty and race.

Race is a highly controversial as well as questionable construction. It is far from being a universally agreed-upon concept. The way that race is construed in the Puerto Rican context is different from the way the concept of race operates in the United States. Given the comparatively higher degree of miscegenation in Puerto Rico, the discourse of race there is more dependent on skin color and other racial markings than on "blood" or heredity. A phenotypically white person who, due to heredity, is considered black in the United States, may be considered white in Puerto Rico since there, phenotypical characteristics carry more weight. Another difference resides in that while the classificatory system of race in the United States places more weight on the dichotomy black/white, racial categories in Puerto Rico take into account a variety of intermediate shadings (Davis 1991:103; Omi and Winant 1991:61; Rodríguez 1991:54).

Racial inequalities in Puerto Rico, although blatant, have been disguised by a discourse of hybridity. We are taught in elementary school that we are "a mix of three races": Spanish, African, and Taíno. But this acknowledgment of racial miscegenation has in fact been used to elaborate a myth of racial harmony where obvious power inequalities are consistently denied. It is around this myth that the dominant racial discourse is built (González 1989:25).

Miscegenation has proven to be a handy flag in Puerto Rico to wave and prove that WE ARE NOT RACIST BECAUSE WE ARE INCAPABLE OF BEING RACIST. Allegedly, we cannot be racist because, after all, anyone's grandmother may be black ("y tu abuela ¿adonde está?"). But even though the dominant racial discourse acknowledges and even celebrates miscegenation, it still privileges the Spanish component. Nuyorican rapper Puerto Rock explains his qualms with the prevailing discourse:

> Everything that's positive the Spaniards [supposedly] created. The Africans created the little negativity, the cooking, this and that, the music-nothing "important." . . . Everybody over here, the Nuyoricans, is more or less up to date on all that. We realize our roots lead back to Africa.

Mayra Santos has accurately argued that the great acceptance and flourishing of rap in Puerto Rico can be explained partly in the fact that it recognizes racial differences that have always existed but have been consistently denied. Rap proposes a discursive revision that pulls blackness in from the margins.

The concept of race in Puerto Rico is profoundly informed by issues of class. When one looks at the skin pigmentation of Puerto Ricans across class it becomes obvious that there are more darker people the lower down one looks in the socioeconomic structure. Predictably, there are more lighter people in the upper social echelons. This has resulted in a perception within the collective imagination of an intrinsic relationship between blackness and poverty. Thus, race in Puerto Rico is not merely a reflection of phenotypic characteristics, but is also dependent on class markings such as dress, attitude, general apperance, and verbal and body language. Most raperos are considered and consider themselves black not only because they gravitate toward the darker side of the phenotypical spectrum, but because they belong to the lower classes.

As was mentioned previously, the rap culture is characterized by the flaunting of the symbols of marginality. Understanding the close link between race and class in Puerto Rican society, rappers loudly proclaim their ghettoness as much as their blackness, and not their "mestizoness". "Mestizoness," in Puerto Rico, has implied the assimilation and silencing of blackness and the privileging of whiteness. Thus, rappers ditch the concept of mestizoness altogether in order to frame the debate on their own terms.

Rappers and D.J.s have taken up names like O.G. Black, Blackie D., Black Mail, D.J. Negro, and Prieto M.C. Others have adopted the word "nigger" as their own. The use and vindication of a word like nigger is undoubtedly informed by U.S. rap. Hip-hop culture in the United States has served as a different frame of reference from which to look at race matters in Puerto Rico; it is, as Mayra Santos has said, the mirror in which the invisible ones seek for their reflection (Santos 1993).

Rap music is a subversive form of cultural expression regarding the question of social class and race, however, it steps right into the homophobic and mysogynistic mold set up by a patriarchal society. On the one hand, it participates in the construction of alternative class and racial identities; on the other, it attempts to enforce compliance with traditional gender and sexual identities. Although these are general characteristics that can be used to describe most of the rap being produced in Puerto Rico, and for that matter all other musical forms, it is important to stress that this genre is not monolithic. Rap is a cultural form engaged in multiple and continuous processes of subversion and communion. It is also in constant internal struggle, dialogue, movement, and change.

Reflections

Youth from impoverished communities of Puerto Rico have used rap as a vehicle of artistic expression for articulating identities and experiences. Social marginality has become a source of pride for rappers; in this way, they subvert the dominant discourse that accuses them of being responsible for the social unrest generated by decades of neoconservative/neoliberal politics. Such subversion takes place through the reappropriation of physical spaces (the street, the media, the market), as well as of symbols (the construction of alternative identities).

Rap is an example of how the negative stimuli surrounding impoverished youth can be transformed into a creative force. Many rappers, such as Prince Komazshi, attest to having chosen to channel their resentment through art since it is useless to respond to "hate with hate."[19]

Educators must come to realize the great importance that educating themselves about youth culture holds. Someone like Prince Komazshi, who is perhaps hardly stimulated by traditional subjects taught in the traditional way, would benefit immensely from exercising and developing his literary and philosophical potentials. Efforts must be made to better relate student interests to academic requirements. This may require quite a bit of effort on the part of the educators themselves who might be tempted to dismiss youth culture as frivolous, vulgar, or deviant.

I am not suggesting, however, that rap is a sacred cow that cannot be questioned. Many positions and attitudes within it need to be, and are being, challenged both from within as well as from outside the genre. The key is in encouraging the production of a liberated, liberating, and politicized rap that elaborates not only on realities but also on histories, causes, and possibilities for change. Recognizing inequalities and debunking myths is a first step, but we must then go beyond by projecting solutions into the future.

Rap, as a genre that contests various form of social oppression, can be a vehicle for building alliances between activists, community organizers, educators, conscientious policy makers, and all others interested in conspiring against inequality. Through it speak the dissident voices of those currently designated to bear the blame for social ills. Rap may indeed serve as a catalyst for building political commitments that strive for a liberating social change.

NOTES

1. The author is grateful to Laura Pérez for her assistance with the English translation of this paper.

2. The Young Lords Party (1969–1972) was an organization of Puerto Rican activists in the United States.

3. Close to one-half of the Puerto Rican population lives in the United States.

4. "De la calle," like "En coma," was recorded in a home studio and was sold on the underground market.

5. Vico C's and D.J. Negro's biographies, courtesy of Prime Entertainment.

6. See the *Sales Report*, October 30, 1993, p.15.

7. Plena is a genre of traditional Puerto Rican music.

8. This event was held on May 27, 1994.

9. A trio is a three-member string and vocal ensemble.

10. Puerto Rock and Krazy Taíno, the duo comprising Latin Empire, gave a lecture at The City College, New York, May 6, 1994.

11. From Sin Parar (N.R.T., 1994).

12. Initially an underground release, it was later remixed and released by Prime Records.

13. This interpretation comes from an underground recording by N.B.H., a rap group, in 1994. The tape which carries no label or song title, was made available to this author while doing research in Puerto Rico.

14. Ana María García, Documentary *Cocolos y roqueros*, 1993. Cocolo is a term used to identify salsa followers. However, the term became a synonym for delinquent youth due to the fact that most young people who

identified as cocolos came from impoverished classes; hence the pejorative use.

15. *El Vocero.* September 23, 1993.
16. *El Vocero.* November 20, 1993.
17. See Master Joe, "Underground Masters" (1995).
18. Vico C., "Base y fundamento" from *Xplosión* (1993).
19. Interview with Prince Komazshi in Old San Juan, February 20, 1994.

REFERENCES

Acevedo, Carmen, E. 1993. "Masacrados cuatro jóvenes." *El Nuevo Día* (October 8).

Borges, Ingrid Ortega. 1994. "Gran tasa de suicidio entre los jóvenes reclusos." *El Nuevo Día* (August 1).

Candela, Carlos Fortuño. 1993. *El auge de la actividad criminal en Puerto Rico.* Levittown: Ediciones Bandera Roja.

Clemente, Fernando. 1994. "Entrando por la salida." *Claridad* (February 18–24).

Davis, F. James. 1991. *Who is Black?: One Nation's Definition.* State College, Pa.: Pennsylvania State University Press.

Flores, Juan. 1988. "Rappin', Writin', & Breakin'." *Centro de Estudios de Puertorriqueños* Vol.II:3 (Spring) (City University of New York).

Flores, Juan. 1992. "IT'S A STREET THING!: An Interview with Charlie Chase." *Callaloo* 15:4.

Flores, Juan. (forthcoming). "Puerto Rocks: New York Ricans State Their Claim." In Juan Flores and Eric Perkins (eds.), *"Droppin' Knowledge" Essays on Rap Music and Hip Hop Culture.* Philadelphia: Temple University Press.

González, José Luis. 1989. *El país de cuatro pisos y otros ensayos.* Rio Piedras: Ediciones Huracán: 25.

Havelock, Nelson and Michael González. 1991. *Bring the Noise: A Guide to Rap and Hip Hop Culture.* New York: Harmony Books.

Hebdige, Dick. 1987. *Cut 'N' Mix: Culture, Identity and Caribbean Music.* New York: Methuen and Co. Ltd.

Interview with Pedro Merced, owner of B.M. Record Distributors. August 5, 1994. Santurce, Puerto Rico.

Interview with Vico C. 1993. San Juan, Puerto Rico.

Interview with Prince Komazshi. March 20, 1994. Old San Juan, Puerto Rico.

Interview with D.J. K-Kemit. February 20, 1994. Old San Juan, Puerto Rico.

Interview with Carlos Adorno (ex-member of the Bayamón electroboogie crew Los Smurfs), June 16, 1994. Rio Piedras, Puerto Rico.

Interview with D.J. Scratch Master E. August 3, 1994. Old San Juan, Puerto Rico.

Lipsitz, George. 1992. "'We Know What Time it is' Youth Culture in the 90s." *Centro de Estudios Puertorriqueños* 5:1 (Winter).

López, María Milagros. 1994. "Post-Work Selves and Entitlement Attitudes in Peripheral Postindutrial Puero Rico." *Social Text* 38 (Spring).

Messerschmidt, James, W. 1986. *Capitalism, Patriarchy and Crime: Toward a Socialist Feminist Criminology*. Savage, Maryland: Rowman and Littlefield).

Omi, Michael and Howard Winant. 1994. *Racial Formation in the United States: From the 1960s to the 1990s*. New York: Routledge.

Ortiz, Sofia. 1991. "Más allá del enfiebre del rap." *Claridad* (March 15–21).

Osorio, Idem. 1993. "Vico: una explosión de crítica social." *Diálogo* (November).

Rivera de Ríos, Trina. 1994. "Derechos humanos y civiles: juventud, trabajo y criminalidad." *Claridad* (April 29–May 5).

Roche, Mario Edgardo. 1994. "Desempleo y falta de orientación afectan la juventud puertorriqueña." *Diálogo* (January).

Rodriguez, Clara, E. 1991. *Puerto Ricans: Born in the U.S.A.* Boulder, Col.: Westview Press.

Rose, Tricia. 1994. *Black Noise: Rap Music and Black Culture in Contemporary America*. Hanover, N.H.: Wesleyan University Press.

Santos, Mayra. 1993. "A veces miro mi vida." *Diálogo* (October).

Silvestrini, Blanca. 1980. *Violencia y Criminalidad en Puerto Rico (1898–1973)*. Rio Piedras: Editorial Universitaria.

Toop, David. 1991. *Rap Attack 2: African Rap to Global Hip Hop*. New York: Serpent's Tail.

Vázquez, Héctor I. Monclova. 1993. "Los comienzos del abogado Brewley." *Claridad* (October 8–14).

Esther I. Madriz

— *6* —

Neoliberalism in Venezuela

From Urban Riots to Presidential Impeachment

In one of his visits, the author Eduardo Galeano referred to Venezuela as *La Civilización del Oro Negro* (The Civilization of the Black Gold). Venezuela has been for many years one of the wealthiest countries in the Americas although, paradoxically, large sectors of the population are deprived of some of the basic services and necessities (Galeano 1992). One of the most stable democracies in South America, Venezuela is also one of the major suppliers of oil to the United States, which has thrown enormous revenues into the hands of the Venezuelan government. But, in spite of the wealth that the petroleum has produced, Venezuela remains a country where poverty and richness coexist; mansions, modern buildings, fancy restaurants and hotels, *avant-garde* fashions, and cellular telephones coexist with the poverty faced by the inhabitants of the *barrios* (poor neighborhoods) surrounding the major urban centers.

The modern design of the Simón Bolivar International Airport, situated approximately thirty miles from Caracas, the capital, sharply contrasts with the sight of thousands of *ranchos* or shacks built on the hills of the mountains that surround Caracas. Piled up in irregular groupings, painted in different colors, the *ranchos* are a reminder of the prevailing poverty that exists in one of the wealthiest countries of Latin America. In spite of the sharp economic inequality, since 1958 Venezuela has been one of the models of democracy in the continent, contrasting with the military dictatorships then and afterwards in existence in other Latin American countries such as Brazil, Peru, Argentina, and Bolivia.

Venezuela has recently occupied the headlines of major newspapers in the United States and all over the globe. Political turmoil is tarnishing the democratic institutions of the country. On February 27, 1989, thousands of people took to the streets of major urban centers such as Caracas, Maracaibo, Valencia, and Maracay, looting supermarkets and small businesses and creating an image of Venezuela that departs from that of a wealthy country and of a "model democracy." Furthermore, on February 4, 1992, a group of middle- and low-ranking military men, under the leadership of Colonel Hugo Chavez, rose up in arms, attempting to overthrow the government of President Carlos Andrés Pérez. Another unsuccessful military coup d'etat took place in December of the same year. These events finally culminated in accusations of corruption against President Carlos Andrés Pérez and his impeachment by the Venezuelan Congress.

The crisis had enormous repercussions all over the world because of the symbolic and real consequences of this event for Venezuela and for other countries (Sonntag and Maingon 1992). If this is happening in Venezuela, the argument went, this can also occur in other countries such as Brazil, Argentina, and Chile, with more recent democracies.

This chapter analyzes the recent events of Venezuela in the context of the country's political economy. It employs a world-system perspective and focuses particularly on the connections between the global, national, and urban dimensions that led to the present crisis. Pointedly, the discussion deals with Venezuela's incorporation into the world economy, its emphasis on the neoliberal model, and the consequences of implementing that model for the Venezuelan people.

Venezuela's Incorporation into the Global Economy

According to Hopkins and Wallerstein (1982), the process of incorporation of a country into the world system constitutes a break with old historical patterns, leading to basic structural changes, especially in the productive processes and in the processes of governance. The terms of the incorporation are of unequal exchange, with the peripheral countries entering into the system as suppliers of raw materials for the industrialization of the core (Hopkins *et al.* 1982). Venezuela's entrance into the economic world system began during World War I, when oil became a major source of energy, making the control of the sources of petroleum a priority for the core countries of the world (Fierro Bustillos 1981). During the first part of the century, Mexico was one of the major providers of oil for the United States. However, the Mexican Revolution and one of its consequences, the nationalization of the Mexican petroleum industry, made finding and securing new sources of oil a crucial matter. In the 1940s and 1950s, the industrialization of the United States, heavily dependent on oil, increased the importance of Venezuela's oil resources. World War II and the Korean War further augmented the reliance of the United States on oil, tightening the economic ties between both countries and making Venezuela a crucial peripheral nation. Consequently, the Venezuelan economy received an influx of foreign capital, mainly from the United States but also from Great Britain, leading to the development of what some authors have called an *enclave economy*, in which production is developed by foreign capital to exploit primary products (Lucena 1980).

One of the structural consequences of Venezuela's incorporation into the global capitalist system as an oil provider was the development of a mono-productive economy, highly dependent on foreign investments and on the ups and downs of the prices of oil in the international markets. From the 1940s until the present, the country's economic dependency on oil as the major source of revenues has greatly increased, from fifty percent of the exports in 1940 to eighty percent in 1990 (Venezuelan-American Chamber of Commerce and Industry 1992: 32). Since then, any shift in oil prices or in the world's demand for oil has had a profound influence on the socioeconomic and political life of the country.

According to world-system theory, one of the patterns existing in the peripheral countries, stemming from their dependent status, is the migration of large sectors of the population from the rural areas toward the cities, resulting in *overurbanization* (Evans and Timberlake 1980; Rubinson 1976; Walton and Ragin 1990). In the case of Venezuela, the growth of the oil industry was paralleled with a neglect of the agricultural sector. Thus, after World War II, peasants left the countryside in massive numbers and moved to the major cities, especially Caracas. According to the World Bank, the Venezuelan urban population increased from sixty-seven percent in the 1960s, to eighty-four percent in 1982 (World Bank 1983: 179). In spite of some efforts such as the *Reforma Agraria* (the Agrarian Reform), attempting to bring people back to the rural areas, most Venezuelans preferred to live in the overcrowded cities of the country—since the urban centers offer at least a few services that are unavailable in the countryside.

Far from improving, this situation has been exacerbated during recent years. In 1993, the Minister of Agriculture, Hiram Gaviria, announced that employment in the agricultural sector had decreased by more than twenty-five percent between 1987 and 1992. This meant that 450,000 peasants lost their jobs and moved into the cities (Regalado 1993). The process of *overurbanization* was further accelerated as immigrants from other countries also moved to Venezuela, and specifically to Caracas, looking for their share of the "Venezuelan dream." Whereas in 1941 the Venezuelan population census reported 55,654 foreign-born, in 1961 their number had risen to 541,563, an increase of approximately 973 percent. Among them, 19 percent were Colombians, 25 percent Italians, and 30 percent Spaniards (Sosa 1979: 437). Given the accelerated urbanization process, the prices of real estate skyrocketed, benefitting oligarchic land and property owners and contributing to the formation of *barrios* where the majority who could not afford the high prices of real estate had to live. This situation accentuated already-existing income inequalities and increased class divisions.

The Urban Crisis

The majority of the Venezuelan people live in cities, with most living in *barrios*. For many Venezuelans, the word *barrio* has a negative connotation, implying that it is a neighborhood where the majority of the inhabitants are lower-class and, one may add, *mestizos*, or a mixture of indigenous, Black, and European. This ideology of *mestizaje* is part of the Venezuelan official and popular discourse. The implication is that all Venezuelans are *mestizos*, and therefore, equal (Trigo 1982). Although there is no official information about racial groups in Venezuela, a few authors have attempted to deal with the issue. For example, Otto Maduro states: "there is discrimination in Venezuela, otherwise, how can one explain the decreasing proportion of Blacks as one moves upward in the social ladder? . . . and vice versa" (1982: 66; *translation mine*). In other words, the lower the class, the higher the proportion of *mestizos*. It should not be surprising, therefore, to find that these groups are overrepresented in the *barrios*, where the majority of the urban poor live. The opposite is also true, in the middle- and upper-class neighborhoods, or *urbanizaciones*, Maduro says (1982), one can expect a larger representation of whites.

Barrios lack basic services such as water, electricity, telephone, transportation, garbage, and sewage collection, social and recreational areas, and adequate housing. *Barrios* and *urbanizaciones* contrast. In Galeano's words (1992), some houses in the wealthiest *urbanizaciones* of Caracas "have kitchens that look like the offices of cabinet ministers," whereas a *rancho* in the *barrios* is often smaller than a single room in a wealthy person's house. While *barrios* have ugly names, Black Cat, Yellow Sewer, Last Shot, *urbanizaciones* have delicate ones, the Marquis, the Woods, Beautiful Mountain.

In Caracas, *barrios* occupy less than ten percent of the land; however, sixty percent of the inhabitants of the city live in them. There are seven areas occupied by *barrios* in Caracas. The estimated total population is 1.5 million and the density of population is approximately 148 persons per acre. The average number of persons per family is 6.4 (Sosa 1993: 438). Due to overcrowding and lack of land, the *barrios* are growing vertically, with some *ranchos* having up to eight floors.

Most *barrios* are located in areas with steep slopes and soft soils, unable to sustain too much weight. Therefore, during the rainy reason, landslides are commonplace, with many *ranchos* falling and people dying every year. Access to the *barrios* is very restricted and cumbersome, and estimates show that some of the inhabitants of the *barrios* have to climb the equivalent of twenty-seven floors in a building to reach their homes. Mobility is very difficult for older people, the sick, and children, and transportation is expensive. In most cases, Jeeps are the only vehicles that can reach these homes (Sosa 1993).

Over the years, the Venezuelan government has developed programs to ameliorate the situation of the *barrios* by creating services such as sewers, electricity, improvement of roads and the facades of some of the most visible houses. However, since the *barrios* were built in a random, unplanned manner, these programs have been only bandaids, because they have not undertaken the radical transformations that are needed to change the infrastructure of the *barrios* into decent habitats. Moreover, these programs were more the result of populist policies, aimed to gain the support of the people during election times, than the product of well-planned housing and urban development programs.

The lack of employment opportunities among the inhabitants of the *barrios* has led to the creation of an urban informal economy, which is shaped by those who work as street vendors, car washers, shoe-shiners, and others (Mendez 1988). The number of persons who work in this informal sector of the economy is unknown, but estimates indicate that fifty-three percent of urban jobs are now classified as informal (Schemo 1996). In addition, some have opted for illegal activities such as drug trafficking and selling. Drug consumption also seems to be very frequent in the *barrios*. Guns and other weapons in the hands of young people have resulted in increased violence, which is reported weekly in the local press under the popularly known sub-heading, *reporte de guerra*, or war report (Sosa 1993).

The Birth of the Liberal State

The impact of dependency on the role and functions of the state is complex. While Wallerstein (1974) argues that dependency weakens the state due to foreign intervention in the domestic economy, lack of autonomy, and loss of legitimacy, O'Donnell (1988) claims that dependency strengthens it, leading to the development of bureaucratic-authoritarian states in some dependent countries. The birth of neoliberal states in Latin American countries offers a good test of these two hypotheses, with the second one being closer to the Venezuelan situation.

The first ten years of democratic rule were particularly important because they led to the emergence of the liberal state, main administrator and distributor of the oil revenues. The highly centralized and disciplined political parties guaranteed the control of major sectors of Venezuela's political and economic life: FEDECAMARAS (the chamber of commerce), unions, student and professional organizations, and even neighborhood associations (Hellinger 1994). After 1963, the increase in oil prices allowed a relative industrial development of the country, able to satisfy the internal demand for manufactured goods. One of the most important economic policies of the time was "import substitution" aimed at replacing imported goods by those produced in the country. But as early as 1966 and 1967, the Venezuelan Central Bank (Banco Central de Venezuela) and FEDECAMARAS, the organization representing Venezuelan major businesses, had manifested their preoccupation with the strangling of the incipient industrial development. In the IV Plan of the Nation, the government announced its sympathy with this opinion, asserting that Venezuela was passing through difficult moments, marked by a squeeze of the economy. The downturn in the economy was attributed to limitations that Venezuelan products faced competing in international and even regional markets. However, the dynamism of the oil market, and especially the increases in the oil prices, contributed to delay the economic crisis, contributing to the democratic stability of the country (Ferrigni 1981).

Exclusive dependency on a single export commodity led to the growth of private commercial activities and employment opportunities in the urban centers, major foci of these activities. In addition, the state embarked on the development of large infrastructure projects, further encouraging the growth of employment. The key role played by the state in commerce and construction opened the door to traffic in influence and corruption (Fierro-Bustillos 1981), since import licenses and construction contracts were, after all, controlled by the government.

The Venezuelan state has been characterized by some as an *estado rentista* or renter state because of its role as main collector and distributor of the oil revenues (Ferrigni 1981; Rosen 1994). It has also been one of the major creditors in the country, favoring some sectors of the population, creating a wealthy consumer class, who could afford the most expensive imported goods and who traveled around the world, especially to Miami, where many owned vacation homes.

The role of the *estado rentista* as provider started to erode when oil revenues began to fall, from $19.1 billion in 1981 to $7.6 billion in 1986, signalling the end of the "Venezuelan bonanza" (Hellinger 1994). The dreamers, however, were late in waking up. Corruption scandals and influence-peddling were commonplace. Capital flight was rampant, with members of the elite sending large amounts of money to numbered Swiss banks accounts and U.S. financial institutions. Some newspapers began to expose links between Venezuelan elites and Colombian drug lords.

In 1988, ex-President Carlos Andrés Pérez—a Social Democrat—returned to power, aided by his populist image and the prestige reached during his previous presidential period in the 1970s. But the reality of the late 1980s was very different from the oil bonanza of 1974. Faced with an enormous debt, Pérez opted for a neoliberal program of liberalization of prices, privatization of major industries, and cuts in state employment. These policies created resentments among both the lower classes and the elite, who were accustomed to the old paternalistic state policies. In 1993, after Carlos Andrés Pérez was impeached for corruption, another ex-president, the Social Democrat Rafael Caldera, returned to power, this time supported by a coalition of Left parties, including the Movement Toward Socialism Party (MAS). Caldera's victory was caused by the discontent of Venezuelans toward the neoliberal policies of his predecessor and by the charges of corruption brought against political leaders, including the previous two presidents, Jaime Lusinchi and Carlos Andrés Pérez. During the years of abundance corruption was tolerated, but it became unacceptable during times of scarcity.

The Economic Crisis and the Crisis of the Democratic Institutions

There are complementary explanations for the crisis that Venezuela is facing, some of which are shared with other countries in Latin America and some of which are unique to the Venezuelan situation. The most common are: the foreign debt and the involvement of international financial institutions in the economic and political life of the country, the creation of the *estado rentista*, the rampant corruption existing among politicians and Venezuelan entrepreneurs, and the process of *overurbanization* (Rosen 1994).

According to Luis Zambrano Sequin (1993), one of the major culprits in the current crisis that Venezuela is facing is the excessive foreign debt that Venezuela acquired in the 1970s, becoming the fourth-largest debtor in Latin America, after Brazil, Mexico, and Argentina. The factors that led to this indebtedness are multifold. Internally, the declining economic growth during the period between 1974 and 1980 led the government and the private sector to finance many of their projects through foreign indebtedness. Abroad, world financial institutions promoted loan programs because they had an excess of capital as a result of the payment surpluses of the OPEC countries (Block 1977; Kuczynski 1982–1983). This led to an increase in credits to Latin America from $16 billion in 1973 to $200 billion one decade later (Saieh 1985: 195). Falling oil prices, together with skyrocketing interest rates, placed a big burden on the economies of Third World countries (Inter American Development Bank 1984). To deal with the impact of the external debt, Latin American countries implemented a series of economic measures such as cuts in imports of commodities, consumer goods as well as capital goods. The impact of these cuts on the economic growth of Venezuela was particularly severe given the country's dependency on imported products. Reduction of imports also caused a decrease in the consumption levels of Venezuelans, creating a sense of discontent.

Venezuela had to postpone debt service payments. In 1983, the government initiated negotiations with the International Monetary Fund (IMF) to refinance or reschedule the payment of the principal. It also negotiated additional funds aimed at paying the interest on the debt. This situation led to a spiralling indebtedness, which became a threat to the country's economic and political stability. In order to obtain additional funds, Venezuela had to accept the IMF's austerity program or *paquete economico* (economic package), which entailed decreasing government spending and eliminating subsidies, increasing taxes, establishing new import duties, and continuing monetary devaluations (Walton and Ragin 1990). The intervention of the IMF in the political and economic life of the country became evident to Venezuelans, who now had a clear and distinguishable "enemy."

Another explanation given for the current crisis has to do with some of the characteristics of the Venezuelan state and their implications. The growth of the *estado rentista*, accustomed to living off its oil rent and to administering and distributing the nation's revenues, led to the development of a *mentalidad rentista*, or renter mentality, in the population. This *mentalidad rentista* implied living under the umbrella of a paternalistic state, which took care of the basic needs of its citizens without demanding the active participation required in most democratic societies (Hellinger 1994). The populist Venezuelan state clearly favored the rich and provided minimal living conditions for some of the poor, who barely benefitted from the "trickle down." Faced with an economic crisis, the paternalistic state lost credibility when the decline in oil revenues meant that it could no longer pay for social programs.

A third explanation commonly offered by Venezuelans for the crisis is the rampant corruption existing in the country. The Venezuelan state has been, simultaneously, collector, distributor, administrator, and creditor of oil revenues, becoming what some authors call an *interventionist state* (Fierro-Bustillos 1981) with ample power to decide what groups will benefit. Rumors of corruption have been commonplace in Venezuela, and the likelihood of punishment for those accused and even charged with corruption or *corruptos* very low. For years, sectors of the population and opposition leaders have demanded, unsuccessfully, a clean-government drive, aimed at eradicating administrative corruption. The passivity of the judicial system in dealing with accusations of corruption against government officials and their protegees has been linked by many to the complicity of the two major political parties—The Social Democratic Party (AD) and The Christian Democratic Party (COPEI)—in many corruption schemes.

Finally, *overurbanization* has also been signalled as one of the factors in the crisis, since the measures contemplated in the *paquete* fall heavily on the shoulders of the inhabitants of the urban centers, especially the dwellers of the *barrios*. These measures have resulted in an increase in unemployment and underemployment, fifty-four percent inflation (Schemo 1996), increases in the prices of basic commodities, including food, transportation, and medicines, and a decrease in social services. Thus, it should not be surprising that the people who live in the *barrios* have been some of the most active participants in the food riots and in the urban protest movement.

From el Caracazo of Feb. 27, 1989, to the Military Insurrection of Feb. 4, 1992

Soon after his inauguration, on February 16, 1989, Carlos Andrés Pérez presented his economic program to the country. Contradicting his pre-electoral nationalistic discourse, he announced that the government had signed an agreement with the IMF. The agreement, known by Venezuelans as *el paquete*,[1] meant increased hardship and sacrifices for the Venezuelan people, including a raise in the price of gasoline, the devaluation of the bolivar, the suspension of subsidies to products that are part of the *cesta basica* (the food basket of basic consumer necessities), the elimination of price controls, increased taxes, and the privatization of many state-owned companies, such as VIASA, the major Venezuelan airline, and CANTV, the telephone company. It also included using one-third of the national budget to satisfy debt payments. From a macroeconomic viewpoint, *el paquete* contributed to lowering the rate of inflation to 31 percent in 1992, down from 36.5 percent in 1990 and 81 percent in 1989 (Herrera-Vaillant 1992). Besides, the country's international reserves and Gross National Product increased and, in general, the economy grew at a 4.4 percent rate (Sonntag and Maingon 1992; Villegas 1992). However, from a microeconomic viewpoint, the social and political cost of *el paquete* was very high, affecting, especially, working- and even middle-class urban sectors, who were confronted with alarming increases in basic goods and commodities. For example, the price of medicines increased 513 percent between 1989 and 1991 (Fajardo 1992; Villegas 1992).

On February 26, a few days after the President announced his *paquete*, the increase in the price of the gasoline was implemented. In the early hours of February 27, the popular protest erupted: thousands of people, in a big wave, flooded the streets of Caracas and other cities of the country for more than twenty-four hours and took over commercial establishments, especially supermarkets, grocery stores, and appliance stores. The individuals involved in the protest, which is known by many as *el Caracazo* (Caracas's riot), included students, urban workers, and housewives, protesting the increase in the price of public transportation. On February 28, the city was virtually paralyzed. To control the situation, the government sent the national guard, the police, and, eventually, the army. Civil rights were suspended and a curfew was imposed. The repression was especially focused on the *barrios*, considered the nuclei of the popular movement (Sonntag and Maingon 1992). While the official toll was estimated to be between 200 and 350 deaths, human rights organizations placed it between 1,000 and 1,300 (Batatin 1994).

One obvious result of the implementation of *el paquete* was the widening of the gap between the rich and the poor (Montes de Oca 1993). Whereas those who depended on a salary saw their real wages shrink, those who benefitted from the privatization of state-owned companies and new taxation saw their capital increase. However, some sectors of the bourgeoisie were also affected, since they heavily depended on imported products, domestic consumption, and domestic borrowing (Walton and Ragin 1990). "The middle class is disappearing," said Andrés Serbin, President of the Venezuelan Institute for Social and Political Studies, a private research institute (Schemo 1996). The general sentiment is that the weight of the austerity measures rests on the shoulders of the working and middle classes and that the upper class and certain sectors of the government have benefitted from the situation. According to Juan Carlos Navarro, coordinator of the Center for Public Policy at the Institute for Advanced Administrative Studies, Venezuelan people feel that they are getting poorer; "and they are right," he concluded (Schemo 1996).

For many Venezuelans, disenchanted with the democratic institutions, the leaders of the two attempted military coups—Colonel Hugo Chavez and the members of his *Movimiento Nacionalista Bolivariano Revolucionario–200*—became popular heroes. A survey done by the Venezuelan newspaper *El Nacional* two days after the attempted coup d'etat gives us a hint of the popular sentiment: Even though many people reported to be against a dictatorship, they wanted the government to take the movement seriously and to start exercising democracy effectively, "guaranteeing better public services, education, security, housing, transportation and the improvement of the quality of life for all" (Gonzalez 1992; *translation mine*).

On the afternoon of February 4, 1992, Venezuela's congress met to approve the temporary suspension of constitutional guarantees. Rafael Caldera, veteran leader of the Venezuelan Christian Democracts asked for permission to speak. Eloquently, Caldera expressed his view that the people should not be blamed for reacting to the hardship they were experiencing, and he called upon the president to modify his economic policies. From that moment on, Caldera would be viewed by Venezuelans as a nationalist and an opponent of the neoliberal reforms imposed by Pérez and the IMF (Alvarez 1994).

After February 4, anti-government sentiments became more manifest. For example, on March 10, sectors of the working and middle class took to the streets of Caracas, banging empty pots, protesting the economic consequences of the *paquete* for their daily lives (El Nacional 1992). The noise produced by the banging was accompanied by slogans in favor of Colonel Chavez and against corruption and by the singing of the national anthem. The President seemed to be oblivious to the mass movements, as he refused to change his economic policies. On December 6, 1992, a second failed attempt to overthrow the government precipitated the imminent crisis for the President and his cabinet.

Political leaders began to press for Carlos Andrés Pérez's resignation, accusing him of using 250 million bolivares from the *partida secreta* (presidential discretionary funds) for his own benefit. Finally, before the end of his five-year presidential term, the Venezuelan Congress impeached President Pérez and elected an economist, Ramón J. Velazquez, who assumed transitory power amidst the rumors of an imminent coup d'etat. The major goal of Velazquez's presidency was to ensure the peaceful transition between presidential terms (Centro Gumilla 1994).

The Elections of December 1993

Rafael Caldera was the victor in the December 1993 presidential elections, this time supported by a coalition of Left parties known as the *chiripero* (the bugs), in which the most important political force was the Movement toward Socialism. Political analysts saw Caldera's victory as a rejection of both *bi-partidismo* and the neoliberal policies implemented by the previous administration and support for a more nationalist platform, which did not strictly follow the mandates of the IMF, and for the positive image of a candidate considered honest by many Venezuelans. Indeed, Caldera campaigned on the promise to change the neoliberal economic strategy followed by Carlos Andrés Pérez. The elected president and his consultants expressed the view that the goal of the government should not be purely economic, but should also work toward social equity (Alvarez 1994). With the plummeting of the price of oil on the international markets and with a fiscal deficit estimated at 300 million bolivares, however, the state is in desperate need of revenues. Thus, financial consultants have turned to one major route to economic health, raising taxation and the privatization of some industries. (Purroy 1994; Schemo 1996).

Among the first emergency measures of the new administration was intervention in the affairs of eight banks that were at the edge of collapse, suspension of some constitutional guarantees including the right to hold private property, negotiations with the IMF, and price and exchange controls to put limits on the flight of Venezuelan capital to foreign banks. *The Washington Post* referred to Venezuela as a "country moving backwards" and to Caldera as an "unrepentant populist" because of his belief in the interventionist role of the state in the economic affairs of the country (Bauman 1994: 1–2).

Conclusions

The mass protests that have taken place in Venezuela have to be analyzed in the context of other mass movements that have occurred in different parts of the world since the early 1980s, with more than eighty countries forced to implement the IMF's "structural adjustments." What is particularly pertinent to the present analysis is that, contrary to the past, when economic growth in Third World countries was concentrated in the cities to the detriment of the rural areas, the neoliberal economic policies affect mainly the urban working and even middle class. Consequently, the food riots of the 1980s and 1990s are fundamentally an urban phenomenon, with some studies linking these movements to the process of *overurbanization* that has occurred in Third World countries. Austerity policies, which have mainly affected the inhabitants of the city, subject the poor and working class more than any other groups to layoffs, inflationary pressures, and the decline in social services. Similarly, the IMF measures are imposed more heavily on those who depend on a salary for their subsistence while some members of the business and financial elites are, in many instances, favored by measures such as privatization of state-owned industries (Loxley 1984; Walton 1987). A consequence of the current scenario is the growing disparity between rich and poor countries and a widening of economic inequalities in Third World countries.

Although there are many factors common to these countries, such as the huge sums of dollars that all of them owe to the international banks, and the IMF negotiations and resulting austerity policies, there are also particularities due to the position that these countries occupy in the global political economy and to the way this has influenced internal institutions, particularly the state. In the case of Venezuela, the role the country plays as supplier of oil for the United States, guaranteeing enormous revenues for the country and its elites, and the role of the state as the major collector and distributor of oil revenues, gives a special character to the crisis.

The neoliberal economic policies considered by some to be the remedy for the world economy's malady are based on the assumption that if the macroeconomic indicators improve, the life of the people will improve: "trickle down economics." This assumption has been challenged by many economists and politicians, and the experience of Venezuela shows how the implementation of these policies is generating broad discontent. Victor Fajardo (1992) argues that the *paquete* is designed for a textbook country: a country with autonomous risk-taking entrepreneurs, perfectly competitive markets, and a submissive working class. This is not the case of Third World countries and particularly of Venezuela.

President Caldera faces three alternatives, none of them without problems. First, to continue the implementation of the pure neoliberal model, which might result in increased urban protests, and possibilities of a military coup d'etat with a strong nationalistic and populist flavor. Second, to keep the strong interventionist and paternalistic role of the state in the economy. This scenario is highly improbable given the plummeting of oil prices and the demands of the international banks. A third, more likely scenario is the selective implementation of some of the previous economic policies together with the creation of social "buffers" aimed at softening the impact of these measures upon the working and middle classes.

The current situation offers the opportunity to develop an economic agenda based more on national priorities than on the requirements of the foreign markets. This economic agenda should include, firstly, state protection of the agricultural sector, specifically of small and medium size landowners. This, in turn, would generate employment in the rural areas, contributing to the control of *overurbanization*. Secondly, given the fact that a small group benefitted from the enormous wealth at the expense of the poor, the government needs to create an income tax system that guarantees that the rich pay their share of the taxes. Nowadays, many wealthy people in Venezuela do not pay taxes because there is not an efficient system of fiscal control. Thirdly, certain companies and industries should be selectively "destatized" and decentralized. The private sector as well as workers must be included as actors in the decision-making process. Other industries that are basic for the economic life of the country, such as the oil industry, should remain in the hands of the state. Finally, the enormous expenditures generated by the inefficient and bureaucratic state apparatus should be reduced, especially those related to conspicuous expenses and privileges for the few. Moreover, the government needs to send clear messages that corruption and the traffic in influence will not be tolerated. Above all, the government can not solve the crisis at the expense of the majority of Venezuelans who, rightfully, are demanding their access to education, transportation, housing, health, and other services, which have been in the past the privilege of a few.

While the long run consequences of the mass movements occurring in Venezuela and other countries of the world are still to be seen, one thing is clear: people are not willing to tolerate passively the imposition of austerity measures upon them. In Venezuela and in other countries, political leaders are using a nationalistic political discourse to placate the masses. Meanwhile, leaders of financial institutions are trying to "stabilize" the crisis, but without much success.

The urban protests of the 1980s and 1990s are, according to some, "the microcosms in which overt struggles over the directions of the contemporary global economy take place" (Walton and Ragin 1990). The results of these struggles are not clear yet, but they are certainly an indication of a mass opposition to intervention by foreign forces in the national affairs of Third World countries and a rejection of the submissive attitude of national leaders to the mandates of the international economic institutions.

--- NOTE ---

1. The word *paquete* in Venezuela has a double meaning. One meaning is the equivalent to the English word packet. Another meaning, though, has to do with a problematic situation. For example, the phrase "esa persona es un paquete" (that person is a packet) means, in slang, that the person is problematic.

--- REFERENCES ---

Alvarez, Federico. 1994. "Deciphering the National Elections." *NACLA Report on the Americas* Vol XXVII No 5: 16–22.

Batatin, Carlos. 1994. "27F: Cronica de lo Insolito." *El Universal* (27 de Febrero): 1–22.

Bauman, Everett. 1994. "Venezuela en Retroceso." *El Universal* (13 de Julio): 1,2.

Block, Fred L. 1977. *The Origins of International Economic Disorder: A Study of United States International Monetary Policy from World War II to the Present*. Berkeley: University of California Press.

Centro Gumilla. 1994. "La Encrucijada en el Camino." *SIC* 561, pp. 2–4. Centro Gumilla: Caracas.

El Nacional. 1992. "El Ruido de las Cacerolas se Escucho en toda Caracas." (Miercoles 11 de Marzo): C/1.

Evans, Peter B. and Michael Timberlake. 1980. "Dependence, Inequality and the Growth of the Tertiary: A Comparative Analysis of Less Developed Countries." *American Sociological Review* 45: 531–552.

Fajardo, Victor. 1992. "Colapso del Paquete Economico: Causas, Efectos y Perspectivas, Venezuela 1989–92." *Cuadernos del Cendes* 20. Caracas: Universidad Central de Venezuela.

Ferrigni, Yoston. 1981. "Estadio de Consolidacion Capitalista de la Sociedad Venezolana." In *Formacion Historico Social de Venezuela*, pp. 162–195. Caracas: Universidad Central de Venezuela, Centro de Estudios del Desarrollo/CENDES.

Fierro-Bustillos, Lourdes. 1981. "Estadio de Condiciones para la Estructuracion Capitalista de la Formacion Social Venezolana." In *Formacion Historico Social de Venezuela*, pp. 132–161. Caracas: Universidad Central de Venezuela, Centro de Estudios del Desarrollo/CENDES.

Galeano, Eduardo. 1992. "The Civilization of Black Gold." In *We Say No*, pp. 111–117. New York: W.W. Norton.

Gonzalez, Aliana. 1992. "Ser Tomado en Cuenta Pide el Pueblo a Gritos." *El Nacional* (6 de Febrero): C/1.

Hellinger, Daniel. 1994. "Democracy Over a Barrel: History Through the Prism of Oil." *NACLA Report on the Americas* Vol XXVII 5: 35–41.

Herrera-Vaillant, Antonio. 1992. "Editor's Memo. The Paradox." *Business Venezuela* 137 (January/February): 2.

Hopkins, Terence K. and Immanuel Wallerstein. 1982. "Structural Transformations of the World Economy." In *World System Analysis, Theory and Methodology*, pp. 121–142. California: Sage.

Hopkins, Terence K., Immanuel Wallerstein, and Associates. 1982. "Patterns of development of the Modern World-System." In *World System Analysis, Theory and Methodology*, pp. 41–82. California: Sage.

Inter American Development Bank. 1984. *External Debt and Economic Development in Latin America. Background and Prospects.* Washington, D.C: Inter American Development Bank.

Kuczynski, Pedro Pablo. 1982–1983. "Latin American Debt." *Foreign Affairs* (Winter): 344–364.

Loxley, John .1984. "Saving the World Economy." *Monthly Review* (September): 22–34.

Lucena, Hector. 1980. "Industrial Relations in an Enclave Economy: The Case of Venezuela." *Labour and Society* 5: 341–354.

Maduro, Otto. 1982. "Clases y Razas." *SIC* 442, pp. 66, 67. Caracas: Centro Gumilla.

Mendez, Domingo R. 1988."El Sector Informal Urbano en Venezuela." *SIC* 504, pp. 152–155. Caracas: Centro Gumilla.

Montes de Oca, Acianela. 1993. "Enzo Faletto. America Latina : un Continente de Privilegiados y Excluidos." *El Nacional* (4 de Junio): C/1.

O'Donnell, Guillermo. 1988. "Bureaucratic Authoritarianism: Argentina 1966–1973." in *Comparative Perspective*. Berkeley, Cal.: University of California Press.

Purroy, Ignacio Miguel. 1994. "Balance 1993 y Perspectivas 1994." *SIC* 561, pp. 16–21. Caracas: Centro Gumilla.

Regalado, Rosita. 1993. "Caida del Empleo Rural es una Bomba de Tiempo." *El Nacional* (26 de Julio): 2/Economia.

Rubinson, Richard. 1976. "The World Economy and the Distribution of Income Within States." *American Sociological Review* 41: 638–659.

Rosen, Fred. 1994. "The Temperature Rises in the Crucible of Reform." *NACLA Report on the Americas* XXVII, 5: 23–28.

Saieh, Alvaro. 1985. "On Latin America External Debt. Is there a way out?" In Jorge Antonio *et al.* (eds.), *External Debt and Development Strategy in Latin America*. New York: Pergamon Press.

Schemo, Diana Jean. 1996. "Whatever Happened to Venezuela's Middle Class?" *The New York Times* (February 6): A/3.

Sonntag, Heinz R. and Thais Maingon. 1992. *Venezuela: 4-f 1992: Un Analisis Sociopolitico*. Caracas: Editorial Nueva Sociedad.

Sosa, Arturo. 1993. "Barrios Humanos." *SIC* 560, pp. 436–439. Caracas: Centro Gumilla.

———. 1979. *Democracia y Dictadura en la Venezuela del Siglo XX*, pp. 436–441. Centro Gumilla: Curso de Formacion Socio-Politica.

Trigo, Pedro. 1982. "Patria, La Mestiza." *SIC* 442, pp. 61–64. Caracas: Centro Gumilla.

Venezuelan-American Chamber of Commerce and Industry. 1992. "The Package Unwrapped." *Business Venezuela* 137 (January/February): 31–34.

Villegas, Mario. 1992. "De lo Macro a lo Mega sin llegar a lo Micro." *El Nacional* (Domingo 2 de Febrero): C/1.

Wallerstein, Immanuel. 1974. *The Modern World System: Capitalistic Agriculture and the Origins of the European World-Economy in the Sixteenth Century*. New York: Academic Press.

Walton, John. 1987. "Urban Protests and the Global Political Economy: the IMF Riots." In Michael Peter Smith and J. R. Feagin (eds.), *The Capitalist City: Global Restructuring and Community Politics*. London: Basil Blackwell.

Walton, John and Charles Ragin. 1990. "Global and National Sources of Political Protest: Third World Responses to the Debt Crisis." *American Sociological Review* 55: 876–890

World Bank. 1983. *Population Change and Economic Development*. Oxford University Press: International Bank for Reconstruction and Development/The World Bank.

Zambrano Sequin, Luis. 1993. "Sobre lo que Hemos Hecho y aun Podemos Hacer en Politica Economica." In Andres Serbin *et al.*(eds.), *Venezuela:la Democracia Bajo Presion*. Caracas: editorial Nueva Sociedad.

Vânia Penha-Lopes[1]

7

An Unsavory Union

Poverty, Racism, and the Murders of Street Youth in Brazil

In Brazil, both the elite and the population at large have long promoted the country as a "racial democracy," despite convincing evidence to the contrary (see Azevedo 1975; Fernandes 1971; Skidmore 1993; Telles 1992). Consequently, among all of the countries touched by the African Diaspora, Brazil alone has the reputation of being an oasis for Blacks (DuBois 1992; Frazier 1992; Freyre 1946). Even when racial inequality is recognized there, it is thought to be much less important than economic inequality (Cox 1948: Chapter 17; Harris 1964).

However, the recent murders of street youth have forced an examination of race relations in Brazil. The most talked-about incident took place on a night in late July 1993, when forty youngsters who called the streets home slept outside of Candelária, a prominent church in downtown Rio de Janeiro. They were suddenly awakened by an imposing man looking for a certain boy. As the boy identified himself, he was fatally shot in the eye. In less than one hour, seven boys between the ages of 11 and 22 were summarily exterminated and two others were seriously hurt. The news left the Brazilian president ashamed, while pictures of the violence appeared in major newspapers the world over (ISTOÉ 1993a:16–17).

Unfortunately, murders like those have become commonplace in large Brazilian cities. As evidence of the significant increase in youth murders during the past twenty years, São Paulo recorded an increase of over 1,400 percent in such violent deaths between 1970 and 1984; in 1989, four youths per day were murdered in Recife, Rio de Janeiro, and São Paulo (Huggins and Mesquita 1996:6). In 1992, 424 minors were murdered in Rio de Janeiro, up from 306 the previous year; nationwide, four children and adolescents are murdered every day (Veja 1993b:20).

While the number of street youth has been increasing, at least partly due to the rampant economic recession that has created 65 million poor in a country of fewer than 150 million inhabitants (ISTOÉ 1992:26), it is worth noting that a majority of street children—including those described above—are Black and mulatto, even though official statistics classify as such only forty-four percent of the total population (IBGE 1992 Table 22.2: 261). How can "racial democracy" explain such figures?

This chapter examines the recent growth of violence against Brazilian children in light of race relations. I argue that so many murdered children are nonwhite because Blacks and mulattos have traditionally occupied the lowest rungs of Brazilian society, and so have been the victims of its pernicious de facto discrimination. Thus, rather than being a racial democracy, Brazil is actually a country where racial inequality is, for the most part, subtle, but widespread nonetheless. The massacres of destitute children bring to the fore not only the substandard social conditions faced by a large proportion of the population, but also the perilous position many Brazilian Blacks and mulattoes occupy today. In the following sections, I will review Brazil's unique history of race relations and its peculiar form of racism. I will then provide a profile of that country's current socioeconomic conditions. Third, I will report on the major characteristics of street youth murders. Finally, I will discuss possible social policy alternatives to the extermination of one of the most underprivileged segments of Brazilian society.

Brazil's Legacy of Race

The unusual Brazilian approach to race relations can be gauged by the impossibility of ascertaining the number of Africans who entered the country; it can be only estimated that about four million

Africans landed in Brazil between 1551 and 1856 (Azevedo 1975: 12). Besides the obvious fact that at least one-sixth of captured Africans died on their forced passage to the Americas, the Brazilian government ordered the burning of all records related to slavery in 1891, just three years after Abolition. The government justified its actions "for honor of the Nation, and in homage to our duties of fraternity and solidarity to the large mass of citizens who, by the abolition of servitude, became part of the Brazilian community" (in Azevedo 1975:12; *my translation*). Unsuspecting individuals may agree that the federal authorities indeed had the best intentions when they took such drastic measure. However, a Brazilian scholar suggests that a more realistic explanation was an effort to prevent former slaveowners from requesting compensation for lost property (Azevedo 1975:12).[2]

The government's intentions notwithstanding, the burning of records may have been correlated to a nascent desire to erase evidence of an African past. During the Abolitionist campaign, many participants shrouded the burning in moral and humanistic terms, but some were openly concerned with Brazil's racial future. After all, in the social-evolutionist climate of the nineteenth century, even some liberals saw the significant Black contingent as a reminder of Brazil's "backward" agricultural reality, and perhaps a hindrance to the achievement of "progress," so important in American and European circles at the time, and eventually adopted as a Brazilian national motto.

Ever since the "scientific" racial theories of the nineteenth century (and their horrified European proponents) determined that Brazil was doomed to deterioration due to widespread miscegenation, the Brazilian elite had been trying to put an end to its "racial problem," namely, a Black numerical majority. At the turn of the century, the government wholeheartedly embraced European immigration in an effort to dilute African and Indian "blood," and thus accelerate Brazil's whitening.[3]

Indeed, the official whitening plan showed results almost immediately. As late as the 1870s, the Brazilian black population exceeded 50 percent (Skidmore 1993:29), which gave travelers the impression of being in Africa. However, according to the 1890 census, the black population that year was less than 15 percent (Azevedo 1975:26–27), while so-called whites accounted for over 40 percent. By 1950, whites constituted over 60 percent of Brazilians, whereas blacks had declined to close to 10 percent. The mulatto contingent, however, went from 41 percent in 1890 down to 30 percent in 1950, and climbed ten years later, to nearly 40 percent (Degler 1971:Chapter 4).

How do we explain such a rapid decrease in the nonwhite population in such a short time? While it is indisputable that a massive European immigration brought to Brazil three million whites starting in 1890 (Skidmore 1993:46), that alone would not have accounted for a significant change in the population in that same year. One possibility would thus be rapid intermarriage and a high rate of light-skinned births. However, large-scale intermarriage has never really taken place in Brazil. According to official records, there were only 5.9 percent marriages between whites and nonwhites in Rio de Janeiro in 1890, and only 3.3 percent Black-white marriages in Bahia in 1933–1934, hardly enough to provoke such a rapid increase in the "white" population.[4] It must be assumed, then, that there was a significant number of illegitimate black-white births, as Freyre (1946) suggested, though it is doubtful that that would have been enough.

Another possibility for the rapid decrease of the Black population was the "low rate of net natural increase," for which there is evidence from the city of São Paulo (Skidmore 1993:46). Apparently, there had been a high Black mortality rate due to the substandard quality of life, in addition to a low birthrate, since at least the early 1800s (Skidmore 1993:42–43). But if we take into account that racial classification in Brazil is quite fluid and that census racial classification is highly subjective—it varies both among interviewers and respondents—then it is also possible that many Brazilians chose to whiten themselves, a process that continues to this day (Penha-Lopes 1996). This would be possible if, in those sixty years, the society became even more amenable to the whitening ideology. Indeed,

[D]uring the high period of racist thought—1880 to 1920—the "whitening" ideology gained scientific legitimacy, because racist doctrines came to be interpreted by Brazilians as supporting the view that the "superior" white race would prevail in the process of racial amalgamation. (Skidmore 1993:46)

By the 1940s, social whitening got an incentive in Freyre's postulation that miscegenation constituted the uniqueness of the Brazilian national character, allowing the best characteristics of the three main races that formed Brazil—whites, native Indians, and Blacks—to emerge. For Freyre, this blending occurred in a context of "racial democracy," because he saw the three races on equal footing. Miscegenation was positive and unavoidable; thus, Brazilians did not have to see themselves as racially inviable on their road to whitening.[5]

And whiten themselves they do. If, on the one hand, Brazil is regarded as the country with the largest black population outside of Africa, on the other—according to official statistics—its black contingent is only 5 percent, compared to 39 percent of mulattos and 55 percent of whites, as of 1990 (IBGE Table 22.2: 261). Again, even considering widespread miscegenation, it is fair to assume that many Blacks and mulattos must change their racial identity.

As for the state of racial democracy in Brazil today, it is still powerful, despite nearly half a century of attacks against it, both from academia and from Black political mobilization (Fontaine 1985:2–5). While most Brazilians "look mixed," at the same time negative stereotypes about Blacks abound, such as the conspicuously racist saying, "If a white man is running, he must be an athlete; if a Black man is doing the same, he must be a thief."

The following case illustrates the widespread belief in such stereotypes: A few years ago, the leader of "Olodum," a famous musical group from Salvador (the capital of the northeastern state of Bahia), was shot by a military policeman at the local airport. "'Eusébio had packed a suitcase and was on his way to London,' said . . . a church human rights lawyer familiar with the case. 'But the policeman saw a black man with a bag and assumed he had stolen it from a tourist'" (Brooke 1991:A4). This happened in a city where about eighty percent of the residents are Black or mulatto. Nevertheless, Salvador's Mayor at the time insisted that he did not know "why the majority of the city council is white, but there is no discrimination in Salvador. Blacks and whites live together peacefully here" (Brooke 1991:A4). Obviously, the proponents of racial democracy base their thinking on the lack of overt racial friction. But it is about time racial democracy was seen not as different races coexisting equally, but as the acceptance of an ideology of racial hierarchy.

Another example of the lower social status of Brazilian Blacks comes from Benedita da Silva, from Rio de Janeiro, who became the first Black congresswoman in 1987:

> I know the position of blacks in this country. . . . From the time I was tiny, *I was made to feel my place.* I learned to go in through the back door. I was told I was ugly because I had crinkly hair and black skin. . . . Yet at the same time this is a country where blacks are always being told there is no discrimination. It's a difficult issue because it's not just a question of changing the law, *it's a question of attitudes.* I might say that so far in Congress I haven't felt the same interest in black issues as in women's issues. (Riding 1987:A3; *my emphasis*)

Indeed, in Brazil, Blacks are constantly reminded of "their place." They know that the requirement of "good appearance" in job advertisements is a euphemism for "Whites Only" (see Azevedo 1975: Chapter II). They know that they risk humiliation if they insist on taking the "social" elevator at a building, for it is common knowledge that service elevators are reserved for maids and Blacks; this custom shows that social class stratification alone does not explain racial discrimination.[6] They also know that, despite its racial mixture, the Brazilian elite is white-oriented; Blacks are noticeably absent, which leads an American observer to ask rhetorically, "If It's 'Black Brazil,' Why is the Elite So White?" (Brooke 1991:A4). In sum, "the supposed racial democracy is really an ideological fiction that both the class barriers and the old and not-yet-forgotten separation between slaves and free men, and between superior and inferior strata prevent from taking place" (Azevedo 1975:29; *my translation*). Unfortunately, as the following section shows, these barriers are still alive and well.

Imperilled Future: A Profile of Brazilian
Socioeconomic Conditions

The myth of racial democracy in Brazil dissolves when confronted
with comparisons of the quality of life between whites on the one
hand, and Blacks and mulattos on the other. In fact, as Hasenbalg
(1985) and Silva (1985) convincingly demonstrate in their analyses
of socioeconomic characteristics from 1976, it makes sense to group
Blacks and mulattos into one category when comparing them to
whites since, in many respects, their social positions are very similar. As of 1990, the median annual income for all employed Brazilians aged ten years and older was $24,956 cruzeiros, but racial
disparities were clear: whites earned more than $32,000 cruzeiros,
as opposed to little more than $13,000 and $15,000 cruzeiros for
Blacks and mulattos (IBGE 1992 Table 22.7: 264).[7] In addition,
"The darkest Brazilians hold the worst jobs, get the lowest pay
(even for the same jobs as light Brazilians), die youngest, . . . hold
very few elected posts, and have few high positions in business,
government, or the military" (Huggins and Mesquita 1996:13).

To be sure, the "country of the future" cares very little for the
future of its children. As of 1993, according to UNICEF, the quality
of life of its children puts Brazil in sixty-fifth place worldwide, behind all developed countries, as well as Costa Rica, Argentina, and
Mexico. Sixty-seven out of every thousand children under five
years of age die each year. In educational terms, the future is also
bleak: Among children in the first grade, only 22 percent finish
elementary school, as opposed to 70 percent for Mexico and 100
percent for Japan (Veja 1993b:20). And it is quite possible that so
few children remain in school because many are too weak to at-
tend: "of five Brazilian children, three are undernourished—and
the meager school lunch is distributed to only 30 percent of the
child population" (ISTOÉ 1992:26).

Brazil's discouraging educational profile is also characterized by
deep racial inequalities, as Blacks and mulattos are overrepresented among the illiterate. While nationwide the illiteracy rate of
persons seven years of age and older is 20 percent, it is 30 percent
for blacks as well as mulattos, but only 12 percent for whites
(IBGE 1992 Table 22.3: 262). Illiteracy is an even more dramatic
social problem when we consider that, among the 7–9 age group,

50 percent of Blacks and 54 percent of mulattos are illiterate, as compared to only 25 percent of whites (IBGE 1992:Table 30.6: 363). Further, significantly fewer nonwhite children between five and fourteen years of age are in school (IBGE 1992: Table 22.4, p.262). It is not surprising, then, that the average schooling for whites, while still dismal (5.7 years), is twice as much as that for Blacks and mulattos (IBGE 1992 Table 30.10: 373). Coupled with the fact that fully 57 percent of Black and mulatto children between the ages of ten and fourteen are economically active (as opposed to 43 percent of whites), it is clear that a whole generation of nonwhite Brazilians is socially neglected (IBGE 1992 Table 22.5: 263). In sum, the difference between mulattos and whites is a lot bigger than the difference between being mulatto and Black, which clearly indicates that Degler's (1971) thesis, that mulattos serve as an "escape hatch" to prevent racism in Brazil, is quite debatable.

Of course, we must see these alarming conditions in the context of the rampant poverty that characterizes Brazil. With one of the widest income gaps in the world, it is a real luxury to find legitimate work there—only one in three Brazilians is so lucky and, in a perennial economic recession, many lose their jobs (ISTOÉ 1992: 26). As a consequence, they join the growing ranks of those who have traditionally worked in the informal economy, thus increasing the competition for precarious jobs, since, "By most estimates, the informal sector employs sixty percent of all urban workers" (Huggins and Mesquita 1996:16). Moreover, the lack of economic resources forces the cooperation of the whole family, including children younger than ten years of age. Many of these live in the streets,[8] some with their own families. In fact, in Brazil's largest cities, it is common to see whole families who live under highways in makeshift cardboard dwellings and wash themselves and their laundry in public fountains. If it is true that a small number of children do resort to petty theft and drug delivery, which leads to general fear and resentment from merchants who see the youth as detrimental to their businesses (Veja 1993a:18), all street children are subjected to the public perception that they are juvenile delinquents, rather than carwashers, shoeshiners, and candy sellers.[9]

Because the life chances for Brazilian nonwhites are so limited, a disproportionate number of the street children are Black and mulatto. In a society where skin color is extremely significant for racial classification, and where darkness is associated with poverty, Blacks and mulattos are highly visible. Racial discrimination against Black men is also apparent in that they are much more likely to be searched by police officers in public places. It is thus no wonder that the majority of murdered youth are not white: "Ethnicity structures the probability of being among Brazil's poorest and of having to live on the streets, and influences who among poor youth is most likely to be murdered" (Huggins and Mesquita 1996: 13). The following section discusses recent street murders.

Death about Town

Huggins and Mesquita (1996:5) note that street murders in Brazilian cities have become so commonplace that they are actually underreported by the media. Indeed, while "Between 1988 and 1991 alone, more than seven thousand poor children and adolescents were murdered in Brazil," others were erroneously classified as the result of "traffic accidents," were not accounted for because the bodies have never been found, or were not reported by relatives for fear of retaliation. In other words, unfortunately, the murder of street youths, like other forms of violence, is not necessarily earth-shaking news.[10]

This probably explains why equally gruesome massacres get less attention than the infamous Candelária murders mentioned above. For example, on July 3, 1993, three black youngsters—fifteen, seventeen, and nineteen years of age—were lynched at the foot of the church of Nossa Senhora da Penha ("Our Lady of the Hill") by an angry crowd, who, upon seeing them running, suspected them of robbery, even though no weapons, witnesses, or victims were found.[11] After chasing the boys, the crowd stomped, kicked, stoned, and beat them before burning them alive. To add to the injury, the corpses were taken to the precarious city morgue where, like other corpses awaiting burial, they proceeded to rot (ISTOÉ 1993a:36).

Contrary to the police's initial assumption—that the murdered boys were indigent—all three lived with their working-class families; two were slum-dwellers, none had police records. The nineteen-year-old had been a factory worker since he was fourteen. According to his mother, the three friends, on their way to playing ball, took a bus without paying the fare. Suddenly, someone shouted "Pega ladrão!" ("get the thieves"), which led to the stampede. An officer of the nearby police precinct told reporters that he is "used to tragedies in which workers are accused of robbery" (see Pereira 1993:36).

How does the public react to such violent crimes? Sadly, many at best are indifferent; at worst, they favor them. While Penha inhabitants expressed horror at the massacre of the three boys, they also complained to reporters that no members of the media showed up when they themselves were robbery victims (see Pereira 1993:36). Similarly, when the state government broadcast a telephone number for any information leading to the solution of the Candelária massacre, twice as many people called to celebrate the murders, some adding that "it was not enough; they should have decapitated [the boys]" (VEJA 1993a:18). In fact, polls showed that the majority of the populations of Rio de Janeiro and São Paulo approved the Candelária murders. In Rio de Janeiro, sixty-five percent of those polled favored the institution of capital punishment to contain street crime. And while most authorities denounced the murders, ordinary citizens were relieved by the fact that robberies in downtown Rio had decreased by thirty percent after the massacre (Alves Filho and Tognozzi 1993:56–57).

However, many other Brazilians show a clearer understanding of the reasons behind both the street murders and the public reaction. According to 4557 Brazilians polled in fourteen states, the main causes of the Candelária murders are "government incompetence" (28 percent), followed by the "economic crisis" (17 percent), "police violence" (15 percent), "social indifference" (10 percent), and "impunity" (8 percent) (ISTOÉ 1993c:61). Each of these causes deserves examination.

On the issue of government incompetence, in December 1990, then-President Fernando Collor de Mello signed the "Estatuto da Criança e do Adolescente" (Statute of Children and Adolescents). A wordy document, it guarantees minors several basic rights, including "the preservation of their image, identity, autonomy, values, ideas, creeds, and personal space and objects" (Veja 1993b:22).[12] Unfortunately, like the Brazilian Constitution and laws in general, this document has had little practical effect, for it has done nothing to stop the systematic murder of poor youths.

As the following pages show, the incompetence of the Brazilian government does not stop in its failure to protect poor children; rather, it manifests itself in a variety of ways. One way, for instance, is the country's continuous economic crisis: Brazil is the country of failed economic plans. From the "Economic Miracle" in the early 1970s to the "Cruzado Plan" in the mid-1980s, high inflation is the perennial feature that defies the economy to work: since 1978, annual inflation has often reached over 1,000 percent (Pereira 1994:38), with a "dizzying" accumulated inflation rate of 146 billion percent (Huggins and Mesquita 1996:21). And in January 1994, annual inflation was expected to reach 5,570 percent (ISTOÉ 1994f).

Between 1980 and 1994, the government introduced roughly ten economic plans, all with limited or no success. At the end of each plan, although Brazil is an industrial power, the purchasing power of most of the population continued to decrease, real salaries all but disappeared, and the number of poor Brazilians increased.[13] One can grasp the extent to which high inflation rates and a disorganized economy affect citizens: shoppers are used to seeing prices increase twofold before their very eyes at the supermarket. These problems are compounded by high unemployment and underemployment. As a result, all but the tiny economic elite are threatened by poverty. Yet, in Brazil, being poor is a major social stigma; being dark-skinned, young, and poor transforms one "into 'symbolic assailants,' seen as potential criminals" (Huggins and Mesquita 1996:13). In this sense, murdered children and adolescents can be seen as scapegoats for the serious inequalities, high inflation, and loss of jobs, which are the responsibility of a failed government (Huggins 1993:37–38).

On the matter of police violence, scholars have noted that "the Brazilian state is as much involved by what it does not do to stop the murders, as by having some of its agents involved in those murders" (Huggins and Mesquita 1996:23). It is widely known that many of the perpetrators of violent crimes such as those at Candelária are police officers—civil and military, on and off duty (see Chevigny 1991; 1995). Some police officers, who on the whole are poorly remunerated, are attracted to merchants' offers to act as "rent-a-cops" or vigilantes, and rid their neighborhoods of those seemingly "feral children."

In at least two recent magazine articles, street adolescents pointed to police officers as directly responsible for their fates. In one case, E.R.S., a fifteen-year-old self-proclaimed thief and drug dealer from the city of São Paulo, told a reporter that he expects to be murdered by the military police for several reasons: on one occasion when he has was arrested for robbery, he was tortured by the police, who fear being recognized by him; he has also stolen the gun of a police officer; for half of his life, E.R.S. lived on the streets, and had to pay off police officers in order to stay free. At the time of the article, however, afraid for his life, he was living at an institution for youth welfare (Prado 1993:62–63).

The other reported case ended even worse. Less than a year before the Candelária murders, one of the victims predicted his own death. Thirteen-year-old Anderson Oliveira Pereira, called "Caolho" (cross-eyed) on the streets, had been living on the streets of downtown Rio de Janeiro for four years. He left his home, where his parents and siblings still live, to be free from their lack of food. On the streets, he made a living working for drug dealers and at petty theft, but any money earned was spent on cocaine and sniffing glue. Like E.R.S., Caolho pointed out police corruption:

> I've tried to sell candy or shine shoes, but when the policemen searched me, they would take my money, saying it was stolen. If I was wearing a good pair of sneakers, bought with my work money, the policemen would take them too. So, what should I work for? Now, if they think I stole my money, they'll be right. . . . There are lots of military policemen who order us to rob and then take our money. It's not possible to be honest. I think I'll never go back home, never go to school or learn a profession. I know I'll never leave the streets again. (Alves Filho 1993:63; *my translation*)

Unfortunately, Caolho's predictions were realized but too soon. On July 23, 1993, he was among the seven youth summarily executed at Candelária. He only left the streets to be buried.

The fact that murders by police officers are unlikely to be investigated, let alone prosecuted, adds to official participation in them. In the aftermath, the suspicion of police involvement was all the more apparent in that some survivors refused to bear witness, for fear of being murdered themselves. A year after the massacre, four accused murderers—among whom there are two military police officers—have been indicted, but survivors believe that other participants continue to walk about the crime scene (*O Globo* 1994:15).

On the issue of social indifference, "The problem is that the Brazilian elites don't see the poor. It's a problem of negation of other people." Thus concludes Herbert de Souza, a Brazilian sociologist who crusades against hunger (Brooke 1993a:E7). His campaign has sparked interest among the general population, including homemakers, students, entrepreneurs, members of the clergy, artists, and workers, who contribute their time, money, and food in thirty-five hundred committees, to try to nourish more than nine million starving families (Penha 1993). Despite these efforts, the extent of the social indifference to malnutrition is visible in the 35,000 tons of grains that proceeded to rot in governmental warehouses in 1993 (Penha 1993:39), and in the national scandal in which six politicians misappropriated 1.7 billion kilos of food between 1987 and 1992, ". . . enough to feed 40 million Brazilians for a year" (Costa 1994:29).

In the aftermath of the Candelária murders, survivors called on Yvonne Bezerra de Mello, a well-to-do artist who has devoted six years to helping street children in Rio de Janeiro. Both in her studio and on the streets, she feeds them, teaches them how to read and write, "reads to them newspaper articles on violence and racial prejudice, and discusses notions of citizenship" (Veja 1993a:19). Like Herbert de Souza, Mello cites "the omission of the elites" (including the government) as partly responsible for the status quo of a large proportion of Brazilian youth. But she adds that "If everyone took care of the abandoned youths by their doors, the situation . . . would be quite different" (Veja 1993a:17; 19).

As for impunity, Roberto da Matta, a Brazilian anthropologist, has said, "Impunity in Brazil is part of a culture that doesn't have a tradition of allocating responsibility" (see Brooke 1993b:E6). If, on the one hand, Brazilians like to joke that "God is one of us," on the other they always remember the words of the late French President Charles de Gaulle upon visiting their nation, "This is not a serious country." One need only consider that, in Brazil, laws are often poorly and subjectively applied, heavily favoring those with important social connections: college graduates have prison privileges, and efficient attorneys virtually guarantee an acquittal to anyone who can pay for it, whereas "Of Brazilians who end up in jail, 98 percent cannot afford a lawyer, according to a Justice Ministry survey" (Brooke 1993b:E6).

In recent times, several incidents of extreme violence that verge on impunity have occurred in Brazil. In August 1993, gold miners in the northern state of Roraima slaughtered at least two dozen Yanomami Indians—mostly infants and women—while in the same month, a gang of thirty vigilante military police officers invaded a slum in Rio de Janeiro and, claiming to be searching for drug dealers, executed twenty workers and one student in about an hour (ISTOÉ 1993e:70–74; Veja 1993c:18–20). In both cases, as in the Candelária case, the victims were either economically or racially disadvantaged. Also as in the murder of street children, in both cases prosecution is made more difficult by witnesses' reluctance to speak up against the perpetrators, for fear of meeting a similar fate (O Globo 1994:15).[14]

Clearly, all factors cited contribute to the proliferation of violent crimes and public response to them. It is also clear that the Brazilian government ultimately figures in each one of these factors: by failing to put an end to the long-term economic crisis, by not providing more effective social services, and by maintaining a climate of impunity, either by directly participating in the murders as police officers, or by ignoring them. Thus, while I agree that "the murders continue because the Brazilian state does little to prevent them or punish the perpetrators" (Huggins and Mesquita 1996:23), I also believe that the interaction of all these causes leads to the pervasiveness of the situation. Disadvantaged Brazilians would not be routinely exterminated if society as a whole did not go along with it. Without much trust in the authorities, and fearful for their lives, citizens at best become desensitized at the sight of yet another street child; at worst, they take the law into their own hands. For if Brazilians are divided as to the causes of the murder of street youth, two-thirds of those polled agree that criminals under eighteen years of age should be tried as adults (ISTOÉ 1993c:61).

But treating children and adolescents as adults in no way solves the problems that millions face today: malnutrition, lack of education, and life on the streets. It is time that society paid attention to the impassioned editorial in a popular Brazilian magazine, which, upon reflecting on the link between the street murders, the killing of Yanomami, and the execution of prison inmates in São Paulo, warned, "Our civil war progresses silently" (ISTOÉ 1993d:15).

Conclusion

The murders of street youth in Brazil must be seen as a result of the complex relation between extreme economic inequality, racism, and impunity. Economic inequality leads a large proportion of the population to absolute poverty and very few opportunities for gainful employment. Racism attaches itself to poverty to make a large category of Brazilians even more vulnerable. Finally, the failure of the legal system to punish criminals allows the murder of less-privileged citizens to be practiced with complete impunity. Two years after the Candelária murders, no one had been convicted.[15]

No child wants to sleep on the streets and steal for a living if he or she has better alternatives. It is thus an international shame that Brazil, the eighth-largest economy in the world, allots so little to its children. Palliative measures such as the "Statute of the Child and the Adolescence" are not enough; particularly in this case, actions speak louder than words.

An obvious first step is a more equitable distribution of resources, since in Brazil "[t]he richest ten percent holds more than half the national wealth, while the poorest fifty percent divide up barely fifteen percent" (Huggins and Mesquita 1996:12). The majority of murdered youngsters represent a large proportion of the country's unemployed and underemployed, who become more vulnerable to the perils of the streets when they supplement their families' income by joining the informal urban economy. It follows that more jobs with real purchasing power must be created for adults, not children. However, whether this will be achieved in the near future, given the long history of economic mismanagement and disregard for the lower strata is anybody's guess.

In a modern economy, access to formal education is a child's right. Unfortunately, so far Brazil has failed to extend that right to a large proportion of its population. It is imperative, thus, that more initiatives such as the Curumim Project, in Minas Gerais state, be sponsored. That program, which has so far served more than five thousand children, encourages poor children to stay in school by rewarding those who stay with support for the practice of sports (Veja 1993b:22). It would also help if all school children were healthy (ISTOÉ 1992:26).

Finally, given that "the vast majority of youth murdered by strangers are dark-skinned" (Huggins and Mesquita 1996:10), Brazil needs to tackle, once and for all, the fallacy of its ideology of racial democracy and acknowledge the dire social situation of its people of color. Therefore, one way to diminish the likelihood of youth murders is to strive at erasing the stigmas of being poor and Black in Brazil, and to debunk the perverse idea that that combination necessarily leads to antisocial behavior. Poor Brazilians in general, and nonwhite Brazilians in particular, need to achieve better representation in the polity. Brazil must lift the barriers between superordinate and subordinate, or many more Candelária incidents are bound to occur.

─────────────── NOTES ───────────────

1. The author is indebted to Diva Penha Lopes for data collection, Dilma Penha Lopes for computer assistance, and Martha K. Huggins for intellectual support.

2. Given that the burning was ordered by Ruy Barbosa, the Minister of Justice, yet another explanation is possible: a mulatto himself (like many of his fellow abolitionists), Barbosa may have wanted to erase his slave past. This idea is even more plausible when we consider that at least one abolitionist—Joaquim Nabuco, who would later become ambassador to the United States—clearly believed that an end to slavery would contribute to a "whiter Brazil" (Skidmore 1993:21).

3. The fact that the elite had such a plan was evidenced by its persistent objection to Chinese immigration, for the Chinese would not "raise the moral level of this country." As Nabuco put it one occasion, "the Negro improves itself, but the Chinaman is impossible" (in Skidmore 1993:26).

4. Even in 1980, of the 21 percent intermarried couples, "16.1 percent were between whites and browns, 3.2 percent between browns and blacks, and 1.4 percent between whites and blacks" (Telles 1992:187).

5. Before Freyre, other Brazilian intellectuals had refuted the theories of racial degeneracy (Skidmore 1993:188). But Freyre's work is unique in that it gives a positive interpretation to the origin of Brazilian culture, and it acknowledges the contribution of races other than whites. On the other hand, by labelling it a "racial democracy," it ignores the attempted eradication of Black as a racial identity, since it appears that not many want to be Black (Nascimento 1989).

6. Telles (1992:194) reached a similar conclusion about residential segregation by color in Brazil: it is not a result of socioeconomic status, because "moderate residential segregation along color lines occurs among members of the same income group." Further, residential segregation is higher among middle-class whites and Blacks than among the poor.

7. In September 1990, the minimum wage that served as basis for these calculations was Cr$6,056.31 (IBGE, personal communication).

8. According to the Municipal Office of Social Development in Rio de Janeiro, there are about three thousand street children in that city, and nearly one million nationwide (Veja 28 July 1993:20).

9. "It would . . . be naïve to overlook the fact that for some kids, the 'school of the streets' has socialized them into a delinquent and predatory lifestyle that puts them and others at great risk" (Lusk and Mason 1994: 171–172).

10. Extreme violence against the young is but the fastest-growing form of overall violence in Brazil: "In most Brazilian cities youth murders have increased much more than adult homicides. According to Rio's Oswaldo Cruz Foundation, between 1985 and 1992 the number of children and adolescents murdered in Brazil grew one hundred and sixty-one percent, while adult murders increased by only seventy-six percent" (Huggins and Mesquita 1996:6).

11. In the purportedly largest Catholic country in the world, it is ironic that incidents of such raw violence would take place right at two of the most famous Rio churches.

12. Partly due to this document, Brazil has been hailed as the country with "one of the most progressive bodies of legislation in defense of children's and adolescents' rights . . ." (Rizzini 1994:15).

13. "The contingent of the poor in 1960 was 41.4 percent of the Brazilian population; in 1988 it reached 39.2 percent, after having shrunk to 24.4 percent in 1980." "[I]n 1990, out of ten Brazilians, 4.4 were poor and 2.3 were indigent" (ISTOÉ 23 December 1992:26)

14. Even when the opposite is true, it is not uncommon for witnesses to be ignored. A year after the Candelária massacre, the mother of thirteen-year-old Caolho (one of the victims) complained to a reporter that no police investigator had contacted her for information that could help solve the

166   *LATIN AMERICA*

crime, even though her son had visited the family only four days before the murders. The woman, who still hopes to see those who killed her son brought to justice, said that she is now "angry and fearful of the police" (Motta 1994:16).

15. In July 1994, the district attorney investigating the case reported the probability of the trial of the four alleged murderers to take place in 1995 or 1996, in case they appeal the judge's latest decision. While then it was said that four or five other persons might be indicted (*O Globo* 17 July 1994:15), in May 1996 only one ex-police officer was convicted of the crimes. A primary offender, Marcus Vinícius Borges Emanuel is likely to serve less than twenty years in jail (Schemo 1996:A5).

──────────────── REFERENCES ────────────────

Alves, Filho Francisco. 1993. "Morte Consumada" (Consummated Death). *ISTOÉ* (August 4):63.
Alves, Filho and Marcelo Tognozzi. 1993. "A Platéia Não se Move" (The Audience Doesn't Budge). *ISTOÉ* (August 4):56–57.
Azevedo, Thales. 1975. *Democracia Racial: Ideologia e Realidade*. Petrópolis: Editora Vozes.
Brooke, James. 1991. "If it's 'Black Brazil,' Why is the Elite so White?" *New York Times* (September 24):A4.
Brooke, James. 1993a. "A Hard Look at Brazil's Surfeits: Food, Hunger and Inequality." *New York Times* (June 6):E7.
Brooke, James. 1993b. "Brazilian Justice and the Culture of Impunity." *New York Times* (August 29):E6.
Chevigny, Paul. 1991. *Police Deadly Force as Social Control: Jamaica, Brazil, and Argentina*. São Paulo: Universidade de São Paulo, Núcleo de Estudos da Violência.
———. 1995. *The Edge of the Knife: Police Violence and Accountability in Six Cities of the Americas*. New York: New Press.
Costa, Raymundo. 1994. "Desperdício Oficial" (Official Wastefulness). *ISTOÉ* (January 12):29.
Cox, Oliver C. 1948. *Caste, Class, and Race: A Study in Social Dynamics*. Garden City: Doubleday.
Degler, Carl. N. 1971. *Neither Black nor White: Slavery and Race Relations in Brazil and the United States*. New York: The Macmillan Company.
DuBois, W.E.B. 1992 [1914]. "Brazil." In David J. Hellwig (ed.), *African American Reflections on Brazil's Racial Paradise*, pp. 31–34. Philadelphia: Temple University Press.

Fernandes, Florestan. 1971. *The Negro in Brazilian Society*. New York: Atheneum.

Fontaine, Pierre-Michel. 1985. "Introduction." In Pierre-Michel Fontaine (ed.), *Race, Class, Power in Brazil*, pp. 1–10. Los Angeles: UCLA Center for Afro-American Studies.

Frazier, E. Franklin. 1992 [1942]. "Brazil Has No Race Problem." In Hellwig, *op.cit.*, pp. 121–130.

Freyre, Gilberto. 1946. *The Masters and the Slaves: A Study in the Development of Brazilian Civilization*. New York: Knopf.

Harris, Marvin. 1964. *Patterns of Race in the Americas*. New York: Walker and Company.

Hasenbalg, Carlos A. 1985. "Race and Socioeconomic Inequalities in Brazil." In Fontaine, *op.cit.*, pp. 25–41.

Huggins, Martha K. 1993. "Lost Childhoods: Assassinations of Youth in Democratizing Brazil." Paper presented at the 88th Annual Meeting of the American Sociological Association, Miami Beach.

Huggins, Martha K. and Myriam Mesquita P. de Castro. 1996. "Exclusion, Civic Invisibility and Impunity as Explanations for Youth Murders in Brazil." *Childhood: A Global Journal of Child Research* 3, 1 (February):77–98.

Instituto Brasileiro de Geografia e Estatística (IBGE). 1992."Seção 2: Características Demográficas e Socioeconômicas da População." *Anuário Estatístico do Brasil*. Rio de Janeiro: Fundação Instituto Brasileiro de Geografia e Estatística.

ISTOÉ. 1992. "65 Milhões de Pobres" (65 Million Poor). (December 23):26.

ISTOÉ. 1993a. "À Queima-Roupa: Pistoleiros Alucinados Fuzilam Sete Meninos de Rua" (At Close Range: Hallucinated Gunmen Shoot Seven Street Boys). (July 28):16–17.

ISTOÉ. 1993b. "Fuga do Pesadelo" (Flight from the Nightmare). (August 4):58–59.

ISTOÉ. 1993c. "Omissão de Mão Dupla" (Double Omission). (August 4): 61.

ISTOÉ. 1993d. "Massacres Cotidianos" (Daily Massacres). (August 25):15.

ISTOÉ. 1993e. "Selvageria de Brancos" (Whites' Savagery). (August 25): 70–74, 79.

ISTOÉ. 1994f. "5.570%: Quem Agüenta?" (5,570 Percent: Who Can Stand it?). (January 12): cover page.

Lusk, Mark W. and Derek T. Mason. 1994. "Fieldwork with Rio's Street Children." In *Children in Brazil Today: A Challenge for the Third Millennium*, pp. 151–176. Rio de Janeiro: Editora Univeritária Santa Úrsula.

Motta, Aydano André. 1994. "Esperança na Punição dos Criminosos Continua Viva" (Hope in the Criminals' Punishment Is Still Alive). *O Globo* (July 17):16.

Nascimento, A. do. 1989. *Brazil: Mixture or Massacre? Esssays in the Genocide of a Black People.* Second Edition. Translation by Elisa Larkin Nascimento. Dover, Mass.: The Majority Press.

O Globo. 1994. "Muitos Mistérios, Poucas Testemunhas" (Much Mistery, Few Witnesses). (July 17):15.

Penha, Gerson. 1993. "A Campanha Feijão e Arroz" (The Rice and Beans Campaign). *ISTOÉ.* (December 22):34–38.

Penha-Lopes, Vânia. 1996. "What Next? On Race and Assimilation in the United States and Brazil." *Journal of Black Studies* 26, 6 (July): 807–824.

Pereira, Raimundo Rodrigues. 1993. "Caldeirão de Ódio" (Caldron of Hate). *ISTOÉ.* (July 14):34–38.

Pereira, Raimundo Rodrigues. 1994. "Na Caixa Preta" (In the Black Box). (June 6):36–41.

Prado, Antonio Carlos. 1993. "Morte Anunciada" (Announced Death). *ISTOÉ.* (August 4):62–63.

Riding, Alan. 1987. "One Woman's Mission: To Make Brasília Sensitive." *New York Times.* (February 19):A3.

Rizzini, Irene. 1994. "Preface to the English Edition." In Rizzini, I.(ed.), *Children in Brazil Today.* Rio de Janeiro: Editora Universitária Santa Úrsula.

Schemo, Diana Jean. 1996. "Rio Ex-Officer is Convicted in Massacre of Children." *New York Times.* (May 1):A5.

Silva, Nelson do Valle. 1985. "Updating the Cost of not Being Black in Brazil." In Fontaine, *op.cit.*, pp. 42–55.

Skidmore, Thomas E. 1993 [1974]. *Black into White: Race and Nationality in Brazilian Thought.* Durham,N.C.: Duke University Press.

Telles, Edward E. 1992. "Residential Segregation by Skin Color in Brazil." *American Sociological Review* 57 (April):186–197.

Veja. 1993a. "A Chacina das Crianças da Candelária" (The Slaughter of the Children of Candelária). (July 28).

Veja. 1993b. "A Morte como Rotina" (Death as a Routine). (July 28).

Veja. 1993c. "O Rosto da Barbárie" (The Face of Barbarity). (September 8).

Part Three

THE CARIBBEAN

Charles Green

8

Urbanism, Transnationalism, and the Caribbean

The Case of Trinidad and Tobago

Throughout the Caribbean[1] as elsewhere in the developing world, population migration from the rural countryside to the towns and cities persists (Gilbert and Gugler 1993; Portes *et al.* 1994). Whether we turn to Kingston, Jamaica, Port of Spain, Trinidad, Bridgetown, Barbados, or even smaller cities like Roseau, Dominica, Kingstown, St. Vincent, and St. Georges, Grenada, the urban poor are a common sight.[2] Behind the congestion and the pavements lined with vendors and street hawkers are a set of related conditions. These conditions are manifested in the forms of rising unemployment and underemployment, inadequate housing, declining family structure, the erosion of traditional values, youth-related problems of crime and violence, and the rise of a drug subculture. Providing a backdrop for the present urban crisis are the Caribbean states' traditionally insecure economies and their increasing marginalization in a troubled global economy.

Scholars and students of development are coming to realize that an accurate analysis of the present crisis cannot be limited to the closeup examination of either the political economies of single states or for that matter the bilateral and multilateral relations between Caribbean states. The present world theatre is increasingly one in which disparate nations are more interconnected than ever before. Gilbert and Gugler's discussion of urban development

171

in a world system has relevance here. They argue that the size, role, and characteristics of individual cities reflect the world roles of the societies of which they form part (1993:15). That would suggest that the properties of a single city cannot be understood solely in terms of its local or even its national functions. Consequently, it demands that the search for causes, effects, and solutions to mounting urban problems in the small island states of the Caribbean take into account global economic and political effects.

But globalization has ensured the increased penetration of ideas, beliefs, and trends from abroad and that has contributed to the dislocation of culture and values indigenous to the people of the region (Mander 1996; Norberg-Hodge 1996). This effect is relevant to any serious discussion and analysis of the present crisis. Commenting on the consequences of the new global economy, political critic Noam Chomsky foresees a strengthening of the international state that will ultimately lead to an international executive. The international state or "de facto world government" will have its own institutions like the IMF, The World Bank, and trading structures like GATT, and will be the property of the G-7[3] and their transnational corporations and banks. For Chomsky, a "democratic deficit" is created by the populations and nations with less influence who stand outside this orbit of decision making (Chomsky 1995:7).

In view of these developments, I will argue in this chapter that the political economy approach, which is widely accepted by progressive scholars and centers the analysis on historical processes of underdevelopment, measures of class mobility, class stagnation, production levels, and so on, is vital but no longer sufficient. A comprehensive understanding of the urban situation in the Caribbean is needed, which will result in the appropriate policy solutions. This can be optimally achieved through an integrative approach that links the political economy model and an incipient model that scholars have come to refer to as "transnationalism." Such an approach, I argue, will further the analysis by exploring the specific sociocultural effects precipitated by the geopolitical and economic forces. Furthermore, it will show that because these social and cultural effects have come to be interpreted as short-term relief measures, as in the case of emigration, or conduits to the superhighway of modernization and development, as in the case of the new consumer products and technology, their dysfunctional effects for the society as a whole tend to be overlooked and accommodated.

In the discussion that follows, the perspective of transnationalism is presented. To demonstrate its function in an integrated analytical approach, an abbreviated examination of the case of Trinidad and Tobago, the site of recent urban and societal-wide dislocation is presented. Finally, state and regional based policy alternatives are considered.

Transnationalism in Perspective

The term transnational or transnationalism is commonly associated with corporations and conglomerates (TNCs, MNCs) whose investments and subsidiaries form an international operating network (See Sassen:1991). The current application of transnationalism to entire societies and specifically to describe behavioral patterns of members of societies is fairly recent. Leading scholars point out that to fully understand transnationalism in the context of the Caribbean, or elsewhere for that matter, it is necessary to situate it within the long-term process of global capitalist penetration (Basch, *et al.* 1994:12). That process has instigated the development of an international division of labor and corporations that developed world-wide systems of production, distribution, and marketing, which have affected the flow of immigrants and their personal outlooks. In this sense, transnationalism can be linked to a world-system theory such as that articulated by Immanuel Wallerstein (1974), Andre Gunnar Frank (1969), and others, in which applications to core regions, to refer to developed economic systems, and peripheral, to refer to subordinate or developing economic systems, are made. A basic tenet behind world-system theory is that the hegemony of the developed economies rests with their ability to manipulate the least-developed economies and keep them dependent on the developed societies. Dependency on, the part of peripheral societies is achieved through various strategies, including aid and loan packages, investment and divestment, control of commodity prices and markets, and the creation of low wage labor.

Transnationalism is also envisaged as a process whereby trans-migrants[4] forge and sustain multi-stranded social relations that connect their societies of origin with the societies of settlement. Consequently, they build social fields that enable them to maintain multiple relationships—familial, economic, social, organizational, religious, and political—that span borders (Basch *et al.* 1994:7). Thus, transnationalism is viewed as both a response and an accommodation to the controlling global capitalist forces.

It is important to note that other scholars have otherwise described this same phenomenon. In their study of Barbados, Sutton and Maiesky (1975) introduced the term "bi-directionalism" to describe the flow of political ideas and racial consciousness between those at home and those abroad. Portes and Rumbault (1990:57) point to the importance of social networks between villagers in places like Mexico and the Dominican Republic and their respective ethnic communities abroad. Because of these linkages, these villagers are able to remain well informed about the current labor market situation and day-to-day life conditions in cities such as Chicago and the boroughs of Queens and the Bronx in New York City.

It has also been observed that rapid transformations in communications technology and international travel, an aspect that will be addressed elsewhere in this chapter, have operated to such a degree in linking the social experiences and activities of people across regions that they appear to constitute a single field of social relations (Basch *et al.* 1994:5). This observation, which is a constant theme for this chapter, is discussed in the sociological literature in terms of cultural diffusion and homogenization or the internationalization of culture.

In their comparison of urban societies across several continents, Gilbert and Gugler (1993: 29–32) note that people are beginning to resemble one another not solely in styles of dress but in patterns of food consumption and other behaviors. Commonly observed names of hotels (e.g., Holiday Inn, Grand Hyatt, and Hilton), accounting firms, banks, and food chains (e.g., McDonald's, Pizza Hut, and Kentucky Fried Chicken) offer convincing evidence. But Gilbert and Gugler are joined by others, including Featherstone (1990:1–14), Smith (1990:171–190), and Norberg-Hodge (1996:20–23) in cautioning proponents of the cultural homogenization thesis to rec-

ognize that in spite of these glaring similarities, important differences exist among societies that have much to do with their position
in the world economy and overall cultural orientation.

While the benefits of the global economy are extolled, the Caribbean states remain outside the playing field as their economies are
tenuous and subordinate to the interests of the metropolitan systems that control the region more than three decades after the
movement for independence began. In the cases of St. Vincent and
Grenada for example, their economic problems have been exacerbated not solely by geography, poor infrastructure, and inefficient
production techniques, but by the absence of reinvestment profits
due to their repatriation to metropolitan capitals (Basch *et al.*
1994:58). It is no wonder that an unprecedented number of Caribbean people today perceive outward migration, whether personally
or by a family member, as the primary means for improving their
material status and future. They eagerly join the ranks of transmigrants with the metropoles of the United States and Canada
and, to a lesser degree, Europe as the chief targets for their migration.[5] In the 1980s, at the height of Trinidad and Tobago's economic
crisis, long lines of visa seekers encircled the U.S. Embassy in Port
of Spain each day. For them, the commitment to home and nationalism could not guarantee food on the table or the prospects for a
good life. Flight became synonymous with hope. The fact of economic hemorrhage that is taking place in major cities across the
United States and other core regions due to deindustrialization
and the outposting of manufacturing jobs in peripheral regions
where labor is cheaper has had little effect on curbing the quest by
new immigrants to enter, in sociologist Nathan Glazer's phrase,
"the clamor[ing] at the gate."[6]

Social and Cultural Consequences of Transnationalism

A recurrent theme for West Indians at home and abroad is the
decline of West Indian civil society as it was once known, with
many pointing to the mid-to late 1970s as a watershed. The bottom
is said to have fallen out by the mid-1980s, with a discernable shift
in familial structure and values, the rise of serious crime, violence,

and youth related problems. This coincided with the period of acute global recession that shook the developing world (Henry and Melville 1989; The South Commission 1990; Portes *et al.* 1994). Following the recession, the demand for such Caribbean exports as bauxite, petroleum products, sugar, as well as tourism, was severely reduced. In some Caribbean countries where growth in the 1970s had already been sluggish, as in the case of Guyana, or negative, as in the case of Jamaica, the crisis of the 1980s wiped out the gains of the decade of the 1960s in terms of average per capita income (Deere *et al.* 1990:18–19). It was also a period that witnessed the introduction of new age technology, albeit not at a pace equal to that taking place in the more advanced countries, but still significant relative to the extent of technological development in the small island states at that time. It should also be pointed out that the pace with which new age technology was introduced was uneven throughout the region. For a country like Trinidad and Tobago, with a fairly well developed petroleum and petrochemical industry, the cadence has been more rapid than in other countries such as Grenada or Dominica, where the economy is based upon the export of small crops like bananas, or upon tourism. While the introduction of computers and new farm technology has occurred at varying degrees in the Caribbean, it is certain that this has altered the nature of work and the daily lives of people in the island societies.

Of all technology, that which has had the most profound cultural impact upon the people of the Caribbean has been in the area of communications. Not to be overlooked is the introduction of VCRs, the satellite dish, and subscription cable television—material symbols of modernization—which have served to sharpen appetites for the consumption of other imported goods. In Trinidad and Tobago and Barbados, for example, cable channels number well over twenty and foreign programming dominates these as well as the local television channels. The extent of this becomes clear when one browses the weekly television and cable listings of most Caribbean countries. Except for minor scheduling differences, one is challenged to distinguish between these listings and their U.S. and Canadian counterparts.

The role of transmigrants as reinforcers is prominent in this process. With each sojourn they pollinate those at home with the latest trends and other aspects of mass culture from abroad. For certain, a dependency has developed around their monetary remittances, but of equal importance are the sturdy cardboard barrels they send that contain many of the items that bombard locals across the media air waves. For most transmigrants, however, the social implications of their gifts are uncalculated. The barrels provide evidence of transmigrants' devotion to their families by ensuring that they are equipped with certain essentials that are unavailable to them. But they also serve as conspicuous reminders of their own success and industriousness abroad (Toney 1992; Bonnett 1990, 1992; Larmer 1996:45–48).

The following account by a St. Kitts national underscores the role of transmigrants and the new technology in the present crisis. He describes an incident that occurred in downtown St. Kitts the day after the Chicago Bulls' third consecutive National Basketball Association title in 1993:

> Dressed in Chicago Bulls regalia (that is to say, caps, jerseys, and expensive Air Jordan Nike sneakers) scores of youth jammed the streets in a carnival like atmosphere bringing traffic to a halt as they celebrated their team's victory. (Interview 1993)

These youths had watched the victory game live via cable television the previous evening. Procuring the Bulls paraphernalia did not present a problem for them, since many were the offspring of transmigrants residing abroad in the United States and Canada, who regularly send home barrels filled with requested items. It was interesting to learn that such a parade by youths in St. Kitts/ Nevis was unprecedented (*Ibid.*). Evidently, these youths have not felt the same urge to honor West Indian cricketers or other local sports heroes. While innocuous on the surface, this incident raises concern about the implications of a global culture or cultural homogenization for the region as a whole and the youth in particular, who are the next generation.

Thus far, the discussion has centered on defining and operationalizing the perspective of transnationalism. At this juncture, it would be helpful to return to the question of analysis and to demonstrate how an approach that integrates the perspectives of political economy and transnationalism might be directly applied in examining the urban challenge in the contemporary Caribbean. For this next section of the chapter, the case of Trinidad and Tobago will be highlighted.

The City of Port of Spain: An Overview

Extremely south at the tip of Venezuela lies the small two-island nation of Trinidad and Tobago, with a population of just over 1.2 million people. In 1956, self-government status was granted by Britain. In 1962, independence from Britain was achieved and under the leadership of Dr. Eric Williams and the People's National Movement (PNM), Trinidad and Tobago voyaged to find its place among the sovereign nations of the world. Despite its stature within the region as a producer of petroleum with other natural resources in its soil, outside the region Trinidad and Tobago is relatively obscure because its economy is not tourist driven as in the case of the larger island of Jamaica or the smaller island of Barbados.

Dr. Eric Williams was a leader in the full sense of the term. As one of the island's brightest minds and a trained economist, his scholarly works, *Capitalism and Slavery* and *From Columbus to Castro* won him international acclaim. Williams the progressive and anti-colonialist nationalist held the vision of a new and strong Trinidad and Tobago that was also the vision he aspired for the region as a whole. Under his leadership, a clear sense of pride and commitment to nationhood emerged from the citizenry of Trinidad and Tobago, and so the young nation grew. But in time, all things do change. Young men with great vision and ideas grow old. Old sentiments and ideas eventually succumb to new ones and it becomes increasingly difficult to sustain a common ideology. Although the discussion that follows falls short of a comprehensive analysis of the PNM and the events that led to its decline in the 1986 elections, we can safely assert that the party of independence that had galvanized the country for more than twenty-five years was not the same. In his final years as leader, Eric Williams had become a weary soldier. The charismatic nationalist had apparently lost his appeal and grip and with that, the party and the internal affairs of the country began to wane. Following Williams's death on March 29, 1981, George Chambers took over as Prime Minister and PNM leader. Allegations of corruption and graft that had engulfed the government failed to disappear. In the midst of this an international recession was brewing.

These facts and events become critical as we unravel the circumstances leading up to the current urban crisis in the country. Moreover, they help to clarify for us the nature of youth rebelliousness and resistance and their growing disregard for authority and the state.

The economic crisis that confronts the nation has affected both the pace of urbanization and the quality of life. Port of Spain, located on the larger island, Trinidad, is the capital city and the hub of much of the observed social unrest.[7] Port of Spain is made up of some older middle- and working-class families who have opted to remain in their well-preserved Victorian-style houses rather than head for the suburbs. Much more visible are the working class and poor residents. The city's main districts of Gonzales, Belmont, Woodbrook, Newtown, St. James, Laventille, and Morvant are tightly populated and there is virtually little available space for residential expansion. From the early 1980s to the present, Port of Spain's population has declined from approximately 52,000 to 42,021 (CSO Bulletin). Some residents migrated out of Port of Spain due to fear of rising street crime and the declining city infrastructure. Still, there were those who chose the route of emigration. A number of poor and working-class persons living in deteriorating housing were relocated to government and private subsidized housing that offered multi-family rental units and small single-family houses at modest monthly mortgages. Several of these housing developments emerged, including Trin City and Maloney on the eastern fringes and the Couva area in central Trinidad. Besides the overflow from Port of Spain, demand for this housing was also registered by persons migrating from the countryside for the purpose of establishing closer proximity to the city. Because the desire to "own house" on a small lot of land is a long-standing aspiration for most people of Trinidad and Tobago, their willingness to take advantage of the opportunity to buy government and private subsidized housing (which for the majority of poor and working-class families was their very first house) was strong.

While no official blueprint for urban renewal and removal has passed through the Ministry of Planning and Development, that has not dispelled the rumors and theories that circulate regarding the country's business elite's interest in commercial expansion in the downtown district and their ability to influence politicians to free up prime space currently occupied by the urban poor. An article that appeared in *The Daily Express* in 1994 entitled "The City's Changing Face" discussed proposals by the City Corporation and the major banks like the Bank of Nova Scotia, Bank of Commerce, and other business concerns, to beautify the city and eventually create a landscaped city center. Officials hoped that through the use of "gentle persuasion" they would be able to encourage an estimated two hundred street vendors, who occupied the most expensive piece of downtown city property, located at the corner of Queen and Frederick Streets, to relocate to a new four-story shopping mall (Marajh 1994:19).The business community and city officials are quick to point out that relocation is in the vendors' best interest and will benefit the city and the nation.

Those areas from which the Maloney development residents were absorbed—the vicinity of George Street and Nelson Street in Port of Spain proper and the nearby East Dry River vicinity—were decaying, high-density areas that were crime-ridden, with many social problems. These residents needed a stimulus to move out, which is where the government stepped in. In fact, the government is proud of its track record in addressing the housing needs of the urban poor. Frequently cited is the plan that emerged shortly after independence to resettle the squatters along the Beetham Highway—a major conduit to Port of Spain.

The debate over a benevolent government versus an intrusive government continues. What is certain is that, government subsidies notwithstanding, the residents of these housing developments are obligated to pay rents, or mortgages as the case may be. What that suggests, in the light of persistent unemployment and the lingering effects of structural adjustment, is that residents must find some means to make ends meet and keep their dwellings. Thus, many of these residents return to Port of Spain each day via private motor car, bus, and maxi-taxi to report not only to government and private sector jobs but frequently to livelihoods in the rapidly growing informal business sector.

Origins of the Urban Crisis

Between 1974 and 1981, Trinidad and Tobago's petroleum-driven economy was booming and generated a foreign exchange surplus of more than TT $75 billion (Abdulah 1988; Henry and Melville 1989). This bonanza, of course, followed the OPEC action of the 1970s. The windfall created by the petrodollars enabled the PNM government to engage in redistributive transfers, to ameliorate certain pressing domestic needs, that had been previously impossible. Chief among them were grants for school uniforms and books, and free bus passes for school children. Unemployment, for example, which had hovered at over fourteen percent since the mid-1960s plummeted to ten percent or less by the early 1980s due to government-developed makework programs (Henry and Melville 1989). During the boom period personal outlooks and expectations continued to rise. Some workers were allocated long-awaited back pay, and generally there was a good feeling all around. With a little additional money in their pockets some workers were able to enjoy certain material "extras" not readily available to them before. Many people today gleefully recall the "boom days" when the beverage taste buds of Trinidadians and Tobagonians called for imported scotches, wines, and champagne rather than local rum. As well, they recall the rising demand for color television sets, satellite dishes, and household appliances. But these heightened expectations could not be sustained in the aftermath of the storm. Theoretical insight drawn from political science and sociology confirm that the consequences of rising expectations and relative deprivation are crucial to understanding the growing frustration and civil unrest in society.[8]

The bottom fell out in 1981. Between 1980 and 1985, the value of petroleum exports declined by an average annual rate of 14.4 percent, with the decline even more severe in 1986 and 1987 (Abdulah 1988:4). Cost of Living Allowance (COLA) was suspended in 1987 and the government also reduced public wages by ten percent in order to control spending (World Bank Report 1996:94). Falling oil prices, declining monetary reserves, and balance of payment problems forced the newly elected National Alliance For Reconstruction (NAR) government into an agreement with the International Monetary Fund in 1988. Between 1989 and 1990, the nation's foreign exchange reserves were depleted and the total public debt was estimated at over TT$10 billion, with foreign debt payments exceeding TT$1.1 billion annually (Deere, et al. 1990:27). Nothwithstanding charges of corruption, which were credited to the former PNM government, a paramount condition leading to NAR's decision to seek IMF assistance was thevery fact of an oil dependent economy and the accompanying failure to sustain a more diversified economy, and the mismanagement of certain state-run operations (Ambursley 1983; Thomas 1988; Ryan 1989). In the past, the state monopolized specific operations including the national airline (BWIA), utilities and communications, and petroleum. Conditions set by the IMF have altered this structure with the subsequent introduction of privatization and deregulation. As a result, the dismantling of (costly and often mismanaged) state-run operations is in full swing.[9]

Social dislocation has been extensive. Renowned calypsonian and loyalist to the free market system, The Mighty Sparrow, captured the despair of the masses at that time when he released the calypso "Capitalism Gone Mad" in 1983. Between 1981 and 1990, the number of individuals and families with children in Trinidad and Tobago receiving direct welfare assistance through the Old Age Pensions and Public Assistance programs rose.[10] Government expenditures went from TT$14.7 million in 1981 to TT$36.2 million in 1990 (Statistical Digest 1990:182). Henry and Melville (1989) reported that by the mid- to late 1980s the poverty rate for the country had risen to 18.5 percent. However, in the urban centers of Port of Spain and Arima, the poverty rate was highest at 41.43, percent with 31.72 percent of families there receiving some form of public assistance. In many households both parents have been forced to seek employment, leaving youths to fend for themselves to a degree unimagined just one generation ago. Television sets, VCRs, and cable network in most households serve as surrogate parents and have become the main pastime for many of Trinidad's idle youths. As noted earlier, the influence of foreign, mainly North American, programming is profound. These technological influences cannot be overlooked in discussing the nation's escalating crime and violence statistics, which will be examined later on in the chapter.

Reduced parental control and the expansion of single-female-headed households functioning at bare subsistence levels, have been associated with other problems. Indiscipline has erupted, notably in the urban schools, accompanied by the lowering of educational standards, secondary school dropouts, teen pregnancies, crime, violence, and drug abuse (Youth Survey 1991:1).

Between 1988 and 1990, the unemployment figure for the nation was roughly 20 percent higher for Port Spain and other urban areas. The rate of youth ages 15 through 19 was 46 percent, and for ages 22 through 25 it was 36 percent. For those without high school diplomas, unemployment affected roughly 27.2 percent, while for those with diplomas the figure was 12.5 percent (*Statistical Digest* 1990:30). In 1994, unemployment in Trinidad and Tobago stood at 18.2 percent of which youth, women and those with limited levels of education continued to be disproportionately represented. If the discouraged job seekers are added to this figure, it would increase to 25 percent (The World Bank 1995:viiii). The double-digit unemployment prevailed throughout 1995 and 1996.

With over 25 percent of its population between fifteen and twenty-four years of age and 33.5 percent under fifteen years of age, Trinidad and Tobago is a youthful nation (CSO Bulletin 1994). It should come as no surprise, therefore, in the wake of the youth unemployment crisis that the incentive to complete school is diminishing among Trinidad and Tobago's youth. Exacerbating this crisis for Trinidad and Tobago and the entire region is the recession in North America and other traditional receiving countries and their more stringent immigration policies, which have limited the flow of migration. Would-be migrants including youth and other prime members from the working age population have, consequently, been forced to remain at home and that has in part explained the increases in this segment of the population over the recent decade (Neil 1992).

To what extent the introduction of new information technology has impacted the nation's unemployment is still being studied. It is true, however, that various government and private sector employers, including the telephone company, banks, and the utility companies are now computerized, with the inevitable need to downsize their labor forces.[11]

In a recent survey of 1,247 young people between the ages of fifteen and twenty-four throughout the nation, 75 percent named unemployment as the second most serious problem for youth. However, 80 percent named drugs and drug-related crime as one of the severest problems facing their communities (Youth Survey 1991: 18). This finding underscores the relationship between unemployment and the escalation of the drug subculture and violent street crime.

Ivelaw Griffith, a specialist on drugs and security in the Caribbean prefers to use the term "geonarcotics" when discussing the global dimensions of contemporary drug operations. Geonarcotics refers to the present dilemma whereby conflict and cooperation among national and international actors are increasingly driven by drugs (Griffith 1994a, 1994b; Booth 1996). Drug transshipment, money laundering, and production are widespread in the urban centers of the Caribbean. No longer is the drug problem perceived as a monopoly of Jamaica, the Bahamas, or Belize. Guyana and Trinidad and Tobago, not known for major drug operations a decade ago, are now producers and transshippers of drugs, with a daunting user population. Much of this can be credited to the Colombian cartels' efforts to locate new bases for shipment. Idle young adult males and school dropouts are particularly vulnerable to becoming involved in the lucrative drug industry. Transmigrants have been major players as transporters of drugs into the region and as clients. Some of these transmigrants are native-born youth themselves who live abroad and travel between countries. Ansley Hamid (1991:615–68) discusses this in the case of Jamaican posse members in New York City.

Accompanying the drug menace is the menace of violent crime. Between 1990 and 1993 Port of Spain led the nation's urban areas in serious crimes (Crime Report 1993). Once safe havens, many of the streets of Port of Spain and other urban areas now throb with lurking fear. Front galleries that were an esthetic addition to most Port of Spain houses, where residents sat and parlayed day and night, have become off limits. They are universally burglar-proof, with iron bars and locks. Comparisons by residents to the streets of New York are common, with statements like:

down here getting real dread boy; just like de STATES. Trinidad ain't no different from Brooklyn an' Harlem. Is

deh T.V. and deh drugs from up deh dat making dis place
so bad.

    Since 1981, serious crimes reported to police authorities, includ-
ing manslaughter, assaults, burglaries, larceny, and drugs, have
soared in Trinidad.[12] There were 11,621 of these combined felonies
reported in 1981, compared to 16,202 in 1990. Minor crimes also
increased during the same period, from 4,605 to 6,535. These offenses have significantly involved juveniles under sixteen years of
age and youth ages sixteen to twenty-five (Statistical Digest 1990).
It is conceivable that the streets of Port of Spain might be compared to those of New York City. It has become fashionable for
youths to cruise the streets in fancy cars with loud speakers blast-
ing the imported sounds of rap and "gangsta" rap. With the exception of reggae, which is regionally appreciated, locally grown calypso
and soca music is seldom heard except during the Carnival season.
No less trendy than their African-American counterparts, these
youth sport gold necklaces, baggy pants, expensive sneakers, and a
body language that projects their indifference and resistance.
    To fully understand the youths' frustration and anger, as well as
these data on crime and violence, we must return to the period of
the oil boom. As we have already noted, some revenues from that
bonanza did manage to trickle down to the masses. That is not to
imply that all classes benefited equally or that the boom signalled
an end to poverty in the nation. It did, however, serve to raise
expectations and stimulate the demand for imported goods and
luxuries. But a major oversight amidst all of the excitement was
the need for long-range economic planning in the likelihood of a
decline. Short-term work programs continue such as the controversial "10 Day" work policy which was begun during the Williams
administration and is officially known as URP or the Unemployment Relief Programme. However, this has been at the expense of
more serious long-term planning and training for the nation's
youth. The secondary school rejection rate was already becoming
noticeable, not to mention the growing number of youth who were
failing to earn the necessary passing grades on their secondary
school exams (G.C.E./C.X.C.)[13] and opting to enter the work force.
Consequently, when the bottom fell out and the holiday was over,

the needs of the nation's youth were left unaddressed. Their environment, which, up to that point, had appeared fairly secure, was disrupted. They saw unemployment and the fear of unemployment disrupt their households and family life. Without the promise of employment after completing school or even part-time work to cushion oneself, and with a growing mistrust for adults, politicians, the government, and the police (who are held in contempt and considered responsible for the upheaval), restlessness and anger have fermented among the youth. This is manifested in their resistance to authority at various levels.

It is no coincidence that the eruption of violence in the streets, in schools, and in homes should occur concomitant with the escalating consumption of violence throughout the society. Violence is ubiquitous; it is displayed on television, seen at the cinemas, sold at video rental shops, and programmed for computers at the video game rooms at urban and suburban shopping malls. High profile acts of violence have proliferated since the July 27, 1990, Jumaat-al-Muslimeen attempted overthrow of the NAR government. The largely youthful Black Islamic group led by Imam Yasin Abu Bakr traded parliamentary politics for terror and gun violence in responding to the austerity measures imposed by structural adjustment policies, policies that threatened to further marginalize and degrade the masses.

In the period preceding the uprising, that is, the latter part of the 1980s, the Jumaat's appeal to the poor and working class centered around the state's take-back measures, the loss of school book and lunch allowances, and the housing crisis and the subsequent rise of vagrants and squatters, mainly in the urban areas. At a time when conventional politicians were in a frenzy and bankrupt for ideas and solutions, the urban sufferers were a ready-made audience for the Jumaat at the various rallies and gatherings they held around town. Many of these gatherings were dispersed by the authorities and some arrests were made because the required applications had not been filed. Although the majority of Trinidad and Tobago's African population are followers of Christianity, the message delivered by these traditionally attired grassroots Islamic brothers offered a reasonable alternative to the lackluster speeches and promises offered by mainstream politicians.

At the end of the Jumaat's six-day siege, at least six persons lay dead on the steps outside the Red House in downtown Port of Spain, where the Parliament is housed. Prime Minister A.N.R. Robinson, who was held hostage along with several ministers, was seriously injured. The urban poor immediately took to the streets, which prompted the government's call for a curfew. The total loss of life was twenty-five people and the losses from several days of looting and damage were unprecedented in the young nation's history. Destruction to the downtown business area was estimated at between $300 million to $500 million and some 4,000 people were put out of jobs (*The Daily Express* 1990:i).

Analyses and postmortems of the uprising converge in noting that although the Jumaat achieved a limited appeal among the masses on the matter of their worsening material and class position, they were less successful, due to their sectarian and ideological orientation, in winning the moral support of most Trinidadians and Tobagonians. The merciless behavior the outlaws exhibited fell outside the experience of most nationals, and although they distrusted the increasingly unpopular NAR government, their sympathies seemed to be with the victims and their families. That innocent people were killed and their corpses left out in the hot sun for the duration of the siege—the militants declined requests by hospital workers to take them away—left a numbing feeling.

Cable News Network (CNN) carried live broadcasts of the events from Trinidad and the international community, including nationals abroad, was awed to see the island of sun, steel pan, and Carnival, as if experiencing some rite of passage, suddenly plunged into the real world of the late twentieth century. The widespread lawlessness in the society, along with political unaccountability, provided a receptive environment for the Muslimeem offensive. The event served as a wake-up call to those who had previously refused to accept the fact that a crisis of violence existed and that the nation was in trouble (Deosaran 1993). Ironically, this very same episode had already been choreographed many times for the people of Trinidad and Tobago on the giant screens in cinema houses and on their television screens at home.

Other high-profile acts of violence involving youth in the past five years are too numerous to mention here. However, two are noteworthy. In 1993, two young males entered a Royal Castle fast food restaurant in Arima and brutally killed the manager for a batch of tickets to the Steel Pulse concert, a popular Jamaican reggae band. They had planned to sell the tickets on the black market. The other incident occurred in 1994 in the upscale suburb of Westmoorings, just outside of Port of Spain. Two young males broke into a home and raped and tortured to death two mothers of small children just for the fun of it. What startled the public in these and other cases was the ease with which those involved were apprehended, but even more that there was little outward expression of remorse for their behavior. In July 1994, shortly after this last case and in response to the citizens' growing fear and increased lobbying, Attorney General Keith Sobion was asked by Prime Minister Patrick Manning to draft the "Bail Bill," which would deny repeat offenders the right to bail for specific offenses. National crime data show that between fifty and seventy-five percent of the serious crimes are committed by repeat offenders (Viarruel 1994:3).

In a recent work, Cornel West (1994) used the term "nihilism" to refer to this same tendency among inner-city African-American youths. It points to a form of psychic numbing[14] resulting from feelings of deep frustration, fear, and the lack of hope about the future. Through numbing, the individual is able to deny fear and other insecurities that roam his environment. In other words, it allows the individual to shut himself off from the fact of his own vulnerablity. The process of numbing also allows the individual to deny responsibility for his actions and behaviors.

The current generation of young people in Trinidad and Tobago are growing up in an era of increasing single-parent households, with most headed by a female who is struggling to make ends meet. A common scenario today is for youths to remain with surrogates—a grandmother or close friends—while their mother is employed in the United States or Canada doing domestic, child care, or some form of hospital work (Bonnett 1990; Toney 1992; Basch *et al.* 1994). Kinship parenting is a common cultural practice in the tradition of African people, which has been observed throughout the Caribbean. However, a problem has arisen today whereby surrogates, who are also preoccupied with their own survival in an uncertain economic climate, are overwhelmed by the additional pressure of a restless youth(s) left in their care. In many cases, remittances from the employed relative abroad are their only source of income. Overall, parental love and the sense of a stable family life are becoming scarce resources for many of the nation's young people. Experiencing this void, it is little wonder that these young people might be incapable of showing remorse for their criminal actions or sensitivity for their victims.

More than two decades ago, sociologist Orlando Patterson noted that the dire conditions that were rapidly unfolding in the United States were emerging as well among Blacks throughout the Americas. He predicted that by the 1990s, though still poor, many Caribbean societies would be more urban than rural, doing so at a time when the prospect of any breakthrough in terms of industrialization still seemed remote. He noted:

> [F]amily unity collapses and the personal dignity of the peasant disappears and is replaced by the fatalism and aggressiveness of the urban masses; the hustler replaces the shrewd farmer; unemployment becomes a way of life and crime and delinquency run rampant, and black unskilled labor becomes a redundant lumpen-proletariat. (Patterson 1972:56–57)

Whether or not Patterson's prediction could have been avoided is a major aspect of the ongoing debate. What appears to be clear at this point is that it will take an emboldened and visionary leadership to help overcome the present crisis and restore a sense of hope for the people of Trinidad and Tobago and the region as a whole.

Exploring the Policy Alternatives

Although this chapter has dealt with the urban condition specific to the English-speaking Caribbean, the issues raised are regional in scope. Tumultuous change that daunts the region's urban territories at this historical juncture appears unrelenting. As the case of Trinidad and Tobago demonstrates, it is the youth—who constitute a majority of the population of that country and the region as a whole and upon whom the future rests—who are critically affected by structural adjustment policies and the sociocultural dislocations discussed throughout this chapter.

The present crisis in Trinidad and Tobago is a classic example of a nation where rising expectations, an outgrowth of the prosperity that accompanied the oil boom era, were left unchecked. The voting-out of the PNM, the party of independence, and the election of a new government, NAR, in 1986 failed to restore economic order. The return of PNM in 1991 and its inability to live up to one of its chief campaign promises, to improve the social and economic conditions in the country, exacerbated the feeling of entrapment felt by many poor and working-class persons.

Policies are urgently needed that will restore a sense of hope and future to the country. A "Bail Bill" and the construction of more prisons do not point to constructive policies. Imperative are employment and training programs that will address short- and long-term needs. In this regard, the needs of the nation's youth come first. The importance of completing school must be instilled in the youth but this claim can only be supported if it is accompanied by a well-planned jobs program that will help to assure youth of their importance to the nation's future and, at the same time, provide a meaningful alternative to the illicit drug industry.

Government programs to alleviate youth unemployment and poverty were inspired by World Bank funding between 1988 and 1990. These programs included Youth Training and Employment Partnership Programme (YTEPP), Apprenticeship In Industrial Mobilization (AIM), Youth Employment Support System (YESS), and Each Community Helping Out (ECHO). YTEPP, the most ambitious of these, was set up to provide a wide range of vocational courses (targeted at eight to ten thousand youths per period) at craft level over a nine month period, at forty-one centers scattered throughout Trinidad and Tobago. The other programs, which functioned as support and placement entities, fell under the Ministries of Education, Industry, and Community Development. A 1992 report by ECLAC stated that the prospects for success of YTEPP and the others remained grim due to the lagging ability of the private sector to absorb sufficient graduates; this, in light of the current privatization and declining public sector employment. Among the many recommendations cited was the need for greater input by independent NGOs and critical, programmatic input from the youth themselves concerning their training needs and desires (Neil 1992).

A firm drug security policy is desperately needed to combat the drug menace in Trinidad and Tobago and other states in the region. This response, therefore, has regional implications, calling for greater cooperation among states in securing their borders and coast lines, interdiction, and promoting more drug prevention programs. Existing policies that call for more policing, stiffer penalties, and incarceration have proven ineffective within and outside the region in the war against drugs. Pressure will have to be brought upon international financial institutions, including the World Bank, IMF, and Inter-American Development Bank, to which many states have outstanding fiscal obligations, to support these measures. While debt relief would be the ideal policy, another approach would be for these institutions to permit countries to use a portion of their interest payments to finance these programs. For certain, these international bodies will need to be pressed at the diplomatic levels, but pressure from grassroots efforts and movements in the countries should not be overlooked.

The recommendations presented for Trinidad and Tobago are not unique and, given the pervasiveness of the crisis, could easily apply to other states in the region. With an eye on the region for the next millennium, it will be crucial to extend the question, "What is to be done?" to include, "By whom?" and, "How can we sustain constructive change?"

The three day Summit of the Americas held December 9–11, 1994, in Miami, Florida illuminates the need for constructive responses. At that summit, U.S. President Clinton met with all of the heads of state from Latin America and the Caribbean (except Cuba) to discuss strategies for reducing trade barriers and increasing international trade. In a pre-summit speech, President Clinton noted that in just seven years, U.S. exports throughout the hemisphere had doubled, rising to nearly US $80 billion in 1993 (IAQ 1994:1). But for some skeptics, this meeting represented the groundwork for an expanded North American Free Trade Agreement (NAFTA), with the disturbing feature of increased penetration of U.S. mass culture through the exportation of new consumer products and various forms of modern technology. The representatives departed with the "Summit Plan of Action" that called for hemispheric free trade, but the other important issues they hoped to have implemented, such as insuring Caribbean Basin Initiative parity with the North American Free Trade Agreement, relief or the reduction of external debt, and the preservation of preferential trade status for Caribbean bananas were left unaddressed.

The Assembly of Caribbean People (ACP), the brainchild of the Trinidad and Tobago Oil Field Workers Trade Union (OWTU), is a potential catalyst for constructive and sustainable change and development. It has emerged at the very time when progressive grassroots movements for change have virtually atrophied, and needless to say, that fact promises to be one of its greatest challenges. Formed in 1992, the first Assembly of Caribbean People convened August 19–21, 1994, at Chaguramas, Trinidad. Represented were delegates from Anglo, Creole or Franco, Spanish, Papiamento or Dutch speaking Caribbean states, and Caribbean persons living in the "diaspora", i.e., North America, Central America, and Europe. Nonpartisan, ACP respects differences among the peoples of the region but perceives the need to bridge divisions among Caribbean people and their nationals abroad as a fundamental step in forging unity that is social, cultural, economic, and political in context. ACP recognizes the bankrupt nature of the current leadership and governments and the failed vision of sovereignty, and that alternatives to the agenda of the respective governments and local elites are desperately needed. One condition for change, therefore, is the active participation by "ordinary people"[15] in the dialogue and debate and ultimately in the decision-making process (ACP 1994:2).

Central to ACP's proposed action plan is the need to organize a regional information center and a Caribbean Cultural Information Centre. Such entities would prove instrumental in buttressing presently frail efforts to neutralize the unflinching penetration of materialistic, dehumanizing values from outside. This is not a call for censorship. Rather, it is a call to encourage critical thinking on the part of Caribbean people about the importance of indigenous cultural resources and to decipher which aspects of external mass culture are expendable to the future growth and development of those resources. While many of the region's policy needs generally overlap with those of individual states, regional-state differences exist and to reconcile these differences will require further creative planning.

Conclusion

In addressing the economic and political upheaval that is taking place in the contemporary Caribbean, and the urban crisis in Trinidad and Tobago in particular, the perspective of cultural transnationalism was introduced. This perspective, concomitant with the political economy approach, was discussed as essential to a comprehensive understanding of the present situation and its solution. Importantly, this discussion pointed to the need to restore national pride and a commitment to home and the development process. As long as the people of the region continue to feel insecure about the ability of their governments and leaders to resurrect their economies and improve their living standards, a superficial or symbolic expression of nationalism will have to be settled for. Restrictive immigration policies may temporarily close doors but rigid policies have not proven effective in containing a people desperate to exit and become transmigrants. In the current atmosphere, persuading the people of the region to strike a balance between their indigenous cultural orientations and mass culture from abroad promises to be a gargantuan task.

The world is a rapidly changing environment and the Caribbean is being transformed. Frameworks and new strategies for analysis must keep in stride with these developments. The initiative taken by the Assembly of Caribbean People, which hopefully will inspire other creative activities, is one reason to be optimistic.

——————————— NOTES ———————————

1. The Caribbean, unless otherwise specified, refers to the anglophone island states of Greater and Lesser Antilles, including Guyana.

2. Poverty in the Caribbean now averages roughly 38 percent of the population, ranging from a high of 65 percent in Haiti to a low of 5 percent in the Bahamas. These estimates place the Caribbean close to a world aggregate average of poverty in developing countries (see The World Bank Report No. 15342 LAC, *Poverty Reduction and the Human Rersource Development in the Caribbean*. Washington, D.C., May 1996, pp. vii–viii).

3. The "G-7" refers to the seven wealthiest industrial countries in the world, i.e., United States, Canada, Japan, Germany, Britain, France, and Italy.

4. Elsewhere in the vast literature on migration, transmigrants have been referred to as "sojourners." See for example Edna Bonacich, "A Theory of Middlemen Minority." *American Sociological Review* 38 (1973):583–594; also, Nancy Foner (ed.), *New Immigrants in New York.* New York: Columbia University Press, 1983.

5. A book in progress by this author entitled, *Manufacturing Powerlessness* compares the urban crisis in the United States, the Caribbean, and East Africa. A survey questionnaire was administered to youth (males and females) in the age group 15–24. Preliminary findings from the survey question on migration indicate that a majority of the Caribbean respondents perceive migration to the United States and Canada as critical for their future.

6. See Nathan Glazer, *Clamor at the Gates: The New American Immigration.* San Francisco: ICS Press, 1985. Also, it should be pointed out that this quest is not new, as West Indians have a history of migration to core regions; but this new immigration is significantly different from the old. See for example, Charles Green and Basil Wilson, *The Struggle For Black Empowerment in New York City.* New York: Praeger, 1989 (especially Chap. 5 on the African-American and Caribbean Dialectic); also, Nancy Foner (ed.), *New Immigrants in New York.* New York: Columbia University Press, 1983.

7. In small island societies and many Third World countries, "urban primacy" or the domination by a central city, most likely the capital city, is common. See: Portes, A., Itzigsohn, J., Cabral-Dore, C., "Urbanization in the Caribbean Basin: Social Change During the Years of Crisis," *Latin American Research Review* (Spring 1994); also, Gilbert, A. and Gugler, J., *Cities, Poverty and Development: Urbanization in the Third World.* New York: Oxford University Press, 1993, p.36.

8. Frances Fox Piven and Richard Cloward (1979) integrate a number of these studies in their analysis and discussion of the structuring of poor people's protest movements. See for example: Karl Marx and Frederick Engels, *Manifesto of the Communist Party.* New York: International, 1948; Ted Robert Gurr, "Psychological Factors in Civil Violence." *World Politics* 29 (January 1968); J.C. Davies, "Toward a Theory of Revolution." *American Sociological Review* 27 (1962); also by Gurr, *Why Men Rebel.* Princeton: Princeton University Press 1970.

9. Various state entities have either been privatized or are in the process being privatized. They include the telephone company, the power company, the water works, the post office, the petrochemical and natural gas industries, and the cement industry, to mention a few. It should come as no surprise that foreigners (e.g., American, British, and Japanese investors) control these buyouts.

10. In Trinidad and Tobago, Old Age Pensions are paid to persons over sixty-five who can prove an inability to maintain themselves otherwise.

Public Assistance is provided to households that are indigent, under very exact criteria. For example, a woman and dependent children if abandoned by a husband or partner or faced with an incapacitated head of household. A male head of household without employment would have to abandon the household in order that his family qualify for assistance. This welfare policy parallels the U.S. public assistance and Aid to Families with Dependent Children programmes.

11. Toward the end of 1989, the government of Trinidad and Tobago entered an agreement with the Inter-American Development Bank to provide institutional strengthening and a major expansion of its computerization and management systems. Throughout 1994, these efforts were continued with several major reports issued (see *Reports on Information Systems Policy And Implementation Plans*. IDB Project No. ATN/SF–3388–TT (September 6, 1993); and IDB Project No. ATN/SF–3388–TT (July 29, 1994).

12. It is worth noting that for approximately 30 years, 1956 through 1886, the average daily prison population was 1,111. From 1987, however, it has climbed steadily to 3,943 in 1994 (see The World Bank Report No. 15 342 LAC. *Poverty Reduction and Human Resource Development in the Caribbean*. Washington, D.C., May 1996, p. 58.

13. In the English-speaking West Indies, after completing Form 5 (equivalent to Grade 11 in the United States), students must take the General Certificate Examination (G.C.E.) or the Caribbean Examination Council (C.X.C.) to obtain a high school certificate (diploma). Students must make at least fivepasses in subject areas that include Math, Literature, English, and Sciences in order to be eligible for advanced education and employment. See Sharon-Ann Gopaul McNicol, *Working with West Indian Families*. New York: Guilford Press, 1993, p. 178.

14. See Robert J. Lifton, "Beyond Psychic Numbing: A Call to Awareness." *American Journal of Orthopyschiatry* 52:4 (October 1982).

15. Ordinary people as defined by ACP refers to workers, farmers, fishermen, the people of the informal sector, the self-employed, the unemployed, students, youth, artists, sportsmen and -women. But it must also include, the intellectual community, NGOs, and members of professional associations.

— REFERENCES —

Abdulah, David. 1988. "The IMF/World Bank And Trinidad and Tobago." Statement by OWTU presented to The People's Tribunal, Berlin.
Ambursley, Fitzroy and Robin Cohen (eds.). 1983. *Crisis in the Caribbean*. New York: Monthly Review Press.

Annual Statistical Digest of Trinidad & Tobago. 1990, 1994. Central Statistical Office, Port of Spain, Trinidad.

Assembly of Caribbean People. 1994. *Declaration and Preamble.* San Fernando, Trinidad, OTWU Headquarters.

Basch, L., N. Glick-Schiller, and C. Blanc-Szanton, 1994. *Nations Unbound.* Langhorne, Pa.: Gordon and Breach.

Bonnett, A. 1990. "The New Female West Indian Immigrant: Dilemmas of Coping in the Host Society." In R.W. Palmer (ed.), *In Search Of A Better Life.* New York: Praeger.

Bonnett, A. and L. Watson (eds.). 1990. *Emerging Perspectives On The Black Diaspora.* Lanham, Maryland: University Press of America.

Booth, Cathy. 1996. "Caribbean Blizzard." *Time* (February 26).

Central Statistical Office. 1994. *The Bulletin.* (July). Port of Spain, Trinidad.

Chomsky, Noam. 1995. *The Prosperous Few And The Restless Many.* Berkeley: Odonian Press.

Crime Research And Assessment Team. 1993. *Report On Crime, Race, And Related Circumstances In Trinidad & Tobago.*

Daily Express. 1990. *Trinidad Under Siege: The Muslimeen Uprising.* Port of Spain, Trinidad: Trinidad Express Newspapers LTD.

Deere, C.D., P.Antrobus, L. Bolles, E. Melendez, P. Phillips, M. Rivera, and H. Safa, 1990. *In The Shadows Of The Sun: Caribbean Development Alternatives and U.S. Policy.* Boulder: Westview Press.

Deosaran, Ramesh. 1993. *A Society Under Siege: A Study of Political Confusion and Legal Mysticism.* St. Augustine, Trinidad: The McAl Psychological Research Centre, University of the West Indies.

Frank, Andre G. 1969. *Latin America: underdevelopment or revolution.* New York: Monthly Review Press.

Gilbert, Alan and Josef Gugler. 1993. *Cities, Poverty and Development: Urbanization in the Third World.* New York: Oxford University Press.

Griffith, Ivelaw L. 1994a. "Drugs Alter the Security Agenda." *Hemisphere* (Winter/Spring).

———. 1994b. "From Cold War geopolitics to post-Cold War geonarcotics." *International Journal* 49 No.1 (Winter).

Henry, Ralph A. and Juliet Melville. 1989. "Poverty Revisited: Trinidad And Tobago In The Late 1980s." Paper presented at Hugh Wooding Law School, St. Augustine, Trinidad (March).

International Affairs Quarterly of Florida International University 1994. Vol.4 No.4 (Fall).

Interview with Dr. Frank Mills at the University of the Virgin Islands. August, 1993.

Kennedy, Paul. 1993. *Preparing for the Twenty-first Century*. New York: Random House.

Larmer, Brook. 1996. "The Barrel Children." *Newsweek* (February 19).

Mander, Jerry. 1996. "The Dark Side of Globalization." *The Nation*. July 15/22.

Marajh, Camini. 1994. "The City's Changing Face." *Daily Express*. Financial & Business Section (Monday, October 10).

Ministry of Youth Sports Culture And Creative Arts. 1991. *Survey of Youth Problems and Perceptions*. Port of Spain, Trinidad & Tobago.

Neil, Joan C. 1992. "Social Programmes For Poverty Alleviation In The Republic of Trinidad and Tobago." (A Working Paper) Port of Spain: Economic Commission For Latin America And The Caribbean

Norberg-Hodge, Helena. 1996. "Break Up the Monoculture." *The Nation*. July 15/22.

Patterson, Orlando. 1972. "Toward a Future that Has No Past: Reflections on the fate of Blacks in the Americas." *Public Interest* 27.

Piven, Frances F. and Richard Cloward. 1979. *Poor People's Movements: Why They Succeed and How They Fail*. New York: Vintage.

Portes, A. and Rubén G. Rumbault. 1990. *Immigrant America*. Berkeley: University of California Press.

Portes, A., J. Itzigsohn, and C. Cabral-Dore. 1994. "Urbanization in the Caribbean Basin: Social Change During the Years of Crisis." *Latin American Research Review* (Spring 1994).

Reich, Robert. 1991. *The Work of Nations: Preparing Ourselves for 21st Century Capitalism*. New York: Knopf.

Ryan, Selwyn (ed.). 1989. *Trinidad & Tobago: The Independence Experience 1962–1987*. St. Augustine, Trinidad: ISER University of The West Indies.

Sassen, Saskia. 1991. *The Global City*. Princeton: Princeton University Press.

Sutton, C. and S. Maiesky. 1975. "Migration and West Indian Racial and Ethnic Consciousness." in H. Safa and B.M. DuToit (eds.), *Migration and Development*. The Hague: Moton & Co.

The South Commission. 1990. *The Challenge to the South*. New York: Oxford University Press.

The World Bank Report No. 14382-TR. October 1995. *Trinidad and Tobago: Poverty and Unemployment in an Oil Based Economy*.

The World Bank Report No. 15342 LAC. May 1996. *Poverty Reduction and Human Resource Development in the Caribbean*.

Toney, J. 1992. "The Perpetuation of a Culture of Migration: West Indian Ties With Home, 1900–1979." A Paper delivered at Annual Caribbean Studies Association Meeting, St. George's, Grenada.

Thomas, Clive Y. 1988. *The Poor and the Powerless: Economic Policy and Change in the Caribbean*. New York: Monthly Review Press.

Viarruel, Alva. 1994. "New Bail Bill to deal with repeaters." *Trinidad Express* (July 19).

Wallerstein, Immanuel. 1974. *The Modern World System*. New York: Academic Press.

West, Cornel. 1993. *Race Matters*. Boston: Beacon Press.

Williams, Eric. 1944. *Capitalism and Slavery*. London: Andre Deutsch.

———. 1970. *From Columbus to Castro: the history of the Caribbean, 1492–1969*. New York: Harper & Row.

Obika Gray

9

Power and Identity among the Urban Poor of Jamaica

In recent years, there has been an outpouring of literature discussing how disadvantaged groups—poor women, slaves, peasants, the urban poor, and workers in communist systems—convert their social marginality into political resources that challenge the powerful in ways the latter find difficult to suppress (Hyden 1980; Scott 1985; Azarya and Chazan 1987: 106–131; Szelenyi et al. 1988).

While disputes exist about the significance of this expression of power-from-below, exponents of this perspective are united in their agreement that subordinate strata living under oppressive state systems are not without significant resources to contest, contain, or even bring about the subversion of state power from below, typically without resort to violence or overt confrontation. These studies insist that repertoires of peaceful, pragmatic, and evasive contestation deployed by disadvantaged groups in the interest of self-defense, material improvement, and personal dignity are fulcrums of social change. Such resources, exponents argue, must be regarded as a basis of popular power. This is the social power of the disadvantaged, who typically lack access to the state and do not possess traditional political resources, but who nonetheless secure some of what they deem important for their lives, in opposition to the designs of predatory and invasive state structures and their agents.

Notwithstanding their value, these studies have their critics. One criticism is the argument that subordinate strata living under oppressive state structures in Third World countries are primarily engaged in survivalist and self-defensive practices of negligible relevance for the organization of power, and as such do not present a real threat to the state. Critics also maintain that in Third World societies current dissident responses from below have come mainly from the ranks of highly vulnerable and politically weak urban social strata—the unemployed, the lumpenproletariat, petty traders, and the rebellious young—whose responses to marginality have often collapsed into nihilistic protests. Where these responses are not savagely crushed or co-opted by the state, the critics contend, they tend to degenerate into crime, lawlessness, or plaintive expressions of hopelessness. Consequently, evidence of dissidence among urban marginals is regarded by these critics as not so much a politics of resistance as a cry of desperation. Their politically relevant responses neither weaken power, present meaningful alternatives, nor offer solutions; instead, the critics argue that such responses should be seen as symptoms of, not answers to the structural crisis in these deeply fractured societies.

These are serious criticisms, and Scott in particular has marshalled a sustained and persuasive response to some of them (Scott 1985). While that debate cannot be rehearsed here, my own view is that even as the critics have offered a useful correction to a perspective that would romanticize the combativity of the poor and exaggerate their capacity to escape the reach of power, the detractors devalue the *potency* of power-from-below in many Third World societies and are too dismissive of the form and etiquette of this dissidence which they regard as inferior politically to an elite-led, state-centric, organized popular movement articulating a universalistic anti-system ideology.

Political realities in many Third World countries and the political actions of subaltern groups refuse, however, to conform to nineteenth-century blueprints of "good" social movements. For all their weaknesses, it is undeniable that the disadvantaged in many countries have adopted unusual and creative techniques to hold invasive state systems at bay. What critics fail to note is that these repertoires can have massive destabilizing consequences for power. Despite their small size and social composition in particular places, anti-systemic movements can dictate the state's agenda; they can cause massive state resources to be tied up in keeping them in check; and they can inflect the discourse of the state toward their concerns. In addition, they can assume forms the state cannot easily expunge. Whether they are mocking the claims of the powerful behind their backs or engaging in fugitive and evasive practices, subaltern dissidents may not only elude the grasp of the state, they can carve out spaces in which to enjoy a relative autonomy from the reach of the powerful and make it impossible for rulers to govern.

But having called attention to the importance of forms of resistance that do not depend on open revolts to be effective, it must be said that a perspective that emphasizes quiet, fugitive resistance from below may be simplifying things too much. Contrary to the claims of their critics, it is not so much that the exponents of "everyday" resistance fail to appreciate the limits of pragmatic and circumspect dissidence from below. Rather, the real shortcoming is that they hold a one-sided view of the politics of the disadvantaged as mostly a politics of circumspection, evasion, and dissimulation. While this safety-seeking mode of opposition captures a major facet of the politics of the disadvantaged, it tends to ignore the capacity for counter-violence and other forms of overt contestation that go beyond dissimulation but fall short of open rebellion. There is a continuum of openly defiant actions transcending footdragging and covert struggle, which subalterns may employ without mass revolt. There are politically militant subordinate strata for whom hostility to injustice is not easily bottled up; in certain locales in the Third World anger is not always throttled and nursed for some distant day of reckoning. Among such groups and in certain locales, repertoires of resistance exist that qualify the model of predominantly quiet, off-stage actions and covert nibbling at power from below. In these other contexts, resistance from below may be more complex and ambiguous, involving a delicate and subtle combination of circumspection, evasion, and engagement with power, as well as stubborn, open defiance not choked back or hidden from the powerful by self-suppressive behaviors.

Taking post-independence Jamaican society as a case study, and looking closely at the politics of the alienated urban poor, this chapter will show that even though this disadvantaged group has been the target of high levels of state repression and is currently regarded as a most dangerous social class, punitive state measures and blandishments have not cowed them into submission, turned them into resigned, circumspect supplicants, or reduced their fierce, open defiance of power.[1]

On the contrary, as the social crisis in Jamaica has deepened over the past twenty years, there has been a discernable increase in the social power of the Jamaican poor, particularly among sections of its rebellious urban contingent. This latter group has shown both a remarkable combativity and a capacity for creatively transforming its social and political marginality in ways that have led to the creation of new antagonistic moral communities characterized by distinctive popular cultural identities and new ego structures. The fluorescence of these subaltern identities has been so extensive, and their influence so compelling among the urban poor, that several of these identities easily compete with the multiracial bourgeois moral culture, which established its hegemony in the late colonial and early post-colonial years.

This chapter will present some evidence from archival research and interviews conducted early in 1994. It will show how the poor accumulate social power out of marginality, and it offers a nuanced view of resistance that shows the poor giving contingent circumspection to power, but also wresting from their tormenters significant spaces for autonomy while advancing initiatives and identities which the state and its agents reluctantly have been forced to accommodate.

Using an approach to power that sees it as reciprocal, dynamic, and unstable in composition, the chapter examines in turn, the following instances for their lessons about the social power of the poor: (1) the massive political weight and ideological influence of the urban poor inside the two-party system; (2) the resort to public demonstrations by the poor to make their needs known; (3) the rise to prominence and quest for autonomy by popular figures among the poor like Claude Massop; and (4) the expansion of a class-antagonistic moral culture among the urban poor. I conclude with some reflections on the future of the urban poor in Jamaica.

Popular Social Power and Politics Inside the Party Space

One way of organizing our understanding of the social power of the poor is to think of their political actions as occurring both "inside" and "outside" state structures. However, this is merely a convenient heuristic device, which enables us to speak about certain occurrences as if they were independent of each other. This shift in perspective is necessary because there really is no "inside" space that is monopolized by the state and from which the presence of the poor can be barred. Similarly, there really is no "outside" non-party space, for example, to which the poor can retreat and from which the state can effectively be proscribed. The predatory state makes its influence felt to some degree in almost all social spaces, and in a reciprocal way, so do the subordinate classes. They too can exert a leverage and a disciplinary compulsion on state institutions ostensibly "designed" to contain and disempower them.

If this is the case, then it is clear that the integration of the subordinate classes into the Jamaican party-union cartel after 1938 could not indefinitely be regarded as the stroke of venal political brilliance that radical intellectuals claimed it was. To be sure, the creation of the two parties with their multi-class memberships did produce the integrative and demobilizing functions that critics attributed to them. The divisive, factional, and alienating character of the parties and their manipulative political leadership confirmed the radicals' critique of party politics, particularly its clientelist expression, as a choke on the political development of the subordinate classes.

Yet the more-than-fifty-year durability and enormous popularity of the parties, against dire predictions of their demise, is a stubborn reminder that, lacking alternatives, the poor see in them a means of achieving at least some of their needs. The history of modern party politics in Jamaica since 1938, particularly its clientelism and rival populisms after 1962, is also certainly the history of the exercise of popular social power inside these ostensibly bourgeois political parties. The late Carl Stone's lonely insistence on this facet of politics in the parties, and his anatomy of the influence of the poor in them, is a useful reminder that neither the incubus of clientelism nor the agendas of political elites are effective barriers to popular pressures inside the political parties (Stone 1980). These pressures from below are now so well institutionalized that they have come to define the political culture of the parties. Indeed, the parties have become so sharply inflected toward representing competing versions of popular needs that social conflict in Jamaica is defined not by the labor-capital antimony, but by party competition to win support from the poor and to bring benefits to them.

This rivalry, responding to the social influence of the disadvantaged classes in the parties' and nationalist elites' sponsorship of popular causes, has led to a bidding war for electoral support from the majority classes. It has spawned an infamous "benefits politics" that established the principle of what can only be called the "customary feeding rights" of the poor. It has triggered rival party populisms, competing people-oriented public policies, and the sponsored ascent of individuals from the working class and the unemployed to positions of prominence and notoriety within the parties and in the country at large. The nepotistic distribution of government jobs, working-class housing, land, contracts for construction projects, tickets for farm work abroad, and support monies and vehicles for the activist vanguard has been a common feature of the Jamaican political landscape for several decades.

But if the class makeup, ideological orientation, and benefits politics of the parties attest to the direct and mediated social power of the poor inside them, then the militant, often-successful independent efforts of partisans from the poorer class who compel the parties to satisfy poor peoples' "customary rights" are also potent demonstrations of subaltern power. This capacity for compulsion is especially evident in circumstances where antagonistic power from below comes into conflict with political elites' attempt to monopolize both the sponsorship and disposition of benefits to the poor.

This bid from below for a role in the sponsorship and disposition of goods has contributed to the contentious politics that flows from subalterns' efforts to intervene in processes that affect them. And in the context of Jamaican benefits politics, this contestation is ultimately about attempts from below to nourish the "partisan political body" of the poor in circumstances where a party is seen as not doing enough for its own supporters and is regarded as being too "soft" in dealing with other sections of the poor whose party happens to be out of power. This is the internecine struggle by activists of the victorious party to satisfy popular partisan appetites, not only by devouring the spoils of war but also by militantly intervening to block any trickle-down of benefits to supporters of the defeated party. Insiders' accounts, news reports, and official inquiries document this nasty civil war inside the parties, as street-level activists and supplicants from poor neighborhoods battle with party officials over the disposition of political spoils. This factionalism within and between the parties, driven by benefits politics, cannot therefore be blamed solely on the party bosses' devious manipulation of their supporters. Poor people's stout defense of their customary feeding rights and their success in blocking party plans for disposition of benefits indicate the enormous leverage they possess over the distribution of political goods in Jamaica, and confirm the potency of their influence on an important area of party policy.

This ability, from within the party space, to derail the plans of party bosses and alter their calculations, is confirmed by other forms of insurgent actions from below. It is useful to think of these actions as governed by the popularly-held image of politics as the process of "eating or being eaten."[2] This imagery is captured in the vivid metaphors in popular language when the poor speak of a government's "share out" of political bounty and the quest by the disadvantaged to "eat out" the bounty of benefactors. This is the language the poor use to characterize their experience of Jamaican politics. In popular parlance, "politricks" is the experience of being eaten up by the parties and dismembered by strategies of the state. To therefore protect the corporeal body of the poor, the latter have adopted the self-defensive strategy of jockeying with others to feast on the state while compelling the parties to satisfy the hunger of only their backers.

This pressure on the parties to "share out" only to their loyal supporters, is matched therefore by poor peoples' insistence on "eating out" the largesse of the state, or that of its unfortunate agents. Desperate for material improvements, their appetites slaked with the meager spoils of scare benefits, many from the ranks of the poor have turned to feeding hungrily on the body of the state itself. In this cannibalizing of the state, the poor gnaw at its vitals, taking huge and unauthorized bites out of its funds, its property, and even its time. The drama of much of contemporary Jamaican politics is really about a Leviathan that masticates the body of the poorer classes by "eating them out" with levies and punishments, while permitting a few to nourish at its body.

Of course, while benefits politics encourages this feasting on the state, it is still the case that contrary values in defense of the public interest are sufficiently strong in the political culture that state agents are sometimes compelled to curb excesses in the feeding frenzy. From time to time, therefore, gormandizers nibbling away from below are inadvertently caught in the act by some lonely public official whose disclosure triggers a mini-scandal which is then pounced on for advantage by an equally complicit opposition party. The outcry surrounding "no shows" for jobs, unfinished work on construction sites, and irregular payments to political contractors for work on projects like the Lilford and Sandy Gullies highlights this steady feasting from below and the public dismay it often provokes.

In the light of public scrutiny, the parties have often had to distance themselves from such embarrassing disclosures. Yet the real embarrassment for the parties is less public dismay than concern with the uncontrolled proliferation of independent initiatives from below, which confiscate state largesse and enervate its functions. This tussle between the parties and their loyalists over how much the poor can siphon off for themselves is not a simple dispute that can easily be settled by forcing the poor to accept unilateral party edicts. On the contrary, the party civil war highlights the growing independence the poor have gained in putting forward their own agendas in opposition to those of party elites. Civil strife in the parties is in large part about the proliferation of these initiatives, the subalterns' battle to defend them, and the parties' episodic and often futile attempts to interrupt this unmolested feeding.

This cannibalistic disposition toward the state is not based, of course, on any inherent moral failure of the poor. Rather, their orientation is anchored in their lived experience of impoverishment, abuse, and marginalization, and in their understanding of the active, as opposed to the official, principles governing politics in the island.

If the party space gave the urban poor broad, if somewhat constrained opportunities to exert a meaningful compulsion with political consequences for the functioning of the state apparatus, then their presence in domains not totally monopolized by the state and the parties gave them numerous opportunities to deploy other repertoires which won for them a modicum of independence from a predatory state. In these other domains they developed self-help strategies, fashioned additional structures of defiance, elaborated norms of subordinate community membership, and advanced alternative ego structures for the recognition of worth, achievement, and honor.

Self-Help Strategies: The Informal Economy

One popular self-help strategy which has caught the attention of several commentators is poor people's well-known retreat to the informal economy. Already a historical feature of the country's economic landscape from slavery times, the informal economy in Jamaica, especially after the 1960s, grew more complex in its configuration, heterogeneous in its class composition, and highly politicized in its functioning. It is an important social space, where the poor and working class have carved out distinct and expanding niches over which they exercise significant control and from which they attempt to exert political influence.

Stimulated by the failure of the formal economic sector to provide jobs at adequate wages for a growing labor force, the informal sector mushroomed in both numbers of activities and the level of citizen participation. Expanding against the background of the 1970s and 1980s, which saw a massive crisis of production, savage IMF-mandated cuts in state spending, reduced state ownership of the economy, as well as drastic cuts in scarce benefits, the informal economy attracted an ever-increasing number of recruits.

Dominated prior to the seventies by street-based traders, vendors, market women, artisans, shopkeepers, and petty hustlers, the informal economic sector saw the entry of new participants and the intensified involvement of others during the turbulent "Wild West" atmosphere of the 1970s and 1980s. Participants included: members of the middle class, particularly its working women, who sought to stem the erosion of their standard of living by buying and selling imported luxury goods out of their homes; independent middle-class freelancers; working-class members of the underworld and politicians connected to the drugs, guns, and contraband trade; state agents and political fixers who took bribes in return for delivering goods or favors; big and medium-sized businessmen who worked outside the law or on its margins to expedite the operations of their firms or to secure the necessary political connections for bringing in contraband and protecting their activities in the trade.

Jostling inside the informal sector with these "respectable" types for advantage and leverage on power were members from the ranks of the urban poor. Among them were: independent commercial traders, primarily poor women, selling imported goods in the streets and from government-built arcades; petty hustlers, street vendors, market women, drug gangs, independent artisans, small shopkeepers, and a dense assortment of self-taught practitioners offering a variety of personal services including cooked meals, hair-care, sexual favors, and sound system music played at the thousands of popular dances in working-class communities across the island each week. The ranks of the poor also included the broad swath of unemployed and unskilled young people from working-class communities, as well as members of the working poor. Among the latter were such social types as barmaids, unskilled workers doing menial work in the service sector, those hiring themselves out as domestics and gardeners, as well as others working in a myriad of jobs for which it was necessary to pass a law establishing a national minimum wage.

It is clear from this description of the class backgrounds of those participating in the informal sector that a significant proportion of the national population from all classes could be found conducting economic activities there. This multi-class composition of the informal sector is significant for both its configuration and its political functioning. The informal sector has three identifiable group structures. These are the state, big business, and people sectors. Political leverage is exercised reciprocally between all three sectors, as state agents, big entrepreneurs, and members of the working class and poor compete for advantage. The informal economic sector, like its formal counterpart, has a structure of power and influence corresponding to the capacities of the agents in it. Unlike the formal economy, which has a similar three-tiered group structure and a preponderance of power exercised by the state and big business, participation in the informal economic sector is weighted demographically in favor of the poorer classes and power there is tendentially exercised to their advantage—precisely because the informal economy is underground, thus making its activities and relations less susceptible to effective policing by the state. Moreover, as sections of the poor grew in confidence they were able to use the *fait accompli* of their massive presence in the sector and their political weight and influence in the parties to turn back, at least in the medium term, efforts of both the state and big importers to rout them.

This is not to say that the state and its agents are not powerfully present in this shadow economy. As observers of the phenomenon remind us, the informal economy is not so uncoupled from the formal economy that the state is barred from acting there. On this point, Robert Fatton's observations with respect to Africa are salutary. As he notes, far from being a major threat to the state, informal economies are significant arenas for state strategies (Fatton 1992:84). These include state agents' use of the informal economy to accumulate capital, the devolution of state functions to the informal sector in times of massive shortages of resources, and the active collusion of rulers in black markets and the contraband trade.

With this caveat in mind, it seems reasonable to assume that although many states may find it necessary to strategically resort to the informal economy, in instances where democratic control of capitalist economic activity retains some usefulness for the state and entrepreneurs—as it does in the Jamaican context—then neither the bulk of economic activities nor the scope of economic regulation will be developed predominantly on the basis of hidden transactions. In such circumstances, economic regulation is premised on the principles of the formal economy and on the transparency of transactions that take place there.

It is precisely the attempt of the poor to hide their economic transactions from the state that gives them a leverage on power, even as this evasion makes them the target of that power. As more and more poor and working people earn their living and conduct much of their economic activities in the informal sector, their activities take on a clear political significance.

Politics in the Informal Commercial Sector

The well-known situation in Jamaica involving informal commercial importers and the presence of street vendors next to commercial establishments selling the same commodities, highlights how this facet of economic activity in the informal sector can quickly become politicized.

Beginning in the 1970s and maturing a decade later, there was a major expansion of commercial vending on the streets of urban Jamaica, and in the capital city in particular. Working-class women and others who had accumulated small amounts of capital invested it in the importation of consumer durables to be sold at high markups in the business districts next to the stores of big commercial enterprises. This development could not long be ignored either by the state or the large commercial importers concerned about their profits being undercut by vendors who stole their customers, paid no income taxes, and avoided duties on their imports.

From the 1970s to the present, a triangular war of attrition involving the state, big business, and the vendors has been fought with no clear victor in sight. In the socialist seventies, the vendors appeared to have had the upper hand, as a populist party, anxious not to alienate the grassroots, turned a blind eye to complaints by big commercial importers who decried this competition as unfair. Emboldened in these years by the People's National Party (PNP's) defense of the poor, and alert to the weaknesses of a cowed and panicked business class, squadrons of sidewalk vendors faced down and intimidated their rivals into frightened retreat.

By the 1980s, however, the tide had turned against the vendors as the more conservative Jamaica Labor Party came to power at the beginning of the decade. Seeking to reverse the pervasive sense of disorder on the streets, and being more sympathetic to the cries of the business class, the JLP dealt with the vendors with the inducements of carrot and stick. The vendors would be recognized as legitimate entrepreneurs, they would be housed in clean and modern arcades in the shopping districts, but they would pay their way by giving the state its dues in the form of fees and import duties. If they chose to ignore these edicts, then their goods would be confiscated at the docks and airports, and any return to prohibited areas would cause the police to be unleashed against them.

As this war wore on into the 1980s, the vendors remained hostile and undeterred by this political offensive against them. As soon as the public relations benefits of the exercise in routing them from the sidewalks wore off, and the vigilance of the authorities waned, the vendors promptly returned to their accustomed places near the big stores. Still, by the late 1980s many from their ranks had resigned themselves to selling to reduced numbers of consumers in government-built arcades; others struck deals with big merchants to import and sell their goods on the sidewalks and in the arcades, while all resigned themselves to paying import duties, though many still evaded them by resorting to bribes.

It is clear from the foregoing that in this area of economic self-help, a section of the hustling urban poor was not only able to create a means for survival, but was also modestly successful in fighting off adversaries with far greater resources. Although the vast majority of the scuffling poor in the informal sector remained untouched by the state's attempts to tax or regulate them, the state's regulation of the *importers* among the poor signalled a major breakthrough for it, as it successfully captured some of the income from the informal sector.

In the meantime, the social relations of marginality would spawn bonds of solidarity in the sector as a community of economic interests sprang up. Lacking the resources used by their bigger competitors, enterprising petty entrepreneurs nonetheless conducted their own "market research" on the needs of the urban poor and discovered needs they could serve. Street hustlers, market women, commercial traders, and artisans invented new markets. And where they did not create needs, they certainly recognized ones they could fill in a declining economy characterized by skyrocketing prices and major shortages in consumer goods. As the case of the informal commercial importers showed, this branch of the entrepreneurial poor recognized the potential of the market for cheap imported goods and brought these goods to satisfy consumers avid for their wares. In so doing, the importers and allied petty entrepreneurs helped secure a community of interests from below for their activities. Poor consumers found cheaper goods in the thriving street trade, many traders in turn made good profits from high markups, and the vested interests of both buyers and sellers in these activities tended to strengthen the relationship and deepen subordinate community commitment to informality as a mode of economic exchange.

Structures of Defiance

In postcolonial Jamaica, major political opposition to the state has come not so much from the ranks of the working class or peasantry but primarily from the vast layer of the urban poor and the unemployed. One instance of this conflict was evident in the struggle over control of poor communities in Kingston. In this struggle, actors from poor and working-class communities found themselves swept into a vortex that pulled them to do the bidding of state agents coveting power and influence in poor communities and pressured them to find spaces for autonomy and even to act against the interests of their sponsors. The case of Claude "Jack" Massop offers an interesting study of this relationship between state patrons, the organization of power in poor communities, and the conflicted role of community notables there. Massop's rise and eventual murder by the state, captures both the capacity of long-time loyalists to break party ranks and the brutal means the state was prepared to employ to keep figures revered by the poor from taking them outside the suzerainty of the parties.

Massop was born in Western Kingston in 1949, in the early, fractious years of electoral competition. The forties and fifties saw the parties fighting nasty wars for the votes of a population desperate for improvements in its circumstances. In many precincts bottles, stones, sticks, and knives competed with lofty appeals and heated, demagogic attacks as freshly-minted, often rowdy politicians competed for votes throughout the country.

Nowhere were those battles fought more bitterly than in the precincts of West Kingston. By the time young Massop had become a teenager in 1962, that war appeared settled for the time being with the electoral victory of Edward Seaga, an unlikely young campaigner of Lebanese origins. The fresh-faced and white-skinned Edward Seaga had apparently done the impossible: as a "white man," with no national name recognition, he had won handily in an electoral district known for its squalor, human degradation, poverty-ridden itinerant population, and no-holds-barred competition for votes from an overwhelmingly Black and despised population. The story of Seaga's early rise to power cannot be told here. However, for young "Jack" Massop, the swath cut by Seaga's passage through West Kingston in this period would be fateful, as the handsome, stockily built dark-skinned youth witnessed the violent, brawling competition for votes in his community and the Seaga victory there.

By the time Seaga next faced the voters and his determined PNP foes in 1967, Massop had become a major player in "holding" the West Kingston constituency for the politician. From his fourteen years of intimate contact with the community, the canny Seaga had established a loyal following among the poor people there. Where other politicians made hollow promises and then moved on to campaign in more hospitable constituencies, Seaga maintained his presence in West Kingston long after his first forays there in 1953 as an anthropologist gathering data for ethnographies of Jamaican religious sects.

Highly knowledgeable about the people, culture, and ecology of the area, Seaga was advantageously poised to plumb the area for votes. Compared to his black-skinned rivals, who tried to discredit him by suggesting that he lacked ambition for wanting to represent so benighted a district, Seaga used his knowledge of the area, and especially his recognition of the role unemployed males played in the social networks there, to advance his political fortunes. It was no doubt this intimate knowledge of male youth culture and the importance of their networks that brought young Massop to Seaga's attention as a figure whom he could mentor and employ in his bid for re-election.

What brought Massop to Seaga's attention in particular was his popularity among the rebellious youths in the area. Massop had apparently earned the respect of community youths by force of his tough reserve, community loyalty, broad and open generosity, and winning ways with women. These qualities counted for much in the ghettos of urban Jamaica, and Massop's early readiness to actively protect his friends in the community and spend his money on them at the popular dances he attended and sometimes sponsored suggested an attractive personality a cut above the rest.

This independent popularity of the unemployed youth was quickly converted into a political resource for the politician as Massop and the emergent "rude boys" of Wellington and Charles Streets fought off waves of assaults launched by PNP partisans in 1967. With reciprocal violence and intimidation, the Seaga youths, backed by seasoned gunmen, defied the PNP's attempt to dislodge them from the enclaves from which PNP adherents could then control the coveted constituency. The violent politics of creating a garrison community by routing supporters of the opposition party from their homes continued in earnest as Massop and his "corner boys" successfully beat back this assault, thereby immeasurably assisting Seaga in securing his 1967 electoral victory.

Now well-entrenched in the constituency, and seen as a rising star in national politics, both Seaga's and Massop's political fortunes increased in the ensuing years. In the case of the latter, he won a special role as a community-based dispenser of patronage for the politician. Whether at the construction site for the modern Tivoli housing complex, which Seaga brought to his constituency in 1963 and extended in 1966, or at the venue for the building of the new National Stadium, Massop played the "broker" role assigned to party loyalists who made sure that their supporters got the choice jobs. Of course, as a veteran party street fighter, Massop would also have had under his command several armed men who comprised the early form of the party militia, which was deployed to protect these sites from jobseekers of the opposing party.

This link to power, and the distribution of largesse it afforded, earned combatants like Massop the title of a "Top Ranking." This was the honorific given by the Kingston poor only to the most seasoned fighters who could bring resources to their communities and who were admired for their cruelty to adversaries and active solicitousness to their natal communities. Bravado, links to the powerful, and respect among the poor defined the place of the "Top Rankings" in these communities.

Despite his growing notoriety as a "badman" among law enforcement officials, Massop's reputation among the poor and working people of West Kingston and its environs remained unsullied. His deceptively gentle mien, which hid the tough inner fighter and merciless partisan for his cause, no doubt endeared him to many in the ghettos. The young males who belonged to rival gangs and the phalanx of unemployed youths who, along with Massop, attended football matches, gambled at the races, and went to the dances to hear the latest recording artists from the ghettos, admired and respected him. And though Massop had his detractors among heady partisans from the PNP, its "Top Rankings" also respected him, and even consorted with him at venues where the poor took their leisure.

While Massop could mete out brutal justice to his political adversaries if provoked, his response to a domestic crisis in 1969 disclosed something about his essential character that tended to confirm the popular reputation he enjoyed. Although he had several run-ins with the police during the sixties, Massop was forced to flee the island in that year not because of a direct altercation with the police or with his political adversaries. On the contrary, Massop took off for England after shooting, in the foot, a man who had been physically abusing his mother. Cruelty and solicitousness therefore sent Massop into exile for more than a year.

Upon his return to the island in May 1971, Massop resumed his links with the Tivoli community. However, by this time the politics of the island had changed significantly. Though Tivoli and West Kingston remained loyal to Seaga, vast layers of the unemployed youths, workers, farmers, and other strata were rejecting the JLP and were turning increasingly to the unfurling popular-democratic banner of the PNP. Moreover, by the time Massop returned things had gotten worse overall for the urban poor. Internecine wars in poor communities, fed by the parties, rocked the capital city. Austerity measures undermined their well-being, and the PNP grew suspicious of their growing discontent. Indeed, as the PNP retreated to a defensive posture to protect itself from escalating political violence, this outlook soon turned into a bunker mentality.

One effect of this siege mentality was that Massop and other JLP supporters inside and outside the ghetto, as well as gunmen of all political stripes, were swept up in the dragnet cast by the PNP in the State of Emergency it declared late in 1976. Like many poor people incarcerated by the PNP at this time, Massop would serve several months in prison.

The declaration of the second such emergency in the island's brief postcolonial history, was justified again in the name of national security. As in the previous declaration in 1967, party warriors were fighting street battles which forced the state to intervene on behalf of law and order. However, in the current instance, an impending election in December cast suspicion on the PNP's motives for arresting members of the opposition. This election therefore produced an ominous development—the interdiction of the opposition during a political campaign. Hence, where the parties had hitherto challenged each other on the basis of a rough and often brutal competitive politics in the sixties, the seventies had now introduced a new element of viciousness. In the competition for power and spoils, both parties had resorted to extreme measures in the 1976 electoral campaign. Conforming to well-rehearsed political scripts from the past, each party attempted to associate the other with political deviltry. The JLP painted lurid images of a PNP that would turn the country into a Communist bastion, and the PNP portrayed its adversary as compradors of Washington, prepared to reverse the people's gains and sell them out to capitalists at home and abroad.

But something far more ominous had also emerged by the mid-to-late seventies. This was the naked resort to terror and violence on both sides in the competition for power. What must have concerned Massop within months after leaving detention was the knowledge that the PNP was prepared to use naked force to curb the political violence. The PNP targeted political gunmen, sought out armed socialist bandits who dreamed of creating their own state in the inner city, and interdicted ordinary people who defied the police in poor communities.

By 1978, the PNP's use of extreme measures to deal with the violence and the rebellious poor produced a state of siege throughout the country. Curfews, interdictions on the streets, patrols, and national security laws became the norm. With the toll of these measures falling heavily on the youth and poor communities, it is clear that the search for political "consent" in more halcyon days had given way to "force" in the seventies. This PNP policy was a real threat to Massop, other "Top Rankings" and independent gunmen. If the PNP had already decided to eliminate gunmen or those they feared would take up arms against them, then those who bore arms for whatever reasons had to be even more careful of the state's assassination squads now pitted against them. As a group of young men from a JLP enclave in Kingston was to discover on January 5, 1978, the PNP was prepared to kill unemployed youths from hostile communities on the suspicion that they were party gunmen. In the short term, this policy produced a paradoxical "success" for the state: it drove the leaders of the various militias to close ranks and forge a separate peace. But in halting the violence, which the state desired, the gunmen also forged an unexpected unity from below, which threatened to undermine a major pillar of party domination in the country—the maintenance of disunity among the poor.

Unity from Below: The 1978 Peace Truce

The killing of five unarmed youths in an ambush by the army, and the miraculous escape of nine others at the Green Bay firing range, became a *cause celèbre*, exposing as it did the terroristic face of the Jamaican state. Ever aware of shifts in state repression, the "Rankings" from several poor communities recognized the massacre for what it was: a turn to death squads to eliminate defiant youths caught up in the gun politics of the time. Within days, community notables of the poor called a halt to their wars on behalf of the political parties.[3]

This noble declaration and the determined effort to put the hopes of the poor into practice was a major threat to the parties. Unanimity and collective action by the poor on their own behalf in this crucial area, could undermine the party pillars holding up the edifice of political domination in the country. The gradual expansion of the truce to other politically volatile areas where hardened, partisan enemies put away their guns and ammunition to embrace, drink, and socialize across formerly "no go" zones was a breakthrough from below of major proportions.

Ras Rupert, a Rastafarian from the area, captured the sentiments of the unemployed poor who stood to benefit most from the truce:

> Unity wonderful but we want better housing, better living standard for all people whether JLP or PNP. We cannot allow politicians to come into West Kingston and divide youths anymore. The situation must remedy. We have to get together. We are the ones living in degrading conditions. This is west and that is what the struggle is all about. The peace is a start. We belong to the poor class. We must defend the poor class. It is not time for politics and selfishness.[4]

As this and similar remarks show, the urban poor, no matter how destitute, were aware of the political traps that ensnared them. These remarks, repeated to the press in several variations, clearly disclosed the "imagined community" to which the poor aspired; one in which they could find an elusive justice, live in peace and unity, find work without discrimination, and be housed in accommodations fit for human beings.

But these common human aspirations could not easily be realized without the cooperation of the political parties. Taken aback by this challenge from below, the parties and their leaders paid lip service to the truce but acted to undermine it. Despite severe internal difficulties, and threats from independent gangs who refused to cooperate, the truce still lasted an astonishing ten months before finally unravelling in November. With Massop bemoaning the presence of "forces out there who are trying to destroy the youth," another attempt by the poor to establish unity from below failed, but not before forcing the parties to the margins in this momentous political initiative, while compelling them to gingerly cooperate, for a time, with an exercise whose agenda was to subvert their dominance.

In this dark moment for the Kingston poor, "Jack" Massop could only be deeply disillusioned by the failure of the initiative he had helped launch. It remains unclear whether Massop had earned the enmity of his mentor for his actions in the truce or had simply become careless in the face of the continuing PNP hunt for gunmen. However, within three months of his cryptic criticism, in October, of unnamed "forces" undermining the people's efforts, and his assertion that "no individual can influence or brainwash [us] into destroying our fellow people," Massop was killed in a hail of police bullets, with his hands in the air, on a busy thoroughfare near the Tivoli enclave from which he ruled.

Bandits, Gangs, and the State

Massop's death in February 1979, was only the latest in a series of police killings in the late seventies. Given free reign by the authorities to curb gun crimes, the police, particularly the brutal Mobile Reserves, had stepped up their surveillance of the youths, many of whom belonged to street gangs. Such juvenile street gangs and their rivalry were long a part of the Kingston underworld. For more than twenty years, the Jamaican state had fought these gangs, but without much success. In the late fifties and sixties some of them, like the Phoenix and Viking gangs, were incorporated into the political parties. But despite attempts to assimilate them, spiralling unemployment drew hundreds of young males into the ranks of the gangs. By the time Massop was killed, several well-entrenched independent gangs, with their membership rituals, had developed alongside the violent, youth-involved partisan militias.

But where the state could sometimes domesticate the political violence of the early gangs, this strategy became less possible in subsequent years. As the economic decline of the seventies and persisting austerity policies of the eighties trimmed benefits politics, the unemployed poor became more resourceful in surviving in the new straitened circumstances. Deeply alienated and having few ties to the parties or their militias, the youths fashioned a new gang culture and improved on the banditry that had always been a feature of criminal gangs in Jamaica.

It should be recalled that in their initial incarnation in the fifties, the early gangs fought the usual turf battles with primitive weapons such as knives, stones, and broken bottles. Occasionally, a gun—stolen in a robbery of a shopkeeper or from delivery drivers for Desnoes and Geddes, the huge bottling company—would find its way into the arsenal of the gangs. But in the seventies, knives had given ways to guns, as new sources for the weapons opened up. These avenues ranged from those smuggled in for the political wars and protected from police interference, to those brought in by the thriving drug trade, which by the late seventies began to include some cocaine. A few weapons came, as well, from the stockpiles of the politicized army and the police, who sold their weapons to political sympathizers. Of course, the open and largely unpatrolled coastal waters and the heavy passenger traffic between the island and the American mainland provided other routes.

With access to guns so relatively easy, it is not surprising that the latter-day gangs had some of the most sophisticated weapons in their arsenal. Unlike their counterparts in the partisan sector who wielded guns on behalf of "politics," the criminal gangs typically employed their weapons to rob and plunder. For both "armies," the gun brought users its own seductive mystique, and possession of the weapon became a source of power in its own right. "Gun power" for the militant poor in the seventies and eighties meant both a source of command over populations and a symbol of swaggering, male bravado.

This conjunction of personal mystique and territorial control afforded by the gun seduced many youths into the gangs. Led by "Rankings" or "Generals," these gangs robbed banks, conducted stickups of big firms, and fought pitched battles with the police and army. That they were fearless in engaging the security forces and often outgunned them to the point where policemen drew back from confronting them in the streets, only increased their notoriety and the "heroic" popularity of their leaders. Indeed, despite the numerous coups claimed by the state in its subsequent killing of notorious gunmen, it remains the case that a tiny minority of outlaw figures had managed to set the terms of the national agenda, divert major resources of the country to crime control, and heighten public disillusionment with the state's inability to stamp out the criminal gangs.

The Subaltern's Identity and Moral Culture

It is clear from the foregoing that in their social relations with the powerful since the seventies, the militant urban poor have altered the Jamaican political landscape. They have exercised a marked compulsion on the designs of the powerful, fashioned innovative strategies of self-help, and formed structures of defiance—all of which have had serious limiting effects on the capacity of the state to exercise an untrammeled sway over groups with far fewer resources.

Despite the remarkable nature of these achievements, the social power of the Jamaican poor is not reducible to the negative influence they exercise over the powerful. The complementary dimension of this aspect of their power is to be found in the production of cultural structures that contribute to the group's self-formation and identity. In this sense, expressions of the group's social power take on a generative and positive dimension with implications for the group's "civilizational" possibilities. Expressed differently, this means that as a subordinate group engages in social relations of power, their activities not only alter the field of power relations but change who they are and what they are capable of achieving as well.

With this other dimension of social power in mind, it is apparent that the social struggles of the urban poor, and the conditions under which they conduct that struggle, are themselves part of the social relations that define them. These social relations alter the subaltern's cultural identity and shape their moral culture. Necessarily, this moral culture, in its turn, alters the social relations, and so on in a continual dynamic.

What this cycle has created among the urban poor in Jamaica is an identity and moral culture informed by responses to *marginality* (social, political, economic, cultural), *migration* (domestic and trans-national), and *repression* (bodily and spatial). While the Jamaican peoples share common cultural traits involving these nodes of identity, only the urban poor experience with acute intensity the conflated pressures of all three nodes. This fact probably accounts for their unusual capacity for political militancy compared to the rest of the population.

For the urban poor, their experience of migration has had a double effect. On the one hand, it has produced a sense of homelessness and wandering. This is represented in the moral culture of the poor which exhibits an exilic sensibility that drastically reduces any sense of commitment to Jamaica as a place worth sacrificing for. The modular identitarian clothing for this sense of homelessness is, of course, the Rastafari. However, since not all youths are Rastafarians, that clothing may change. As the sixties showed, the identitarian clothing worn by the poor ranged from "sufferer" to "rude boy" to the "raggamuffin" and so on. These are exilic clothing within domestic social space and ego-structures for personality formation.

On the other hand, the experience of migration yields a sense of worldliness. It is expressed in the morality of the poor as cultural cosmopolitans who express a hybridity in which global culture is synthesized with local culture. The renowned cultural cosmopolitanism of the Caribbean people, for example, is reproduced within the ranks of the Jamaican poor. Living in global time and space, they imbibe all the historic data in global space whether it is knowledge of events in Africa or developments concerning the latest breakthroughs in scientific knowledge. These resources are then synthesized within the "local" cultural space. In this sense, the urban poor partake of a New World cultural modernity that finds them shaping and being shaped by developments in global space. As several commentators have noted, Bob Marley's music remains the model for the cultural expression of this modernity among the poorer classes.

Similarly, the experience of repression yields its own moral culture and identitarian forms. From the review above, it is clear that repression has produced a moral culture characterized by the struggle for control of free physical and mental spaces. With respect to the search for autonomous physical space, the moral culture here is one of asserting authority; seeking to "run things" without interference, whether it be a gang, neighborhood, business, or street corner, or control of the body. The mental analog would be control over thoughts, ideas, and cultural possibilities.

For the most part, the existential responses to repression seem to find expression in demonstrations of prowess, hardiness, courage, and aggressiveness. Their identitarian clothing are familiar: gang leader, political and drug "Donmanship," and mercenary crime figure.

Marginality in its turn captures the general experience expressed in the other two nodes. Marginality's impact on moral culture is contradictory, exhibiting both centrifugal and centripetal norms. The former leans toward group annihilation, internecine conflicts, and beggar-thy-neighbor attitudes. The latter contains communitarian impulses produced by common circumstances and powerful loyalties to neighborhood and natal communities. As I have shown above, marginality is productive; it yields repertoires of self-defense, defiance, and innovation. The cultural, political, economic forms expressed within the ranks of the poor, some of which have been described here, are powerful testimonies to their inventive brilliance.

Lessons from the Social Power of the Urban Poor

I have argued above that the social actions of the urban poor produce a social power and that this power has been a fulcrum of change in Jamaica over the last thirty years. The power of the poor has been a fulcrum because of the effects it has produced on the state and on the field of power. The power of the poor has also been a fulcrum of change by contributing to the self-formation, and "making," of the urban poor in terms of their identities, moral culture, and politics.

It is evident from the foregoing that the urban poor have exercised some leverage on both the state and power in Jamaican society. This compulsion has expressed itself in several ways. By their disobedience, non-cooperation, and "indiscipline," the poor have dictated, from the margins, one of the major concerns and agendas of the Jamaican state—the suppression of non-cooperation from below. This concern, produced by the actions of the poor, has caused the state to devote significant resources and energy to dealing with this dissidence. That the Jamaican state and its agents have not decisively expunged the myriad forms of such dissidence, has contributed to the perception that it has lost control of the society. The state's attempts to reverse these perceptions by launching violent and largely ineffective campaigns to stamp out these forms of opposition, have only deepened public cynicism and disgust. By making it difficult for the state to rule, its opponents have intensified the crisis of the state.

This does not mean, however, that the state is about to topple in the face of such difficulties. On the contrary, its agents have used this very crisis to secure the reproduction of their power. The inability to curb violent crime, for example, is used to justify further security measures to protect public order.

But while the poor may be reduced to achieving only small victories over the state, the social relations in which they participate also contribute to their cultural formation. Their struggles have disclosed the capacity for unity, albeit fleeting. They have also developed the hard-to-suppress structures of defiance and modes of political self-help described above. In addition, the ego-structures and the moral culture produced by their local struggles and participation in world culture and global space have formed them as cultural moderns having a hybrid sensibility with all its advantages and discontents. Complementing the protean structure of this cultural makeup is an equally heterogeneous moral culture. From the cases discussed above, that moral culture seems to have core values defined by a trademark quest for mastery, self-ownership, leadership, respect, and the taking of risks to achieve group needs. This core in the various expressions of their moral culture holds the key to any meaningful response from the top to the needs of the urban poor in Jamaica.

Lastly, the militant urban poor have paid a high price for their defiance. Confronting power in the ways they have has taken a severe toll. Whole communities have been destroyed; thousand of women have been widowed and children orphaned. The oppositional response to alienation in Jamaica is often more destructive to the poor than to those whom they challenge. For all their bravery and defiance, popular figures like Massop and hundreds of other young men are dead. They may be martyrs to their communities, but a community's struggle cannot long be waged in this form lest it result in the ruin of that community.

Similarly, a popular moral culture that has as one of its elements the politics of "feasting" on those at the top who have more, may not open up onto a platform for taking power and using it to address the urgent needs of the subordinate classes; the politics of feasting may instead produce a social cannibalism in which the vulnerable poor become the likely targets of opportunity. Likewise, outlawry-as-politics, "indiscipline"-as-resistance, and solidarity based on identity-in-warmaking may not produce the ends the urban poor desire in the long run, or open a path to progress; instead, it may simply lead to a descent into chaos, a degeneration into barbarism, and the ruin of the contending classes.

Unfortunately, the return to draconian measures such as hangings, the demand for floggings in prisons, and tolerance for state terror are more likely to hasten, rather than forestall these ominous prospects. In a society where official corruption is extensive and where white collar criminals routinely flout and escape the disciplinary effects of the law, re-imposing these odious measures on the rebellious poor can only deepen their cynicism, intensify their hatred, and provoke their active rejection of official authority.

The remedy for such ills will be found neither in unconvincing moral appeals for the poor to "behave" themselves, nor in half-hearted and inconclusive debate about constitutional reform. What is required is an end to benefits politics with its violence-incurring, and dependency-inducing, culture of victimization. Depoliticizing the delivery of basic services to poor communities will improve prospects for social peace and save lives. Despite the parties' extreme reluctance to take this step, spiralling social violence—which is now a real threat to the economy, especially the tourist sector—and the growth of numerous economic self-help initiatives among the poor, are now inexorably pressuring the parties to re-assess their fealty to benefits politics.

The content of urban poor people's protests dramatizes the need for community development without the heavy hand of partisan-ship and the closure of free space for political expression. Poverty, joblessness, and lack of opportunity in poor urban communities produce frustration, alienation, and resentment, especially among the young. This alienation is aggravated by the monopoly and abuse of power at the center, by its neglect of local needs, and by its creation of captive populations. Power must be devolved to local communities and resources transferred to them in the context of a national plan for urban community reconstruction and political re-form.

The negative consequences of the appalling denial of political freedom and citizenship rights to significant segments of the na-tional population are now acutely evident to Jamaicans, and espe-cially to the political class. Whether they will move beyond indirec-tion, footdragging, and hypocrisy to adopt meaningful reforms in the immediate future remains to be seen.

NOTES

1. I have tried to avoid using the term "underclass" to describe the ur-ban poor in Jamaica. The concept has all kinds of unfortunate connotations associated with American politics and theorizing which simply do not fit the Jamaican situation. For the urban context, I prefer using "the poor" or "the ranks of the poor" to describe not indigents, but that vast subordinate strata that can be defined not only by their role in production but also their social status. The "poor" therefore includes the lower ranks of the working class, the unemployed, and the self-employed. These are the so-cially oppressed who can be defined by a common status of overwhelming marginality, victimization, and repression.

2. In Jamaica Talk, the correct word is "nyam" which carries a richer connotation of the feast, as in the following typical exchange among poor Jamaicans: "How yu do?" "Bwoy, de govament ah nyam me out!"

3. See the editorial section of *The Daily Gleaner*, January 11, 1978, p.1.

4. See the editorial pages of *The Daily Gleaner*, January 13, 1978, p.11.

REFERENCES

Azarya, Victor and Naomi Chazan. 1987. "Disengagement from the State in Africa: Reflections on the Experience of Ghana and Guinea." *Comparative Studies in Society and History* 19:1.

Fatton, Robert Jr. 1992. *Predatory Rule*. Boulder: Lynne Rienner.

Hyden, Goran. 1980. *Beyond Ujaama In Tanzania: Underdevelpoment and an Uncaptured Peasantry*. London: Heineman.

Scott, James. 1985. *Weapons of the Weak*. New Haven: Yale University Press.

Stone, Carl. 1980. *Democracy and Clientelism in Jamaica*. New Brunswick: Transaction Books.

Szelenyi, Ivan *et al.* 1988. *Socialist Entrepreneurs: Embourgeoisement in Rural Hungary*. Madison: University of Wisconsin Press.

Joyce Toney

10

Women, Urbanization, and Structural Adjustment in St. Vincent

Since the decline of the sugar industry in the nineteenth century, the island of St. Vincent has been largely mired in economic poverty and deprivation. For most of that period, St. Vincent was a colony of Great Britain, and to a large extent its welfare was dependent on the economic and political policies of that country. In 1979, the nation of St. Vincent and the Grenadines declared independence. Although it remained a member of the British Commonwealth, its newly acquired status presupposed that the people would be responsible for their own economic and political destinies.

Unfortunately, the major period since independence has coincided with the economic crisis that began in the 1970s. Most of the crisis was the result of conditions originating in the larger international arena. St. Vincent and the Grenadines had no control over the Arab oil boycott, for example; and the island was simply another pawn in the global Cold War games. Nevertheless, the international scenario had a major impact on any potential economic and political policies that the government planned to develop.

Thus, the nation was going through birthing pains at a time of global economic retrenchment. The people had to learn to provide for themselves in a world that was not necessarily accommodating to their needs. The government tried various stopgap solutions, ranging from an emphasis on tourism to offshore banking and widespread emigration of the people. Any relief that came from these activities quickly dissipated in the face of the global economy.

As a consequence, the government joined other developing nations in accepting the economic measures referred to as structural adjustment.

Although the Prime Minister of St. Vincent and the Grenadines, James Mitchell, was not at the meeting in Nassau, Bahamas, in 1984, like other Caribbean Community (CARICOM) heads of government he accepted the report, "Measures for Structural Adjustments in the Member States of the Caribbean Community." The document was prepared primarily by the Caribbean Development Bank, but the sentiments were essentially the dictates of the United States government, the International Monetary Fund (IMF), and the World Bank (Deere *et al.* 1990).

This so-called Nassau Understanding committed the leaders to recognizing that "structural adjustment is an integral part of the development process. It essentially involves a conscious and determined shift to a new development path to accelerate development, while adapting to major external or internal shocks to the economic system" (CARICOM Perspective 1984). Governments were to try to boost exports, which, because of the low wages in the Caribbean, would eventually help the entire population. At the same time, the governments would rely on the free market to set prices, internally and externally. Emphasis was to be put on privatization, because the assumption was that the private sector is more efficient than the state (Deere *et al.* 1990). It was also assumed that the private sector would find capital mainly from foreign investments. As far as the Caribbean population was concerned, the implementation of these policies called for a tremendous amount of financial restraint, as well as cuts in social programs (McAfee 1991).

On the whole, the economic problem was interpreted to be a direct result of the shortage of foreign exchange. The origins of the economic crisis could be directly linked to rising oil prices of the 1970s. At the same time, Vincentians, like other Caribbean people, continued to import more food and other items (Deere 1990:133). The external debt incurred by the government of St. Vincent and the Grenadines escalated from $3 million in 1975 to $42 million in 1988 (*Ibid.*: 34).

In the Nassau Understanding, governments promised to steer their countries away from a situation of economic and social breakdown, but the success of that promise is highly debatable in the case of St. Vincent. True to the worst fears of the leadership, there was an upsurge of the chronic discontent, crime, violence, and political extremism that they had hoped to avoid as a consequence of their policies. In St. Vincent, all segments of the society suffered under the burdens of the new economic order, but the group that suffered most were women, who were at the direct receiving end of the fallout of economic adjustment.

As the economy worsened, Vincentian and other Caribbean people were forced to make do with less in response to mandates from the IMF and other banking agencies (Senior 1991). Women, in particular, experienced tremendous changes brought about by the new political status, and by the economic restructuring that was taking place around them.

From the time of their inception these policies were found to be biased against women and "fundamentally exploitative of women's time, labour and sexuality" (Antrobus 1989:17–35). At least two of the criteria for structural adjustment, cuts in social services and the removal of price controls and subsidies, had direct impacts on women's role and status. The reduction in social services had a drastic effect on the lives of children and the elderly, who are generally under the care of women.

Much has been written about the general conditions that confronted the women in the region as their leaders tried to balance budgets and maintain democracy at the same time (Mohammed 1988; Antrobus 1990; Deere *et al.* 1990). This chapter examines the condition of Vincentian women in the capital city of Kingstown. Although other census areas in St. Vincent are growing at a more rapid rate than Kingstown, the capital with its adjacent suburbs has a population of more than 27,000 people and a density of 8,140 persons per square mile, compared to 733 persons per square mile for the remainder of mainland St. Vincent (St. Vincent and the Grenadines Statistical Office Ministry of Finance and Planning 1991).

The problems resulting from structural adjustment affected all parts of the island, but the major effects were felt in this urban area. The population had come to expect some of the material benefits that accompany economic development, and that cushion was being slowly removed in the 1980s. Unlike their rural counterparts, Kingstown people had to buy all of their food, because they could not turn to the land to tide them over hard times. It is not difficult to understand, therefore, why the urban women were at the forefront of the struggle against the increasing economic deprivation that was affecting the nation. They, more than any other group, articulated the grievances and found ways of confronting the increasing social and economic problems.

The methods used by these women to cope with these issues are examined with the specific objective of determining the extent to which gender consciousness affected their responses. Bunche and Carillo (1990: 70–82) recognize a distinction between two types of female response to economic problems in the Third World. Initially, women were mainly interested in inclusion in the ongoing development process in their countries. As international feminism advanced, however, women began to recognize the need for a specific feminist response to their problems. They saw their connections with the larger world of feminism as it was articulated by women in predominantly Western societies. Thus, it will be important to examine the activities of Vincentian women in order to determine to what extent their movement reflected the pattern described by these scholars.

Urban Women and Work in St. Vincent

The nation of St. Vincent and the Grenadines has a total population of about 110,000, of which fifty percent is female. The country is a member of the Organization of Eastern Caribbean States (OECS) and the Caribbean Community (CARICOM). St. Vincent and the Grenadines occupies the unfortunate position of being the poorest country in the Caribbean after Haiti. The island's main economic sources are the banana industry and foreign assistance (World Bank 1992: 2). Furthermore, in 1984, forty percent of the island's population was unemployed, thus sharing with Grenada the status of highest unemployment in the region (Deere et al. 1990).

In the 1990s, St. Vincent continues to be a predominantly agricultural society. 22.8 percent of the entire population and 13.9 percent of the women are agricultural workers. However, the late 1960s and early 1970s saw a rise in manufacturing, particularly in light industry. By 1990 that sector accounted for 8.4 percent of the entire working population and 9.1 percent of women workers. Many former agricultural workers moved into factories established in industrial parks (Ryan 1987:5).

At first the women appeared to be pleased with the new type of labor. It was more reliable than agriculture, and they earned more than the $7.80 EC per day that they received in agricultural work. Female unemployment was declining in relationship to male unemployment. These new industries, mostly owned by foreign companies, saw this unskilled pool of labor as a target for the low wages that would help their industry (Ryan, 1987:4). Once they were employed, the women began to recognize the low wages and the bad working conditions that existed in the factories.

The female workers in The Island Glove Factory were particularly vocal in expressing their grievances against that company, and they called for the recognition of the National Worker's Movement as their bargaining unit. The women complained that they "had been restricted from doing basic necessary things, like using the toilet and speaking to one another during work" (*Ibid.*). The government was reluctant to alienate the company by taking the side of the workers.

As the country continued to fall into debt, conditions deteriorated. The dictates of the Nassau Agreement of 1984 coincided with the decline and departure of the same factories that had helped women find employment. The ten year tax holiday for many factories came to an end, and the foreign investors folded and left the country. The manufacturing sector declined by 12 percent and more than 800 employees lost their jobs (World Bank 1992:3). Once more, female unemployment escalated.

Other forms of economic adjustments made by the government in St. Vincent directly affected women. In the early 1970s, St. Vincent appeared to have a thriving agro-lab business that employed many women. This lab was closed down in the 1980s. Similarly, a crafts market that employed women underwent tremendous decline. This period also coincided with the closing of the garment factories, which provided employment for women. In 1991, over sixty percent of the female heads of household were unemployed or economically inactive.

Yet from the point of view of feminism, the economic problems had important ramifications. The predominance of women in light industry brought together women who could recognize their lowly positions in the economic scheme of things. Throughout the 1980s they protested and unionized as a result of the terrible conditions under which they had to work. Furthermore, they recognized their marginality even more clearly when the factories were abruptly removed and they were further deprived of making a living. These events marked the beginning of working-class feminist consciousness in St. Vincent.

The Family

Much as women's working lives were disrupted by the new economy, perhaps the most drastic effects were imposed on the family. As is the case in the other English-speaking Caribbean countries, the family in St. Vincent takes varied and complex forms. The middle class adheres more closely to a system that emphasizes marriage in a formal sense. This type of marriage carries prestige for the couple and the children, and it is held in high esteem by all segments of the society.

The majority of working class Vincentian women are themselves the heads of single-parent families. They comprise 39 percent of the families in St. Vincent and the Grenadines. Many women live in common-law relationships that generally do not have the stability, and certainly do not have the respectability of legal marriage. In some cases the male head of that household is the absent father in another woman's household. In 1991, "never married" comprised 56 percent of the households in St. Vincent and the Grenadines, an increase from 53.5 in 1980. Married households comprised 33 percent of the population, a decrease from 37 percent in 1980.

In spite of the social realities of marriage and family living in St. Vincent and the Grenadines, it was not until 1980 that the Status of Children Act No. 18 addressed the situation by granting some rights to children born outside of marriage. Today, those children can claim the same property inheritance rights as those born in marriage. The common-law wife, however, has no legal status, and she cannot automatically claim property that is only in the man's name at his death. If a woman wants to lay claim she must resort to legal action to determine if indeed she has any rights (Campbell 1986).

This situation works against women, since most times the woman's contribution to the home is not quantifiable. The amount of work spent caring for the home and making it possible for the man to earn his wages is not considered. In general, therefore, out-of-wedlock relationships operate to the disadvantage of women (Packness 1988). As a result, most women still see a Christian marriage as the preferred situation for themselves and their children, but for economic and social reasons they seldom achieve it.

Much as marriage is an ideal, it is not considered an essential requirement for childbearing. Many women in St. Vincent raise their children without live-in husbands and fathers. Only 19 percent (464) of the children born between 1990 and 1991 were born to a married couple. The other 81 percent (1, 988) were born mostly to women who had never married or were in common-law relationships. Because many of these women have no job or any form of economic stability, they continue to live in their parents' homes or with a member of the extended family. (St. Vincent and the Grenadines Statistical Office Ministry of Finance and Planning 1991).

Although the erratic family structures always had debilitating economic consequences for women, the presence of a supportive extended kinship system minimized much of the social and personal damage that one would expect from such a system. Generations of unmarried Vincentian women raised their children to adulthood with the same type of security and family cohesiveness that one finds in the traditional "Western" family. This survival mechanism, however, is now under siege. Instead of sending a child to live with a more affluent relative, families must keep their children at home. Between 1970 and 1980, the number of families living in a one room house decreased from 8.4 percent to 5.8 percent; in 1991, that figure had again risen to 7.6 percent. Similarly, houses with only two rooms increased by 12.3 percent between 1980 and 1991 (St. Vincent and the Grenadines Statistical Office Ministry of Finance and Planning 1991).

The scarcity of food and other commodities means that family members are no longer able to keep extra people around. In the past when a rural relative did not have cash they compensated their urban kin in kind. Today, however, even in the rural areas traditional gift items such as eggs, chickens, and ground provisions are as expensive as in Kingstown. The mandates of the international organizations created new problems by destroying some of the accepted aspects of small island existence, such as family support and the mutual exchange of goods and services (Tinker 1976; Antrobus 1990:130–136).

Structural adjustment programs led to rising unemployment, political tensions, and an increase in alienation, particularly among the youth. The daily routines connected with the household became more burdensome as income decreased and prices increased. Women had to spend more time planning and preparing because it was so much more difficult to obtain the basic supplies for the home. They had to juggle their time between their breadwinning roles and their care giver roles, as increased pressures disrupted traditional customs.

Cuts in health care spending presented a particularly pressing problem. The general hospital in Kingstown was perceived to be in perpetual shortage of basic supplies. Private wards that existed as early as the 1950s were virtually eliminated, and the hospital had returned to an open-ward system with no sense of privacy. The middle class looked for health care in Barbados, the United States, and other places. The poor and those who needed emergency treatment had to resort to the Kingstown hospital. Criticism of health care helped to unite disparate members of the female population, especially when wrangling between the government and medical personnel led to the departure from the hospital of one of the most popular and efficient gynecologists on the island.

Migration

Women have come to regard migration as one method for coping with the economic problems (Marshall 1981). With the passage in the United States of the favorable Immigration Act in 1965, and the new obstacles to immigration in the United Kingdom, the United States became the favorite country for Vincentian emigrants. There was one major change in immigration patterns, however. In the past most migrants were men, but in this new migration stream, women emigrated and left the men and children behind (Toney 1989).

This situation had its origins partially in the economic conditions that existed in the United States. In the earlier part of the century men left home to find work in industry, which then existed in New York City, for example. In the late twentieth century there is a shortage in this type of male-oriented factory work and an increase in traditional female jobs such as nursing, domestic work, child care, and home health care (Toney 1989). As the Civil Rights movement opened new opportunities for native Black women, Caribbean women stepped in to fill the void. At the same time the women's movement in the United States encouraged white and Black middle-class women to work outside the home, thus increasing the demand for child care and domestic workers.

The female migrant leaves her children with other women at home, and she is expected to send remittances to maintain the children and the others left behind. Sometimes grandmothers and relatives at home receive little or no help from the relatives abroad. Although women who neglect their children become the objects of ridicule and social stigma in the migrant and home communities, some of them for different reasons are unable or unwilling to send the support that their relatives expect. In such cases, the relatives at home must cope with the children who often grow up with a feeling of being unwanted (International Development Research Center 1982).

These social and economic conditions are not new to St. Vincent or elsewhere, but because emigration is more available as an avenue to economic and socal liberation, more women from St. Vincent view it as an option. They are usually encouraged by husbands and family, because they recognize the economic benefits and perceive that female emigration is a sacrifice to be made for the family. It frequently turns out that men cannot fill the role that the mother vacated, and the family suffers from the absence of the mother.

Women and Violence

The breakdown in the family structure inevitably leads to crime and violence against women. In the 1980s, concerned individuals perceived violence against women to have increased, even if they had no concrete statistics to support their views. This concern led the government to pay some attention to the situation and address the precarious position of women in the society. In 1984, the government passed two pieces of legislation that related to the issue. The "Domestic Violence and Matrimonial Proceedings Act, 1984" was meant to discourage violence against all women in their homes, and "The Matrimonial Homes Act" gave both married and common-law-wives some degree of protection against eviction from their homes.

The new emphasis on domestic violence also led the public to realize how little information they had on the subject. A 1971 report conducted by the Inter-American Commission on Women (CIM), called "Background on Statistical Information on Violence in the Region," revealed that there were no data available for St. Vincent on domestic violence (St. Vincent and the Grenadines Women's Affairs Division 1991). As a result, in 1989 the Canadian University Service Organization (CUSO) and the St. Vincent and the Grenadines Women's Affairs Division sponsored a research project on this issue. There were participants from the police department, the medical profession, and the social welfare agencies. The aims of the project were to: (1) "[D]etermine the extent of violence perpetuated against women particularly in the areas of rape, incest, and wife battery; (2) Investigate the socioeconomic status of the women affected; (3) Investigate areas where it occurs; (4) Investigate causes of abuse and how they can be combatted" (*Ibid.*).

The project also aimed to educate the public through programs that would be viewed by institutions and by the public at large. A study of 702 cases in police files revealed that although violence pervades all economic strata, it was much more evident in the "lower socio-economic bracket." Dilys Peters, a high-ranking police officer, concluded that persons in the upper and middle strata of society would be less likely to disclose incidents of battery and other types of abuse. The report spoke to incidents of violence including punching, kicking, slapping, and hair pulling. Women reported fractures, swollen faces, and bites on ears and neck. They were assaulted with instruments including cutlasses, broomsticks, blocks, chairs, buckets, hammers, and bottles. Some women were thrown on the ground after being lifted into the air. In addition, there was continuous verbal and psychological abuse.

Although most violence against women was inflicted by husbands, women were also abused by step-mothers, step-fathers and guardians. The report demonstrated that the laws put into effect five years earlier were either inadequate or constantly being broken by the men. The report mentioned that violence against women was socially acceptable in Vincentian society.

The report called for several measures, including deeper research into the problem and special training for police offficers, the establishment of a Domestic Violence Board, special training for victims and counselors, and strengthening of the women's movement. The findings were used in producing a video documentary on violence against women, and a comic booklet written by Nelcia Robinson called "Belling the Cat," which dealt with the well-kept secret of domestic violence and the ways in which women could protect themselves.

The new discourse surrounding women as victims of crime has had the positive effect of forging links between women of different strata in the society. All women recognize that gender makes them vulnerable to rape and other types of assault. The newly formed, vocal, Committee for the Development of Women led the first demonstrations against violence in December 1985. One of the major supporters of the protest was Norma Keizer, the headmistress of the prestigious Girls High School. The need to address the issue was emphasized when one of the students in the school was brutally murdered by a man in her village. Suddenly, the words and tactics of the supposedly militant CDW would begin to fall on fertile soil within the middle class.

Structural Adjustment and the Development of Women's Organizations

One of the recommendations of the Committe on Violence was a strengthening of the women's movement. While it may be argued that the suggestion had some concrete results, it is more logical to believe that the women's movement was already thriving in 1989. The study itself was an indication that women were willing to organize around gender issues, and that they were willing to bring pressure on the government. One of the results was the increased politicization and radicalization of women's formal organizations in St. Vincent and the Grenadines.

In keeping with the general feminist movement sweeping the Caribbean in the 1970s, Vincentian women organized the National Council of Women (NCW) in 1975. This organization, led by Sheila Douyon, a returned migrant from New York, was a response to the International Year of Women. Although NCW was an umbrella group of mostly middle-class groups such as the Anglican Church Mothers Union and the YWCA, the working-class Rosehall Working Group was also a member. Douyon remained in the leadership until 1983, when she was succeeded by Nelcia Robinson. Robinson helped to change the image of the organization from a traditional women's organization to one that was more political and activist in its orientation.

When the New Democratic Party was elected in 1984, the creation of a women's desk promised a more responsive attitude to women's affairs than the leadership had experienced under the previous Labour Party administration. These expectations were enforced because the head of the Women's Desk was Yvonne Francis-Gibson, an activist member and leader of the Teacher's Union, one of the most outspoken groups on the island.

Soon after, however, the Minister in charge of women's affairs, Burton Williams, made statements that were considered insulting to women. In a public speech, he stated that women needed only to be liberated from "cobwebs and commess (gossip)." The CDW and other organization in the NCW protested vehemently against the insults, and as a result the relationship between the government and the women's movement declined drastically. Furthermore, the Women's Desk appeared to be subject to the whims and fancies of the government, and was unable to take a firm stand on behalf of women's issues. In the next election, in 1989, Francis-Gibson was herelf elected to government, but the relationship between the government and organized feminist groups continued to deteriorate.

The CDW, led by Nelcia Robinson, continues to be in the forefront of any militant women's activity. Much of its focus is on research, and the organization, in conjunction with the Caribbean Association for Feminist Research (CAFRA), was responsible for the well-received "Women in Agriculture" project. They also conducted a study on "Women and the Law" in 1988. However, because there was a vacuum in feminist activism, CDW led the banner in protesting violence against women. It also spawned other militant groups, including POWER (Political Women for Education and Redirection). In addition to Robinson, prominent members are Earlene Horne, Theresa Daniels, Valcina Ashe, and Shirley Byron-Cox.

The women's organizations in St. Vincent have been able to maintain a level of independence largely because of funding from external non-governmental organizations. Robinson in particular maintains contacts with regional and extra-regional groups, and her work is well respected by donors and sympathizers.

The Caribbean People's Development Organization (CARIPETA) and its Vincentian affiliate, Projects Promotion, have been particularly cooperative in women's activities. These groups are funded by the Canadian concern CUSO. The women's organizations in St. Vincent have also received support from Caribbean feminist organizations such as WAND (Women and Development) with headquarters in Barbados. As a result of CDW's demonstrations against violence and the subsequent CUSO sponsored research, the Commonwealth Women's Desk through the St. Vincent and the Grenadines Women's Desk conducted a series of workshops on gender planning.

Some of the more traditional organizations are also managing to hold their own in the quest to find answers for the current financial problems. Some have recognized that women can participate in enterprises that they had formerly accepted as within the male domain. Recently, the Rotary Club published a set of guidelines for women interested in small businesses. Such organizations are less likely to run into confrontations with the government.

Activist women recognize that in order to bring about genuine progress they must work with less vocal members of the society. At all levels of the society, the women in St. Vincent, whether by force or by choice are actively involved in resisting the effects of economic structural adjustment. Their tactics include day-to-day struggles to make ends meet, working with the government to change legislature, emigration, and feminist activism. In the 1970s, very few of the organizations could be considered feminist as such, and it was not until the formation of the CDW in 1984 that some organizations within the NCW began to recognize the particular oppression of women because of their gender.

Feminism also received a major boost because of the politics of individual women who were leading the women's movement at the time. Nelcia Robinson, in particular, had maintained contact with outside feminist organizations such as WAND and CAFRA as they were making their presence felt on the Caribbean scene. Robinson was one of the few women to be actively involved in electoral politics, when in 1984 and 1989 she ran as a candidate for the left-leaning United Progressive Movement. She entered the women's movement from a more politicized position than many of her contemporaries and she interpreted the position of women in the society from a class, as well as a gender perspective.

Conclusion

In the decades of the 1980s and 1990s, women in St. Vincent, like their counterparts elsewhere in the developing world, have had to make major adjustments to the optimism that followed political independence in the 1970s. Aided by a history of struggle against poverty and oppression, Vincentian women found several ways of attacking their decreasing income. The methods that they tried have had mixed results, but they have brought into public light the horrendous effects of structural adjustment on women in the society.

The problems incurred by the economy coincided with an incipient feminist movement among urban women in St. Vincent and the Grenadines. It is possible that world trends would have eventually led to to a gender-based interpretation of women's problems, but the peculiar results of the economic setback called structural adjustment ensured that women had to address the tremendous hardships that they faced. As they examined these issues the question of fairness arose, and inevitably led to a questioning of the position of women in the society.

Because women bore the worse brunt of the failing economy they had to use their own resources. As jobs became more scarce and the hope of ever having meaningful employment decreased, they could not depend on men for support. Migration helped to empower them in their relationships with men and gave an added boost of self-confidence, but that phenomenon provided its own set of problems. The question of their vulnerability to violence also wove a common thread among all segments of the female society. By marching and demonstrating together, women perceived the extent to which gender made them vulnerable to crimes such as spousal abuse and rape.

By the 1990s, the women's movement, if it was not a full-fledged feminist movement, was imbued with a strong dose of feminist consciousness. In her 1993 International Women's Day Address, Izalene Nickie, head of CARIPETA, mentioned that women were resisting not only their local government, but were in opposition to an internationally organized, mostly male-dominated system. "In this man's world, women have been constrained by . . . a male-biased ideology . . . . gender must be at the centre of development ideology, policies and programmes."

The NCW was organized so that women could come together to help build the society. In the beginning there was little discussion of inequality between the sexes. The benign attempt to be included in development programs escalated into more openly feminist organizing as the economy deteriorated and structural adjustment led to declining social conditions. It was natural that the new militancy for gender and justice would begin in the urban area of Kingstown, for these women tend to be better educated and organized than their rural counterparts. As time progressed they took their message to rural women so that they too could make their voices heard on the national scene. Women in St. Vincent and the Grenadines were forced to organize along gender lines to protect themselves and their children from losing all that they had gained in the recent past, and to prevent their society from falling victim to what they perceived to be anarchy and chaos. At this juncture, the greatest challenge facing the women of St. Vincent will be to maintain this momentum.

--- REFERENCES ---

Antrobus, Peggy. 1989. "Crisis, Challenge, and the Experiences of Caribbean Women." *Caribbean Quarterly* 35: 17–35.
———. 1990. "Gender Relations in the Caribbean in the Year 2000." *Caribbean Affairs* 3:130–136.
Bolles, Lynn. 1985. "Economic Crisis and Female Headed Households in Urban Jamaica." In June Nash and Helen I. Safa (eds.), *Women*

and Change in Latin America. South Hadley, Mass.: Bergin and Garvy Publishers.

Bunch, Charlotte and Roxanne Carollo. 1990. "Feminist Perspectives on Women in Development." In Irene Tinker (ed.), *Persistent Inequalities.* pp. 70–82. New York: Oxford.

Burnic, Mayra and Nadia H. Young. 1978. *Women Headed Households: The Ignored Factor in Developing Planning.* Washington, D.C.: International Center For Research on Women.

Caribbean Association for Feminst Research and Action. Report on the Regional Meeting on Women, Violence, and the Law.

Campbell, Parnel R. 1986. The Law of Maintenance and the Law Governing Property Rights. Paper Presented at the National Council of Women of St. Vincent and the Grenadines, International Women's Day Seminar.

CARICOM Perspective. 1984. Closer Integration for Accelerated Development in the Caribbean Community, Nassau, the Bahamas, July 7, 1984.

Cornia, Giovanni and Richard Jolly. 1987. *Adjustment With a Human Face.* Oxford: Clarendon Press.

Deere, Carmen Diana, Peggy Antrobus, Lynn Bolles, Edwin Melendez, Peter Phillips, Marcia Rivera, and Helen Safa. 1990. *In the Shadows of the Sun: Caribbean Development Alternatives and U.S. Policy.* Boulder: Westview Press.

Document of the World Bank. 1992. St. Vincent and the Grenadines Country Economic Memorandum. Report No. 10374-STV.

International Development Research Center. 1982–1984. International Migration Project. Ottawa.

Marshall, Paule. 1981. *Brown Girl, Brown Stone* . Old Westbury, N.Y.: Feminist Press.

Massiah, Joycelin. 1986. "Women in the Caribbean Project: An Overview." *Social and Economic Studies* 35.

McAffee, Kathy. 1991. *Storm Signals.* Boston: South End Press.

Mohammed, Patricia and Catherine Shepherd. 1988. *Gender in Caribbean Development.* UWI Women and Development Studies.

Momsen, Janet, ed. 1993. *Women & Change in the Caribbean.* Bloomington: Indiana University Press.

Packness, Ella and Committee for the Development of Women. 1988. Working Papers on Laws Affecting Women.

Ramsaran, Ramesh E. 1992. *The Challenge of Structural Adjustment in the Commonwealth Caribbean.* New York: Praeger.

Robinson, Nelcia. 1991. *Belling the Cat.* St. Vincent amd the Grenadines, Women's Affairs Division.

Ryan, Cecil (ed.). 1987. *Women, Work, Income: Doing Social Work For Change.* 8. Kingstown: Projects Promotion Limited.

Senior, Olive. 1991. *Working Miracles: Women's Lives in the English Speaking Caribbean.* Bloomington: Indiana University Press.

Sistren and Honor Ford Smith. 1986. *Lion Heart Gal: Life Stories of Jamaican Women.* London: The Women's Press.

St. Vincent and the Grenadines, Statistical Office Ministry of Finance and Planning Kingston. 1991. Population and Housing Census Report Volume 2.

St. Vincent and the Grenadines, Statistical Unit. 1989. Digest of Statistics, No. 39.

———. 1990. No. 40.

———. 1991. No. 41

St. Vincent and the Grenadines Women's Affairs Division and CUSO. 1991. Final report on Research on Violence Against Women:

Tinker, Irene. 1990. *Persistent Inequalities.* New York: Oxford.

——— and Bo Brasser (eds.). 1976. *Women and World Development.* New York: Praeger.

Toney, Joyce. 1989. *The Changing Relationship Between Caribbean Men and Women in New York City In Establishing New Lives: Selected Readings on Caribbean Immigrants in New York City.* Brooklyn, Caribbean Research Center, Medgar Evers College, CUNY.

University of the West Indies, Wand and Development Unit. 1993. Whither the Family.

Part Four

NORTH AMERICA

Gerald Horne

11

The Political Economy of the Black Urban Future

A History

Generally speaking, changes in the global economy and the international situation have had a major impact on the destiny of African Americans, particularly those who are young and of the working class. This has notably been the case since the end of World War II and the dawn of the Cold War. But now the Cold War is over, or at least has eroded, and there is some question of what this all portends for a Black community that is overwhelmingly working-class and disproportionately under the age of thirty.

California, the most populous state in the United States, has frequently played a vanguard role in the nation, foreshadowing trends that ultimately embrace the whole country. Thus, a historical context is useful when seeking to ascertain what the future holds.

The "HOLLYWOOD" Mode of Production

If the U.S. moguls have their way, the future of all too many workers in this nation—if not the world—will be akin to the fate of workers in Hollywood (Chanan 1976; Staiger 1981). The producer raises capital and hires the writers, actors, technicians. When film-

247

ing is completed, all return to the jungle of the marketplace, waiting to be called for the next picture.

If the glamour of Hollywood makes that image too alluring, consider another vision from Southern California. In Los Angeles there are active labor markets on a number of streets. Predominantly Mexican, El Salvadorean, and Guatemalan workers wait to be chosen for a day's worth of labor by disproportionately Euro-American contractors in trucks. And on a facing corner, it is not unusual to view workers who are predominantly Black—African-American, Belizean, continental African, and others—also waiting to be chosen, in a visual representation of an ethnically and racially divided work force.

As the United States faces the next millennium, it is apparent that significant changes in the international correlation of forces do not necessarily augur well for those people who now call themselves African-American—especially those who happen to be young workers. The LA (Los Angeles) model, which might be called the "Hollywood Mode of Production," is the inexorable product of interwoven domestic and global factors. Stiffening global competition, the changing nature of work (more part-time and contingency workers), the scientific and technological revolution, and "downsizing" by the private and public sectors all interact and spawn ever-newer developments.

In the aftermath of the Cold War, the steroids of military spending, which kept the California economy particularly pumped up artificially, are being redeployed (Leslie 1993). In the new international dispensation—Iraq and Panama aside—it is unclear what will be the contours of a U.S. foreign policy that drives military spending. Simultaneously, the 1992 explosion in Los Angeles in the aftermath of the beating by police officers of the Black motorist Rodney King, was suggestive of what might happen if the problem of racial discrimination were simply left to fester.

The civil unrest in Los Angeles in the spring of 1992 was also illustrative for another reason. It was obvious that those participating in this carnival of the oppressed were not exclusively of African origin; there were a range of racial and ethnic groups represented. Yet it remained true that the Black Question was the kindling that sparked the conflagration.

The immediate cause of the explosion in Los Angeles was the

failure to convict the officers who beat Mr. King, despite the fact that the incident had been videotaped—unbeknownst to those involved—by a young Euro-American man trying out a new camera. The recording of fifty-six blows by officers aimed at the body of Mr. King, as other officers stood by, was not sufficient to convince a suburban jury with no African Americans to issue a conviction. The officers' counsel achieved this result in part by decontextualizing the video of the beating, showing the jury each static frame, as opposed to a continuous showing. This was done repetitively as well, and it served to desensitize the jury to the monstrosity of what had befallen Mr. King. Of course, an existing precondition of racial bias no doubt was a factor in triggering this process of desensitizing and decontextualization. Alas, this has been the fate of Black workers in the United States. Their plight has been decontextualized, ripped cruelly out of the flow of global events, and the monstrosity that has befallen a people once enslaved has been represented in a static fashion designed to deprive the jury of public opinion of sensitivity to this matter.

By focusing on such issues as the global economy, the "prison industrial complex," education, the law, and other factors, this chapter will seek to provide a historical context for comprehension of what has happened and is happening to Black workers in the United States in the hope that perhaps this will be a factor in aiding this nation in the emulation of our counterparts in South Africa by moving toward a future that involves a larger role for unions and parties of the Left. For I would argue that if this does not occur, Black workers will not be the exclusive victim. Like the proverbial canary in the mine, the fate of Black workers may be indicative of the future of this nation, the working class generally, and Africans of the diaspora.

The "Underclass" Revisited

The fate of young Black workers has not gone unexamined. However, too often this complex question has been bogged down in sterile debates about a so-called "underclass." To its discredit, this debate does not draw clear lines between and among the unemployed, the underemployed, and those who might be characterized as a "lumpenproletariat" (Wilson 1987; Katz 1993). Nor does this discourse often note that the distinctions between the Black employed, unemployed, underemployed, and lumpen is more akin to a film dissolve than a snapshot, that is, the fluidity of the economy and the stain of bigotry ensures that Black workers are in constant motion and are not a static formation. Moreover, what is often being examined is precisely the lumpenproletariat (a heterogeneous band of rapists, suppliers of certain illicit drugs, scam artists, and others who prey on the Black working class and rarely prey directly on the elite of this country). This salient factor is discussed in the absence of similar developments taking place in the nation generally. It is as if Blacks do not exist in North America and are not subject to similar forces facing others, for example, Italian Americans and Jewish Americans.

The fact is that organized crime—or hyper lumpen criminality—at times has overridden potential Black competitors. One example of this is Harlem during the 1930s. Thus, this form of primitive accumulation has escaped the Black community, in part because of what might be called "white skin privilege" (Allen 1994). This has been one of the major differences between those who had been slaves in the Deep South and those who faced hostile U.S. immigration laws and subsequent stigmatization at Ivy League universities and the major citadels of finance capital.

This historic defeat for Black primitive accumulation took place primarily in the entertainment industry, gambling and its handmaidens, the music and film sectors of the economy. Along with armaments, music and film may be the only areas where the United States remains hegemonic in the global economy (Schatzberg 1993). Moreover, entertainment, including sports, is one of the few areas where African Americans have been allowed to participate in sizeable numbers (and, naturally, this diversity has helped to ensure that this is one of the few areas where the nation has remained competitive globally).

Dorothy Wade and Justine Picardie detail how there was an effort to "integrate" an African American, Nathan McCalla, into a noted Italian-American crime family (Wade and Picardie 1990:177, 258). Given the role that blood plays in defining family—not to mention the social construction of "whiteness"—this was even more surprising. Historically, later entrants into the "hallowed halls of whiteness," for example, Jewish and Italian Americans were barred from the higher echelons of capital and consigned to areas of capitalism that were not perceived as being as lofty, such as entertainment (Korman 1988). Wade and Picardie describe the evolution of the "Fairplay Committee," an organization composed primarily of African-American men, who sought to redress what was correctly perceived as gross exploitation of Black artists. In the deeply rooted tradition of violence in the United States, they were not above using strong-arm tactics (Brown 1991).

But the murder of McCalla in 1980 marked the close of this movement toward integration. This also happened to be the year that Ronald Reagan, a former trade union leader in the entertainment industry, was elected President of the United States. He then went on to preside over an attempted dismantling of civil rights laws and affirmative action concessions, not to mention presiding over the increased reliance on organized crime globally (Horne 1992a; Vaughn 1994).

Robert Lacey has noted that Meyer Lansky, a premier leader of organized crime who happened to be Jewish, also happened to be a Zionist and a nationalist. He contributed heavily to Israel over the years and sought to immigrate there in the 1970s, when he perceived that some of his Italian-American colleagues were turning against him on bigoted grounds. When he was called to testify about his nefarious activities before the United States Congress, he anticipated Clarence Thomas by claiming that the panel was grilling him not because he was a mobster but because he was Jewish (Lacey 1991:190–207). Gangsters of whatever hue have leaned toward nationalism.

In Los Angeles after the Watts Uprising of 1965, African Americans who had a nationalist orientation were attracted to the Black Panther Party, which was militant and generally progressive (it was certainly not "anti-white"). However, after this party was bludgeoned out of existence, Blacks were less able to confront their class and race antagonists; in addition, this was part of a process of ideological disarmament and marginalizing of the Black Left that created a vacuum filled by narrow nationalism (Seale 1991; Brown 1992). This pattern of undermining the Left helped to foment increased chauvinism, as has been seen in South Africa, Palestine, Afghanistan, and elsewhere (Said and Hitchens 1988).

Like the defense's use of the video in the Rodney King beating, this relentless attempt to segment and balkanize has had a disastrous impact on race relations most notably. It has served to perpetuate that historic trend marked from the times of Bacon's Rebellion in Virginia in the 1660s, when dispossessed Euro-Americans were made to break ranks and flee from their erstwhile African and indigenous comrades in exchange, in some instances, for seizing of the land of the latter and stocking that land with African chattel (Washburn 1962). "Divide and conquer" is a tactic basic to political and military science. Furthermore, Blacks in the United States have found themselves checkmated on all fronts: barred from expressing their discontent through the militancy of Left formations like the Black Panther Party, and barred from seeing a lumpen transformed into "organized crime" and then more legitimate enterprise, like their Jewish and Italian-American counterparts.

In this context it should not be surprising that Los Angeles has been the scene of a profound renascence of the phenomenon known as "gangs." It is not just that the heavily Italian-American and Jewish-American mob in that city provided a deft example of how to profit handsomely by dominating the entertainment industry, hiring relatives and comrades. It is also that these social organizations have increased in number significantly over the past few decades as youth who might have drifted into the Black Panthers in the 1960s saw that option foreclosed by the 1990s. This limitation was accompanied by a fierce socioeconomic assault, the results of which the state of California and the United States generally are just beginning to assess. And it is this assault that has led some to invoke the term, "underclass." In many ways, what has happened to the Black employed, unemployed, underemployed, and some lumpen is the end result of a process that includes restriction on opportunities for Black "gangsters" and the close association of this trend with the demise of the Left. The latter factor has left the unemployed unarmed and the former has placed increased pressure on lumpen, which has resulted in internecine factionalism and some self-destructive violence, and there has been cross-fertilization of this negativity as well (Anderson 1990; Horne 1992b:65–72; Shakur 1993).

Unlike the trajectory of the Jewish-American and Italian-American mobs, which evolved from illegal, bootleg liquor during the Prohibition era to staid corporations like Seagram's and Schenley's, the Black lumpen and closely allied Black petit bourgeoisie were not allowed to progress similarly. Movements toward equality did not include equal opportunity for Black lumpen to spread beyond the Black community, and the same holds true, largely, for the Black business community. This is even more ironic given the widespread perception that it is the Black petit bourgeoisie that has been the dominant ideological force among Blacks and the primary beneficiary of the civil rights movement (Sigleman and Welch 1991).

The decline of the material well-being of many African-American workers reached a nadir during the presidency of Ronald Reagan, with his binding and refining white racial identity in the secular church of anti-communism. He also, not coincidentally, presided over an escalation of "Afro-phobia" which was facilitated by the difficulty Blacks had in endorsing a global policy that had as primary victims countries such as Angola, Mozambique, Grenada, Panama, and Cuba. As analysts have begun to examine the wreckage of this era, they have discovered that this so-called "underclass" is not only sweeping inexorably beyond African Americans, it is also deepening its bite among Blacks globally.

Engineering Depression

In December 1993, the legislature of California issued what was described as "the first comprehensive look at the status of Black men in [the state]." The findings were startling. One-sixth of California's 625,000 Black men age sixteen and older are arrested each year, records that hamper job prospects. It was discovered that men of African descent are more likely than Euro-Americans or Latinos to be arrested on drug charges and later released for lack of evidence. Black men comprise forty percent of the felons entering state prisons and they are three times more likely than Euro-Americans to drop out of high school. And those with less than a high school education are twice as likely to be unemployed as Euro-Americans with the same education.[1]

It is apparent that in California, the nation's largest state, with

a population of over thirty million and a penchant for foreshadowing national trends such as general strikes in San Francisco, uprisings in Los Angeles, and "gangsta rap," the political economy has
undergone significant transformation. Most significant is the erosion of semi-skilled jobs in which Blacks were employed disproportionately. This has set in motion a rapid slide in the income,
education, and opportunities not only for Black men (as the legislature's report indicated) but for Black families generally. The state's
heavy dependence on military spending meant that, inevitably,
downsizing would occur once the Cold War subsided. In any case,
African Americans historically have had difficulty in securing work
in this important sector of the state's economy, and the entertainment industry, the other engine of the state's economy, has been
similarly inhospitable to Blacks (Olin and Daniels 1972). In addition, the auto and rubber industries, which have been so important
to the destiny of California, have been moving south of the border
and to even more distant climes and this has served to undermine
what had been a growing Black proletariat (Davis 1990; Starr
1990).

Of course, the plight of Black families in California is not necessarily an act of God. There is a subjective element in the form of a
virulent racial bias imbedded in commercial, legal, and social sectors that reduces the life chances of peoples of African descent in
this pivotal state and, ultimately, the nation. But, again, California
represents trends that may subsequently sweep the nation. For
racism there is not simply a videotaped replay of the binary Black-
white mode, there are also color conflicts between and amongst
Blacks, based in part on the over-representation of Louisiana migrants, and there are color conflicts in the Mexican community and
the Pan-Asian community as well. This helps to engender a compounded racism that presents multiplied possibilities for dividing
and conquering the working class, a conquest that is of value to
Blacks least of all.

Certainly Black men in California are not singular in their
community in suffering through a de facto economic depression.
For the fact is that Black women are likewise afflicted (Zinn and
Dill 1992). Many Black women happen to be found in areas of the
economy that have undergone or are about to undergo profound
transformation (Malveaux and Wallace 1987). The teaching pro-

fession is under siege from the relentless forces of privatization, which could lead to the decline of unionism and concomitant fall in wages and working conditions for many Black women (Gerstner 1994).

This attack on African-American women inevitably has a sexist edge. Not only are they being undermined in the labor market, there is a constant effort to erode their self-esteem via the projection of Eurocentric standards of beauty, color, and hair (Morrison 1970; Busby 1992). This roughly serves the social purpose that lynching of Black males once served, that is, to intimidate a sector of the population in order to force them to work for less and under harsh conditions (Hall 1993).

The point is that if the United States' pattern of trends developing in the West and then sweeping East continues, California may present a model for what is to come elsewhere. The binary Black-white mode of race relations is breaking down. It is well known that the fastest growing sectors of the U.S. population are Asian Americans and Latinos (particularly Mexican and Central Americans) and these sectors are found heavily in the Golden State. With a deficit of Left influence and a concomitant deficit of class consciousness, there is a distinct possibility that the continued decline in the material well-being of the Black and non-Black working class could lead to sharpened ethnic and racial conflict. Unfortunately, such a prospect becomes more likely when U.S. relations with Asian nations, notably Japan and China, along with the importance of the North American Free Trade Alliance, or NAFTA, combine to provide an image that affects domestic perceptions of Asian Americans and Mexican Americans particularly.

New World Coming

As World War II was coming to a close, the progressive Afro-Caribbean journalist Roi Ottley, then toiling in Harlem, penned a book highly popular among Blacks entitled *New World A-Coming* (Ottley 1943). It signalled his belief and the belief of many more that Black sacrifice during the war inexorably would lead to the devolution of Jim Crow. What was not widely envisioned at that moment was that a Cold War would follow that would remove the African-American sentry, the Black Left, and this would leave the community ideologically defenseless.

This ideological disarmament could not have occurred at a worse moment. For now, with the Cold War ended, yet another pervasive transformation is sweeping through the economy of the United States, which is likely to change radically the role and status of Black workers. With the dissolution of the Soviet Union and the collapse of the socialist camp in Eastern Europe, not only has a new pool of labor been opened that will compete directly with the U.S. working class but further, this has been a material and psychological boost to capital generally with no immediate benefit to African-American workers particularly (Horne 1992c, 1994).

Analysts like Paul Kennedy, Lester Thurow, and Michael Garten have peered into the crystal ball and come forth with prognostications about what the future holds. It does seem that one of the most lasting effects of the Cold War has been to place Japan and the European Union in the passing lane (Reich 1991; Thurow 1992; Kennedy 1993).

But it is another "futurist," Frances Fukuyama, who has sought to assess what this may mean for the working class of the United States. Best known for his provocative prediction about the "end of history," the former U.S. State Department analyst most recently explored the class dimension, interestingly in the *Japan Times* of April 11–17, 1994. Bluntly he avers, "the traditional working class will face unremitting competition from workers with similar skills around the world, competition that will either deprive them of their jobs or drive down their wages, even as their higher-skilled countrymen prosper." Hinting obliquely at the future of the United States, he noted, "Those [nations] that fail to move their populations up the skill ladder and into higher value-added occupations will see growing income inequality and marginalization of their working classes, with all the social turmoil this implies" (Fukuyama 1992).

Previously, enforcement of civil rights laws and certain affirmative action concessions softened the blow that fell on Black workers. But the context that produced affirmative action has been transformed with the fall of the USSR and the rise of a new international situation. Thus, while the sons and daughters of alumni and alumnae of prestigious Ivy League schools receive de facto affirmative action "points" when considered for admission to these institutions, this does not attract controversy, although it locks in a generational advantage for well-placed Euro-Americans (Dreyfuss and Lawrence 1979). And though Washington pushed for legislative quotas to protect the interests of the white minority in Zimbabwe, there has been decided hostility to the imposition of quotas to protect the interests of the an African minority on these shores.

But likewise, the U.S. Special Trade Representative has little problem in arguing for quotas for Lee Iacocca and Chrysler in Japan while arguing against quotas aimed at Hollywood exports to the European Union. This failure or inability to deal forthrightly with the quota question not only jeopardizes domestic race relations, apparently this omission also has infected or made possible the confusion of this issue on the international scene. In particular this has complicated relations with Tokyo (Tyson 1993).

At the same time, relations with Beijing are not becoming simpler with the passing of time. During the Cold War, it did appear that Washington was quite adept at manipulating Moscow against Beijing and vice versa. Now there appears to be not only a new post–Cold War triangle, with Tokyo taking the place of Moscow, there are also attendant and not necessarily dependent tensions with the European Union that make it more difficult for rank anticommunists to continue the epic crusade against ruling Communist Parties (Chang 1990; Lardy 1994).

Georgi Arbatov, a former leading Americanist for the Soviet Communist Party, has written about the United States' need for a new enemy to replace the now-departed USSR (Arbatov 1992). It seems at this point that in addition to what is called "religious fundamentalism," Tokyo and Beijing are rapidly becoming the prime concern, if not antagonists, of Washington, and at various times historically when this has occurred, race relations domestically have been affected (Kearney 1991). Thus, it should not come as a surprise that the quota question is now of concern to "people of color" at home and abroad; the danger is that the politically unsophisticated U.S. majority, which has a long history of racism, could conflate these two issues, thus worsening race relations at home and harming diplomacy abroad in a symbiotic fashion.

Given this context, a primary question is whether African-American workers will join an incipient crusade in the U.S. labor movement that seeks to blame the decline of heavy industries like auto and steel on Tokyo. The fact that real and imagined "Black-Korean" tensions have been given prominence in the news suggests that a deficit of class consciousness may mean that a crusade against Tokyo or Beijing may be more likely at this point than a campaign against Wall Street. This also suggests the overlap between tensions with Asians at home and abroad becoming mutually reinforcing, just as anti-communism at home and abroad was similarly reinforcing. If that is the case, even Wall Street may wind up paying a heavy price as a result of the deterioration of race relations.

American Apartheid

It is ironic that just as the African majority in South Africa is attaining a measure of freedom, the plight of the African minority in the United States seems even more dire. Again, the former resisted the Cold War bargain of excommunicating the Left in exchange for a fistful of concessions, while the latter felt constrained to accept this deal. But now with the Cold War concluding, recent reports indicate that the South African economy may enjoy some of the more significant growth rates in the world with much of that fuelled by internal consumption, while African Americans face the future with uncertainty. It is even more ironic that just as apartheid seems on its deathbed in South Africa, it seems to be undergoing a renaissance on these shores.

What is called the "ghetto" is not just a metaphor for residential segregation, although obviously it subsumes this ostracism. It also indicates a spatial isolation that the presence of television and radio cannot overcome. It involves distance from developing industries in suburbs, as federal and state policies have encouraged the building of expressways and even mass transit to facilitate the construction of areas far-flung from urban cores dominated by darker peoples. It involves a separate civil society and, to an extent, a separate culture of religious institutions, block associations, and parent-teacher associations (Daniels 1990).

This "hypersegregation" is an essential component of the construction of what has been called the "underclass." In other words, the prospects for the Black unemployed and underemployed are circumscribed, while the Black lumpen are unable to expand to newer markets (as did their Jewish-American and Italian-American counterparts) and engage in further primitive accumulation. Instead, all of these groups increasingly become cast into prisons and jails for crimes that may or may not have been committed. There, a sector becomes subject to various millennial and messianic religious groupings whose teachings serve to further isolate or become more adept at plying trades that directly soak the Black working class (Massey and Denton 1993).

Increasingly, the legal system has become a decisive factor in perpetuating "American Apartheid"; judicial decisions create the legal basis for zoning and city planning edicts that maintain lines of segregation. Judicial decisions, as Lani Guinier has noted ably, simultaneously balkanize the polity and jeopardize minimal political gains by African Americans in the U.S. Congress, state legislatures, city councils, and the numerous other political bodies that have been created to fragment the public sector and hamper a concerted response against the private sector (Guinier 1994). Furthermore, judicial decisions, particularly decisions of the U.S. Supreme Court, have served as symbol and barrier, consigning an overwhelming majority of the Black working class to a fate worse than purgatory.

Further evidence of the impact of the demise of the Black Left was the appointment of Clarence Thomas as the only African American on the high court and, perhaps, that body's most right-wing member. Thurgood Marshall, whom Thomas replaced, a noted liberal and the court's first African-American, collaborated with the Left—as did many Black lawyers—most notably the National Lawyers Guild. At this point, the U.S. elite was quite content with not confronting Jim Crow and, like South Africa, it was only the Left that tried to bring Euro-Americans into conflict with this institution (Davis and Clark 1992).

Marshall's work with the NAACP, which purged their Left wing after the onset of the Cold War, culminated with *Brown v. Board of Education* in 1954, and his prominence ensured that President Johnson would nominate him to the high court subsequently. But with his untimely death, President George Bush saw fit to replace him with the right-wing Thomas. More than that, it was foreseeable that this bolstering of the Right at some point would serve to erode the life chances of the Black working class and galvanize "American Apartheid."

In my recent book *Reversing Discrimination: The Case for Affirmative Action*, I detailed the torturous struggle that led to the passage of the Civil Rights and Women's Equity Act of 1991 and the reversal of a series of anti–civil rights decisions of the high court. The bone and sinew behind this titanic struggle were individuals like Terrell McGinnis, a Black man who had worked for an equipment company in Birmingham, Alabama; he was removed from his foreman's post for blatant racist reasons, he was threatened with violence by his supervisor, and was subjected to frequent racial epithets. Yet, because of the machinations of the law, he was not able to prevail in court (Horne 1992a:102).

The devolution of the law and its impact on African-Americans is a matter that soars far beyond its immediate surroundings. For the fact is that there was an implicit promise to African-Americans that they should not hesitate in casting aside the Black Left, left-wing CIO unions, and other important realms of civil society, because the law and lawyers would preserve their rights (Fraser 1991; Rosswurm 1992). But what happened was that the preservation of legal gains, contrary to popular opinion, was much more dependent on the correlation of forces at a particular moment than the wizardry of legal technicians.

A glancing examination of case studies involving Black workers indicates that in this post–Cold War environment they are ironically facing a recrudescence of "American Apartheid" while its presumed counterpart in South Africa is spiralling toward devolution (Kischenman and Neckerman 1991:203–232). The correlation of forces has changed and with it the destiny of Blacks on both sides of the Atlantic.

What is especially troubling about this development is that it appears to be negatively affecting Black workers in the United States at a much more pervasive rate than others. This was the conclusion of an exhaustive study that appeared in the September 14, 1993, *Wall Street Journal*. According to that report, Blacks were the only racial group to suffer a net job loss during the 1990–1991 economic downturn at the companies reporting to the Equal Employment Opportunity Commission. Whites, Hispanics, and Asians, meanwhile, gained thousands of jobs, according to an analysis of EEOC records. At Dial Corporation, for instance, blacks lost 43.6 percent of the jobs cut, even though they represented 26.3 percent of Dial's work force going into the recession. At BankAmerica Corporation and ITT Corporation, blacks lost jobs at more than twice the rate of their companies' overall work force reductions.

Up to date reports from across the country substantiate the point that despite—or perhaps because of—the Cold War bargain, those who now call themselves African-American are the most affected victims of the new international situation. *The New York Times* of June 20, 1993, observed that "since 1990 complaints of racial harassment filed through local and regional offices of the Equal Employment Opportunity Commission and state human rights agencies increased nearly 17 percent to 6,038 filings last year." *The Los Angeles Times* of March 31, 1994, reported that there has been a staggering increase in the ranks of the "working poor" and, necessarily, the nation's Blacks are among those most severely affected. The Black Brooklyn, New York–based weekly, *The City Sun* of April 6–12, 1994, averred that downsizing in the city bureaucracy has amounted to an "ethnic cleansing" of Black workers.

It does seem that Black workers have a reputation for militancy and a penchant for joining unions. In response, major corporations increasingly are moving to oust these workers disproportionately, while corporations establishing facilities are moving far from urban centers where Blacks are concentrated. This increases the numbers and visibility of what has come to be called the "underclass" and heightens the spatial isolation of "American Apartheid" that undergirds this tendency. This spatial isolation, like the defense's use of the Rodney King video, rips Blacks out of context and predisposes bias against them among the jury of public opinion. This forced march to balkanization and "American exceptionalism" has happened as the world, in so many ways, has changed dramatically.

New World Here?

Keep in mind, what is happening to Black workers in the workplace is disproportionate, not singular. For the fact is that in today's global economy, U.S. workers are not only subject to a U.S.

elite that is probably stronger vis á vis the working class than Japanese and European rivals, they also are forced into direct competition with millions of workers from Eastern Europe, India, Brazil, Indonesia, Malaysia, Korea, and elsewhere. "Reinventing Government" is the mantra driving a downsizing of the federal labor force, as privatization motors on buoyed by the right-wing notion that sees the public sector as nascent socialism (Osborne 1992). That Black workers are over-represented in the ranks of state sector workers and, thus, more likely to be hurt by this trend is somehow glossed over.

Meanwhile, in the private sector, the situation is appreciably worse as recent gains are threatened by the operation of the "first hired/first fired" principle as businesses rush to be "virtual corporations" akin to Hollywood film projects. Michael Hammer and James Champy outline the future in their *Reengineering the Corporation: A Manifesto for Business Revolution.* Job classifications are being eliminated, a process that is eased by the impact of computers; one person handles a task from beginning to end; work is contracted out vitiating the need to keep staff on board (Hammer and Champy 1993).

"Reengineering" is seen most clearly in telecommunications, insurance, and manufacturing companies. But it is in hospitals, that one-seventh of this nation's GDP, that this tendency is highly visible. The thrust to "reform" health care has obscured the possibility that in New York State alone, 60,000 jobs of hospital workers may be lost in the process. These jobs are held disproportionately by Black women in the New York metropolitan area, who belong to one of the few remaining Left-led unions, Local 1199 of the Hospital Workers Union (Fink 1989; Starr 1992).[2]

A clear example of reengineering is "Patient-Focused Care," which is now in use in a number of hospitals that attach a good portion of patient services, including bedside services, to computer terminals. "Non–value-added work" such as walking, is curtailed. Workers are reorganized into "care teams" with the aim of doing away with specialists (read: workers) and creating the "generic health care worker." Despite the assurance that service workers were relatively immune from the force of the global economy because hospitals, unlike auto plants, do not necessarily abandon the country in search of cheaper labor, the fact is that the relentless drive for profit combined with the scientific and technological revolution will serve to deprive more Black workers of employment, whether or not they're in the service sector (Richardson 1994). In any case, Black workers—be they in the service sector or otherwise—are subject to the national trend toward hiring part—time workers with low salaries and meager benefits. In 1993, the Milwaukee based company, Manpower Incorporated, employed about 600,000 people in the United States; that is more than the labor force of General Motors and McDonald's combined. Manpower happens to be the premier temporary employment agency in the nation.[3]

The challenge confronting Black workers is an unanticipated negative international situation, an unfriendly high court that was supposed to have been their guardian in exchange for dumping Left allies, corporate and government downsizing, the proliferation of contingency work with no continuity or future, and the proliferation of computers and robots that are eliminating even more jobs. Meanwhile, the labor movement was, for a number of years, under the leadership of regressive leadership at the top in the person of Lane Kirkland, which did not bode well for a sharp challenge to this gloomy destiny.

Not surprisingly, homelessness seems to be disproportionately impacting Blacks while the welfare rolls have more than their share of Black faces as benefits continue to decline (Jencks 1994). Overall, the U.S. working class continues to obtain an ever-smaller share of the national wealth, while heads of corporations continue to wallow in the filthy lucre of super-profits. In 1994, *Business Week* reported that Michael Eisner, CEO of the Disney Corporation, had a take-home pay of over $203 million in 1993.

At the same time, prisons continue to be constructed at a record pace to house the expanding ranks of the Black unemployed, underemployed, and lumpen. In a sense, the military-industrial complex is being supplemented, if not supplanted, by the development of a "prison-industrial complex" (Rideau 1992). Not only is there money to be made by privatizing prisons, there are also jobs in these institutions as prison guards, cafeteria workers, counselors, and administrators, not to mention jobs manufacturing prison uniforms, firearms, bullets, bulletproof vests, surveillance equipment, and the like. Moreover, prisoners are not left idle in prisons. Despite U.S. criticisms of China for using prison labor to make goods, a similar process takes place on these shores. In Oregon prisons, popular jeans known as "Prison Blues" are made for domestic and export markets.[4] This is not an isolated example but instead is indicative of a national pattern.

Conclusion

Thus, the future of Black workers on these shores appears to be bleak. Like the laborers who congregate on the streets of Los Angeles, the U.S. working class is increasingly divided and segmented by race and ethnicity, a process that is particularly harmful to the African-American sector. Like extras in a Hollywood film, Black workers are called to work briefly on certain projects, then released to the jungle of the marketplace. Those who are unemployed or underemployed face the murderous attraction of drifting into the lumpenproletariat or the so-called "underclass" where they face even further restriction on opportunity and, worse, a possible stint in prison factories. But a people who have faced slavery are not daunted by the downside of capitalism; worse has been faced and surmounted.

The Black working class—and indeed the entire U.S. working class—must devote more attention to organizing unions and building a Left political party. The Cold War mandate dictated the dismantling of unions and the Left, and that is what has led the Black working class to the precipice of disaster. Emulating the example of South Africa is what will lead us away from an impending catastrophe and offer us hope for a glorious future beyond this perilous economy.

NOTES

1. According to a *Los Angeles Times* editorial of December 12, 1993, the net worth of African-Americans in the state averages $9359 compared to $44,980 for Euro-Americans. More than one-third of Black men in California grow up in poverty; about thirty-one percent of Black families in the state make less than $15,000 per year compared to twenty-five percent of Latinos and sixteen percent of Euro-Americans.

2. I formerly served as Special Counsel to Local 1199 and remain close to this union. These workers nationally are concerned that impending health care reform could lead to the erosion of tens of thousands of jobs that Black women have held in this industry.

3. For an interesting discussion of this, refer to the *New York Newsday* editorial of April 24, 1994.

4. This was mentioned in a *New York Newsday* editorial of April 24, 1994.

REFERENCES

Allen, Theodore. 1994. *The Invention of the White Race*. New York: Routledge.

Anderson, Elijah. *Streetwise: Race, Class and Change in an Urban Community*, Chicago: University of Chicago Press.

Arbatov, Georgi. 1992. *The System: An Insider's Life in Soviet Politics*. New York: Times Books.

Brown, Elaine. 1992. *A Taste of Power: A Black Woman's Story*. New York: Pantheon.

Brown, Richard M. 1991. *No Duty to Retreat: Violence and Values in American History and Society*. New York: Oxford University Press.

Chanan, Michael. 1976. *Labour Power in the British Film Industry*. London: British Film Institute.

Chang, Gordon. 1990. *Friends and Enemies: The United States, China and the Soviet Union, 1948–1972*. Stanford: Stanford University Press.

Daniels, Douglas Henry. 1980. *Pioneer Urbanites: A Social and Cultural History of Black San Francisco*. Philadelphia: Temple University Press.

Davis, Mike. 1990. *City of Quartz: Excavating the Future in Los Angeles*. New York: Verso.

Davis, Michael D. and Hunter R. Clark. 1992. *Thurgood Marshall: Warrior at the Bar, Rebel on the Beach*. Seacaucus, N. J.: Carol.

Dreyfuss, Joel and Charles Lawrence. 1979. *The Bakke Case: The Politics of Inequality*. New York: Harcourt Brace Jovanovich.

Fink, Leon. 1989. *Upheaval in the Quiet Zone: A History of Hospital Workers' Union, Local 1199*. Urbana: University of Illinois Press.

Fukuyama, Frances. 1992. *The End of History and the Last Man*. New York: Free Press.

Fraser, Steve. 1991. *Labor Will Rule: Sidney Hillman and the Rise of American Labor*. New York: Free Press.

Gerstner, Louis V. Jr. 1994. *Reinventing Education:Entrepreneurship in America's Public Schools*. New York: Dutton.

Guinier, Lani. 1994. *The Tyranny of the Majority*. New York: Free Press.

Hall, Jacqueline. 1993. *Revolt Against Chivalry: Jesse Daniel Ames and the Women's Campaign Against Lynching*. New York: Columbia University Press.

Hammer, Michael and James Champy. 1993. *Reengineering the Corporation: A Manifesto for Business Revolution*. New York: Harper Business.

Horne, Gerald. 1992d. *Reversing Discrimination: The Case for Affirmative Action*. New York: International.

———. 1992b. "Hell in the City of Angels: 1965–1992" *Guild Practitioner* 49:3 (Summer).

———. 1992c. "Imperialist Rivalries," *Political Affairs* 71:11 (November).

———. 1994. "Race: Ensuring a True Multi-Culturalism." In Richard Caplan and John Feffer (eds.). *State of the Union 1994: The Clinton Administration and the Nation in Profile*. Boulder: Westview.

Jencks, Christopher. 1994. *The Homeless*. Cambridge: Harvard University Press, 1994; Mark Robert Rank, *Living on the Edge: The Realities of Welfare in America*. New York: Columbia University Press.

Katz, Michael. 1993. *The "Underclass" Debate: Views from History*. Princeton: Princeton University Press.

Kearny, Reginald. 1991. "Afro-Americans and Japanese, 1905–1941," Kent State University, Ph.d.

Kennedy, Paul. *Preparing for the Twenty-first Century*, New York: Random House.

Kirschenman, Joleen and Kathryn M. Neckerman. 1991. "'We'd Love to Hire them, But . . .': The Meaning of Race for Employers." In Christopher Jencks and Paul E. Peterson (eds.), *The Urban Underclass*. Washington, D.C.: Brookings Institution.

Korman, Abraham. 1988. *The Outsiders: Jews and corporate America*. Lexington, Mass.: Lexington Books.

Lacey, Robert. 1991. *Little Man: Meyer Lansky and the Gangster Life*. Boston: Little Brown.

Lardy, Nicholas R. 1994. *China in the World Economy*. Washington, D.C.: Institute for International Economics.

Leslie, Stuart. 1993. *The Cold War and American Science: The Military-Industrial-Academic Complex at MIT and Stanford*. New York: Columbia University Press.

Malveaux, Julianne and Phyllis Wallace. 1987. "Minority Women in the Workplace." In K.S. Koziara, M.H. Moskow, and L.B. Tanner (eds.), *Working Women: Past, Present, Future*. Washington, D.C.: Bureau of National Affairs.

Massey, Douglas S. and Nancy A. Denton. 1993. *American Apartheid: Seg-*

regation and the Making of the Underclass. Cambridge: Harvard University Press.

Morrison, Toni. 1970. *The Bluest Eye.* New York: Holt, Rinehart and Winston.

Olin and Roger Daniels. 1972. *Racism in California: A Reader in the History of Oppression.* New York: Macmillan.

Osborne, David. 1992. *Reinventing Government: How the Entrepreneurial Spirit is Transforming the Public Sector.* Reading: Addison-Wesley.

Ottley, Roi. 1943. *New World a-Coming Inside Black America.* Boston: Houghton Mifflin.

Reich, Robert. 1991. *The Work of Nations: Preparing Ourselves for 21st Century Capitalism.* New York: Knopf.

Richardson, Trudy. 1994. *Patient-Focused Care.* Alberta: United Nurses of Alberta.

Rideau, Wilbert. 1992. *Life Sentence.* New York: Random House.

Rosswurm, Steve (ed.). 1992. *The CIO's Left-Led Unions.* New Brunswick: Rutgers University Press.

Said, Edward and Christopher Hitchens. 1988. *Blaming the Victims: Spurious Scholarship and the Palestinian Question.* New York: Verso.

Schatzberg, Rufus. 1993. *Black Organized Crime in Harlem 1920–1930.* New York: Garland.

Seale, Bobby. 1991. *Seize the Time: The Story of the Black Panther Party.* Baltimore: Black Class Press.

Shakur, Sanyika. 1993. *Monster: The Autobiography of an L.A. Gang Member.* New York: Atlantic Monthly Press.

Sigelman, Lee and Susan Welch. 1991. *Black Americans Views of Racial Inequality: The Dream Deferred,* New York: Cambridge University Press.

Staiger, Janet. 1981. "The Hollywood Mode of Production: The Construction of Divided Labor in the Film Industry." Ph.D. dissertation, University of Wisconsin.

Starr, Paul. 1992. *The Logic of Health Care Reform.* Knoxville: Whittle.

Thurow, Lester. 1992. *Head to Head: The Coming Economic Battle Among Japan, Europe and America.* New York: Morrow.

Tyson, Laura. 1993. *Who's Bashing Whom? Trade Conflict in High-Technology Industries.* Washington, D.C.: Institute for International Economics.

Wade-Gayles, Gloria. 1994. *Pushed Back to Strength.* Boston: Beacon.

Washburn, Wilcomb. 1962. *The Effect of Bacon's Rebellion on Government in England and Virginia.* Washington, D.C.: Smithsonian Institution.

Wilson, William J. 1987. *The Truly Disadvantaged: The Inner City, the UNDERCLASS, and Public Policy.* Chicago: University of Chicago Press.

Kevin Arlyck

—————— *12* ——————

By All Means Necessary

Rapping and Resisting in Urban Black America

In the twenty-odd years of its existence, rap music[1] has been a consistent locus of controversy, and has suffered innumerable attacks from commentators situated all along the political spectrum. Rap artists have been routinely lambasted for what is perceived to be a glorification on their parts of violence, misogyny, and homophobia, and their general preoccupation with money; hip-hop is often characterized as the misdirected and pathological venting of ghetto anger (Gates 1990; Klinghoffer 1994). However, there is a growing constituency of critics who see rap as having the potential to be a positive force for social change, within both the Black community and the greater society. They view the anger present in rap as being a legitimate response to the oppression that African Americans, particularly young males, suffer in a society that at its core is still fraught with both personal and institutional racism. While these responses may not always be as progressive or constructive as some commentators might hope, they are nonetheless seen as both honest and representative of the feelings of young African Americans. As critic Michael Eric Dyson notes, "The values of memory and social criticism connect it [rap] to a powerful history of African-American cultural resistance, rebellion, and revolution" (Dyson 1993: 280). It is this expression of resistance, rebellion, and revolution in rap music that I am interested in exploring here.

In order to better understand the role that rap music plays in the lives of young Black people and in American popular culture, it is necessary to critically examine rap music's performance as a "voice" for young African Americans in the public discourse. Artists, fans, and supporters of the music contend that the ideas being articulated in the music are representative of the attitudes of young Black people. Critics counter that artists are simply out to make money and produce music specifically, and solely, designed to appeal to a mass consumer market. Proponents of both views make interesting and worthwhile points; unfortunately, the few nuggets of insight that have emerged from this debate have been buried under an avalanche of platitudes that are largely facile and reductionistic. If contemporary scholars are going to engage in any serious and, more importantly, helpful discussion of rap and its broader political, social, economic, and cultural significance, they need to take a more nuanced view of the phenomenon and explore these issues in ways that are as constructive as they are critical.

While many commentators occupy themselves with scrutinizing the professional and personal lives of rap artists, I believe that by taking a look at the songs they write we can better understand how different rappers have reacted, through their music, to the social, political, and economic inequality that young African Americans suffer from. Poverty, racism, inadequate education, severely limited employment opportunity, violence, drugs, and alcohol—the interlocking problems of the ghetto[2] have been thoroughly documented and analyzed by a range of social scientists and need not be reexamined here. It is also important to note that by no means do these hardships comprise the entirety of the urban African-American experience. By many accounts there is much joy, friendship, success (however one chooses to measure it), and love in the ghetto, a fact that is all too often ignored by those who write about it. And these positive aspects of urban life manifest themselves in rap music as well. However, I would suggest that many of rap's most powerful moments (some of which I have tried to capture here) have come when an artist is creating music in order to express his or her discontent with many of the harsh realities of ghetto life, especially when that life compares so unfavorably to that enjoyed by many within the larger, more affluent, white society.

Just as with other genres of popular music, rap music has always been sorted into sub-genres by its fans and critics; more recently, as these people have begun to view the form with a greater historical perspective, certain periods along the hip-hop timeline are understood to be characterized by specific attributes. Therefore, what was formerly seen simply as "rap music," an undifferentiated and contiguous whole, has been given ages similar to those assigned to classical, jazz, or rock music. The period that runs from approximately 1987 to 1991 has often been called the "Golden Age" of hip-hop by older (twenty-something) fans. Though commentators may disagree as to why the period deserves such acclaim, it is agreed that the era was characterized by artists who made music that was not only aesthetically pleasing but meaningful. For a time, it was hip for rap artists to discuss politcal and social issues in their music in complex and thought-provoking ways; hip-hop was no longer simply party music, and rappers were the conscience of a generation of African Americans.

It is this Golden Age that I will focus on in this chapter, for a number of reasons. Of all the periods in hip-hop, it is in the music of this era that we can find the most lucid expression of black resistance. Before 1987, few rap artists were articulating any sort of deliberate resistance to racism and oppression; by the early 1990s such protestations were omnipresent. Unfortunately, as often happens in popular culture, the ideas of the Golden Age were rapidly reduced to their lowest common denominator, and formerly thoughtful elaborations of resistance were dumbed down into dime-a-dozen homilies about killing cops. This is not to say that there are no contemporary artists who approach the same subjects critically and intelligently. In the public eye, however, they are overshadowed by the wanna-be gangsters who toss a verse about hard times in the ghetto into the stew of blunts, gats, and hoes. Although the Golden Age may have been an eternity ago in the chronology of popular music, I hold that the music from that time still holds much relevance today. All the artists featured here express the idea that the plight of African Americans has been caused, by and large, by white people, and that an angry and perhaps violent reaction to white racism is a valid one. Each artist has adopted a "persona" that is developed in his music and used as a means of expressing resistance to perceived white oppression. My examination of personas will focus on several rap artists and the ways in which they present themselves to their respective audiences.

All the artists I will be focusing on produce what I identify as resistive hip-hop, music that expresses an oppositional attitude toward perceived oppression by white society, and which recommends, directly or indirectly, a course of action to be taken in resisting. I have identified two basic categories that I believe will serve as useful analytical tools for discussing the rappers: the militant and the gangster.³ Of course, none of the rappers fall neatly into either category; fortunately, all of them are versatile and creative enough to defy simple categorization. My reason for employing these groupings is not to pigeonhole the rappers I have selected, but to provide a new way of looking at the ways in which they attempt to communicate with their people. I would argue that each persona represents for young African Americans a way of simultaneously relating to and resisting a racist white society. The songs these artists produce can provide valuable insight into how young African Americans view the society they live in.

Militant Messages from the Ghetto

The music produced by militants has often been referred to as "message" rap; theoretically, those artists who produce it are consciously attempting to impart some knowledge to or inspire a certain realization in their audience—essentially, an effort at consciousness raising. The first rap song to be explicitly conceived as such an attempt at communication was Grandmaster Flash's "The Message" (hence the term); at the time of its release, its depiction of urban life was not only the most realistic to date, but it also contained a sort of moral for listeners. The artists were clearly concerned about the vicissitudes of urban life and unambiguously advised that if one did not stay on the straight and narrow he or she was headed to an even more difficult life or possibly a premature death. "The Message" set the standard for a genre of rap music that directly confronts the problems of the ghetto in a way that acknowledges their seriousness and emphasizes how crucial it is that African Americans, particularly young people, deal with them wisely. Militant rap is also often referred to as "nationalist," meaning that it espouses the formation of an autonomous black nation through which African Americans will be able to reclaim the cultural heritage stolen by slavery and modern racism. Jeffrey Louis Decker has observed that "[h]ip-hop nationalists provide black youth with an indispensable history lesson concerning African-American militancy unavailable in public school curriculum" (Decker 1989: 66).

Public Enemy is widely recognized by hip-hop writers and historians as the foremost purveyor of "message" rap, and is often considered to be the most innovative and influential rap group in contemporary hip hop; in my opinion, it is the embodiment of militant and nationalist rap. Ever since its emergence in the mid-1980s, Public Enemy has been a continual, controversial presence in the hip-hop world. The group's leader and spokesperson, Chuck D, has never shied from expressing his anger over the racist oppression that he feels white people have subjected African Americans to for the past four centuries; most of Public Enemy's songs discuss this racism and what Chuck believes to be the appropriate response from his fellow African Americans. The lyrics are generally focused on the importance of self-sufficiency for African Americans, as a means to self-determination and freedom from dependence on white people. Public Enemy's basic philosophy is that white people have historically oppressed African Americans, and that Black people must take the responsibility for freeing themselves from the constraints of racism; white people will not do it for them. This sentiment is clearly expressed in the title of their second album, *It Takes a Nation of Millions to Hold Us Back.*

According to the Public Enemy world view, U.S. society is fundamentally racist and hypocritical; therefore they reject the validity of its anointed authorities (government, police, army, etc.). In their song "Black Steel in the Hour of Chaos," Chuck D tells of a fictitious encounter with the law after he receives a summons from the Federal Government. He boldly declares that "They wanted me for the army or whatever/Picture me giving a damn—I said never." After his imprisonment for refusing to join, Chuck recounts how he and his cellmates instigate a riot in reaction to their unjust incarceration, using deadly force when necessary. He justifies this violence by arguing that there is no other way to achieve justice in a society that continually perpetrates violence against African Americans. Equating incarceration with white oppression is a common theme in rap music, and one that makes sense, given the fact that

African Americans make up a disproportionate percentage of the nation's prison population.

Chuck's philosophy of violence is quite similar to the one expressed by Malcolm X some twenty-five years earlier—when used in self-defense, it is justified. The "Black Steel" in the title of the song is a reference to the gun Chuck takes from the prison guards and uses on them in his escape; he is clearly serving notice that the Black use of violence while resisting white oppression is potentially quite productive and perhaps necessary. Never mind whether Carlton Ridenhour the celebrity would actually use a gun or not; the threat is coming from Chuck D the militant rapper, and he is well aware that the imagery of armed African Americans (particularly men) has historically been a powerful and disturbing one in American society. The Public Enemy image is a conscious emulation of the Black Panthers and other black nationalist groups, who realized that being threatening in an intelligent way was more productive than simply being threatening. This lesson has not been lost on Public Enemy. As cultural critic Greg Tate puts it: "I dig these college-educated-and-proud-of-it-homeys because they're stomp-down and dissonant innovators of the form [rap music] who promote black nationalism with panache" (Tate 1992: 121–22).

The members of Public Enemy may be a pioneers, but by no means are they an exception; the theme of armed resistance by African Americans to violence being perpetrated on them is quite prevalent in rap; unsurprisingly, it is mostly directed toward the police. Boogie Down Productions (BDP) is one group that deals with the issue in this way. In the song "Bo! Bo! Bo!" rapper KRS-One tells of a (presumably fictitious) run-in with the law in which he uses a glass bottle and a shotgun to defend himself against a "redneck cop." And on the track "Who Protects Us From You?" KRS dictates an open letter to the police from all African Americans, listing the grievances that he has with them and their methods of law enforcement. Actually, at no point in the song does KRS specifically indicate that he is addressing the police, but the substance of his lyrics leave little doubt about who the "You" is. KRS challenges the authority of the police in much the same way that Public Enemy does that of the government and the army, by questioning their legitimacy. As Tricia Rose points out, KRS accuses the police of both selectively enforcing existing law and essentially creating their own. At different points in the song he accuses them of "Killing blacks, and calling it the law" and wonders whether "Every time you say 'That's illegal'/Does it mean that it's true?" (Rose 1994: 107–108).

Both groups are expressing the same sentiment, yet on different levels. While BDP is concerned with the day-to-day abuse that young African Americans in Los Angeles, New York, and other urban centers suffer at the hands of the police, PE is focusing on the larger issue of whether African Americans have any obligation to a nation in which they have historically been treated as second-class citizens. Both are reacting forcefully to what they perceive to be illegitimate and repressive authority. This militant attitude is the result of what the rappers see as the abuse of power by those who have authority in society. This attitude is by no means unfounded. The beating of Rodney King by four Los Angeles police officers is simply the most visible manifestation of a behavior that, for rap artists and their fans, is common in the inner city. African Americans have been universally criminalized because of the color of their skin; as Jeru the Damaja puts it: "the fact that I have melanin/Automatically makes me a felon." Because of this, police officers and other agents of authority have lost their legitimacy as upholders of the law and are no longer respected as such.

Reaching and Teaching

For the more sophisticated rapper, however, physical resistance is not enough, for violence will not bring real change. For him or her, education is the key; specifically, education for young African Americans about their history and culture, as opposed to the whitewashed education they receive in the public school system. Most of the rappers that I discuss contend that a Black-focused educational curriculum is crucial for the advancement of African Americans. KRS-One is its most persistent and forceful advocate, and he portrays himself as a teacher of young African Americans (his name is an acronym for Knowledge Reigns Supreme Over Nearly Everyone); although he qualifies as a militant, his main interest is in imparting knowledge to his African-American brothers and sisters. In the song "Why Is That?" he explains how the majority of the important Biblical figures came from Africa (primarily Egypt), and are not the white-skinned, straight-haired people they are traditionally depicted as.

In "You Must Learn," KRS opens the song with a conversation with a friend about how he was suspended from school. He goes on to indict the school system for teaching him useless information that has little to do with his life, and explains that his failure to achieve good grades is a direct result of the irrelevance of what is being taught in the schools. KRS contends: "It seems to me that in a school that's ebony/African history should be pumped up steadily," and proceeds to run down a list of famous African Americans and their achievements, from Garrett Morgan to Madame C.J. Walker, with the express purpose of showing the African-American that he or she is "more than a janitor." He is advocating for an educational system that will do more than present white history and culture as the sole heritage of all Americans; he wants African-American schoolkids to be taught about their own heritage, and to have it be respected. KRS is so enamored with the idea of African-American self-education that on BDP's fifth album one song is a plea to Black drug dealers to use their profits to reinvest in the community and open Black-controlled schools that give primacy to an educational curriculum that is directly relevant to Black youth.

Obviously, rappers do not want African-American students to be taught simply how to succeed in what is often referred to as a "white-dominated world." As the lyrics included earlier demonstrate, KRS-One's arguments go beyond exclamations about how African Americans are undereducated. He is also concerned about what it is that African Americans are being taught, and shares suspicions similar to those that Public Enemy puts forth. Both are attempting an examination of how the disadvantaged situation of African Americans has contributed to their further oppression. They are exposing the ways in which white racism not only manifests itself as physical repression but can infiltrate the consciousness of African Americans and radically affect their own self-image.

The ultimate result is that militants are highly distrustful of white people and white institutions, and reject the interracial cooperative ethic of the civil-rights movement. No self-respecting militant rap artist would be caught singing "We Shall Overcome" or hoping that someday all men will be judged by the content of their character. This is not to say that militants do not want Black and white people to live in harmony and equality, but they are not going to wait around in poverty until that day comes. These artists are both investigating the ways in which white society and its institutions oppress African Americans through physical and economic means and exposing how negative white conceptions about "Blackness" have affected the collective Black self-image. In a *New York Times* article focusing on this strain of hip-hop, music critic Jon Pareles states that the

> only militant messages headed for the pop charts appear in rap songs: a new contingent of self-described "radical" rappers are determined to carry serious ideas onto tape decks and dance floors . . . [radical rap's] vision of America as a racial and economic battleground is apocalyptic From the inside looking out, radical rap assigns the blame for the situation to powerful outside forces and promotes self-help as the only solution. (Pareles 1990: 1)

Those rappers who fall into the militant/educator categories are primarily concerned with freeing African Americans and their culture from white hegemony. Not all of them believe that white people are inherently evil, although all believe that white society is inherently racist. They stress the culpability of white people in creating the current desperate situation that many African Americans find themselves in, yet are not asking white people and white institu tions for help. They know of the victories of the civil rights movement, when whites and Blacks cooperated in the struggle for African-American equality, and they now seem rather empty. The new brand of resistance will require a show of force, as KRS-One asserts in the following quote:

> I'm looking in the face of negativity, hatred, violence, nigger, bitch, ho. I'm looking in that face, and I'm gonna pull a flower out and say, "I'm for peace, I'm for love"? Sorry. If negativity comes with a .22, positivity comes with a .45. If negativity comes with a .45, positivity comes with an Uzi:

The light has got to be stronger than the darkness. (Touré
1993: 61)

According to these militants and educators, it is not until African
Americans reclaim for themselves all the roles necessary for the
formation of a healthy society that they will truly achieve a version
of equality and will be able to effectively resist the white racism
that they feel may very well never disappear.

Illegitimate, Illegal, and Justified

The issue of crime in urban America has been thoroughly discussed
in many different forums, and there is no need to belabor the point
here. Suffice to say that just as violent crime is a fact of life in the
ghetto, so is it featured in much (though certainly not all) of rap
music. Crime is used both metaphorically and literally, for different reasons and with different effects. This distinction is often lost
on critics, who are either not familiar enough with the medium to
correctly interpret it, or who willfully ignore the subtleties of the
music in order to make a point. Although there are many rap artists who tend to glorify crime (particularly violent crime) in order
to get noticed, there are many who are not simply trying to be
shocking, but are trying to express some of the realities they are
faced with. There are many different types of gangsters, and although the endless parade of guns, drugs, alcohol, and misogyny
has become quite tiresome, there are those who use the medium
quite effectively. In this section I want to take a look at the ways in
which gangsters conceptualize the project of resistance, and how
their tactics differ from the militants.

Ice-T is the self-styled "Original Gangster" from Los Angeles,
though his tone is less heartless and uncompromising than the
gangsters who followed him. He has always presented his music in
a pseudo-illegal context; he generally characterizes his musical
production as a criminal enterprise, for which he is continually
persecuted by the so-called authorities that so many other rappers
have difficulty with. Ice hates the police like BDP does and hates
the government like Public Enemy does; however, he is less concerned with the general uplifting of African Americans as a group

than he is with removing the societal fetters that prevent individual players from "getting theirs." Ice seems most interested in reclaiming for African Americans the role of a "productive" member of society, one that has been stolen as they have been forced to serve the needs and interests of whites. He portrays himself as such a producer, giving the people a product (his music) that they cannot do without. In the song "I'm Your Pusher" from *Power*, Ice likens his music to a highly addictive drug, and he tries to convince a junkie to get hooked on his dope instead of the chemicals that are killing him, while bragging about how successful his business is: "I'll be the biggest dope dealer in history/'Cause all the fly'll be high off that Ice-T'". Although Ice may be breaking the law, from his perspective he has been left with few options in a society that denies Black men opportunities for legitimate, independent economic activity.

Ice-T may be the Original Gangster, but Niggas With Attitudes (NWA) is widely considered to be the group that embodied the gangster ethic, and their classic recording, *Straight Outta Compton*, is the definitive gangster rap album. Although they were preceded by a handful of self-identified gangsters like Ice-T, it is the NWA style that has inspired the current generation of gangsters. Loud, obscene, and confrontational, NWA burst upon the scene in 1989 and introduced hip-hop fans to an attitude towards life that had not been articulated in rap music: the "I don't give a fuck" attitude. The members of NWA portrayed themselves as violent, dangerous, materialistic, and uncaring young men who were content to live in the moment, as long as that moment promised quick cash, alcohol, sex, and freedom from harassment by either the police or their rivals on the street. As Greg Tate notes, they expressed the L.A. gang mentality "non judgementally, without any sense of moral distance" (cited in Cross 1993: 36). And group founder Eazy-E states that "[w]e wanted to do some shit that would just shock everybody, that we could relate to, and obviously everybody else could relate to" (Cross 1993: 201).

Despite this careless attitude, NWA did more than glorify violence and crass materialism on their album. *Straight Outta Compton* was the first rap recording to express how many young, urban-dwelling African Americans feel about the police in an explicit and boldly confrontational manner. Many listeners were shocked not

only by the utter lack of respect that the members of NWA evinced
for the police (which had been hinted at by other artists) but also
by the sheer anger and contempt they expressed. The most explicit
manifestation of this feeling is found in the appropriately-titled
"Fuck Tha Police." The song is literally an indictment of the Los
Angeles Police Department, which is being tried by the group—
prosecuting attorneys Ice Cube, MC Ren, and Eazy-E present their
personal police experiences as evidence before judge Dr. Dre. They
express considerable anger over the ways in which police need-
lessly harrass, abuse, and even kill young Black males, simply because of their race. The rappers advocate violence as a means of
defense against police abuse, and show little respect for the forces
of law and order. Unsurprisingly, this song created quite a stir
when it was released in 1989, even prompting a senior agent of the
Federal Bureau of Investigation to write a letter to NWA's record
company, criticizing the song for its supposed advocacy of violence
against police officers. This was followed by a nationwide, informal
attempt among urban police departments to prevent NWA from
performing the song on their summer tour, an effort that was partially successful (Marsh 1989: 33–37). The irony of the whole episode was that by trying to censor the group, police around the
country only succeeded in proving NWA's point about police harassment. Although the group's members did not respond to police
action at their concerts with gunfire, it is clear that their music
had inspired apprehension and perhaps some fear in the police. As
with Public Enemy, it is the implication that tolerance (or submission) has ended and violence will follow that makes the music so
powerful.

On the surface, it may seem as if NWA's response to police harassment and brutality is not much different from the ways in
which Public Enemy and BDP respond to similar oppression; all
three advocate the use of violence against a force that is unjustly
and unnecessarily hostile toward young African Americans. What
is different among the three is that while Public Enemy and BDP
take care to present their situations as critical instances of the
abuse of authority that must be responded to intelligently and decisively, NWA sees their experience as simply being part of their
everyday reality; there is little drama or tension in their narrative.
Consequently, they do not instill a sense of urgency in their lis-

teners; NWA is not so much responding to their situation as they are reacting to it, the best way they know how. Also, both Chuck D and KRS-One express a sense of responsibility in their music, a belief that they are not only fighting racism on their own behalf, but on the behalf of all African Americans. The members of NWA, on the other hand, are quite clear in their assertions that they are looking out for themselves, and others should get out of the way. In "Gangsta Gangsta" Ice Cube alerts the listener that he and his cohorts are utterly unsentimental and are not asking anyone to admire them: "Takin' a life or two/That's what the hell I do/You don't like how I'm livin"?/Well fuck you!"

While many West Coast gangsters are almost nonchalant about their violence, the ones from the East Coast take a more serious and fatalistic view of the business in which they are engaged. Kool G. Rap and DJ Polo are a duo that are, in my opinion, the best example of the East Coast gangster rap artists, and who discuss crime in ways similar, though not identical, to Ice-T. The song "Crime Pays" is the clearest expression of the East Coast gangster ethic that I know of. In it, Kool G. pleads his case, explaining that white people commit high-stakes crime all the time—white-collar crime—and that gangsters like himself are targeted by the authorities simply because of the color of their skin. He also recognizes that "the authorities" are simply agents of a powerful elite who go to great lengths to keep their privilege, and that a poor Black man cannot get ahead "Cause they came up with a law/To keep the rich motherfuckers rich and the poor motherfuckers poor." Kool G. in particular is careful about his image as not simply some hoodlum, but as a real criminal. I think this is an important distinction, because while a group like NWA is simply reacting to the intense pressures of urban life in the only way they see possible, Kool G. is making a conscious choice about his lifestyle as a response to a society that systematically obstructs the advancement of young African Americans like himself. And while Ice-T tries to give his legitimate enterprise an air of illegitimacy, Kool G. has no illusions that not only is the business he raps about illegal, but it is also immoral on some level. However, in a white-dominated, racist society, he has no choice.

Although all three gangster rap artists have militant qualities, I would be hesitant to place them in that category, for one basic reason. They are quite committed to such favorite American pastimes as earning money, misogyny, driving expensive cars, and killing people. None of them advocate for a significant alteration of American society the way groups like Public Enemy and Boogie Down Productions do. Gangsters embrace a materialistic lifestyle, while radicals warn against it. BDP has a song in which KRS-One raps from the perspective of an underprivileged inner-city teen who is lured into drug dealing by the prospect of quick cash. By the end of the song, his brother has been shot in a battle with a rival, his crew has been gunned down by the police, and he is under arrest. The moral of the story: "It's alright to like or want a material item, but when you fall in love with it and you start scheming and carrying on for it . . . just remember . . . it's gonna get you!" For the gangsters, the name of the game is not working to uplift the race, but simply surviving and perhaps prospering in a perpetually hostile environment. This is not to say that the militants are always above such concerns. However, they define themselves in opposition to society in ways that are potentially constructive; for the gangsters, opposition is simply a means of survival.

Conclusion

In general, all the rappers featured in this chapter share a common trait: they are all reacting forcefully (and often violently) to what they perceive to be an unjust society dominated by a racist elite that is expressly concerned with keeping African Americans in a position of subjugation. Their reactions take as many different forms as there are artists, and even songs. I think it is possible, though, to place the artists I have selected along two major axes: the militant/educator axis and the gangster axis. The reason I say this is because I see a fundamental difference between the approaches taken by PE and BDP, and those taken by NWA, Ice-T, and Kool G. Rap. The former are generally devoted to what I see as being a proactive approach to the goal of advancement of African Americans as a whole, whereas the latter are concerned with survival and getting what material benefit out of life they are able to. This is not to say that the gangsters are simply amoral killers looking to make a quick buck, or that the militants are above all material considerations. I see it essentially boiling down to a question of consciousness; each rap artist, through his music, is reacting differently to the difficult situation that is common to too many African Americans.

One of the major questions that remains is what possibilities there are for using hip-hop as a tool in the rebuilding of African-American urban civil society and as a means of affecting serious change in the broader American society, in order to transform it into a more equitable one. Andrew Ross has noted, writing about rap music's importance for African-American youth, that "while socially denied people do not express rage just as they please, or under circumstances of their own choosing, they do tend to opt for vehicles that are the least likely to be culturally influenced by the powerful" (Ross 1994: 193). I agree that rap is, and will continue to be for some time, the vehicle of choice; it also has tremendous potential as a tool, both as a means of educating and empowering African-American young people and as a line of communication between those young people and a larger society that generally ignores their achievements and focuses on their failures. However, if rap is to play a positive role in this regard, it will require a deliberate and determined effort on the part of those African-Americans who are involved in the hip-hop business; it will not happen inevitably, nor by accident.

If we are to accept the idea that many, if not most, contemporary rap artists are using hip-hop to communicate a message to the larger society, then we must also realize that this goal places artists in a difficult position. In order to reach the largest audience possible, as well as fulfill their obligations as artists under contract, they must tailor their art such that it is as accessible to as many different kinds of people as possible without comprimising its core values. Ross has in fact argued that the commercialization of what once was strictly Black music that had no audience other than African Americans has played a vital role in the promotion of African-American culture to a larger population: "These commercial forms [of music] were, after all, the actual historical channels through which 'black' meanings were made widely available, and were received and used by a popular audience, even a black audience" (Ross 1989: 71). Similarly, Chuck D of Public Enemy has stated that rap music is the CNN that African-American kids never had. For him, rap music is a flash bulletin from the front of Black America's fight against a racist society, an ever-changing series of snapshots capturing the essence of the African-American urban experience.

However, rap music is most certainly not a pure communication between rap artists and the disenfranchised African-American youth of the inner city, but one that is significantly mediated by financial concerns. Consequently, rap music's usefulness as a tool to be used in the rebuilding of African-American civil society will necessarily be lessened due to its inextricable (and unavoidable) association with corporate America. Record companies are most concerned with selling their commodities, and little they do is oriented toward any other goal; revolutionary messages from the ghetto are not going to be given very much consideration unless, of course, they move a lot of units. Thus, rap artists who wish to promote positive change and growth in African-American civil society must find ways to couch their message such that it will appeal to a large music-buying public.

Many rap artists express frustration over the ways in which their music is compromised by their record company's desire to release a product that is seen strictly as a commodity, and one that must appeal as much to a white audience as an African-American one. If hip-hop is truly going to act as a messenger from the inner city for African Americans, they must have total control over its production. One of the more encouraging developments in the hip-hop industry over the last few years is the growth of Black-owned and Black-controlled record companies, and a continuation of this trend is crucial for the evolution of hip-hop. Of course, African American-owned record companies will be no more exempt from the demands of capitalism than their white-owned counterparts, and will still need to sell records; commercial viability will still be an important consideration. Even in its current nascent stage, the African-American hip-hop industry consists of entrepreneurs who differ significantly in their commitment to rap music as a positive social force.

And critics should be careful in their condemnations of those artists who are primarily committed to making money and who do so by exploiting themes of drugs, violence, and misogyny; while we may deplore the imagery they use, we should not assume that they represent the attitudes and ideas of most young African Americans. As Chuck D says, "You've got to pick and choose your role models. Some rappers should be, and some choose not be" (Small 1992: 41). There are a number of intelligent, dedicated, and concerned rap artists who see the promotion of positive social values such as education, non-violence, respect for women, and commercial success not as mutually exclusive, but as naturally compatible. Music critic Alan Light explains that

> even when not explicitly issues-oriented, rap is about giving voice to a black community otherwise underrepresented, if not silent, in the mass media. It has always been and remains (despite the curse of pop potential) directly connected to the streets from which it came. It is still a basic assumption among the hip-hop community that rap speaks to real people in a real language about real things. (Light 1991: 868)

In their vision of the future, the one they will help shape, rappers will no longer be forced to respond to such oppressive and denigrating conditions as have been currently imposed upon them, and African Americans will be able to create lives for themselves that are not subject to the depredations of a racist society. Until then, however, the artists I have discussed and their emulators will continue to resist, in the words of KRS-One (taking his cue from Malcolm X), "by all means necessary."

——————————— NOTES ———————————

1. The terms rap and hip-hop are often used interchangeably. While I use them interchangably in this discussion, it should be mentioned that the term "rap" is the preferred term when referring to the music, and "hip-hop" to denote the broader urban youth culture (dance, clothes, language, attitude, etc.) that is associated with the music.

2. I use the term "ghetto" to signify an area of a city characterized by poor housing, little local business or industry, high incidence of crime, inadequate educational resources, and populated primarily by non-white people whose income often places them below the poverty line.

3. Admittedly, these categories are somewhat narrow and are not meant to be definitive. They are used here because they reflect how I generally think about "resistive" rap music. I would encourage others to develop their own archetypes, according to their own perspective on hip-hop.

REFERENCES

Cross, Brian. 1993. *It's Not About a Salary . . . Rap, Race, and Resistance in Los Angeles*. London: Verso.
Decker, Jeffery Louis. 1989. "The State of Rap: Time and Place in Hip Hop Nationalism." *Social Text* 34.
Dyson, Michael Eric. 1993. *Reflecting Black: African-American Cultural Criticism*. Minneapolis: University of Minnesota Press.
Gates, David. 1990. "The Rap Attitude." *Newsweek* (March 19).
George, Nelson. 1993. "Hip-hop's Founding Fathers Speak the Truth." *Source*.
Hacker, Andrew. 1992. *Two Nations: Black, White, Separate, Hostile and Unequal*. New York: Ballantine.
Klinghoffer, David. 1994. "See No Evil." *National Review* (January 24).
Light, Alan. 1991. "About a Salary or Reality?—Rap's Recurrent Conflict." *South Atlantic Quarterly* (Fall).
Marsh, Dave and Phyllis Polack. 1989. "Wanted for Attitude." *Village Voice* 34 (October 10).
Pareles, Jon. 1990. "'Radical Rap': Of Pride and Prejudice." *The New York Times* (December 16).
———. 1993. "Ice-T's Latest Gangster-Rap Caper Finds Him Alone and On His Own." *The New York Times* (March 29).
Rose, Tricia. 1994. *Black Noise: Rap Music and Black Culture in Contemporary America*. Hanover, N. H.: Wesleyan University Press.
Ross, Andrew. 1994. "The Gangsta and the Diva." *The Nation* 259 (August 22/29).
———. 1989. *No Respect: Intellectuals and Popular Culture*. New York: Routledge.
Shecter, Jon. 1992. "Liner notes to Street Jams: Hip-Hop From the Top," Part I. Rhino Records.
Small, Michael. 1992. *Break It Down: The Inside Story From the New Leaders of Rap*. New York: Citadel Press.
Staples, Brent. 1993. "The Politics of Ganster Rap." *The New York Times* (August 27).
Tate, Greg. 1988. "Titty Boom-A-Rooney." *Village Voice* 33 (September 13).

————. 1992. *Flyboy in the Buttermilk: Essays on Contemporary America.* New York: Simon & Shuster.

Touré. 1993. "KRS-One." *Rolling Stone* 672 (December 23).

Will, George F. 1990. "America's Slide Into the Sewer." *Newsweek* (July 30).

Kwando M. Kinshasa

13

Crisis and Lifestyles of Inner-City Bloods

Youth Culture as a Response to the Urban Environment

> I am a going-and-coming-back being
> I am Because I was and Re-Was Before
> I am Because I will Be and Re-Be Again.
>
> *The African Book without A Title*
> —Fu-Kiau, K. Bunjeki

My grandmother often used a large black iron pot to cook a delicious stew of roast beef, potatoes, carrots, onions, and parsley. Ever so tenderly she would add her own brew of hot sauce, which was made with cayenne, vinegar, red peppers, and a dash of Red berry wine. Her stew was always cooked on the rear right burner of an upright four-burner stove. Rice, a major aspect of this Sea Island dish, was cooked separately on the left burner in a metal pot resembling an old silver helmet, with the top canted just enough so that it wouldn't boil over—yet allowing the stew's aroma to seep in. A kettle of hot water for home-grown peppermint tea always sat on the front left burner, while golden fresh corn bread—kept warm by steam coming from the kettle—sat on the front right burner, . . . thereby completing her dinner arrangements. This was a symphony of food conducted by a chef waiting for her audience to enjoy its possibilities.

I often wondered what ever happened to that old iron pot, and if found, would I be able to prepare a stew, not similar, but exactly the way it was done some years ago? I suspect not for several reasons.

For one thing, not only have stoves and ovens changed but also the very structure of society, and those intended social and communal relationships generally associated with eating. Even the concept of the dinner hour has dramatically evolved into a commercialized corporate production sanctioned by non-familial interests whose primary concern is in production cost. In effect, the iron pot as a symbol of communal breaking of bread has been supplanted by the resilient teflon-coated receptacle of a fast-food industry. Nowhere is this more apparent than in the growing impersonal centers of America's inner city areas where culture has been reduced to an artifact of power and authority, and where the notion of social consciousness is premised upon self-interest and psychic needs.

This chapter examines the condition of contemporary Black urban youth who, as products of this changing culture, are increasingly less concerned with the welfare of others and preoccupied with self-interest and the use of aggression and violence in satisfying their immediate needs. These developments, it will be argued, do not occur in isolation and are very much linked to the current process of economic and cultural globalization. The chapter concludes with some policy recommendations for change.

Children of Crisis

In Alex Kotlowitz's book, *There Are No Children Here*, challenges faced by today's urban youth are delineated in a manner that indicates that for a large segment of American inner-city "young bloods"[1] or "homey's," growing up within an urban environment poses immense social as well as psychological challenges, especially for those youths of African-American background. The problem, as Kotlowitz implies, is not simply one that highlights a lessening importance of the nuclear family structure among a growing segment of American youth, nor is it exclusively youth's perennial challenging of an older generation's value system. It has more to do with a multitude of social variables whose impact upon the general urban environment is exacting a horrendous cost for both the victims and the perpetrators and, concomitantly, are bringing traditional American mores and values into question. In this context, inquiries into the possibilities of a youth culture's forever changing the landscape of America have become more than a homily on the generation gap; they are a succinct examination of the fundamental concept of what America's urban centers symbolize.

Inner-city youth's response to the urban environment occurs on the individual as well as the societal level. For instance, one cannot separate the exigencies of low income, poor housing, and poor health from an individual's social personality and/or social attitude. Though this troika of poverty often lands on the shoulders of many American youth in the form of failed dreams while sparing their inner concepts of self, among inner-city youth these realities often explode upon a consciousness already saturated by the exacting torture of a depersonalized environment. This is abundantly clear in the public school systems, where national figures indicate that while free education has traditionally been the vehicle for upward mobility by Americans, today, forty to sixty percent of students in inner cities drop out of school before graduation (Marnet 1993).

Similarly, statistics reflecting the interactive modes of inner-city youth tend to define the urban environment as an arena of mayhem, in which only in rare cases are issues aimed at understanding youth addressed from a cultural perspective. For example, "while in 1991, 10 to 17 year olds accounted for 17 percent of all violent-crime arrests, and more than 2,200 murder victims in 1991 were under 18 (an average of more than six young people killed every day), juvenile arrests for murder increased by 85 percent between 1987 and 1991. The Justice Department also estimates that each year, nearly 1 million young people between 12 and 19 are raped, robbed or assaulted, often by their peers (U.S. Justice Department 1991).

Social disorder as implied by the above statistics is indicative of a troubled environment, where youth having the power neither to create nor to sustain disorder do so as an act of defiance. However, an attempt is being waged in various quarters of Western society to develop a political agenda that asserts that increases in American inner-city violence is directly and solely associated with the ethnic and racial phenotypes now predominating those centers. Such a proposition points to the most rebellious segment of any group, its youth, and then defines that segment's inability to assimilate as further proof of the group's anomic cultural and social relationship to society. The criminalized urban youth is then identified and labeled as the sponsor of innate violence. Their clothing style, language use, radios, body language, and what is assumed as their general disregard for social norms and mores becomes a part of what is defined as "inner city youth culture." By doing so, social observers can, without further investigation, subjectively note that for these youths, violence is in their heads, and that the culture of aggression shows up in their speech, their play, and their entertainment.

The notion of young "inner-city youth" or "bloods" as being undisciplined and unruly has received much attention from proponents of this viewpoint. One response proclaims that the question of order versus disorder within any environment, particularly the inner city, is critical if society and personal liberties are to be protected. This view also asserts that when social services such as garbage collection seldom occur, when alcoholics drink in doorways and urinate in the street, when broken windows are not repaired or graffiti is not removed, when abandoned cars are allowed to disintegrate on the street—a sense of community is lost. The result of such a development is a neighborhood vulnerable to pathological nuances of disorder, which in turn helps to create an atmosphere for violent street crime. Disorderliness, so it is argued, arouses much fear among city dwellers and as a consequence entices the proliferation of criminal elements (Wilson 1985).

By extension, this perspective also suggests that a community's inability to monitor itself in those areas that would suggest order and a level of empowerment is indicative of a breakdown in a neighborhood's infrastructure, primarily within the family. Often proponents of this position also allude to a questionable proposition that suggests that a failed family structure leads to disorderly youth and criminal behavior (Wilson 1985).

Within this arena of so-called "inner-city pathology," youth's response to the violence of deferred power relationships is to reject in forceful terms the possibility of their own powerlessness. Defensive posturings appearing often as aggressive pronouncements of the "make my day" ethic are prime examples of a syndrome that youth have adopted from several quarters of the larger society. For instance, while the "Don't mess with me," "I don't give a shit," "Back the F___k Off," "Bitch," and "I'm Deadly" T-shirts may in fact be "a window to the actual feelings and mores of the larger culture," this kind of profanity is also an attack upon what many youth feel is a non-responsive, insensitive society (Kantrowitz 1993).

Dr. Robert Phillips, Director of Forensic Services for the Connecticut Department of Public Health has observed that violence of this sought is not invented by specific segments of the American populace, but that "they learn it." And that "it shows up in our speech, in our play, more than ever in the entertainments we fashion and fancy, in business style . . . there's an extraordinary degree of violence in the language, and it's the window to the actual feelings and mores of the culture" (Kantrowitz 1993).

Assistant Dean of The Harvard School of Public Health Deborah Prothrow-Stith opined that American culture is becoming "aggressively on the defensive, . . . our national icons tend to be men who excel at violence, from John Wayne to Clint Eastwood. When President Clinton ordered a retaliatory air strike on Baghdad, Iraq, because of an alleged plot against ex-president George Bush, his popularity rating took a leap [upwards], just as Bush's had when, as president, he ordered up the Gulf War, in which an estimated 100,000 Iraqi civilians were killed by bombs and missiles" (*ibid.*). If this is so, youthful resistance to societal abnormalities occurs on a variety of levels, of which verbal use is only one indicator of much deeper social exigencies.

Structural Arrangements and Inner-City Youth

In Kotlowitz's (1992) ethnographic study of a Chicago family, the mother, Lajoe Rivers, her eight children, a husband, Paul, who was physically and emotionally absent from his family after seventeen years of marriage, found themselves living in an environment which can only be described as a war zone or a prison in revolt. In this setting, Lajoe's youngest boys, Lafayette and Pharaoh, increasingly developed a perception of the world as being bounded by the public houses in which they live, and the implicit socialization processes of the "projects" as one premised upon maximum and minimum security relationships.

Not simply a play on words, the living conditions of Lajoe and her children in the Henry Horner housing complex in South Chicago suggest a life style similar to what might be expected in Houses of Detention throughout America, such as Division four of the Cook County Jail, which housed Lajoe's other sixteen-year-old, Terrance. It is in the physical construction of public housing and Houses of Detention or jails where correlations between the two structures is apparent. For instance, an incarcerated youth coming from the projects would note that the thick wire mesh lobby windows, plated elevator windows, ceramic-tiled hallways, and cell-like rooms and mint green or pastel wall colors are not only similar to, but exactly what he would find at home. With this reality in mind, specific questions come to mind, such as what social psychological factors impact upon a child born within an environment that suffers from administrative neglect, rodent infestation, fires, increasing levels of drug use, stairwells filled with the odor of urine, assaults and homicides, in buildings containing sixteen families per 18, 20 or 24 floors? And how strong are the coping mechanisms of inner-city youth who must live within this cultural milieu? Succinctly stated, city housing or "projects" have become holding pens for people whose dreams for a decent life have been systematically or intentionally deferred.

A longitudinal study conducted by Dr. Thomas Achenbach, Director of the Center for Children, Youth and Families at the University of Vermont from 1976 to 1989, identified four symptoms as indicators of youths' hard times: withdrawal from social problems, attention or thinking problems, delinquency and or aggression, and anxiety and depression. However the limitations of the study should be pointed out. Chiefly, the authors suggest that, "by setting aside the financial status of their [youth] families, . . . Black children had no greater problems than White children." If taken prima-facie one would conclude that, however extraordinarily, a level of measured "equality" could be found between the cultural life styles of inner-city Black and white youth if class issues were resolved. Such a conclusion is not only spurious but as we shall see, potentially problematic for inner-city Black youth survival.

To understand the cultural matrix of inner-city youth is to come to grips with what Jonathan Kozol has defined as the "savage inequalities" white America has perpetrated upon urban America (Kozol 1991). For example, tragic social inequities are evidenced by statistics from a recent study by the not-for-profit United Hospital Fund of New York, which indicate that in the South Bronx, one of New York City's lower income areas, "531 infants out of 1,000 neonatals require neonatal hospitalization, compared to 69 infants in 1,000 in the middle and upper class mostly white community of Riverdale in the North Bronx. Similarly when the death rate in Central Harlem among Black children is the same as in Malaysia, or when in East Harlem the rate is even higher than for many so-called "Third World" countries, at 34 per thousand, or further still when a child's chance of surviving to age five is better in Bangladesh than in East Harlem, urban rage is better understood" (Kozol 1991:115–116; NYC Dept. of Health 1992).

Altruism and the Social Drama

Consequently, social economic arrangements as presented by Kozol elicit questions about youth's social status and the roles they fulfill within society. Critical to this analysis is understanding the role of altruism in this social drama. Although altruism is generally defined as "an unselfish concern for the welfare of others" (Stein 1980:25), it also suggests the striving for social attainment and social responsibility, a sense of unlimited possibilities for the individual, and a positive reproduction of the unselfish personality in service to society at large. Whereas this is important for youth if they are to develop within a given social structure, any modification, dissatisfaction, or loss of these altruistic possibilities will have dramatic implications for their sense of commitment and positive social involvement with the larger society. It is a logical deduction, therefore, that there would be a marked absence of altruistic sentiment among youth who live within a battleground environment where social policies ignore issues of inequity. A culture of resistance is bound to develop (Barrett 1993:73).

Addressing this issue, pyschologist Hope Hill at Howard University postulates that concern for personality development or damage is critical for those inner-city children and youth we do not notice for one reason or another. Hill then identifies five major areas that appear to be affected by exposure to community violence: erosion of the sense of personal safety and security; disruption of lifestyle and the major agents of socialization; generalized emotional distress; depersonalization; diminished future orientation (Isaacs 1992:58).

In this regard, one must also begin to examine the possibility that inner-city youth are being acclimated to a reality of *maximum* incarceration by a society that sanctions official neglect and exploitation within an urban environment of *minimum* security. April Allen, a fifteen-year-old who lives in Boston's Roxbury section, has friends who think of jail as a kind of sleepaway camp. "The boys I know think it's fun to be in jail because other boys they know are in jail too," she says. Prison is a way of looking: the dropped-waist, baggy-pants look is even called "jailing" in Miami. And prison is a way of acting. "In prison, the baddest, meanest guy runs the cell," says H.T. Smith, a lawyer and African-American activist who practices in Miami's Overtown ghetto. "Your neighborhood, your school—it's the same. You've got to show him you're crazy enough so he won't mess with you" (Kantrowitz 1993:44–45). Keep in mind, conclusions drawn from this process may have little to do with *who* becomes labelled a criminal, yet everything to do with *how* one becomes criminalized.

A glaring example of this is drawn from a 1989 law in Illinois which mandated that juveniles living in the Chicago Housing Authority [CHA] buildings arrested for selling drugs will be tried as adults. That is to say, youths in Illinois under seventeen cannot be charged as adults unless they live in Public Housing, and as reported in a local newspaper, "in the past year every young person prosecuted under the CHA provision has been African American." Maria Woltjen, an attorney for The Lawyer's Committee for Civil rights Under the Law, commenting on this particular law stated, "the Illinois legislature made a decision that there is nothing we can do with 'these young people,' and in making this decision condemned these youth. In other words, when they get out of prison, they will be prone to do much more violent crimes because of what our criminal justice system has condemned them to" (see Kobernick 1993).

Segregation Patterns and Inner-City Youth

The social plight of many inner-city youth can be directly associated with the de facto racial and class segregation patterns of urban America (Roberts 1992:1). Historically, American segregation patterns have impacted upon the African-American community, and specifically its youth, in two violent ways. The first is that it evokes upon the individual and eventually the community a sense of being marginalized, labelled, stigmatized, and finally criminalized. In doing so, this process creates a historical scenario that deems Blacks as Americans only when they have periodically advanced through a "legitimizing" ritual of judicial fiats or legislative procedures, which in turn leads to an enactment of Civil Rights Bills theoretically aimed at alleviating social inequities. The painful reality for Black Americans is that their status as Americans has always been open for review and adjustment by white Americans, consequently their social well-being has always been contingent upon successful review by one legal or extra-legal judicial body or another. Social violence on this level has ironically created among Blacks a cynical yet strong attachment to the material ethos of American consumerism, while simultaneously rejecting any strong spiritual attachment to society beyond that of a faith in the future (Walters 1993).

African Americans are not, therefore, surprised by the latest economic Census Bureau data from 1992, which underlines the fact that economic inequality between the races is widening: The median Black family income of $21,761 was only 55.3 percent of the median white family income of $39,320, and a greater disparity existed in employment, poverty, housing ownership rates, and in quality housing. But greater still is the disparity in the area of economic reproduction, i.e., ownership of income-earning resources and organized enterprises to create jobs and financial capital. Deficient in this area, Blacks are largely dependent upon others for employment. In 1987 for example, "Blacks owned fewer than 15 businesses per 1000 persons compared with more than 72 businesses per 1000 persons for whites. Moreover, black-owned business generated only $775 in revenues per employee, compared with $56,120 for white businesses. Consequently, black per capita net worth was only $10,651, and 80% of these holdings were in home and motor vehicle equity. Whites had a net worth of $51,191 per capita, and less than half of that was in the same types of equity" (Swinton 1994:24).

Some ninety years ago, W.E.B. DuBois noted that Blacks' divided sense of loyalty, that is to say, to themselves as a people and as Americans, was a source of serious social and political disorientation due to their day by day marginalizing within society. This kind of social denigration, DuBois argued, forced blacks to camouflage their hatred, fears, and anxieties in the face of American racism by developing a non-threatening social personality when around whites. He defined this phenomenon as "twoness," a tactic of accommodating oneself to one's sense of social political impotence yet exercising limited control in those areas beyond the pale of the dominant power (DuBois 1969:17). This concept of the split social personality cannot be fully assessed in today's terms unless we evaluate the explicit social psychological cost paid by the African-American community, and specifically its youth, as a result of this psychic implosion of frustration and rage, or what C.L.R. James defined as, "passion not spent but turned inward" (James 1963:148).

The second major way in which American segregation has impacted African-American youth is through inner-city marginalization and isolation. These patterns have created an atmosphere of violent confrontation and resistance as each succeeding generation of black youths increasingly disavow any allegiance to a social-cultural agenda whose values appear to be hypocritical and harmful to their sense of self-esteem and self-worth. Inner-city youths have constructed a cultural matrix outside society's conventional notions of the peer group. Identified as "crews," these constructs are in many instances urbanized versions of communal family networks vying for power and status in society, yet challenging the traditional notion of sub-cultural groups' dependency upon a dominant social structure.

If, as psychologist Amos Wilson suggest, "feelings of power, competence, mastery, self-control, self-determination and autonomy are of essential importance in positive mental health and prosocial behavior," inner-city youth are quickly becoming cognizant that efforts for growth in these areas are fraught with dangers and risks (Wilson 1992:68). Moreover, for some inner-city youths, striving for a sense of control within an urban environment largely distressed by de facto segregation in social institutions such as education, is a learning experience. For it gives credence to the nihilistic concept that the essential difference between those who have power and control over others and those who don't is simply the question of who can aspire successfully regardless of the cost to others. In this analysis, morality and power as such are simply relative to the task at hand. Moreover, while humanitarianism, patriotism, and philanthropy become associated with the gloved hand of the power elite, immorality and powerlessness become a cliche for the disadvantaged. It is the latter development that contemporary inner-city youth reject and in doing so challenge the traditional mores of social behavior.

Inner-city youth's assertiveness in defining a new reality based upon their perceptions invariably forces them to come face to face with the rawness of material-based urban lifestyles. Within this cauldron of expectations and nihilistic role models, violence in its numerous configurations and disguises becomes not only a way of life but the very meaning of life. Life becomes a contest for survival, where the leader is whoever demonstrates the most guile, cunning, and power.

The problem becomes even more complex when we realize that violence in African-American communities affects not only the victims but also the survivors. More and more young African-American children and family members witness or are exposed to violent behavior in their daily lives. In her research on this subject, Mareasa Isaacs cites several studies conducted in major cities across the nation. A recently completed study of fifth graders in a school located in an economically deprived area of New Orleans found that 40 percent of these ten-year-olds had seen a dead body, 72 percent had witnessed weapons being used, and 49 percent had observed a wounding. A similar study conducted in 1990 in a school in Washington, D.C., located in an area considered to be only "moderately" violent, found that 12 percent of the fifth and sixth graders had been shot, stabbed, or sexually assaulted, and 22 percent had witnessed someone else being shot, stabbed, or sexually assaulted. It was also reported that on an average day, 21,800 young Black men in the nation's capital are involved with the criminal justice system. Of those, 7,800 were in jail or prison; 6,000 were on local probation; 3,700 were on parole; and 1,300 were on

Federal probation. The report estimated that 3,000 others were awaiting trial on bond or being pursued on felony or misdemeanor warrants. In the city of Chicago, a recent survey of 1,035 children ages ten to nineteen in several public schools reported that 75 percent of the participating boys and 10 percent of the participating girls had directly witnessed the shooting, robbing, or killing of another person. Most of these children never received any type of screening or mental health intervention to determine the impact of this violence on their social and emotional development. Certainly, the implications for the normal development and functioning of these children raise enormous issues for the African-American community and the larger American society in general (Isaacs 1992:45; DeParle 1992:11).

These studies suggest that the impersonal, almost nihilistic life style of many urban youth negates most altruistic expressions of group concern unless it is directed toward the immediate experiential group, the crew. The nuclear family unit, once believed to be the fount of positive creative expression, now becomes a corralled and inverted illustration of the previous generation's inability to demonstrate social control of their lives and communities. These developments have engraved a humiliating if not devastating effect upon those African-American children who correctly sense that their social worth is viewed disparagingly by much of American society.

In addition, one recognizes that inner-city youths' sense of powerlessness is actually altruism turned inward, and like suppressed passion promotes feelings of rage, which when acted out further labels Black youths as marginalized, dysfunctional, destructive social misfits. Inward rage of this sort exhorts youth to demean those symbols of society that are considered representatives of this external " force." Accordingly, inner-city youth are labelled with charges of "self hatred" and "demonization" as they, the victims of social oppression, become further victimized by their resistance to a social order that is viewed as antithetical to their best interest. As a consequence of this development, we see that youth's resistance to racial devaluation is not pretty, nor is it acceptable by those who have "bought" in to the dominant social order's notion of social change. Similarly, their rejection of self-devaluation, dramatized in their urban attire, is reminiscent of Ralph Ellison's comments in

Invisible Man: "When they approach me they see . . . everything and anything except me . . . [this] invisibility . . . occurs because of a peculiar disposition of the eyes . . ."

Fear of devaluation and alleviation of altruistic endeavors on a national level occurs "from the first grade onwards," in schools whose sole purpose is to propagate a feeling that Blacks are squatters in white America's social institutions. So much so that "blacks have the extra fear that in the eyes of those around them their full humanity could fall with a poor answer or a mistaken stroke of the pen" (Steele 1992:75). Conversely, the inner-city "crew" provides an opposite sense of worth, and in doing so develops a feeling among its members that goals can be established and obtained, albeit juxtaposed to those of the general social order.

Ultimately, we must conclude that inner-city violence is spurious when correlated *solely* with urban poverty. One must instead consider the saliency of social structural factors that help to maintain a more pernicious form of violence, i.e., poor housing, insufficient medical facilities, poor health care, inappropriate educational system, joblessness, drug importation, and gun manufacturing. Yet it is the poor inner-city residents of America who are viewed as the problem due to their alleged laziness, constant "complaining," and criminality.

In this regard, one notes that in conjunction with America's ongoing culturally traditional love of violence, where large segments of its populace are inundated by profit-making ventures of drugs and guns, it is the disenfranchised African and Spanish-speaking American youth along with their class and racial competitors, white American youth, who are targeted as potential consumers of games of violence. As one promoter of a particular violent video game proclaimed, "one came in two versions, with or without extreme violence"; and that, "players choice depends on what game system they have at home" (Kantrowitz 1993).

The spectacle of social violence and homicides in urban and, increasingly, suburban communities has reached a level where many argue that it threatens to desensitize a fearful and potentially victimized populace much in the same way a therapist desensitizes a phobia patient. Although one can document Post-Traumatic Stress Syndrome in Vietnam veterans as a definitive reaction to crisis, war-like conditions within numerous inner-city areas have also created a similar response in residents. One psychologist has observed that, "like soldiers who have seen too much combat, increasing numbers of children in the nation's capital are beginning to show battle fatigue." He further notes that, "some children cry uncontrollably, and keep their shades drawn in their room." A medical doctor at a local hospital in Washington, D.C., observed that "we're seeing more and more kids who are simply overwhelmed, not unlike people who have experienced shell shock." Another doctor calls them, "children under siege. . . . They are always suspicious . . . fatalistic and impulsive . . . they live surrounded by the vivid symbols of their undesirable status: drugs and death, decay and destitution" (see Ayers 1989).

Herein lies America's social-political predicament; instead of restructuring those systemic institutional inequities within its inner cities, a policy of benign neglect appears to be the methodology for governance. The resulting criminalization of urban population centers through ineffectual policies has bestowed upon inner-city youth an environment defined by drug importation, prostitution, gun running, political corruption, high infant mortality, retardation, mental illness, alcoholism, homelessness, and the ever-increasing likelihood that they will come into contact with America's criminalization process.

What Needs to Be Done

Inner-city African-American youth need to be encouraged to adhere to Afrocentric community based institutions, that is, educational, economic, religious, and social, that would provide them an independent cultural and philosophical outlook. The nucleus of this effort would be the establishment of *community-funded* programs, which would function as a counterbalance to illicit community-based activities like drug operations. An expansion of the alternative school model, utilizing community-based resources such as religious institutions, is essential in this process. At present, the public school system is simply a battleground where impressionable youth come into contact with various forms of malicious and racist neglect, whose traditional philosophical intent runs counter to the interest of African Americans' empowerment.

With the development of alternative educational structures an opportunity to discuss, organize, and then implement specific programs to enhance cultural, economic, and political roles in society will occur. This would be the impetus for a rebirth in African-American altruism, selflessness, and economic-political growth. Failure to address these issues, and/or to confront what appears to be a destructive pattern within the African-American community, will force millions of inner-city youth to rely solely upon the limited possibilities of system-based survival programs that emanate from a hostile conservative political structure. The innate failure of these programs will simply exacerbate a cruel inward self-destructive cycle of violence within African-American communities, which ultimately provides solace only to others.

It is apparent that the present tension-filled living conditions of many American inner-city residents will not disappear on their own accord. A shriking urban tax base, a reluctant and often malevolent governing elite, and a growing xenophobic atmosphere among the populace is indicative of greater social conflict in the near future. One hears among the parents of inner-city youth that "the teachers are not going to educate our children to replace theirs," . . . and so the die is cast. Expressions of rage, the manifestation of acrimony and despair, become a part of inner-city youth's response to a negative environment.

So while the glory of grandma's stove and its balanced potpourri has been seriously threatened by the plagues of selfishness, individualism, and cultural-historical amnesia, her "symphony of food" awaits the hungry mouths of eager youth. However, we must first resensitize them to the glories of self-nourishment.

NOTES

1. "Bloods," a term that exhorts racial camaraderie among African Americans, was used extensively in the nineteenth century by Black Civil War soldiers. Migrating southern Blacks in the early 1920s introduced this term into northern urban centers.

—————————————— REFERENCES ——————————————

Ayres, Drummond. 1989. "Drug Wars Scar Capital's Children." *The New York Times* (May 15).

Bunjeki, K. Fu-Kiau. 1994. *The Source: Magazine of Hip-Hop Music, Culture & Politics* No. 55. (April).

Barrett, Ronald K. 1993. "Urban Adolescent Homicidal Violence: An Emerging Public Health Concern." *The Urban League Review (Spring)*.

Brown, Claude. 1994. "The Language of Violence." *The Los Angles Times* (March 24).

De Parle, Jason. 1992. "Forty-Two Percent of Young Black Males Go Through Capital's Courts." *The New York Times* (April 18).

DuBois, W.E.B. 1969. *The Souls of Black Folk*. New American Library.

Issaacs, Mareasa R. 1993. "Violence: the Impact of Community Violence on African American Children and Families." *Mental Health*. Publication of the Maternal and Child Health Bureau, Arlington, Va.

James, C.L.R. 1993. *The Black Jacobins: Toussaint L'Ouverture and the San Domingo Revolution*. New York: Vintage Books.

Kantrowitz, Barbara. 1993. "Wild in the Streets." *Newsweek* (August 2) [with a special report on statistics from Office of Juvenile Justice and Delinquency Prevention, U.S. Justice Dept.]

Kobernick, Corey. 1993. "Challenge Drug Law as Racist." *People's World* (February 6).

Kotlowitz, Alex. 1991. *There Are No Children Here: The story of two boys growing up in the other America*. New York: Anchor Books.

Kozol, Jonathan. 1991. *Savage Inequalities: Children in America's Schools*. New York: Harper Perennial.

Marnet, Myron. 1993. "No Escape for the Underclass." In *The Dream and the Nightmare: The sixties legacy to the underschool*. New York: William Morrow & Co.

New York City Department of Health. 1992. *Infants Mortality Rate*. Provisional data. (7 July).

Roberts, Sam. 1992. "Shifts in 80's failed to Ease Segregation." *The New York Times* (July 15.).

Steele, Claude M. 1992. "Race and the Schooling of Black Americans." *The Atlantic Monthly* (April).

Stein, Jess, ed. 1980. *the Random House Dictionary*. New York: Ballantine Books.

Swinton, David. 1994. "The Key to Black Wealth: Ownership." *Black Enterprise* (July).

Walters, Ronald. 1993. "A Strategy for Redeveloping the Black Community." *The Black Scholar* 23:1.

Wilson, Amos. 1990. *Black on Black Violence: The Psychodynamics of Black Self Annihilation in the Service of White Domination*. New York: Afrikan World Infosytems.

———. 1992. *Understanding Black Adolescent Male Violence: Its Remediation and Prevention*. New York: Afrikan World Infosystems.

Wilson, James Q. 1985. *Thinking about Crime*. New York: Vintage.

Carl E. James

——— *14* ———
The Distorted Images of African Canadians

Impact, Implications, and Responses

Social images or stereotypes held of a particular population have implications for their participation and success in any society. In response, members of that population develop ways of dealing with such images in order to ensure their survival and well-being. In the case of the African-Canadian population, specifically the youth, the social images or stereotypes which are held of their group evidently influence their experiences and opportunities. Their responses to the social images or stereotypes that may operate as barriers to their achievements, give us insights into the ways in which they intend to secure their educational, occupational, economic, cultural, and political future in Canadian society.

This chapter explores some of the historical and contemporary social images of Blacks[1] in urban Canada and the impact and implications the images have had on their experiences. Starting with a brief historical overview of Africans' early experiences in Canada, we proceed by discussing the constructed images; how Toronto youth counter the images; and conclude with a look at the role that institutions should play in helping to reconstruct the images.

The African-Canadians: Some Background Notes

The first known record of the Africans' presence in Canada is 1605, when former Portuguese slave Matthieu De Costa sailed to Canada as a Micmac interpreter for French traders Pierre Du Gua and others. But it was not until the 1620s that Africans began living here. It is believed that in 1628, a young Madagascan male of about ten years was the first African to be sold into slavery to a Quebec resident and given the name, Olivier Le Jeune (Walker 1980; Hamilton 1994: 13–40). Slaves were bought and sold in those parts of Canada now known as Quebec, Ontario, New Brunswick, and Nova Scotia. Slavery ended officially in the British colonies in 1834; however, in 1793 the parliament of Upper Canada (now Ontario) passed an Act "to prevent the further introduction of slaves."

During the American Revolution, Blacks who fought for the British as Loyalists came to Canada, where they were promised freedom, land, and fair treatment as their white counterparts. But in Canada they were treated badly, and the "land that they were promised turned out to be infertile and the plots too small to support a family—if indeed they received any land at all" (Ashworth 1988:3). In June 1796, about 546 Maroon men, women, and children were deported from Jamaica to Nova Scotia (Walker 1980). They were descendants of slaves who had been fighting the British colonial government in Jamaica to maintain their freedom.

During the fugitive slave era of the nineteenth century, thousands of escaped slaves, mainly from the southern United States, came to Canada, primarily to Ontario, via the "underground railroad." It is not known how many came to Canada via this route, but it is estimated that perhaps 20,000 entered Canada in the decade between 1850 and 1860 (Krauter and Davis 1978: 44). Many free Africans also migrated to Canada during this time (see Perry, 1967; Winks 1971; Hill 1981; Robbins 1983).

Overt and covert exclusionary immigration policies prior to 1967 limited the number of Blacks who came to Canada. Their low numbers in Canada in part reflect the principles of selection and admittance. That is, according to the government, only the numbers of people who "could be absorbed by the economy" and at the same time preserve "the fundamental composition of the Canadian population" (Burnet and Palmer 1989:39) were admitted into the country. As late as the 1950s, the federal government felt justified in restricting Black immigration to Canada because they were seen as "mentally, morally, physically and socially inferior and a potential social problem in Canada" (Calliste 1994: 131–148). Furthermore, immigration ministers would argue that "it had been 'scientifically proven' that Blacks could not endure cold climates" (Burnet 1984: 19).

Notwithstanding the restrictive immigration policies, limited numbers of Caribbean immigrants did enter Canada during the first half of the twentieth century. They were recruited as a cheap source of unskilled and domestic labor. Despite their skills in carpentry and mechanics, most of the men who came in those early years were restricted to jobs in the coal mines of Nova Scotia and "the steel plants' coke ovens because of the segregated workforce and the myth that blacks [sic] could withstand the heat better than whites" (Calliste 1994:135).

Women from Guadeloupe and the English-speaking Caribbean were recruited through the Caribbean Domestic Scheme, 1910–1911. Nevertheless, because of the perception that these working-class Caribbean women were immoral, likely to become single parents and eventually public charges,[2] the number that were allowed to enter Canada were significantly controlled (Calliste 1994). The subsequent "Household Service Worker's Scheme," established in 1955 through agreements between the Canadian and some Caribbean governments, e.g., Jamaica, Barbados, Antigua, and Trinidad, continued to bring hundreds of women each year to work in the homes of middle- and upper-class families. These women were expected to be between the ages of eighteen and thirty-five, single, and have at least a grade eight education. Applicants were also interviewed by a team of Canadian immigration officials who visited the islands once a year for this purpose. Many of the women who came to Canada through this scheme were sole support mothers (Silvera 1984:13). It is estimated that between 1955 and 1965 about 2,700 women came to Canada from the Caribbean under this scheme (Ministry of Education 1983:12).

While Blacks are to be found throughout Canada, most are concentrated in the urban areas of Toronto, Halifax, and Montreal—with metropolitan Toronto being home to the majority of Blacks. On the basis of the 1986 census, Statistics Canada estimated that there were about 133,035 Blacks in metropolitan Toronto, representing about six percent of the population. But some Black community members estimate the population to be as high as 300,000 which is over ten percent of the metropolitan Toronto population.[3] Statistics Canada also reported that sixty-one percent of all Ontario Blacks live in metropolitan Toronto, making them one of the largest segments[4] of the racial minority population in the city.

The composition of the Black population is particularly significant because of the large number of young people. The available data show that a greater proportion of the population (45 percent), compared to the total population (34 percent), was under the age of twenty-four in 1986 (this includes 20 percent between 15–24 years), and most (83 percent) under the age of fifteen years were born in Canada. The majority of Blacks living in Toronto (72 percent) were born outside of Canada, mainly in the Caribbean; and most immigrated between 1966 and 1986. Coming from many regions of the world, the population is linguistically and religiously diverse. The majority is Christian and about 96 percent speak English as their first language. The 1991 census data calculated the African-Canadian population at 504,290. In Toronto alone Blacks were (291,000) or 6 percent of the population; in Montreal, (101,390) or 3 percent; and in Halifax, (10,390) or 3 percent of the population. It is projected that the racial minority population of metropolitan Toronto will increase by 30–40 percent by the year 2001 (Samuel 1992). Given this projection, and with reference to 1986 statistics, Turner (1994:2) suggests that "if Blacks continue to comprise 30 percent of metropolitan Toronto's racial minority population, they could comprise between 10 and 14 percent of the city's population by the 2001, or between 240,000 and 340,000."

Constructing Black Stereotypes

How and when a group of people is permitted to enter a new country, and the ways in which they are accommodated and expected to participate economically, politically, socially, and culturally, set the stage for their eventual success. Mythologies or "overgeneralized truths" help to construct social images or stereotypes that justify the treatment that the "outsiders" receive. These social images or stereotypes along with ethnocentrism, prejudice, racism, and discrimination operate as control mechanisms to ensure stability and maintenance of the hierarchical structure. Ultimately, these mechanisms help to structure the laws, shape the institutions, and inform the cultural norms and values of the society. Institutions such as immigration, education, justice and legal system, employment, recreation, and media carry out the dictates of the system through the process of socialization and acculturation of the members of the society.

In the case of African Canadians, who came, and the periods during which they came to Canada, are a result of the mechanisms that were established to create a population mix that would serve the cultural and economic interests of the society and at the same time maintain the status quo, and, hopefully, preserve stability. Initially, Africans entered Canada as slaves, and in later years as laborers and domestics because they were regarded as undesirable immigrants. This has contributed to the images of them as Canadians. Such social images of African people would then justify the treatment they receive, and would also legitimize the social status or position that they occupy in the society.

That Canada is located next door to the United States, where twenty to thirty million Blacks live, has a significant impact on the conditions and perceptions of Blacks in Canada. Therefore, not only are the social images or stereotypes of African Canadians a product of racism and discrimination, rooted in the historical development of Canadian society, but also a result of the U.S. imperialist cultural export to Canada. Images of Blacks come into Canada through the media and educational materials. According to the Saskatchewan Coalition Against Racism: "the ever present American television programs have given White Canadians their stereotype of the American urban Black, usually at the caricature level in situation comedy. . . . They fail to present any information or role model relevant to the history and accomplishments of Black people in this country" (cited in Armour 1984:27).

In essence, how African Canadians are perceived, treated and positioned in the society is based on the historical legacy and the social images that have been constructed over the years and sustained through policies, programs, and practices. These images are so embedded in the social structure that it is inevitable that all African Canadians will be affected by them. It is left to individuals, and the African-Canadian community as a whole, to decide what images of themselves they are prepared to live with. Dissatisfaction with the images and stereotypes will propel members of that community to initiate actions that will bring about change. Evidently, generations of African Canadians have struggled against the social images/stereotypes in order to gain respect and acceptance—in short, equity. Before proceeding to discuss the contributions that today's youth are making to this struggle, the following section examines some of the historical and contemporary events and issues that help to shape the social images and stereotypes of African Canadians. We will specifically examine the construction and stereotyping of these Canadians as immigrants, service workers, low achieving students, athletes, and criminals.

As Immigrants

Like most other racial minorities in Canada, Blacks in Canada are most often identified as immigrants. This commonly held perception is a result of: their absence from the "mainstream" historical accounts; lack of "visibility" in major political, economic, social, educational, and cultural institutions, particularly the media; and the change in 1967 of the discriminatory immigration policy which had made it possible for racial minorities to enter Canada.

The failure to see Blacks as integral to Canada's history has had a profound effect on how Blacks are perceived and on how they relate to the society. Perceiving Blacks only as immigrants negates the fact that they have been present in Canada for nearly 400 years. It means that with the "immigrant label," they are considered new to Canada, and therefore they cannot expect to have the same opportunities as fourth-, fifth-, and sixth-generation Canadians. It also means that the Black community is usually defined more in terms of its Caribbean immigrant population. When viewed as immigrants, the issues and/or problems that are experienced tend to be attributed to their adjustment to a new society. The Report of the Special Committee on Visible Minorities in Canadian Society expresses this sentiment. It stated that the majority of visible minorities in Canada are comparatively recent immigrants and many are experiencing the stresses and strains of moving not only from one country to another, but also from a rural background to an urban center. Adaptation is a long, ongoing process and is especially difficult for people who are members of visible minority groups (1984:12).

Perceived as "newcomers" to Canada, as with all immigrants, Blacks are expected to occupy what prominent Canadian sociologist John Porter (1965) refers to as "the entrance status." This implies that they will be expected to be in the lower level stratum of the society, and in most cases hold lower level occupations. They are also subjected to the process of acculturation[5] to the host or majority group culture since their culture would have been judged by the majority group—white Anglo-Celtic—as incompatible with the "Canadian culture." Such status positions get reinforced by expectations, stereotypes, and social images which often harden and become perpetuated over time.

As Service Workers

Well into the 1960s, most African-Canadian women made their living primarily in domestic work (Shadd 1987; Calliste 1994). The population of these workers increased when English-speaking Caribbean women came to Canada as domestics on the Household Service Workers Scheme (1955). Writing about the experiences of the Caribbean workers, Silvera (1983:19) tells us of their "frustration of never having enough money and the humiliation of being a legal slave . . . of working overtime for no pay, of sharing rooms usually with a baby or the family pet, of shaking off the sexual advances of their male employer, and . . . of being raped . . . manipulated and degraded by female employers."

Like the women, Black men also had limited employment opportunities. During the early 1900s, they were largely employed as porters on the railway (Shadd 1987:4–31), and in limited numbers as coal miners and steelworkers (Calliste 1994). In more recent times, Blacks tend to be employed in manual, clerical, and service occupations (Reitz *et al.* 1981). That they are primarily employed in lower level occupations is in part a product of, and a mechanism which has helped to sustain, the social images that Canadians have of Blacks as unskilled immigrants.

But this image of the work habits of Black people is different from that held by a white young man who, talking about his summer job and how hard he had to work, said: "I only work the trucks in the summer . . . but I fuckin' hate it, . . . it's nigger work, . . . all the lifting and shit . . . and it's dirty, fuckin dirty job. . . ." (O'Bireck 1993:91). In terms of why Blacks tend not to be employed in senior positions, *The Toronto Star Minority Report* quotes "Black community leaders" as saying: "senior company and government managers question the ability of a black man or woman to exercise effective authority and discipline over whites" (Ward 1985:12).

As Low Achieving Students

The social images that have been presented of Black people is a product of an educational system that is primarily Western and Eurocentric (Henry, 1994; Dei 1995; Dei et al. 1995). The Consultative Committee on the Education of Black Students in Toronto Schools (1988) points out that the negative portrayals of Blacks in educational materials and curriculum tend be racist. The Committee cited the novel *Huckleberry Finn* and the play *Othello* as examples of racist portrayal of Blacks.

As a result of these social images and stereotypes, Black students tend to receive differential treatment from teachers who often perceive them as more likely to do well in vocational rather than academic school programs (Head 1975; D'Oyley and Silverman 1976; James 1990; Solomon 1992; D'Oyley 1994). As one parent expressed it: "Students are forced into non-academic courses leading to dead-end jobs. The school expects the students to be low achievers. The school focuses on the failures of Black students" (Consultative Committee on the Education of Black Students in Toronto Schools 1988: Appendix E, p.1).

A sample of students' comments from one school board in the western suburban area of metropolitan Toronto illustrates Black students' experiences within the school system. The report on Student Perspectives on Current Issues quotes students as saying:

[P]eople look down on blacks. Whenever they have good performance in school they assume they cheated.

. . . black kids are picked to be team captain in sports in gym, but teachers often assume their marks are bad.

I had taken an enriched French class which was a level higher than advanced. I was the only black student in that class. One day, my teacher had asked me, literally if I considered myself black. I found that remark very offending since what he basically meant was that black people weren't smart enough to take that particular level (Board of Education for the City of Etobicoke 1993: 52–56).

In commenting on the experiences of Black students within the school system, Brathwaite (1989: 195–216) and Dei *et al.* (1995) point out that the idea of low achievement among Black students is a result of their experiences within the Canadian school system, for Black parents generally have confidence in the school as an institution that has the capacity to open opportunities for their children. But this belief and hope of many parents has been eroded by the predominant picture of the Black student as failures.

As Good Athletes

Research shows that Black students are perceived often by teachers as making "good athletes" (Head 1975; Solomon 1992; James 1995a; 1990; Dei *et al.* 1995; Black Learners Advisory Committee (BLAC) 1994). For example, in his study of Blacks in Toronto, Head (1975) reports that one of his respondents disclosed that:

[W]hen discussing his desire to become an engineer, the teacher commented that he was not suited to that field. "You are a good basketball player and the school needs basketball players. Why don't you become a professional and forget about the engineering?" (89).

In her 1978 study of Torontonians, anthropologist Frances Henry found that Blacks were stereotyped as poor and more religious, more humorous, and less ambitious than whites but at the same time better at sports. But this does not mean that Blacks are good at all sports, only specific ones. For example, they are not seen to be good at hockey, Canada's national sport; but good at basketball, baseball, football, track and field. And even within the sports in which they participate, they face limitations. For instance, with reference to soccer in Ontario, researchers White and Willits (1992:10) have shown that Blacks are less likely to play in central positions where intellectual and leadership skills are viewed as important in facilitating performance. Consequently, they are over-represented in non-central positions which "rely more on physical and motional traits."

Ben Johnson is an excellent example of the image that is held of Black athletes. Johnson won the 100 meters gold medal at the 1988 Seoul Olympics, only to lose it when it was discovered that his urine sample showed "traces of anabolic steroids." Writing about the incident in the *Globe and Mail* newspaper, Toronto journalist Meredith Levine, noted that many Canadians believed Johnson when he said "he was duped, given steroids without his knowledge." Levine suggests that "this view may be popular because it coincides with a common stereotype of black athletes: dumb and naive." And as a letter writer to a local newspaper suggested, "Mr. Johnson's lack of education gives him a kind of childish aura, a charm" (Levine: A 7). In the same article, Levine also draws to readers' attention the "animal imagery" that appears in newspaper articles of Ben Johnson. "He is compared to a racehorse. . . . Even his coach, Charlie Frances, was quoted as saying: Ben does what he wants. He is like a very well-timed, 800-pound gorilla" (*ibid*.:A7). Finally, as Levine "bluntly" stated, "There is little in Ben Johnson with which Canadians can identify," he "is black; he was born in Jamaica; he speaks English with a thick accent. For the 97 per cent of Canadians who are not black, this is not the idealized version of themselves they have envisioned presenting to the world" (*ibid*.:A7). This idea is captured in the cartoon statements accompanying Levine's newspaper article on Ben Johnson. They read: "Canadian wins Gold medal"; "Jamaican-Canadian accused of steroid use"; "Jamaican stripped of Gold Medal" (*ibid*.:A7).

As Criminals

Stereotypes of Blacks as lawless and therefore "a most undesirable element" as citizens of Canada are well recorded in historical accounts.[6] The image of Blacks as lawless is further illustrated by what happened in Edmonton, Alberta, in April 1911, shortly after the arrival of a large number of Blacks from Oklahoma. At that time, newspapers reported that a fifteen-year-old girl who was found by a neighbor unconscious on the floor of her Edmonton home reported that she had "been attacked and overcome by a big, black burly nigger who was intent on robbing the house." This incident was used as evidence to show that "negroes misuse young girls and women and killed them." The story, titled "The Black Peril," was believed by citizens because, as Shepard (1991:25) writes: "These reports would indicate that the age-old sexual mythology surrounding the black man was being reinforced in many white western Canadian minds."

Many members of the Black community note that the criminal images of Blacks, particularly males, have persisted over the years. They believe that these images help to reinforce police stereotypes, particularly those of young Black males who are portrayed as making money primarily through hustling, pushing drugs, or pimping for prostitutes (Ward 1985; Ginzberg 1985). This idea is also expressed in the following comment by a young male participant in a recent study (see James 1995b) I conducted.

Like if you see a lot of white youth, males or females driving a Jaguar, you don't usually stop them. You think that their father is a doctor. But if you see a Black youth driving a Jaguar, they think something's gotta be wrong, it's a stolen car, a drug dealer.

Dei *et al.* (1995: 51–52) in their report on Black high school dropouts also quote one female study participant as saying: "When you're a Black male, . . . you don't have to do anything. . . . You could be a good student, you could be a good father or whatever, [but] when you're out on the street, [you're seen as] a criminal . . . a drug dealer, whatever, you beat your wife. . . ." But as one Toronto high school student wrote, the police are not to be totally blamed for the image they have of Blacks, for "in today's society . . . there is no positive image of Black people. As a result of their bias against Blacks, they assume all Black people are the same" (Frater 1991:67).

In examining the social images of Blacks as criminals, attention must be paid to the role the media have played in constructing and perpetuating these images. This is important because the media continue to play a significant role in communicating to Blacks what the society thinks of them by their absence from, or in the way they are portrayed in, the media. Commenting on the message Blacks receive by their absence from the media, one person said: "It is deeply troubling and dispiriting for a young Black to grow up in a place like Toronto. They have no identity. All of the values of success are white values" (cited in the Special Committee on Visible Minorities in Canadian Society 1984:92). Further, according to a Working Group of African Canadians and Government representatives, when Blacks do appear in the media it is usually in "bad" news stories: "The media seldom feature 'good' news stories involving African Canadians . . . (Hence) the image of the African Canadian Community is distorted and its contributions diminished" (Four Level Government/African Canadian Group 1992:107).

The stereotypical images of Blacks are not specific to Blacks of a particular social class. Studies show that middle-class Blacks are just as likely as working-class to be stereotyped in the same way (Head 1978; James 1990; Dei *et al.* 1995). Olivia Ward in *The Toronto Star Minority Report* mentions that participants stated that "affluent or poor, educated or not, blacks often find they have to deal with a pre-fabricated image, one distorted by stereotypes of black people as criminals, layabouts and disruptive elements" (Ward 1985:6). One participant was quoted as saying: "You're always under suspicion" when shopping in a store or when you move into a neighborhood (*ibid.*:6).

Confronting the Social Images: The Perspectives of Toronto Youth

How Blacks, and youth in particular, respond to these social images will be the focus of this section. I shall make use of findings from studies I conducted with youth in Toronto in 1985 and 1991 (see James 1990 and 1993).[7]

Generally, the findings show that these youth organized their lives with the knowledge that there are particular images and resulting expectations that society had of them. They believed that they had to "be realistic," that because they are Black, they were likely to be perceived as less intelligent and less ambitious. They understood that Blacks are not expected to excel in education, and so when they do, they are regarded as "less Black." They are likely to be "labelled" or stereotyped as athletes, immigrants "from the islands," "dancers," and "pimps." The youth suggested that it is important that they were aware of how they are perceived or stereotyped because only in so doing will they be able to understand why whites reacted to them in particular ways.

Education was identified as the most important means by which they would be able to neutralize or remove such obstacles as stereotyping, racism, and discrimination, which they expected to experience. They believed that once they demonstrated that they are "smart," they would be able to change people's perceptions of them, and in turn ensure that they, and Blacks generally, were judged on merit rather than on the color of their skin. They thought of education as a "kind of security. . . . Something to hold on to," and a necessary means of breaking down stereotypes if they are to achieve their "future" goals.

Many of the youth reported that they used the stereotypes as sources of motivation. For example, being seen as unintelligent was their inspiration to prove to others that they have the skill, brains, momentum, and energy to push themselves. In situations where Blacks might have helped to create "negative images," in workplaces for example, the respondents reported that they willingly undertook the task of "making up" for the "ignorant" behavior of some Blacks. They admitted that this was a "responsibility," a "burden" that they undertook in the hope that their behavior would prompt employers to think "that the next Black they hire would be like me."

Many of the employed youth admitted that to challenge stereotypes and change the social images of Black is "quite stressful." Nevertheless, they felt that they had an "obligation" and a responsibility to play their part, and "in concert with their community" help to make changes; because, as Sonia suggested: "you can't take on the system by yourself, even if you prove to be the brightest or best. . . . I do not think, no matter how optimistic and brilliant I may be, I am not getting anywhere unless it's with other people."

Some of the youth in the studies referred to themselves as change agents, advocates, educators and crusaders who were pioneers and representatives within their workplaces with the responsibility to educate their naive fellow students, bosses, and co-workers about Black people. However, many of them did not expect that non-Blacks would simply observe that their distorted images were inappropriate or inaccurate, and did not represent their individual experience. For this reason, they felt that they had to consistently shatter the negative perceptions of Blacks by their exemplary behavior and achievements. Also, the youth understood that it takes more than individual and community efforts; they argued that social institutions which have been responsible for the construction and perpetuation of the social images and stereotyping of Blacks must also change what they do. The young people were well aware that as long as the school system, the media, the justice system (particularly the police), and workplaces continue to communicate, project, and act on the stereotypical images of Blacks then their efforts and that of the community will yield very little results.

Constructing Positive Social Images

The historical and contemporary social images and stereotypes of African Canadians are a reflection of how they have been represented and accommodated in the society from the very beginning. In many cases, their negative representations have overshadowed the positive aspects of their economic, cultural, and political contributions to Canadian society. From the very beginning of their lives in Canada, generations of Blacks have actively attempted to reverse the negative images and situations, through their writings, activist work, and community educational and social programs. Evidently, their efforts have not produced the full results that would enhance their social images and eliminate some of the stereotypes. Consequently, we need more concerted and aggressive efforts from social institutions such as education, media, and justice in helping to reconstruct the distorted social images.

In terms of education, this reconstructing of the social images of

African Canadians must go beyond the February "Black shows" in schools (see Prince 1996:167–178) to one that places their experiences at the center of their educational process. African-centered education (Asante 1990; Dei 1994; Henry 1994; Wright 1995) would provide African students with a perspective of education and themselves that is grounded in African values. It would validate their experiences and histories as well as engage them in a critique of their marginalization and exclusion in text books, reading materials, and curricula (Dei 1994). Such an education need not be exclusionary, for all students can benefit from critically examining what has been presented to them as representative of minority groups' experiences, and that of Blacks in particular.

Similarly, the media must present more diverse and positive images of Blacks. Presently, athletes and criminals appear most often on the pages of newspapers (see Ginzberg 1984) and on the television screens. Blacks need to be represented in many roles and occupations. The media must not only report the news but must be responsible for helping to inculcate in all Canadians a sense of voice, belonging, accomplishment, and possibilities. Featuring programs on African Canadians that reflect their diversity and their significant contributions to the economic, political, and cultural development of Canada would help to address the negative social images and break down the stereotypes, as well as address their marginalization in society. It is not sufficient for Canadian media to rely on American programs to feature Blacks. It is important that the media feature the African-Canadian experience, for while similar in many ways to that of Americans, it is also different. It is not only up to the "Black media" to report or feature Blacks in a positive light, for the larger community needs the same education and information. The National Film Board and government licensing and monitoring bodies have a responsibility to ensure that the media play a very instrumental role in helping to build positive race relations in Canadian society. For their part, the Black community must use its political influence to ensure representation and positive media representation.

Insofar as the education system and the media become more responsible in their representation of African Canadians, then it is possible that institutions such as the justice system, specifically the police, will be more informed about Africans generally, and about those in Canada particularly. However, this must be accompanied by anti-racism education and equity programmes for the police and other members of the justice system (see Report of the Commission on Systemic Racism in the Ontario Justice System 1995). As human service workers, responsible to "serve and protect" the community, the police cannot afford to act on the negative social images and stereotypes of Blacks. Therefore, governments must ensure that the police are aware of, and sensitive to, the issues and needs that are to be found in today's ethnically, racially, and religiously diverse urban communities. In addition, having police forces that are community-based, and advised by a board or committee made up of community members would help to educate and build better relations between the community and police.

In sum, when educational institutions, the media, the justice system and workplaces (through employment equity programs[8]) recognize that they too have a responsibility to build more positive social images of African Canadians, then the society as a whole will benefit. Canadians generally will come to recognize and respond to Blacks, not based on the negative social images or stereotypes that have existed over the years, but as hard-working, intelligent, long-time citizens of Canada. In turn, Blacks will feel better about themselves and therefore the energies that they expend on "proving themselves" and "dispelling myths" to counteract the negative social images and stereotypes can be directed to more productive pursuits of contributing to the educational, cultural, economic, social, and political development of Canadian society.

--------------------------- NOTES ---------------------------

1. The terms Black and African Canadian are used interchangeably. The useage also reflects ways in which the terms have been or are used, both in everyday language and literature. "Black" (unless within a quotation) is capitalized because as Cheryl Harris, quoting Professor K. Crenshaw, states: "Blacks, like Asians, Latinos, and other 'minorities,' constitute a specific cultural group and, as such, require denotation as a proper noun." Using the upper case "B", in reference to racial identity has a particular political history, it is "part of counterhegemonic practice" (Cheryl Harris 1993: 1710).

2. Calliste (1994) reports that even though their work was reported to

be satisfactory (in the words of one employer) "in every respect," and they were "clean, docile, attentive to their work, and their moral conduct leaves nothing to be desired" (141), this did not change the portrayal of Black women as undesirable immigrants.

3. The discrepancies in the estimations of the number of Blacks in Canada is largely due to the fact that no specific data exist. The census does not ask a particular question on race. The estimates that are put out are based on the question of ethnicity and place of birth. Given that Blacks come from different nations and many are born here, it is difficult to rely on these figures. Furthermore, Europeans, South Asians, Asians, and others from the Caribbean reporting place of birth are likely to get counted as Black.

4. Estimates indicate about thirty per cent.

5. Elsewhere, I have argued that the process of acculturation and assimilation are not necessarily engaged willingly, nevertheless, immigrants and minorities cannot escape the pressure of the dominant ethno-racial group to conform (James 1996).

6. Shepard (1991) reports that Blacks were the only group prior to World War 1 that was barred from entering Canada by an order-in-council. He goes on to say that "even Orientals [*sic*] were allowed to enter provided they paid a head tax" (31).

7. These were qualitative studies that were conducted in 1985 with 60 Toronto youth ages 17–22; and the 1991 follow-up was with 22 (ages 24–29) of the original participants (see James 1993 and 1990).

8. The Federal Government has an Employment Equity Act (1986) which applies to Crown Corporation and federally-regulated businesses (such as banks, and telecommunications and transportation companies) with more than 100 employees. Some provincial governments have similar programs (Stephenson 1996:231–243). But these programs need to be expanded to include the private sector.

REFERENCES

Armour, Monica. 1984. "Visible Minorities: Invisible: A Content Analysis of Submissions to the Special Committee on the Participation of Visible Minorities in Canadian Society." *Currents: Readings in Race Relations* The Urban Alliance on Race Relations 2:1 (Spring).

Asante, Molefi Kete. 1990. *Afrocentricity and Knowledge.* Trenton, N.J.: Africa World Press Inc.

Ashworth, Mary. 1988. *Blessed with Bilingual Brain.* Vancouver: Pacific Educational Press.

Black Learners Advisory Committee (BLAC). 1994. *BLAC Report on Education: Redressing Inequality—Empowering Black Learners.* Volume 3: Results of A Socio-Democratic Survey of the Nova Scotia Black Community. Halifax: Black Learners Advisory Commitee.

Brathwaite, Keren. 1989. "Black Student and the School: A Canadian Dilemma." In S. W. Chilungu *et al.* (eds.), *African Continuties/Leritage african.* Toronto: Terebi.

Burnet, Jean. 1984. "Myths and Multiculturalism." In R. J. Samuda, J.W. Berry, and M. Laferriere (eds.), *Multiculturalism in Canada: Social and Educational Perspectives.* Toronto: Allyn and Bacon, Inc.

Burnet, Jean and Howard Palmer. 1989. *Coming Canadians: An Introduction to a History of Canada's Peoples.* Toronto: McClelland & Stewart Inc.

Calliste, Agnes. 1994. "Race, Gender and Canadian Immigration Policy: Blacks from the Caribbean, 1900–1932." *Journal of Canadian Studies* 28:4. (Winter).

The Report of the Commission on System Racism in the Ontario Criminal Justice System (1995). Toronto: Queen's Printer for Ontario.

Consultative Committee on the Education of Black Students in Toronto Schools. 1988. *Education of Black Students in Toronto Schools.* Toronto: Toronto Board of Education.

Dei, George J. S. 1994. "Afrocentricity: A cornerstone of Pedagogy." *Anthropology & Education Quarterly* 25:1.

———. 1995. "Examining the Case for "African-Centred" Schools in Ontario." *McGill Journal of Education* Vol. 30, No. 2 (Spring): 179–198.

Dei, George, J, S., Holmes, L., Mazzuca, J., McIsaac, E., Campbell, R. 1995. *Drop Out or Push Out? The Dynamics of Black Students' Disengagement from School.* Toronto: Department of Sociology in Education, Ontario Institute for Studies in Education, October.

D'Oyley, Vincent (ed.). 1994. *Innovations in Black Education in Canada.* Toronto: Umbrella Press.

D'Oyley, Vincent and Harry Silverman (eds.). 1976. "Black Students in Urban Canada." *TESL Talk* 7:1.

Frater, Tara. 1991. "Just My Opinion." *Our Schools/Our Selves: Racism & Education* 3:3.

The Four-Level Government/African Canadian Community Working Group. 1992. *Towards a New Beginning: The Report And Action Plan.* Toronto. November.

Ginzberg, Effie. 1985. *Power without Responsibility: The Press We Don't Deserve.* Toronto: Urban Alliance on Race Relations.

Hamilton, Sylvia. 1994. "Naming Names, Naming Ourselves: A Survey of

Early Black Women in Nova Scotia." In P. Bristow *et al.*, *We're rooted here and they can't pull us up: Essays in African Canadian Women's History*. Toronto: University of Toronto Press.

Harris, Cheryl I. 1993. "Whiteness as Property." *Harvard Law Review* 106:1709–1791.

Head, Wilson. 1975. *The Black Presence in the Canadian Mosaic: A Study of Perception and the Practice of Discrimination Against Blacks in Metropolitan Toronto*. Toronto: Ontario Human Rights Commission.

Henry, Annette. 1994. "The Empty Shelf and Other Curricular Challenges of Teaching for Children of African Descent." *Urban Education* Vol. 29 No 3: 298–319.

Henry, Frances. 1978. *The Dynamics of Racism in Toronto: Research Report*. Toronto: York University.

Henry, Frances and Effie Ginzberg. 1985. *Who Gets The Work: A Test of Racial Discrimination In Employment*. Toronto: The Social Planning Council of metropolitan Toronto. January.

Hill, Daniel. 1981. *The Freedom Seekers: Blacks in Early Canada*. Toronto: The Book Society of Canada Limited.

James, Carl E. 1990. *Making It: Black Youth, Racism and Career Aspirations in a Big City*. Oakville, Ontario: Mosaic Press.

———. 1993. "Getting There and Staying There: Blacks' Employment Experience." In P. Anisef and P. Axelrod (eds.), *Transitions: Schooling and Employment in Canada*. Toronto: Thompson Educational Publishing, Inc.

———. 1995a. "Negotiating Schooling Through Sports: African-Canadian Youth Strive for Acadamic Success." *Avante: Journal of the Canadian Association for Health, Physical Education, Recreation and Dance* Vol 1 No. 1: 20–36.

———. 1995b. "Up to no good: The Street, Racial Minority Youth and Police." Paper presented at the 30th Annual Meeting of the Canadian Sociology and Anthropology Association. Montreal.

———. 1996. "Race, Culture and Identity." In C.E. James (ed.), *Perspectives on Racism and the Human Services Sector: A Case for Change*. Toronto: University of Toronto Press.

Krauter, Joseph F. and Morris Davis. 1978. *Minority Canadians: Ethnic Groups*. Toronto: Methuen.

Levine, Meredith. 1988. "What if he'd kept the gold? There is little in Ben Johnson with which Canadians can identify." *The Globe and Mail* (October 13).

Ministry of Education. 1983. *Black Studies: A Resource Guide for Teachers*. Toronto: Government of Ontario.

326   *NORTH AMERICA*

O'Bireck, Gary M. 1994. *Riches and Reggies: The Family, The School, Peer Associations, Socio-Economic Status, and Adolescent Deviance Patterns*. PhD Dissertation. Toronto: York University.

Perry, Charlotte B. 1967. *The Long Road: A history of the coloured Canadian in Winsdor, Ontario 1867–1967*. Windsor: Summer Printing and Publishing Company Ltd.

Porter, John. 1965. *The Vertical Mosaic: An Analysis of Social Class and Power in Canada*. Toronto: University of Toronto Press.

Prince, Althea. 1996. "Black History Month: A Multi-Cultural Myth or 'Have-Black-History-Month-Kit-will-travel.'" In K.S. Brathwaite and C.E. James, *Educating African Canadians*. Toronto: James Lorimer & Company Ltd., Publishers.

Reitz, Jeffrey G., Calzavara, Liviana, and Dasko, Donna. 1981. *Ethnic Inequality and Segregation in Jobs*. Toronto: Centre for Urban and Community Studies, University of Toronto.

Robbins, A.C. 1983. *Legacy to Buxton*. Chatham, Ontario: Ideal Printing.

Samuel, John T. 1992. *Visible Minorities in Canada: A projection*. Ottawa: Carlton University Press.

Shadd, Adrienne. 1987. "Three Hundred Years of Black Women Canadian History: Circa 1700–1980." *Tiger Lily* 1:2.

Shepard, R. Bruce. 1991. "Plain Racism: The Reaction Against Oklahoma Black Immigration to the Canadian Plains." In O. McKague (ed.), *Racism in Canada*. Saskatoon: Fifth House Publishers.

Silvera, Makeda. 1983. *Silenced: Talks with working class West Indian women about their lives and struggles as Domestic wokers in Canada*. Toronto: Williams-Wallace Publishers Inc.

Solomon, R. Patrick. 1992. *Black Resistance in High School: Forging a Separatist Culture*. Albany: State University of New York Press.

The Board of Education for the City of Etobicoke. 1993. *Student Perspectives on Current Issues*. Etobicoke: Board of Education.

The Ontario Black History Society. 1986. *Black History in Early Ontario*. Toronto.

The Special Committee on Visible Minorities in Canadian Society. 1984. *Equality Now*. Ottawa: The Queen's Printer for Canada.

Stephenson, Cynthia. 1996. "The Nuts and Bolts of Employment Equity: A Quick Primer for Social Service Agencies." In C.E. James *Perspectives on Racism and The Human Services Sector: A Case for Change*. Toronto: University of Toronto Press.

Turner, Tana. 1994. "A Summary Profile of Blacks in Metropolitan Toronto." Unpublished paper. Toronto.

White, Philip G. and Kevin Willits. 1992. "Race as a Predictor of Playing

Position in Ontario Youth Sccer." Unpublished paper, Department of Kinesiology, McMaster University, Ontario.

Walker, James W. 1980. *History of Blacks in Canada: A Study Guide for Teachers and Parents*. Ottawa: Minister of State for Multiculturalism.

Ward, Olivia. 1985. *A Minority Report*. Toronto: *The Toronto Star*.

Winks, Robin W. 1971. *The Blacks in Canada: A History*. Montreal: McGill-Queen's University Press.

Wright, Handel Kashope. 1994. "Like Flies in Buttermilk: Afrocentric Students in the Multicultural Classroom." *Orbit: Working Across Differences* Vol 25 No. 2: 29–32.

Part Five

EUROPE

Loïc J. D. Wacquant

15

Urban Outcasts

Stigma and Division in the Black American Ghetto and the French Urban Periphery[1]

Over the past decade or so, the visage of Western European cities has been reshaped by the rise of urban inequalities and the crystallization of novel forms of socioeconomic marginality accompanied by surging xenophobic ideologies and tensions. The coincidence of new forms of urban exclusion with ethnoracial strife and segregation has given *prima facie* plausibility to the notion that European poverty is being "Americanized."

Many European scholars (though by no means all) have turned to the United States for analytic assistance in an effort to puzzle out the current degradation of urban conditions and relations in their respective countries. Thus, we observe the transatlantic diffusion of concepts, models, and sometimes ready-made theories from recent (and not-so-recent) American social science. This is visible in the worried and confused public discussion in France—and in other countries such as Belgium, Germany, and Italy—about the presumed formation of immigrant "ghettos" in degraded working-class neighborhoods harboring large low-income housing tracts known as *cités*. It can be detected also in the spread of the notion of "underclass" in Great Britain and in its smuggling into the Netherlands to address the strain put on citizenship by the emerging concatenation of joblessness, ethnic discrimination, and neighborhood decline. Such conceptual borrowings, however, stand on shaky analytical grounds inasmuch as they presume exactly that which needs to be established: namely, that the American conceptual idiom of "race relations" has purchase on the urban realities of Europe—leaving aside the question of whether conventional American categories (or newer concepts such as the mythical notion of "underclass") pack any analytical power on their own turf to start with.

The best way to answer, or at least productively reframe, this question is through a systematic, empirically grounded, cross-national comparison of contemporary forms of urban inequality and ethno-racial/class exclusion that (1) does not presuppose that the analytical apparatus forged on one continent should be imposed wholesale on the other and is sensitive to the fact that all "national" conceptual tools have embedded within them specific social, political, and moral assumptions reflective of the particular history of society and politics in each country; (2) attends consistently to the meanings and lived experiences of social immobility and marginality; and (3) strives firmly to embed individual strategies and collective trajectories into the local social structure as well as within the broader national framework of market and state.

This chapter is part of a broader attempt to contribute to such a comparative sociology through an analysis of the social and mental structures of urban exclusion in the American "Black Belt" and the French "Red Belt" (Wacquant 1992a, 1992b, 1995a). Black Belt is used here to denote the remnants of the historic "dark ghetto" (Clark 1965) of the large metropolis of the Northeast and Midwest of the United States, that is, the dilapidated racial enclaves of the metropolitan core that have dominated recent public and academic discussions of race and poverty in North America. The expression Red Belt refers not simply to the townships of the outer ring of Paris that form(ed) the historic stronghold of the French Communist Party but, more generally, to the traditional mode of organization of "workers' cities" in France (Magri and Topaloff 1989), anchored by industrial male employment, a strong workerist culture and solidaristic class consciousness, and civic incorporation of the population through a dense web of union-based and municipal organizations creating a close integration of work, home, and public life (Stovall 1990). It is in such peripheral working-class neighborhoods that urban inequalities and unrest have coalesced, making the question of the *banlieue* perhaps the most pressing public issue in the France of the 1980s (Jazouli 1992). It should be noted that the term *banlieue* originally referred to a peripheral urban township or county attached to a larger urban center. Over time, however, it has come to designate any working-class area containing large densities of public housing (or projects known as *cités*) considered repositories for urban ills such as crime, physical dilapidation, economic deprivation, and immigration.

The analysis that follows uses data from a variety of primary and secondary sources and combines observations drawn from censuses, surveys, and field studies of the American ghetto and the French banlieue. On the French side, I concentrate on the Red Belt city of La Courneuve and its infamous public housing concentration called the Quatre mille (after the nearly 4,000 units it originally contained). La Courneuve is an older, Communist—governed, northeastern suburb of Paris with a population of 36,000 situated midway between the national capital and the Roissy-Charles de Gaulle airport, in the midst of a densely urbanized, declining industrial landscape. Like most Red Belt *banlieues*, La Courneuve harbors a high proportion of public housing (about half of the city's stock) and immigrants. The presence of foreigners (half of them from Algeria and thirteen percent from sub-Saharan Africa and Asia) has doubled since the mid-1970s to reach one-fifth of the city's population. Black French citizens from overseas dominions in the Caribbean and Pacific are also a growing and visible presence. On the American side, I focus on the South Side ghetto of Chicago where I conducted ethnographic fieldwork in 1988–1991. The South Side is a sprawling, all-Black zone containing some 100,000 inhabitants, the majority of which are unemployed and live under the official federal "poverty line."

I presented elsewhere a detailed sociography of both sites, which highlighted a number of parallel morphological traits and trends (Wacquant 1995a). In summary, both locales were found to have a declining population with a skewed age and class structure characterized by a predominance of youths, manual workers, and deskilled service personnel, and to harbor large concentrations of "minorities" (North African immigrants on the one side, Blacks on the other) that exhibit unusually high levels of unemployment caused by deindustrialization and labor market changes. This comparison also turned up structural and ecological differences suggesting that the declining French working-class *banlieue* and the Black American ghetto constitute two different sociospatial formations, produced by different institutional logics of segregation and aggregation and resulting in significantly higher levels of blight, poverty, and hardship in the ghetto. To simplify greatly: exclusion operates on the basis of color reinforced by class and state in the Black Belt but mainly on the basis of class and mitigated by the state in the Red Belt (Wacquant 1992b: 98–99), with the result that the former is a racially and culturally homogenous universe characterized by low organizational density and state penetration, whereas the latter is fundamentally heterogenous in terms of both class and ethnonational recruitment with a strong presence of public institutions.

The purpose of this chapter is to flesh out some of the invariants and variations in the social-organizational and cognitive structures of urban exclusion by contrasting two dimensions of daily life salient in both the French banlieue and the Black American ghetto, though, as we shall see, with significantly discrepant inflections, degrees of urgency, and sociopolitical dynamics.

The first part of the chapter addresses the powerful territorial stigma that attaches to residence in an area publicly recognized as a "dumping ground" for poor people, downwardly mobile working-class households, and marginal groups and individuals. Poverty is too often (wrongly) equated with material dispossession or insufficient income. But, in addition to being deprived of adequate conditions and means of living, to be poor in a rich society entails having the status of a social anomaly and being deprived of control over one's collective representation and identity: the analysis of public taint in the American ghetto and the French urban periphery serves to stress the *symbolic dispossession* that turns their inhabitants into veritable social outcasts.

The second part of the chapter takes up the question of the social divisions and bases of conflict operative in stigmatized neighborhoods of concentrated poverty in France and the United States and identifies some of the factors that account for the lack of social potency of ethnoracial divisions in the Red Belt in spite of their discursive proliferation in the public sphere.

TERRITORIAL STIGMATIZATION

Any comparative sociology of the "new" urban poverty in advanced societies must begin with the powerful stigma attached to residence in the bounded and segregated spaces, the "neighborhoods of exile" in which the populations marginalized or condemned to redundancy by the postfordist reorganization of the economy and state are increasingly being relegated. Not only because it is arguably the single most protrusive feature of the lived experience of those assigned to, or entrapped in, such areas but also because this stigma helps explain certain similarities in their strategies of coping or escape and thereby many of the surface cross-national commonalities that have given apparent validity to the idea of a transatlantic convergence between the poverty regimes of Europe and the United States.

"it's like a plague here"

Because they constitute the lowest tier of that nation's public housing complex, have undergone continual material and demographic decline since their erection in the early 1960s, and received a strong inflow of foreign families from the mid-1970s on (Barrou 1992), the *cités* of the French urban periphery suffer from a negative public image that instantly associates them with rampant delinquency, immigration, and insecurity. So much so that they are almost universally called . . . "little Chicagos," both by their residents and by outsiders. To dwell in a Red Belt low-income estate means to be confined to a branded space, to a blemished setting experienced as a "trap" (Pialoux 1979:19–20; Bachman and Basier 1987). Thus the media and its inhabitants themselves routinely refer to the Quatre mille as a "dumpster," "the garbage can of Paris," or even a "reservation" (Avery 1987:13), a far cry from the official bureaucratic designation of "sensitive neighborhood" used by the public officials in charge of the state's urban renewal program. In recent years, the press of stigmatization has augmented sharply with the explosion of discourses on the alleged formation of so-called *cités*-ghettos, widely (mis) represented as growing pockets of

"Arab" poverty and disorder symptomatic of the incipient "ethnicization" of France's urban space.

It should be noted however that the Quatre mille does not exist as such in the perceptions of its residents. The indigenous taxonomies the latter use to organize their daily round distinguish numerous sub-units within the large estate which in effect has only an administrative and symbolic existence—though with real consequences. What appears from the outside to be a monolithic ensemble is seen by its members as a finely differentiated congery of "micro-locales": those from the northern cluster of the project, in particular, want nothing to do with their counterparts of the southern section, whom they consider to be "hoodlums" (*racaille* or *caillera* in the local youth slang), and vice versa. "For the residents of the Quatre mille, to change building sometimes means to change lives" (Bachmann and Basier 1989:46; Dulong and Paperman 1992). Yet it remains that *cités* dwellers have a vivid awareness of being "exiled" to a degraded space that collectively disqualifies them (Pétonnet 1979:211). Rachid, a former resident of the Quatre mille, gives virulent expression to this sense of indignity when asked about the eventuality of moving back into the project: "For us to return there, it would be to be insulted once again. The Quatre mille are an insult. . . . For many people, the Quatre mille are experienced as a shame." When the interviewer inquires about the possibility of salvaging the housing project through renovation, his answer is no less blunt:

> To renovate is to take part in shame. If you agree to play this game, then in a way you're endorsing shame. We've come to a point of no return where you got no solution but to raze the whole thing. Besides the people here agree there's only one solution: "Gotta blow it up." Go and ask them. . . . When you don't feel good inside, when you don't feel good outside, you got no jobs, you got nothing going for you, then you break things, that's the way it is. The shit they're doing trying to fix the garbage disposal and the hallway entrance, the painting, that's no use: it's gonna get ripped right away. It's dumb. It's the whole thing that's the

problem. . . . You gotta raze the whole thing. (cited in
Euvremer and Euvremer 1985:8–9)

The verbal violence of youths, as well as the vandalism they invoke, must be understood as a response to the socioeconomic and
symbolic violence they feel subjected to by being thus relegated in a
defamed place. Not surprisingly, there is great distrust and bitter-
ness among them about the ability of political institutions and the
willingness of local leaders to rectify the problem (Aïchoune 1991;
Jazouli 1992).

It is hardly possible for residents of the *cité* to overlook the scorn
of which they are the object since the social taint of living in a low-
income housing project that has become closely associated with
poverty, crime, and moral degradation affects all realms of existence—whether it is searching for employment, pursuing romantic
involvements, dealing with agencies of social control such as the
police or welfare services, or simply talking with acquaintances.
Residents of the Quatre mille are quick to impute the ills of their
life to the fact of being "stuck" in a "rotten" housing project that
they come to perceive through a series of homological oppositions
(*cité*/city, us/them, inside/outside, low/high, savage/civilized) that
reproduce and endorse the derogatory judgment of outsiders. When
asked where they reside, many of "those who work in Paris say
vaguely that they live in the northern suburbs" (Avery 1987:22)
rather than reveal their address in La Courneuve. Some will walk
to the nearby police station when they call taxicabs to avoid the
humiliation of being picked up at the doorstep of their building.
Parents forewarn their daughters against going out with "guys
from the Quatre mille."

Residential discrimination hampers job search and contributes
to entrenching local unemployment, as inhabitants of the Quatre
mille encounter additional distrust and reticence among employers
as soon as they mention their place of residence. A janitor in the
cité relates a typical incident in which he helped new tenants contact firms by telephone only to be told that there no longer was any
position open whenever he revealed where he was calling from:
"It's like there's a plague here," says he in disgust (in Bachmann

and Basier 1989:54). Territorial stigmatization affects interactions not only with employers but also with the police, the courts, and street-level welfare bureaucracies, all of which are especially likely to modify their conduct and procedures based on residence in a degraded *cité*. "All youths recount the change of attitude of policemen when they notice their address during identity checks" (Dubet 1987:75), for to be from a *cité* carries with it a reflex suspicion of deviance if not outright guilt. A high-school student tells of being stopped by subway controllers in the Paris metro: "We took out our identity cards. When they saw that we were from the Quatre mille, I swear to you! They went . . . they turned pale" (in Bachmann and Basier 1989:65).

"People Really Look Down on You"

In America, the dark ghetto stands similarly as the national symbol of urban "pathology," and its accelerating deterioration since the racial uprisings of the mid-1960s is widely regarded as incontrovertible proof of the moral dissolution, cultural depravity, and behavioral deficiencies of its inhabitants. The journalistic reports and academic (pseudo) theories that have proliferated to account for the putative emergence of a so-called "underclass" in its midst have accelerated the demonization of the Black urban (sub)proletariat by symbolically severing it from the "deserving" working class and by obfuscating—and thereby retroactively legitimating—the state policies of urban abandonment and punitive containment responsible for its downward slide (Katz 1989; Gans 1992; Wacquant 1992d:115–122, and 1992e).

Today, living in the historic Black Belt of Chicago carries an automatic presumption of social unworthiness and moral inferiority which translates into an acute consciousness of the symbolic degradation associated with being confined to a loathed and despised universe. A student from a vocational high school on the city's South Side voices this sense of being cut off from and cast out of the larger society thus:

People really look down on you because of where you come from and who you are. People don't want to have anything to do with you. . . . You can tell when you go places, people are looking at you like you are crazy or something. (In Duncan, 1987: 63)

The defamation of the ghetto is inscribed first in the brute facts of its physical dilapidation and of the separateness and massive inferiority of its resident institutions, be they public schools, social agencies, municipal services, neighborhood associations, or financial and commercial outlets (Orfield 1985; Monroe and Goldman 1988; Wacquant 1992d). It is constantly reaffirmed by the diffident and contemptuous attitudes of outsiders: banks, insurance companies, taxis, delivery trucks, and other commercial services avoid the Black Belt or venture into it only gingerly; kin and kith are reluctant to visit. "Friends from other places don't want really to come here. And you yourself, you wouldn't want to invite intelligent people here: there's markings and there's writing on the wall, nasty, whatever," says an unemployed mother of three who lives in a West Side project.

Desmond Avery (1987:29), who lived in both the Cabrini Green project in Chicago and in the Quatre mille, remarks that residential discrimination is at least as prevalent in the Windy City as in the Parisian periphery. Ghetto dwellers are well aware that living in a stigmatized section of town penalizes them on the labor market: "Your address, it's impression for jobs." Residing on the South Side, and even more so in a public housing project whose name has become virtually eponymous with "violence and depravity," is yet another hurdle in the arduous quest for employment. A jobless woman who lives in the ill-reputed Cabrini Green housing development remarks:

It's supposed to be discrimination, but they get away with it, you know. Yes, it's important where you live. Employers notice, they notice addresses, when that application's goin' through personnel, they are lookin' at that address: (worried tone) "Oh, you're from here!?"

Over and beyond the scornful gaze of outsiders and the reality of exclusion from participation in society's regular institutions, the thoroughly depressed state of the local economy and ecology exerts a pervasive *effect of demoralization* upon ghetto residents. Indeed, the words "depressing" and "uninspiring" come up time and again in the description that the latter give of their surroundings. The possibility of accumulating resources in preparation for upward mobility is further eroded by the predatory nature of relations between residents and by the pressure toward social uniformity that weighs on those who try to rise above the poverty level common to most inhabitants of the area: "They won't let you get ahead. Stealin' from you and robbin' you and all that kinda thing," laments a twenty-seven-year-old machine operator from the far South Side. Given the inordinate incidence of violent crime (Wacquant 1992e:106–109), living in a ghetto neighborhood also entails significant physical risks and, as a corollary, high levels of psychic stress which tend to "drag you down" and "wear you out." No wonder that life in the Black Belt is suffused with a sense of gloom and fatality, a social *fatum* that obstructs the future from view and seems to doom one to a life of continued failure and rejection (Monroe and Goldman 1988:158–159, 273; Kotlowitz 1991; Wacquant 1992c:56–58).

From Social Stigmatization to Social "Dis-integration"

Paradoxically, the experiential burden of territorial stigmatization weighs more heavily on the residents of the French *banlieue* than it does on their counterparts of the American ghetto, in spite of the fact that the latter constitutes a considerably more desolate and oppressive environment (Wacquant 1992a). Three factors help account for this apparent disjuncture between objective conditions and the subjective (in) tolerance of those who evolve in them.

First, the very idea of relegation into a separate space of institutionalized social inferiority and immobility stands in blatant violation of the French ideology of unitarist citizenship and participation in the national community, an ideology fully embraced and forcefully invoked by youths from the Red Belt, especially second-generation immigrants of North African origins in their street protest and marches of the past decade (Jazouli 1992). By contrast, the color line of which the Black ghetto is the most visible institutional expression is so ingrained in the makeup of the American urban landscape that it has become part of the order of things: racial division is a thoroughly taken-for-granted constituent of the organization of the metropolitan economy, society, and polity. Second, residents of the American ghetto are more prone to embracing a highly individualistic ideology of achievement than are their counterparts of the French *cités*. Many if not most adhere to the social Darwinistic view that social position ultimately reflects one's moral worth and personal striving so that no one, in the long run, can be consistently held back by his or her place of residence.

A third and most crucial difference between Red Belt and Black Belt is found in the nature of the stigma they carry: this stigma is only residential in the former but *jointly and inseparably spatial-cum-racial* in the latter. The French banlieue is but a territorial entity which furthermore contains a mixed, multi-ethnic population; it suffices for inhabitants of the Quatre mille or any other *cité* to hide their address in order to "pass" in the broader society. No readily perceptible physical or cultural marker brands them as members of the Red Belt and use of simple techniques of "impression management" (Goffman 1963) enable them to shed the stigma, if only temporarily. Thus, adolescents from poor Parisian banlieues regularly go "hang out" in the upscale districts of the capital to escape their neighborhood and gain a sense of excitement. By traversing spaces that both symbolize and contain the life of higher classes, they can live for a few hours a fantasy of social inclusion and participate, albeit by proxy, in the wider society (Calogirou 1989:64–69). This "consciousness switch" renders more intolerable the idea of permanent exclusion and the outcast status associated with consignment to a degraded *cité*.

Residents of the American Black Belt are not granted the luxury of this dual awareness context. For the ghetto is not simply a spatial entity, or a mere aggregation of poor families stuck at the bottom of the class structure; it is a uniquely racial formation that spawns a society-wide web of material and symbolic associations between color, place, and a host of negatively valued social properties (Pettigrew 1971:91–92, 179–182). The fact that color is a marker of identity and a principle of vision and division that is immediately available for interpretation and use in public space and interaction (Feagin, 1991) makes it nearly impossible for in ner-city dwellers to shed the stigma attached to ghetto residence. Ghetto Blacks in America suffer from *conjugated stigmatization*. They cumulate the negative symbolic capital attached to color and to consignment in a specific, reserved, and inferior territory itself devalued for being both the repository of the lowest class elements of society and a racial reservation. In a race-divided society such as the United States where all spheres of life are thoroughly color-coded and given low chances of escaping the ghetto, the best one can do is make a virtue of necessity and learn to live with a stigma that is both illegitimate and unacceptable to French working-class youths of the Red Belt *cités*.

Yet the main effect of territorial stigmatization is similar in both countries; it is to stimulate practices of internal social differentiation and distancing that work to decrease interpersonal trust and undercut local social solidarity. To regain a measure of dignity and reaffirm the legitimacy of their own status in the eyes of society, residents of both *cité* and ghetto typically overstress their moral worth as individuals (or as family members) and join in the dominant discourse of denunciation of those who undeservingly "profit" from social assistance programs, *"faux pauvres"* and "welfare cheats." It is as if they could gain value only by devaluing their neighborhood and their neighbors. They also engage in a variety of strategies of social distinction and withdrawal, which converge to undermine neighborhood cohesion. These take three main forms: mutual avoidance, reconstitution and elaboration of "infra-differences" or micro-hierarchies, and the diversion of public opprobrium onto scapegoats such as notorious "problem families" and foreigners or drug dealers and single mothers.

To sum up, residents of the French *cité* and of the American ghetto each form an *impossible community*, perpetually divided against themselves, which cannot but refuse to acknowledge the collective nature of their predicament and who are therefore inclined to deploy strategies of distancing and exit that tend to validate negative outside perceptions and feed a deadly self-fulfilling prophecy through which public taint and collective disgrace eventually produce that which they claim merely to record namely, social atomism, community "disorganization," and cultural anomie.

SOCIAL VISION AND DIVISION
IN GHETTO AND *CITÉ*

We have seen that the nexus between territorial stigma, insecurity, and public abandonment is highly distinctive in the Black Belt by virtue of the racial isolation inflicted upon Blacks in America. This is reflected in the caste consciousness and cleavages that structure life in the ghetto, where the division between Blacks and whites is all encompassing. In the Parisian Red Belt, by contrast, the dominant opposition pits not native French residents and immigrants but youths versus all others. Though foreigners and especially families of North African descent have become more concentrated in peripheral Red Belt *cités* since the shutting off of legal immigration in 1974, the French banlieue remains a highly heterogenous universe in which racial or ethnic categories have little social potency.

American Apartheid and Split Racial Consciousness

As a result of the historic experience of two centuries of slavery followed by one century of near-total racial separation and multifarious forms of discrimination, many of which persist into the present, African Americans have carved out a rich expressive culture that provides them with a distinctive set of practices, idioms, and signs through which to construct themselves and to impart meaning to the world about them (Abrahams 1970; Levine 1977; Jones 1985). The United States are also unique for having what Orlando Patterson (1972: 28) calls a "classificatory racial system" in which "anyone who is not completely white and has the slightest trace of black ancestry is considered black." Strict application of this rule of "hypo-descent" has blocked the emergence of a socially recognized mixed-blood or mulatto category despite the widespread genetic mixing of the Black and white populations, resulting in an unbridgeable division between them. As one might expect, race forms the pivotal axis around which the African-American cultural matrix revolves. The inflexible, dichotomous racial boundary that whites have imposed on Blacks across society, most visible in the enduring spatial segregation between the "races" and exceedingly low interracial marriage rates, finds its expression in forms of consciousness anchored in a rigid "us/them" opposition between Blacks and whites mirroring the objective caste relations that have historically prevailed between them.

Race is inscribed everywhere in the ghetto: in the objectivity of space and of the separate and inferior institutions that entrap its population, and in the subjectivity of categories of perception and judgment that its residents engage in their most routine conduct. Indeed, color consciousness in the Black Belt is so ubiquitous and suffusive as to go without saying—so much so that it can go unnoticed even by careful observers because, precisely, it is embedded deep in what Alfred Schutz (1970) calls the "natural attitude" of everyday life. In the Black Belt, racial categories have an immediacy and pervasiveness that make them central cognitive tools (Gwaltney 1990). The fact that most residents of the ghetto have little occasion to interact on a one-to-one basis with whites (and, increasingly, with middle-class Blacks) further increases the perceptual omnipresence of color. Kotlowitz (1991:161) tells the story of a child living in a project on Chicago's West Side who, at age ten, "began to wonder aloud about being black. 'Do all black people live in projects?' he asked his mother. 'Do all black people be poor?'" I am the only white friend that the young Black men I met during my three years of fieldwork in a Woodlawn boxing gym ever had.

That residents of the Black Belt should take the color line for granted is not surprising given that their life is almost entirely self-contained within the racially uniform world of the ghetto and, for many of them, in a small section of it: their street, block, or "stomping ground" of the immediate vicinity. The white world "out there" remains largely unknown, for it is virtually inaccessible, save via the mass media.

So powerful is the racial prism through which ghetto residents see the world that those of them who manage to climb up the class structure and leave the Black Belt are widely perceived as trying to "become white" and as "traitors" to their community—irrespective of the fact that nearly all of them end up moving into all-Black neighborhoods elsewhere in the city or in segregated suburbs. Class differences among Blacks thus find themselves couched in the idiom of race. As long as the residential and interactional structures of "American apartheid" (Massey 1990) persist, the dichotomous opposition existing between whites and Blacks in objective reality has every reason for being replicated in consciousness.

'Jeunes des Cités' Against the Rest of the World

If there is a dominant antagonism that runs through the Red Belt *cité* and stamps the collective consciousness of its inhabitants, it is not, contrary to widespread media representations, one that opposes immigrants (especially "Arabs") and autochthonous French families but the cleavage dividing youths (*les jeunes*), native and foreign lumped together, from all other social categories. Youths are widely singled out by older residents as the chief source of vandalism, delinquency, and insecurity, and they are publicly held up as responsible for the worsening condition and reputation of the degraded banlieue. Avery (1987: 112) reports that:

> [T]he bands of youth that congregate in the stairways [of the Quatre mille] are a favourite topic of conversation: "They bust the light bulbs so we can't see what they do," says one. "They shoot drugs in broad daylight," "they sit there and smoke reefers all night long"; "they piss in the stairwells," "we don't like to encounter them at night, we are prisoners of our own apartments."

Mixing fact with fiction, such accusations are based on the reality that youths are demographically preeminent in projects like the Quatre mille and that they typically take over the streets and the few public spaces available, including building hallways and porches, which makes others feel they are misappropriating a collective good for their own particular uses. Whether founded or not, these grievances invariably portray young people either as themselves troubled or as generators of trouble. Bachmann and Basier (1989:100) point out that, in La Courneuve, "in every incident, youths are both the cause and the victims of violence in the *cité*; they stand way out in the foreground."

For their part, youths from stigmatized Red Belt neighborhoods feel that they are being subjected to a pervasive pattern of anti-youth discrimination that prevails both inside and outside their estate. They complain that governmental programs and public authorities neglect them, reject their queries and input, and promise much but deliver little or next to nothing of value to them; that police harass them or subject them to unwarranted suspicion and surveillance; and that adults more generally fail to recognize their plight and concerns. But, most of all, youths feel none of the above accord them the recognition and respect they feel entitled to: "'We don't exist, nobody sees us.' 'They treat us like rats'" (Lapeyronnie 1992:11). The burning rage that many experience at being durably shut out from employment and at being denied the individual dignity that comes with economic self-sufficiency finds an outlet in a nihilistic discourse glorifying predation and violence as means of access to the sphere of consumption and which, for want of being able to put a face on the mechanisms that exclude them, fastens on the police as the target of enmity (Dubet 1987:80–89; Jazouli 1992: 148–149).

Because the findings of the researchers who have investigated tensions in the housing projects of the degraded banlieue up close are strikingly at odds with the vision that has come to dominate the media and public debate, they are worth quoting at some length. Avery (1987: 21), for instance, "never observed during [his] years in La Courneuve . . . situations of open racial intolerance, of blatant collective scorn" of the kind he witnessed on Chicago's West Side or in a British working-class city where he previously resided. Although 14.5 percent of the electorate of La Courneuve voted for the xenophobic National Front in the 1986 legislative elections, he insists that "there is no racist climate here, habitually. I find on the contrary a lot of mutual respect and solidarity in the daily life of the *cité*" (Avery 1987:21–22). In an isolated working-class project in the western suburbs of Paris, Calogirou turned up slightly more "ethnicized" forms of perception of space; separate sections of the estate and specific buildings tend to be identified, and referred to, by the assumed racial or ethnonational membership of its most visible tenants. Nonetheless, "[t]olerance is the most widespread attitude" and "those who establish national or religious restrictions in their network of friends are few and far between" (Calogirou

1989:144). For youths from these projects, personal characteristics override "ethnic" membership and they often use humor to deflect the derogatory denotation of racist insults.

Group Intermixing, Collective Trajectory, and "Racial" Tension

What explains the muted character of racial or ethnic consciousness in the working-class estates of the Red Belt in spite of the growing concentration of immigrant families into the most degraded housing projects of the urban periphery—their representation in La Courneuve doubled between 1968 and 1982 to reach twenty-two percent—and the expanding place accorded the theme of racism in the public sphere as the 1980s wore on? Three reasons may be adduced briefly.

First, as we noted above, Red Belt *cités* are very heterogenous ensembles in terms of their ethnoracial recruitment. No *banlieue* is the exclusive or even predominant "turf" of a particular group as there is no "ordered segmentation" (Suttles 1968) of space in France and immigrant families are rather widely distributed across neighborhoods, with the exception of select locales monopolized by (higher class) natives. French *cités* are not ghettos if by that we mean a racially and/or culturally uniform sociospatial formation based on the forcible relegation of a negatively typed population to a specific territory (Wacquant 1992a, 1992b, 1995b). Their makeup typically brings together a majority of French native families and a mixed grouping of households from fifteen to forty different nationalities and more. True, residents of foreign descent are disproportionately represented in the Quatre mille compared to their national or regional weight (around 30 percent compared to 11 percent nationwide, and up to 40 percent in the Southern cluster of the project). But this results from their skewed class composition, not from the ethnoracial segmentation of the housing market. Nor do the poorest and most destitute Red Belt neighborhoods overlap closely with the *cités* sporting the largest proportions of foreigners, as the thesis of "ghettoization" would imply.

This mixing of populations is decisive in accounting for the overwhelming likeness in the experiences and strategies of Red Belt youths of native French and North African background, a

point made most effectively by Dubet (1987:326; also Bourdieu
1991: 8):

> In no group did youths introduce immigration as a funda-
> mental cleavage of relations among themselves in a given
> neighborhood. Never, in the cités where we went [three of
> them in the Parisian Red Belt, a fourth in the suburbs of
> Lyons], did youths talk in terms of "us," immigrant youths,
> and "them," French youths, and conversely. Relations and
> friendship ties are multi-ethnic. This does not necessarily
> derive from anti-racist beliefs; it springs, rather, from the
> basic fact that, since their childhood, youths have had the
> same experiences in cités which are not racial ghettos.
> These youths attend the same schools, have the same lei-
> sure activities, and go through the same "horseplay" and
> misdeeds.

Secondly, LePen's recent electoral surge notwithstanding, racial
or ethnic differences do not constitute legitimate principles of construction of social reality in the French tradition of nationhood.
The historical institutionalization of French citizenship as a state-
centered, territorial community, as opposed to a community of descent expressed in cultural terms, as prevails in Germany, for
instance (Brubaker 1990), has—thus far—prevented ethnoracial
categories from becoming the organizing medium of social perceptions and relations by blocking their usage as bases of social mobilization and political claims-making in the public sphere. The timid
attempt to conscript the Beurs (second-generation "Arab" immigrants) into a distinct voting "pressure group" during the 1986 legislative campaign foundered on the shoals of a party system and
electoral regime structurally designed to erase all intermediary affiliations.

Thirdly, and most importantly, second-generation immigrants
from the Maghreb, on whom the recent "moral panic" on integration has fastened, are in spite of everything fast assimilating into
French society. They have largely adopted the cultural and behavioral patterns of the French and have failed to form a distinct
"community" constituted around their unique cultural heritage

(Lapeyronnie 1987; Jazouli 1992). Indeed, they and the leaders of their associations "forcefully reject any idiom of [ethnic] specificity and assert that the problems they pose are quintessentially French and social" in nature (Dubet and Lapeyronnie 1992:143).

Not only are most second-generation "Arabs" being rapidly assimilated culturally; a variety of empirical indicators also reveal an overall improvement of their social position and living conditions, in spite their much higher unemployment rate and lower income than native French households. There is no evidence thus far that the spatial separation of so-called Arabs has risen. On the contrary, the increased presence of North Africans and other immigrants in HLM *cités* represents not a status decline on the housing market but a material improvement over a previous situation of genuine segregation into shabby "guest workers' wagon-estates" run by the special housing authority of SONACOTRA and illegal "shanty towns" (*bidonvilles*) that were much more isolated and dilapidated than are today's low-income housing projects (Sayad 1975; Barrou 1992). The immigrant population is also becoming more similar to the native one in terms of occupational distribution, family size, and other demographic characteristics such as fertility and mortality. Intermarriage rates with autochthons are rising, especially among females of North African descent who have higher upward mobility rates than their male counterparts via the school. Scholastic inequality between ethnonational groups in France has likewise decreased since the 1970s, and students of foreign origin have augmented their representation at all levels of the educational system. In fact, differences in academic achievement between them are negligible once class origins are controlled for (Bastide 1982).

This is not to gainsay the cruel reality of joblessness, exclusion, and discrimination that weighs disproportionately on a growing number of immigrant urban youths, nor the undisputable ascent of venomous expressions of xenophobic enmity that are loudly echoed on the national political stage. It is to suggest that, unlike in America where hostility and violence are fed by the deepening spatial and social schism between poor Blacks (and other minorities) and the rest of society, urban unrest in the French periphery is fuelled by the mixing of ethno-national categories—especially in housing and schools—and by the closing of the economic, social, and cul-

tural distance between immigrants and the stagnant or downwardly mobile fractions of the native working class stuck in the
banlieue. In sharp contrast to the Black (sub)proletariat of the
American metropolis, then, North African families of the French
urban periphery are not uniformly travelling on a dark journey to
the nether region of social space. Contrary to the claims of Hollifield (1991:141), they are not in the process of forming a distinct
"Muslim underclass"—whatever that may mean. Rather than signalling the crystallization of properly ethnic cleavages in the
French city, the seemingly "racial" animosity and simmering tension observed in the banlieue over the past decade are expressive of
the social crisis brought about by persistent underemployment and
by the spatial conjugation of educational exclusion, housing blight,
and poverty in areas where native and immigrant working-class
families compete over diminishing collective resources in the context of the breakdown of the perennial mechanisms that used to
translate such conflicts into class demands in the realm of politics
at both the firm and state level.

Conclusion

The purpose of this chapter has been to uncover some of the similarities and differences between the "new urban poverty" in France
and in America as it is locally structured and experienced by those
whom the term (or its equivalent) has come to designate in these
two countries. Rather than compare national aggregate statistics
on income, standards of living, or consumption patterns, which often measure little more than properties of the survey bureaucracies and procedures that generate them and take no account of
the specific welfare-state and sociospatial environments in which
individuals and groups actually evolve in each society, I have proceeded by way of an examination of two master aspects of life in a
stigmatized neighborhood of concentrated poverty. They are territorial indignity and its debilitating consequences upon the fabric
and form of the local social structure; and the principal cleavages
that organize the consciousness and relations of their inhabitants.

Drawing out the organizational and cognitive texture of everyday living in the Parisian Red Belt and in Chicago's Black Belt,

how the residents of these blighted areas negotiate and experience social immobility and ostracization in "the ghetto"—as social myth in one case and enduring historic reality in the other—highlights the distinctively racial dimension of inner-city poverty in the United States. It also points to the uncertainty in the process of collective identity formation in the Red Belt caused by the demise of traditional agencies of class formation. Whether France and America converge or continue to differ in the future with regard to the social and spatial patterning of inequality in the city, there can be little doubt that racial separation, where it prevails, radicalizes the objective and subjective reality of urban exclusion. And that state support (or tolerance) of segregation and recognition of ethnoracial divisions only serve to intensify the cumulation of urban dispossession and to exacerbate the destructive consequences of socioeconomic marginality, not only for those upon whom it is imposed and their neighborhoods, but for the broader society as well.

NOTES

1. This chapter is an abridged and revised version of an article originally published in *International Journal of Urban and Regional Research* 17 (1993): pp. 366–383. Permission to reprint with revisions was granted by Basil Blackwell Ltd. Oxford, UK.

REFERENCES

Abrahams, Roger D. 1970. *Positively black*. Englewood Cliffs, N.J.: Prentice-Hall.

Aïchoune, Farid. 1991. *Nés en banlieue*. Paris: Editions Ramsay.

Anderson, Elijah. 1991. *Streetwise*. Chicago: The University of Chicago Press.

Avery, Desmond. 1987. *Civilisations de La Courneuve: Images brisées d'une cité*. Paris: L'Harmattan.

Bachmann, Christian and Luc Basier. 1989. *Mise en images d'une banlieue ordinaire*. Paris: Syros.

Balibar, Etienne. 1991. "Es Gibt Keinen Staat in Europa: Racism and Politics in Europe Today." *New Left Review* 186 (March-April):5–19.

Banfield, Edward C. 1970. *The Unheavenly City: the nature and future of our urban crisis*. Boston: Little Brown.

Barrou, Jacques. 1992. *La place du pauvre. Historie et géographie sociale de l'habitat.* Paris: L'Harmattan.

Bastide, P. 1982. "Les enfant immigrés et l'enseignement français: enquête dans les établissements du ler et 2ème degré." *Travaux et documents.* 97, INED/PUF.

Bourdieu, Pierre. 1991. "L'ordre des choses. Entretien avec des jeunes gens du Nord de la France." *Actes de la recherche en sciences sociales* 90 (December): 7–19.

Brubaker, William Rogers. 1990. "Immigration, Citizenship, and the Nation-State in France and Germany: A Comparative Historical Analysis." *International Sociology* 5–4 (December): 379–407.

Calogirou, Claire. 1989. *Sauver son honneur.* Paris: L'Harmattan.

Clark, Kenneth B. 1965. *Dark Ghetto: Dilemmas of Social Power.* New York: Harper.

Dahrendorf, Ralf. 1989. "The Underclass and the Future of Britain." Windsor: St George's House Tenth Annual Lecture.

Désir, Harlem. 1992. "Villes ou ghettos. L'édito de Harlem." *Le mensuel de SOS Racisme* (May 1992): 3.

Dubet, François. 1987. *La galére. Jeunes en survie.* Paris: Seuil.

Dubet, François and Didier Lapeyronnie. 1992. *Les quartiers d'exil.* Paris: Editions du Seuil.

Duncan, Arne. 1987. *The values, aspirations, and opportunities of the urban underclass.* Cambridge, Mass.: Harvard University, unpublished B.A. Honors Thesis, 132 pp.

Dulong, Renaud and Patricia Paperman. 1992. *La réputation des cités HLM: enquête sur le language de l'insécurité.* Paris: L'Harmattan.

Engbersen, Godfried. 1989. "Cultures of Long-Term Unemployment in the New West." *The Netherlands Journal of Social Sciences* 25:2 (October): 75–96.

Engbersen, Godfried, Kees Schuyt, Jaap Timmer, and Frans Van Waarden. *Cultures of Unemployment.* Boulder: Westview Press.

Euvremer, L. and Y. Euvremer. 1985. "La honte." *Archivari* (July): 6–9.

Feagin, Joe R. 1991. "The Continuing Significance of Race: Anti-Black Discrimination in Public Places." *American Sociological Review* 56:1 (February): 101–116.

Gans, Herbert H. 1992. "The positive functions of the undeserving poor: the use of the underclass in America," special issue, *Sonderheft* 32: 48–62.

Goffman, Erving. 1963. *The Presentation of Self in Everyday Life.* Harmondsworth: Penguin Books.

Gwaltney, John Langston. 1980. *Drylongso: A Self-Portrait of black America*. New York: Vintage.

Hollifield, James F. 1991. "Immigration and Modernization." In James F. Hollifield and George Ross (eds.), *Searching for the New France*. New York: Routledge.

Jazouli, Adil. 1992. *Les années banlieue*. Paris: Seuil.

Jencks, Christopher and Paul E. Peterson (eds.). 1991. *The Urban underclass*. Washington, D.C.: The Brookings Institution.

Jones, Jacqueline. 1985. *Labor of Love, Labor of Sorrow: Black Women, Work and the Family from Slavery to the Present*. New York: Vintage.

Katz, Michael B. 1989. *The Undeserving Poor: From the War on Poverty to the War on Welfare*. New York: Random.

Kepel, Gilles. 1987. *Les banlieues de l'Islam. Naissance d'une religion en France*. Paris: Seuil.

Killian, Lewis M. 1990. "Race Relations and the Nineties: Where are the Dreams of the Sixties?" *Social Forces* 69–1 (September): 1–13.

Kluegel, James R. and Eliot R. Smith. 1986. *Beliefs About Inequality: Americans' views of what is and what ought to be*. New York: Aldine de Gruyter.

Kotlowitz, Alex. 1991. *There are no children here*. New York: Doubleday.

Laë, Jean-François et Numa Murard. 1985. *L'argent des pauvres: La vie quotidienne en cité de transit*. Paris: Seuil.

Laë, Jean-François and Numa Murard. 1988. "Protection et violence." *Cahiers internationaux de sociologie* 84 (January-June): 19–40.

Lapeyronnie, Didier. 1987. "Les jeunes Maghrébins nés en France: assimilation, mobilisation et action." *Revue française de sociologe* 28:2: 287–318.

Lapeyronnie, Didier and Marcin Frybes. 1990. *L'intégration des minorités immigrées: Étude comparative France-Grande-Bretagne*. Issy-les-Moulineaux: ADRI.

Lapeyronnie, Didier. 1992. "L'exclusion et le mépris." *Les temps modernes* (December): 2:17.

Levine, Lawrence. 1977. *Black Culture and Black Consciousness*. Oxford: Oxford University Press.

Magri, Susanna and Christian Topalov (eds.). 1989. *Villes ouvrières, 1900–1950*. Paris: L'Harmattan.

Marklund, Stephan. 1990. "Structures of Modern Poverty." *Acta Sociologica* 33:1: 125–140.

Massey, Douglas S. and Nancy A. Denton. 1990. "American Apartheid: Segregation and the Making of the Underclass." *American Journal of Sociology* 96:2 (September): 329–357.

Mead, Lawrence. 1992. *The New Politics of Poverty*. New York: Basic Books.

Miles, Robert. 1992. "Explaining Racism in Contemporary Europe: Problems and Perspectives." Paper presented at the Annual Meetings of the American Sociological Association, Pittsburgh, August.

Monroe, Sylvester and Peter Goldman. 1988. *Brothers: Black and Poor: A True Story of Courage and Survuval*. New York: William Morrow.

Orfield, Gary. 1985. "Ghettoization and Its Alternatives." In Paul Peterson (ed.), *The New Urban Reality*, pp. 161–193. Washington, D.C.: The Brookings Institution.

Patterson, Orlando. 1972. "Toward a Future That Has No Past: Reflections on the Fate of Blacks in the Americas." *The Public Interest* 27 (Spring): 25–62.

Pétonnet, Colette. 1979. *On est tous dans le brouillard*. Paris: Galilée.

Pétonnet, Colette. 1982. *Espace habités: Ethnologie des banlieues*. Paris: Galilée.

Pettigrew, Thomas F. 1971. *Racially Separate or Together*. New York: McGraw-Hill.

Pialoux, Michel. 1979. "Jeunesse sans avenir et travail intérimaire." *Actes de la recherche en sciences sociale* 26:27 (April): 19–47.

Pinçon, Michel. 1982. *Cohabiter: Groupes sociaux et modes de vie dans une cité HLM*. Paris: Plan Construction, Coll. 'Recherches.'

Rieder, Jonathan. 1985. *Canarsie: The Jews and Italians of Brooklyn Against Liberalism*. Cambridge: Harvard University Press.

Sayad, Adbelmalek. 1975. "Le foyer des sans-famille." *Actes de la recherche en sciences sociales* 32:33 (June): 89–104.

Schutz, Alfred. 1970. *On Phenomenology and Social Relations*. Chicago: The University of Chicago Press.

Stovall, Tyler. 1990. *The Rise of the Paris Red Belt*. Berkeley: University of California Press.

Suttles, Gerald. 1968. *The Social Order of the Slum*. Chicago: The University of Chicago Press.

Touraine, Alain. 1991. "Face à l'exclusion." *Esprit* 168. (February): 5–13.

Vieillard-Baron, Hervé. 1987. "Chanteloup-les-Vignes: le risque du ghetto." *Esprit* 132 (November): 9–23.

Wacquant, Loïc J.D. 1992a. "Pour en finir avec le mythe des 'cités-ghettos': les différences entre la France et les Etats-Unis." *Annales de la recherche urbaine* 52: 20–30.

——. 1992b. "Banlieues françaises et ghetto noir américain: éléments de comparaison sociologique." *French Politics and Society* 10:4 (Fall): 81–103.

——. 1992c. "'The Zone': Le métier de 'hustler' dans le ghetto noir américain." *Actes de la recherche en sciences sociales* 92 (June): 38–58.

——. 1992d. "Redrawing the Urban Color Line: The State of the Ghetto in the 1980s." In Craig Jackson Calhoun and George Ritzer (eds.), *Social Problems*. New York: McGraw-Hill.

——. 1992e. "Décivilisation et démonisation: la mutation du ghetto noir américain." In Christine Fauré and Tom Bishop (eds.), *L'Amérique des français*. Paris: Editions François Bourin.

——. 1995a. "The Comparative Structure and Experience of Urban Exclusion: 'Race', Class and Space in Paris and Chicago." In R. Lawson, K. McFate, and W.J. Wilson (eds.), *Urban Marginality and Social Policy in America and Western Europe*. New York: Russell Sage.

——. 1995b. "Pour comprendre la 'crise' des banlieues." *Revue* 2 (December).

Wieviorka, Michel. 1992. "Racism and Modernity: The Contemporary European Experience." Paper presented at the Annual Meetings of the American Sociological Association, Pittsburgh, August.

Wilkinson, Daniel. 1992. "Isolating the Poor: Work and Community in the Inner City." Cambridge, Mass.: Harvard University, unpublished B.A. Honors Thesis, 147p.

Williamson, John B. 1974. "Beliefs About the Motivation of the Poor and Attitudes Toward Poverty Policy." *Social Problems* 21:5 (June): 634–647.

Wirth, Louis. 1964. *On Cities and Social Life*. Edited and with an introduction by Albert J. Reiss, Jr. Chicago: The University of Chicago Press.

Stephen Small

—16—

Racism, Black People, and the City in Britain

In many respects, the Black community in urban Britain remains victim to the same forces that have historically constrained the activities of Blacks throughout the diaspora. But the 1990s has seen a new configuration of forces, especially global political and economic forces, which threaten to engulf the Black community. In their struggle for survival the Black community in Britain has always sought inspiration from other diasporic communities. As such, they have drawn on the same community strength, institutions, and organizations—from churches and community groups to schools and self-help organizations—for sustenance and support. The challenges today call for more intense action and greater inter-diasporic support. Although the forces are immense, it is not at all clear that they will prevail over the community's collective will.

This chapter provides an overview of the circumstances and experiences of Black people in Britain in the 1990s.[1] The first section provides a social profile of Black people in the 1990s with a particular focus on the extent of their urban concentration. Section two examines the key factors that shape Black people's lives. These are the forces and factors that must be confronted if significant numbers of Blacks are to escape the racialized inequality and discrimination which threaten the Black community.[2] The final section outlines some of the options (political and policy-wise) available to the Black community as they confront these problems.

357

Historical Background

The history of Britain's relationship with Black people via slavery, colonialism, and the empire has been abundantly documented and there is no need here to rehearse in detail that history (Williams 1944; Fryer 1984). What is important is to document some of the legacy of that history in terms of the institutional arrangements and collective (white) British mindset the empire created. This legacy is one that has seen the systematic underdevelopment of the colonies and the development of systematic racist ideologies of white superiority. It is against this background that the small Black population in Britain's ports (Liverpool, London, and Cardiff) and the immigration of African Caribbeans since the 1950s must be understood.

This experience is one that is dominated by "racialized" hostility predicated on economic and political domination.[3] Racism, violence, discrimination, and abuse have characterized this history, which has seen British institutions, culture, and language forcefully imposed on Black people across the diaspora. But if "racisms" and "racialized" hostility are vital factors in understanding our history, then economic and political domination are also indispensable. Slavery, colonialism and imperialism cannot be understood without an appreciation of the sometimes simple, sometimes complex, interrelationships of racialized and other forces.[4]

The history of British slavery has also been told in detail elsewhere (Jordan 1968; Walvin 1993). It is a history that saw the systematic appropriation of the lands of Africa and the Americas, the forced transportation and enslavement of millions of Africans, and the relentless exploitation of the colonies for imperial profit (Williams 1944). Colonialism left Africa and the Caribbean with economic and political structures incapable of meeting population needs, and this history has been largely characterized by migration for work (Castles and Miller 1993). Resistance to slavery and colonialism has also been described, in particular the diasporic connections between these struggles (Robinson 1983; Bonnett and Watson 1990).

The history of Blacks in Britain is less well known, though recent decades have seen the development of a significant literature about the Black presence (Walvin 1973; Shyllon 1977; Fryer 1984; Ramdin 1987) and about white attitudes toward them and Africans generally (Bolt 1971). Blacks in Britain remained a tiny population numbering only several thousands until after World War II (Fryer 1984). The Black population grew substantially when successive British governments turned to the colonies as a source of labor (Miles and Phizacklea 1984). Since the 1950s several major differences have occurred: prior to the 1950s all Black people in the colonies shared one passport with white people in Britain, but in the 1990s there are three passports, with many Black people having been deprived of their right to settle in Britain (Miles and Phizacklea 1984). The number of Black people in this country has increased from several thousand to several hundred thousand. Black people who were mostly immigrants, are now mostly indigenous, and a Black population that was overwhelmingly working-class has seen greater stratification (Brown 1984).

But several things have remained consistent in this experience: Black people have faced relentless racialized hostility (discrimination, abuse, violent attacks) and have been stigmatized and constrained by multiple racialized ideologies. Successive governments have encouraged and manipulated white fears of Black people for purposes of electoral success, and Black people have sustained communities of resistance, particularly via their diasporic links and identification. Blacks thus remain systematically disadvantaged, but their resolve to survive and succeed has never deserted them (Brown and Gay 1985; Braham et al. 1992).

Young Blacks have been a central part of strategies of resistance via riots and rebellion (Benyon 1984). Sometimes spontaneous and sporadic, they have had an impact on social policy and the social consciousness of both Blacks and whites (Cashmore and Troyna 1982; Small 1983; Jenkins and Solomos 1987).

A central aspect of community resistance has been diasporic links and identification. Nationalism and Pan-Africanism reverberate throughout the Black community in various ways, via the exchange of ideas and ideologies, institutions and individuals (Gilroy 1987; Sivanandan 1990). From the civil rights movement and Black power during the 1950s and 1960s, to Rastafari and reggae since the 1970s. The Pan-African Congress Movement has maintained a consistent presence (especially via its organization of African Liberation Day) since the 1970s. Diasporic Black music (and music from Africa) as communication and ideology—from blues and soul to reggae and rap and high-life—reverberate throughout the Black British population (Small 1983; Oliver 1990).

The Urban Black Presence in the 1990s

The Black population is only a tiny percentage of the British population but it is a highly visible population because of the politicization of "racism" and because Black people are overwhelmingly concentrated in urban areas (Miles and Phizacklea 1984; Smith 1989). Data are available for the 1980s and 1990s, and these data reveal a consistent pattern.[5]

The total Black population in 1981 was just about 700,000, of whom 550,000 were African Caribbeans, 123,000 Africans, and 26,000 so-called "British Born Blacks," from England's long-standing Black communities such as Liverpool and Bristol (Bhat *et. al.* 1988). The majority of African Caribbeans were from the British West Indies (Jamaica, Trinidad, Guyana, Barbados) while the Africans were mainly from West and East Africa. Around 47 percent of the African-Caribbean population in the early 1980s was born in England (LFS 1982:33). Data from the 1991 Census, the first to have a question on "ethnicity," indicate the size of the Black population at the end of the 1980s[6] (Owen 1992). These data indicate that there were 496,000 African Caribbeans, 203,200 Africans, and 172,900 "other" Black people in England (Owen 1992:1). For all persons of African-Caribbean ancestry about twelve percent were of "mixed African-Caribbean/White ethnic group," with a much larger proportion of this mixed group being young (Population Trends 1985:8).

The most recent population data for Britain are available from the 1991 Census (Owen 1992, 1994). The 1991 Census counted nearly 54.9 million people in Britain. For Great Britain the total number of Blacks was 890,700, (1.6 percent of the total population). For England, it was 874,900 (Owen 1992:1 Table 1). For Great Britain this included 500,000 Black Caribbeans (0.9 percent of total population), 212,400 Black-Africans (0.4 percent of total population) and 178.400 Black-Others (0.3 percent of total population) (*ibid.*).

African-Caribbean families added up to less than one per cent of all families in Great Britain (Haskey 1989:12). The total number of African-Caribbean families was 144,000, while the total number of African families was 28,000 (*ibid.*:12). A total of 112,000 (1 percent) of all couples in Britain are ethnically mixed, of whom 29,000 have an African-Caribbean member of the couple, and 21,000 have a person of mixed origins (LFS 1987:38). By the end of the 1980s, four in every ten African families, were headed by a female (Haskey 1989:13). On average, Black families contained 2.2 dependent children, whereas white families contain 1.8 (*ibid.*:12). By the late 1980s, more than twenty percent of African-Caribbean couples were couples with dependent children (Social Trends 1992:42). The highest proportion of single-headed families is among African Caribbeans (forty-two percent), while twenty-four percent of African families were single parented families (Haskey 1989:12–13).

The residential settlement of Black people in the 1990s was more or less set by 1961 (Smith 1989:27). In general, Black people were more likely to be urban, to live in certain sections of the inner-city, and to be residentially segregated from whites (Rex 1988:31). They are disproportionately located in London, West Midlands, the North West, Yorkshire, and Humberside. These five metropolitan areas account for a huge proportion of all Black people in the country.

In 1991, the Greater London area alone had 535,000 Black people, adding up to 8.5 percent of London's population (Owen 1992:4 Table 4). The West Midlands area (main cities are Birmingham, Wolverhampton, and Coventry) has 102,200 (2 percent of the region's population) (*ibid.*). The North West concentration (main cities are Manchester and Liverpool) is 47,000 (adding to 0.8 percent). Yorkshire and Humberside (main cities Leeds, Bradford) has 36,600 (totalling 0.8 percent of the region's population) (*ibid.*).

Despite the fact that Black people display such a heavy regional concentration, they comprise a relatively small proportion of the total population in the respective areas. The highest concentration is in London. In inner London, Blacks make up 13.4 percent of the population; in outer London they total 4.8 percent of total population (Owen 1992:6 Table 7). Outside London, the highest urban concentration is to be found in West Midlands (3.6 percent). All other counties have Black populations of 2.5 percent or less.

What are the social-economic characteristics of the Black population? The best way to understand the economic and political circumstances of Black people in Britain is to say that a "color line" prevails, that is, compared to white people, Black people are worse off by just about every major economic and social indicator. Data from the 1980s and 1990s indicate that this is true in wealth and health, as it is in education and employment. There are some notable exceptions, and some striking impressions of apparent success, but these do not change the overall picture.

Black people in Britain are more likely to be unemployed, to receive low pay, and more likely to be claiming welfare benefits. For example, Black males earned ten to fifteen percent less than whites in the early 1980s (Field 1986). And almost twice as many Black households as compared with white households were likely to be reliant on child benefits during the 1980s; 60 percent of African-Caribbean households, as compared with 34 percent of white households were more reliant on child benefits (Brown 1984:242).

Compared to white people, Black people are more likely to be self-employed, and more likely to be in manual and lower paid jobs (Owen 1994). Around eighty-five percent of African-Caribbean males were economically active in the late 80s; for women the figure was seventy-six percent (Employment Gazette 1991:61). White men are more likely to be employed as corporate managers and in skilled and semi-skilled jobs. For example, Brown reported that while nineteen percent of whites were found in the top SEG category (socio-economic group), only five percent of African Caribbeans were; and the proportion of whites in other "non-manual" jobs was double that for African Caribbeans (Brown 1989: 157).

Recent evidence suggests the growth of a small but significant group of wealthy and educated Blacks often referred to as a "Black middle-class" (Cashmore 1991:347–358; 1992:169–172). This array of individuals is made up of business owners and managers, the self-employed, professionals such as academics, doctors and social workers, and local and central government workers and civil servants; politicians, and a small but highly visible number of rich individuals such as sport personalities and musicians. Around seven percent of African-Caribbean men were self-employed in the 1980s (for women it was one percent); while amongst the top categories of employees (employers, managers, and professional workers) only five percent were African-Caribbean (for women, the proportion was one percent) (Brown 1984:198 Table 92.). So the numbers remain small—it is considerably smaller proportionately than that of its white counterparts—and there are small but significant numbers of women in it. It seems highly unlikely, in the present economic climate, that these numbers will grow to any significant extent. I have suggested elsewhere that the size and political affiliations of this group has yet to be fully assessed, but they do make the picture more complex (Small 1994b).

Data on success in education display considerable racialized disparities, with Black people generally less likely to receive qualifications (Brown 1984). Black people do tend to stay in education longer than whites, though it may be that they take longer to get the same qualifications. There is some evidence that Black women have earned higher qualifications than Black men and even higher than white men (Mirza 1992). Similarly, whites are more likely to live in owner-occupied housing than Blacks (66 percent of whites own their own homes while 42.3 percent of Blacks do) (Owen 1994:6 Table 5). As well, Black households are more likely to be overcrowded and less likely to own cars.

Key Issues in the 1990s

In the 1990s, Black people in urban Britain find themselves at a significant disadvantage, deprived of many basic resources, facing systematic "racialized" hostility and a harsh economic climate. A series of developments, many simply persisting from earlier decades, but changing form and often more severe, alongside some new developments, pose considerable challenges. Some of these developments are internal to Britain, others are international. Many of the developments are racialized, others appear to be without racialized intent but their effects impact disproportionately on different racialized groups.

Although many of these national and international forces are complex and multifaceted, their impact on Black people will be relatively straight forward: patterns of racialized inequality seem most likely to become exacerbated and the factors that maintain them will become more complex and difficult to pinpoint. The impact on Black women will be especially adverse (Mama 1989,

1992:79–101). In addition, these forces will relegate issues of justice and equal opportunity to a secondary status in a country and world in which concern with free trade and competition, individual initiative, and the enterprise culture will predominate. This means that policies to combat racialized inequality in the city will be more difficult to formulate, market, and implement. However, there are clear signs of determined resistance to these adverse factors.

What are the particular developments of the 1990s, and how do they impact on Black people? The first is the growing stratification within the Black population, as mentioned above. The increasing evidence of more successful Black people, alongside large numbers of unemployed and never-employed Black people, and those in poverty, will make for more diverse political affiliations. It will also lead to different priorities and conflicts over goals and policies.

The second is the changing nature of "racisms" and racialized hostility, as direct individual and institutional racisms are accompanied by indirect and furtive types. This means overall a continued move from direct, overt, and conspicuous racial discrimination, in which it was easy to identify motives predicated on racial beliefs (for example, immigration legislation), to indirect, covert, and inconspicuous racial discrimination in which motives and intentions are less obvious.

Race-related violence and other forms of abuse are escalating. (Thompson 1989; Hesse *et. al.* 1991). Racialized discrimination in employment and education persists at significant levels, as does racialized intimidation by the police (Brown and Gay 1985). The state and employers publicly and officially embrace equal opportunities, but by postponement, prevarication, and delaying tactics, ensure it is not implemented! (McCruddon *et. al.* 1991). For example, given the challenge to racism there has been an increase in more furtive and surreptitious methods of discrimination, vilification, and exclusion as racists employ codewords, double entendres, and the like to camouflage the vehemence and virulence of their attitudes and actions. Locutions such as "our own kind" or "British people" appeal to white nationalism, while a greater emphasis on networks, word of mouth, internal adverts, the criteria for recruitment in employment, continues to keep Black people out.

Black people continue to be subjected to the most pernicious degradation and vilification of their color and culture, a culture that is deemed primitive and a family structure that is dismissed as pathological. Images like these continue to be disseminated by the press, television, literature, and other popular media, even to the extent that Black people are also perpetrators. Each set of problems reinforces the other—racialized discrimination causes material hardship, and in a society in which a premium is placed on material possessions Blacks doubt their self-worth, while racialized images disparage their very being. The pattern of discrimination, and the hostility or indifference to equal opportunity policies amongst most whites, and often government, is a considerable barrier that must be overcome if Black people are to move forward.

There are more Asians[7] than Blacks nationally and in all regional concentrations. For example, the total number of Asians in Great Britain is 1,479,600 (that is, 2.7 percent of the total population) (Owen 1992:2 Table 2). In England they number 1,431,300 (3 percent) (*ibid.*). Asians are almost equal in number to Blacks in Greater London (520,600 or 7.8 percent of the total population); and they outnumber them in the West Midlands (276,800 or 5 percent of the total population); Yorkshire and Humberside (143,900 or 3.0 percent of the total population); the North West (147,500 or 2.4 percent of the total population (Owen 1992 Tables 2,3,4). The Asian population is more economically and ethnically diverse, with significant proportions of educated and occupationally advantaged groups (Modood 1988:397–404). There are important differences within the Asian population—Indians do best economically, followed by Pakistanis and Bangladeshis (see also Jones 1993). There is evidence that Asians generally are more likely to vote conservative, a political action reflecting their class background.

A key countervailing factor is the fact that young, especially British-born Asians, show signs of solidarity and commitment to a shared common identity, and goals with Black people, though this is not entirely free from tension. Strong alliances have been developed in key urban areas, especially around white racists, racialized violence, and community needs (Hesse *et. al.* 1991).

Overall, this means that there is no single minority voice or experience of racism, it raises issues of allegiances, and it allows for the manipulation of difference and cooptation by the state (Sivanandan 1982, 1990).

The economic climate, and the response to it, is equally threatening with high levels of unemployment, homelessness, and poverty, and low levels of investment in health and education. For example, labor markets have been transformed, and companies demand more credentialled workers; employers and government have changed their strategies in a bid to maintain high profits; the new technology, especially in service industries, has led to the restructuring of work processes and the reorganization of industries; the growth in the informal economy has led to dramatic transformations and an invigorated emphasis on ideologies supporting the free market economy, economic efficiency, and enterprise culture (Taylor 1989:18–34; Castles and Miller 1993).

"Racialized" ideologies have always been a feature of political ideology in Britain, given the centrality of slavery and colonialism to Britain's economic and industrial growth, but on the whole, the power and hegemony of Britain enabled it to keep such matters in the background of political discussion until the middle of this century, and certainly to contain most opposition (Rich 1986; Harris 1991:1–30). Because of the immigration to Britain of several hundred thousand Black people since the 1950s, and the political and (white) public response to them, this has changed, and since that time racialized ideologies and discourse have most often been explicit aspects of the political agenda. The domination of the Conservatives since 1979, itself largely a result of its manipulation of racialized attitudes, has seen them try to move overt discussion of racism to the background.

Since taking power in 1992, John Major's government has tried to take a low profile on explicitly employing racialized rhetoric, though much key legislation remains exclusionary. Several incidents highlight the continued ways in which manipulation of racisms remains an important element of state activities, for example, suggestions by government ministers that "foreign scroungers" are burdening the welfare system.

More dizzying in proportions, more difficult to identify and difficult to contain, are the new set of international forces around which the term, "the New World Order," has been applied (Taylor 1989:18–34). Most central has been the European Union (Wrench and Solomos 1993). This dizzying array of economic and political changes present new complexities. The 1990s has seen the consolidation and growth of multinationals; a shift in manufacturing jobs from Europe and the United States to South America and the Far East; changing European Union priorities, policies, and markets; the restructuring of labor markets, especially part-time work; implementation of new technologies; migration flows and the movement of refugees (Cohen 1987).

Alongside economic changes we have seen the disintegration of the Soviet Union and the ethnic struggles in the former Yugoslavia, the unification of Germany, the consolidation of the European Union, and the Gulf War. The end of apartheid in South Africa has raised expectations of democracy, and made for new promises of economic delivery. But the funds have not always been forthcoming, especially given the greater domestic role of President Clinton and the need to work out a new position for the United States. More recently, war in Somalia and massacre and carnage in Rwanda have added to the worries.

These issues are external to Britain; nevertheless, they continue to impact Britain in fundamental ways. They adversely impact on existing patterns of racialized inequality and they make government demands for color-blind policies more appealing to the non-Black population. This means that measures such as equal opportunity policies will find less favor with the non-Black population, and such efforts will become marginalized. A trend of this sort has been particularly strong, and is growing, since the early 1980s when former Prime Minister Margaret Thatcher opposed such policies, arguing they were contrary to free market mechanisms and free choice (Gordon 1990:175–190).

All these developments, of course, have to be understood and interpreted in the context of the Conservatives' domination of British politics for the last fifteen years, and its right-wing policies of free market enterprise, privatization, anti-trade unions, and individualism (Gamble 1988). All, of course, firmly buttressed by notions of the inherent superiority of (white) English culture and institutions, not infrequently reflected in mutterings for the "green and pleasant" land of the past.

But it is also important to identify some trends that make it possible for Black people to confront and resist these forces. First of all, Black people, inside and outside formal channels, continue to demand and campaign for equal opportunities. For example, there is a small but significant number of Black and Asian people in local authorities, education, and private sectors to act as precipitants. A number of procedures have already been established in public and private sectors as examples of good practice, and these can be expanded.

The letter of the law, in terms of the provisions of the 1976 Race Relations Act, still provides a foundation for policy. Though it is stronger on paper than in practice, significant precedents have been taken and can be developed further. In addition, since demography favors Blacks as a younger population, the government and employers may respond accordingly, or be pressured to respond accordingly, in terms of providing education and training.

Black organizations and institutions, locally, regionally, and nationally, continue to demonstrate great determination as they consolidate the Black infrastructure that has been developed over the last decades. Institutions, conferences, campaigns, community centers, are all part of this. International links have been maintained, some developed further. Groups like the Standing Conference on Racial Equality in Europe (SCORE) exemplify this approach. Other Black organizations have developed European and world networks. Central to such activities are diasporic borrowings—ideas, institutions, and individuals—as Black people continue the international dialogue with others throughout the diaspora and continent. The United States figures prominently in such discussion (Small 1991: 3–55, 1993).

One final aspect to note has to do with the political strength of the Conservatives. Recent years have seen significant internal strife among the Conservatives over the European Union, and attempts to change the Prime Minister which, combined with the lack of support for government policies, have threatened to tear the party apart. Whether the momentum is there for Labour to take government remains unclear, but they do pose a significant threat. A change of government would certainly see a shift in "racialized" policies, and greater benefit for Black people. However, the Labour Party's record in government indicates it is unlikely that any policies they propose would fundamentally overcome the barriers to urban Black progress.

The magnitude of the problems confronting Black people far outshadows the promising features of the situation, and many aspects of strength can be developed only with great determination and resilience. But this harsh reality must be confronted, and the work being done by Black communities is testimony to their determination.

Approaching the 21st Century

Given this array of forces, what might be done? At the moment so many Black people are simply struggling to survive against "racialized" attacks and violence, and against the hardships of unemployment, disadvantage, and poverty, that developing an agenda for securing longer term goals often seems secondary. Many of the problems confronted by Black people have given rise to significant mobilization around specific and immediate problems, for example, racialized violence and attacks, police harassment, immigration controls. But there is clear evidence of the existence of an infrastructure of Black groups and organizations that are concerned with longer term strategies. The Black community has several broad options available to it. These options have both policy and political elements, and involve both short-term and long-term strategies. Given the embracing of each of these options by different sections of the Black community, it is unclear which option is likely to prevail, or even whether one option will prevail over others. Of course, it is also difficult to separate the rhetoric from the substance. Two broad options are available to Black people, mobilization around class or around racialized identities. Before the options are discussed, it is important briefly to discuss goals. I believe that there are several key goals pursued by Black people and I have articulated them around the concepts of racialized integration, harmony, and parity (Small 1991:3–55, 1994b). I would add to these goals that of psychological well-being.

Racialized integration usually means the physical and social interaction of Blacks and non-Blacks in a range of social areas— housing, education, employment; racialized harmony suggests nonantagonistic social interaction; while racialized parity suggests similar access to, and/or ownership of resources, economic, educational, or otherwise. These goals, or institutional interests, are usually central to discussions of equal opportunities and anti-racism. A barrage of stereotypes, negative images, and discourses continue to portray Black people as inferior, of limited intelligence, and even animalistic. Black women especially are portrayed as exotic, sexual, and promiscuous (Bryan *et al.* 1985). Containing and replacing such images with more accurate representations of Black experiences and aspirations remains central to strategies for success and the goal of psychological well-being.

These goals are predicated largely around full participation within British society, and seem largely to accept the essential principles of capitalist society. This goal reflects the socialization of Black people into capitalist society. But some Black people clearly want more than equal opportunities in capitalist society (Gilroy 1987). Some Black people thus seek to go beyond capitalist society, to a socialist political and economic system, one that ensures a more equitable distribution of resources, and is not predicated on racialized notions of superiority.

What is the case for mobilization around class and racialized identities, and what are their strengths and limitations? Mobilization around class identities seeks to forge links with whites (and Asians)[9] along class lines. It has several versions. A mainstream element seeks election of the Labour party to Parliament, an approach reflected in Black participation in trade unions and the Labour Party (Anwar 1986; Phizacklea and Miles 1992:30–45). And a more radical element, reflected in the activities of groups such as the socialist workers party, seeks the overthrow of capitalism (Taaffe and Mulhearn 1988).

Both of these approaches are based on the notion that racisms and racialized identities are secondary to the identities of class. One aspect of this are multi-racial alliances, such as between Blacks and Asians and whites, particularly among young people. This group downplays the racialised and cultural differences between Blacks and whites and emphasizes the shared experiences of class disadvantage and common goals for justice and a more equitable distribution of resources. Because they fail to address as a primary matter the continuing centrality of racialized hostility in all aspects of Black people's lives, and especially in shaping their class position, these approaches are bound to leave Black people wanting more. In fact, one element of this approach is efforts by

Black people to get non-Blacks to accept the continuing significance of racialized hostility.

The second approach is that of racialized identities. By 'racialized'
identities is meant mobilizing Black people around a commonly defined identity and goals, building on the strengths of Black-only or
Black-led organizations, and forming alliances with other racialized groups on the basis of common terms and priorities (Goulbourne 1990). Mobilization around racialized identities offers a
number of strengths, including ensuring that policies are based on
a recognition of the links between racialized and economic inequality and injustice. Again, this has several different versions; some
may be called Black nationalism, while others seek to benefit from
the provisions of the 1976 Race Relations Act, which allows for
Black community groups. This approach sees racisms and racialized identities as being of primary importance and envisages the
building of Black community autonomous institutions as the best
way to advance the material interests of Black people. This approach is reflected in the work of the Pan African Congress Movement.

One aspect of this goal is the development of a Black middle
class of the sort that has developed in the United States (See Cashmore 1991:347–58, 1992:169–72). Commonly embraced by Black
people involved in business and enterprise, the aim is for full participation within British society, usually articulated around integration and equal opportunities. This is reflected in the growth of
Black businesses and the provision of services by government to
encourage their growth (Sawyer 1983:55–62).

It is clear that Black people are committed to different strategies
in different numbers, with commitment to class-based strategies
reflected in their level of involvement in the Labour party (Goulbourne 1990). The approach articulated around class identities is
the most favored among Black people in Britain, though many
Blacks retain some overt commitment to making the challenge to
racism more central to this strategy.

These strategies are not mutually exclusive, and there is often
overlap between them. The strategies being pursued by Black
people are being pursued in a climate of harsh economic realities
and Conservative political hegemony. The Conservatives have been
in government for fifteen years, but recent conflict within the Con-

servative government and its lack of popularity in the polls suggest a weakness in their domination.

Conclusion

The goal of this chapter has been to examine some of the conditions in which the Black community in Britain finds itself in the 1990s, and to consider some of the policy and political options that might be pursued in the future. In many respects, as we stand at the foot of the twenty-first century, what we face in the Black community in Britain is a crisis of tremendous proportions. In many respects it is worse off, given the state of economic, educational, and political disadvantage, than ever before. In other respects, there are clear signs of strength. Black community institutions persevere relentlessly in spite of tremendous institutional, ideological, and financial obstacles; some Black people have risen in the system to positions of political and economic importance and strength.

The bewildering array of forces that shape the community's experience, which must be confronted and analyzed if it is to shape policy and politics, has never been so extensive, nor so intricate. National and international forces have marginalized the Black struggle and made it more difficult. A key problem is how to recognize the necessity of maintaining a broader and international vision of diasporic identification—one that acknowledges how global forces shape group experiences and builds on the strengths and struggles of other Black people across the globe—while confronting the immediacies of local and national contexts.

I believe that the best way forward is one that builds on the strength of racialized identities. Only this approach can begin to confront and surmount the range of material and ideological forces that confront us, and sustain a realistic challenge to the psychological devastation such forces continue to inflict. A key aspect of this approach is the development of a Black agenda for the Black community; an agenda that enables it to confront the complexities and even contradictory processes, disentangle the intricacies, establish priorities, and formulate and implement strategies in the short, medium, and long term. The matter of allies must also be considered. Black agendas are currently being developed by local and national groups—from the Society of Black Lawyers to the Black Perspectives Group, from the National Black Caucus to the Standing Conference on Racial Equality in Europe. Only this will enable Blacks to rise to the challenge and to engage and surmount the obstacles that threaten to overwhelm them.

NOTES

1. In this chapter, the word "Black" refers to people from Africa, and their descendents, including those called African, African Caribbean, West Indian, and "mixed race."

2. I analyze the experience of Black people in terms of processes of "racialized" interaction, rather than "race relations." The concept of "racialization" facilitates an analysis of the interplay of ideologies and institutional practices predicated around notions of "race" with economic and political practices. For a discussion of the concept, see Omi and Winant 1986; Small 1994b.

3. I use the term "hostility" to refer to attitudes and actions whose intentions and/or outcomes are detrimental to Black people, rather to mean aggression.

4. The essential issues are reflected in C.L.R. James's frequently quoted axiom: "The race question is subsidiary to the class question in politics, and to think of imperialism in terms of race is disastrous. But to neglect the racial factor as merely incidental (is) an error only less grave than to make it fundamental" (1980:283).

5. There are discrepancies between the data for the 1980s and the 1990s because different definitions of "Black" were employed.

6. The 1991 census was the first to have an ethnic question; until that time, data on the size of the Black population were inferred from data on the nationality of the immigrants, and from sample surveys (Smith 1976; Bhat *et al.* 1988; Brown 1994).

7. The term Asian refers to people in India, Pakaistan, and Bangladesh, and their descendants, including those from Kenya, Uganda, Tanzania, and Malawi.

REFERENCES

Anwar, Muhammad. 1986. *Race and Politics: Ethnic Minorities and the British Political System.* London and New York: Tavistock Publications.

Ben-Tovim, Gideon, J. Gabriel, I. Law, and K. Stedder. 1986. *The Local Politics of Race*. London: Macmillan.

Benyon, John (ed.). 1984. *Scarman and After: Essays Reflecting on Lord Scarman's Report, the Riots and their Aftermath*. Oxford: Pergamon Press.

Bhat, Ashok, Roy Carr-Hill, and Sushel Ohri. 1988. *Britain's Black Population: A New Perspective*. Aldershot: Gower.

Bolt, C., *Victorian Attitudes to Race*. 1971. London: Routledge & Kegan Paul.

Bonnett, Aubrey W., and G. Llewellyn Watson (eds.). 1990. *Emerging Perspectives on the Black Diaspora*. New York and London: University Press of America.

Brown, Colin. 1984. *Black and White Britain: The Third PSI Survey*. London: Heinemann Educational Books.

Brown, Colin and Pat Gay. 1985. *Racial Discrimination: 17 Years After the Act*. London: Policy Studies Institute.

Braham, Peter, Ali Rattansi, and Richard Skellington. 1992. *Racism and Antiracism. Inequalities, Opportunities and Policies*. London: Sage.

Bryan, Beverley, Stella Dadze, and Suzanne Scafe. 1985. *The Heart of the Race. Black Women's Lives in Britain*. London: Virago Press.

Cashmore, Ernest and Barry Troyna (eds.). 1982. *Black Youth in Crisis*. London: Allen & Unwin.

Cashmore, Ellis. 1991. "Flying business class: Britain's new ethnic elite." *New Community* Vol. 17:3 (April).

———. 1992. "Black Entrepreneurs: No More Room at the Top." In Anthony Giddens (ed.), *Human Societies: A Reader*. Cambridge: Polity Press.

Castles, Stephen and Mark J. Miller. 1993. *The Age of Migration. International Population Movements in the Modern World*. Basingstoke: Macmillan.

Cohen, Robin. 1987. *The New Helots: Migrants in the International Division of Labour*. Farnborough: Avebury.

Fryer, Peter. 1984. *Staying Power: the History of Black People in Britain*. London: Pluto Press.

Gamble, Andrew. 1988. *The Free Economy and the Strong State: The Politics of Thatcherism*. Basingstoke: Macmillan.

Gilroy, Paul. 1987. *There Ain't No Black In the Union Jack: The Cultural Politics of Race and Nation*. London: Hutchinson.

Gordon, Paul. 1990. "A Dirty War: the New Right and Local Authority Anti-Racism." In Wendy Ball and John Solomos (eds.), *Race and Local Politics*. Basingstoke and London: Macmillan.

Goulbourne, Harry. 1990. *Black Politics in Britain*. Farnborough: Avebury.

Hacker, Andrew. 1992. *Two Nations: Black and White, Separate, Hostile and Unequal*. New York: Charles Scribner's Sons.

Harris, Clive. 1991. "Configurations of Racism: the Civil Service, 1945–60." *Race and Class* Vol. 33:1.

Haskey, John. 1989. "Families and Households of the Ethnic Minority and White Populations of Great Britain." *Population Trends* 57. Her Majesty's Stationary Office, London, Autumn.

Hesse, Barnor, Dhanwant K. Rai, Chritine Bennett, Paul McGilchrist. 1991. *Beneath the Surface: Racial Harassment*. Aldershot: Avebury.

James, CLR. 1980. *The Black Jacobins: Toussaint L'Ouverture and the San Domingo Revolution*. London: Allison and Busby.

Jenkins, Richard and John Solomos (eds.). 1987. *Racism and Equal Opportunity Policy in the 1980s*. Cambridge: Cambridge University Press.

Jones, Trevor. 1993. *Britain's Ethnic Minorities*. London: Policy Studies Institute.

Labour Force Survey, 1985, Office of Population Census and Surveys, HMSO, 1987.

Labour Force Survey, 1990–91, Office of Population Census and Surveys, HMSO, 1992.

Mama, Amina. 1989. *The Hidden Struggle: Statutory and Voluntary Sector Responses to Violence against Black Women in the Home*. London: Race and Housing Research Unit/Runneymede Trust.

———. 1992. "Black women and the British State: Race, Class and Gender Analysis for the 1990s." In Peter Braham, Ali Rattansi, and Richard Skellington (eds.), *Racism and Antiracism. Inequalities, Opportunities and Policies*. London and Newbury Park, Cal.:Sage Publications Ltd.

McCruddon, Christopher, David J. Smith, and Colin Brown. 1991. *Racial Justice at Work*. London: Policy Studies Institute.

Miles, Robert. 1982. *Racism and Migrant Labour*. London: Routledge & Kegan Paul.

Miles, Robert and Annie Phizacklea. 1984. *White Man's Country: Racism in British Politics*. London: Pluto Press.

Miles, Robert. 1989a. *Racism*. London and New York: Routledge.

Mirza, Heidi. 1992. *Young, Female and Black*. London and New York: Routledge.

Modood, Tariq. 1988. "'Black', Racial Equality and Asian Identity." *New Community* Vol. 14:3.

Oliver, Paul (ed.). 1990. *Black Music in Britain: Essays on the Afro-Asian Contribution to Popular Music*. Milton Keynes and Philadelphia: Open University Press.

Omi, Michael and Howard Winant. 1986. *Racial Formation in the United States. From the 1960s to the 1980s*. London and New York: Routledge & Kegan Paul.

Owen, David. 1992. "Ethnic Minorities in Great Britain: Settlement Patterns." National Ethnic Minority Data Archive, Centre for Research in Ethnic Relations, November.

———. 1994. "Black People in Great Britain: Social and Economic Circumstances." National Ethnic Minority Data Archive, Centre for Research in Ethnic Relations, February.

Phizacklea, Annie and Robert Miles. 1992. "The British Trade Union Movement and Racism." In Braham, Peter, Ali Rattanis, and Richard Skellington (eds.), *Racism and Antiracism*. London, Newbury Park, and New Delhi: Sage and Open Unversity.

Population Trends. 1985. Her Majesty's Stationary Office, 57, London.

Rex, John. 1988. *The Ghetto and the Underclass: Essays on Race and Social Policy*. Aldershot: Gower.

Rich, Paul. 1986. *Race and Empire in British Politics*. Cambridge: Cambridge University Press.

Sawyer, Ade. 1983. "Black-controlled business in Britain: particular problems and suggested solutions." *New Community* Vol. 11:1–2 (Autumn/Winter).

Shyllon, Folarin. 1977. *Black People in Britain, 1553–1833*. London: Oxford University Press.

Sivanandan, A. 1982. *A Different Hunger*. London: Pluto Press.

———. 1990. *Communities of Resistance: Writings on Black Struggles for Socialism*. London and New York: Verso.

Sklair, Leslie. 1991. *Sociology of the Global System*. New York: Harvester Wheatsheaf.

Small, Stephen. 1983. *Police and People in London. II A Group of Young Black People*. Policy Studies Institute, London, (November).

———. 1991. "Attaining Racial Parity in the United States and England; We Got to Go Where the Greener Grass Grows!." *Sage Race Relations Abstracts* Vol. 16:3 (May).

———. 1993. "Unravelling Racialised Relations in the United States of America and the United States of Europe." In JohnWrench and John Solomos (eds.), *Racism and Migration in Europe*. Oxford and New York: Berg Publishers Inc.

———. 1994. "Racialised Ideologies, Class Relations and the State in England." *Discussion Papers in Sociology*, University of Leicester.

———. 1994b. *Racialised Barriers*. London and New York: Routledge.

Smith, David J. 1976. *Racial Disadvantage in Britain*. London: Political and Economic Planning.

Smith, Susan J. 1989a. *The Politics of 'Race' and Residence. Citizenship, Segregation and White Supremacy in Britain.* Cambridge and London: Polity Press.

Social Trends, *Central Statistical Office,* London, 1992.

Solomos, John. 1989. *Race and Racism in Contemporary Britain.* Basingstoke and London: Macmillan Education.

Taaffe, P. and T. Mulhearn. 1988. *Liverpool: A City that Dared to Fight.* London: Fortress.

Taylor, Peter J. 1989. "Britain's Changing Role in the World-Economy." In John Mohan (ed.), *The Political Geography of Contemporary Britain.* Basingstoke and London: Macmillan Education.

Thompson, Keith. 1988. *Under Siege: Racial Violence in Britain Today.* London: Penguin Books.

Walvin, James. 1973. *Black and White: The Negro and English Society 1555–1945.* London: Allen Lane.

———. 1993. *Black Ivory: A History of British Slavery.* London: Fontana.

Williams, Eric. 1944. *Capitalism and Slavery.* London: Andre Deutsch.

Wrench, John and John Solomos. 1993. *Racism and Migration in Europe.* Oxford and New York: Berg Publishers.

Charles Green

Conclusion
Beyond the 21st Century

The findings from this study give overwhelming support to the existence of a global Black urban crisis. Whether we begin the analysis from the African continent and proceed outwardly to London, Paris, Rio de Janeiro, Kingston, New York City, or Toronto or reverse our steps, the socio-cultural, economic, and political realities of the crisis are unmistakable. Persistent racism alongside the intensification of global economic structures constitutes the new urban challenge. Worrisome is the finding that the coping strategies by the urban poor that seemed to work in the past are tenuous at best at this historical juncture.

In the United States, the confluence of postindustrialism and persistent racism (Hacker 1992; Bell 1993; West 1993) operates to shut out scores of Blacks from opportunities promised under the banner of the free market system. Recently, in the midst of economic austerity and political frenzy, neo-conservative Republicans were able to wrest control of the Congress from their Democratic opponents. Their formula for a new America, or "The Contract With America," is a slash and burn policy that advocates an end to the welfare safety net and the excesses of big government. It is unsympathetic to the historic situation of America's Black constituents, in particular those unfortunate souls who happen to be lodged at the bottom in the inner cities. As the essays on Britain and France reveal, the situation there is not much brighter for urban Blacks and other persons of color.

It is not coincidental that the present crisis has had a partic-

379

ularly shattering effect on the institutional arrangements and cultural life of Blacks, browns, and persons of mixed races who reside in the developing regions. This can be attributed to the peculiar structuring of race in these societies. But it can also be attributed to these societies' historic dependency on the more advanced countries, major economic shifts in the dominant capitalist systems, and the increased involvement in the domestic economic affairs of these societies by external institutions like the International Monetary Fund, the World Bank, and the Inter-American Bank For Development. Consequently, as the essays on sub-Saharan Africa, Latin America, and the Caribbean reveal, there has been an observed shift in familial structures, social roles, cultural values, the nature of work, and the extent of nationalistic commitment among the people of these regions. As well, the relationship of young people to authority figures, and the general outlook on life by diasporans, was reported to have significantly declined.

For many residents of developed countries in the post–World War II period, the insurmountable hardships of life have come to be equated with the peoples of the Third World. Distorted television and other media accounts of despondent and hopeless men, women, and children, the victims of famine, internecine ethnic warfare, and unstable governments helped frame their worldview and false sense of security and privilege. Moreover, this prompted responses like "it can't happen here" and "not in our backyard." But awed by the pervasiveness of present day social and economic dislocations that are unravelling in the urban areas, North Americans and Europeans alike are being forced to reexamine these lofty attitudes.

The findings also point to the limited role of state governments across the regions covered to arrest the dislocation. The United States, burdened with an unprecedented trade deficit and a national debt in excess of $5 trillion, is incapable of arresting capital flight that has affected plant closings, chronic unemployment and underemployment, and the crumbling social infrastructure in its central cities. In the Third World, the state is subordinate to foreign (investment) capital, but more to the interests of local elites and corrupt officials who, in many cases, are the dangling puppets of foreigners. The politics of greed rather than the politics of empowerment and human development is the operating ethos for far too many of these statesmen. This was illustrated for example in the essays on Kenya, Venezuela, Panama, and Jamaica. Consequently, a bankrupt state apparatus in the diaspora coupled with the emphasis on market forces has left the poor and working classes to fend for themselves, and thus the proliferation of street hawking, informal economic activities, squatting, school rejection, street crime, and gang and drug related violence.

Because emphasis is placed on macro level problems and solutions throughout the essays in this volume, analysis of the impact of the crisis on interpersonal relations between individuals and groups was limited. In a recent article, Samuel Huntington referred to the present spectacle of inter-ethnic rivalry as the "clash of modern civilizations."[1] This was considered in the essays by Joe L. P. Lugalla and Kinuthia Macharia on Tanzania and Kenya respectively, where competition between Africans, Asians, and Arabs in those urban arenas has increased. Stephen Small and Loïc J. D. Wacquant also dealt with this in their respective essays on Britain and France, where the conflict involves these very groups. Rivalry between the African and the East Indian populations has surfaced in parts of the Caribbean, with Trinidad and Tobago and Guyana the most obvious cases. The election on November 6, 1995, in Trinidad and Tobago of Basedo Panday as the first Prime Minister of East Indian descent has left many Africans with a feeling of uneasiness about their future. In major U.S. cities like New York and Los Angeles, demographic and immigration trends have sparked the arrival of newer residents (e.g., Koreans, Asian Indians, and Latinos) and has been a major source of conflict between them and African Americans who see the newer residents as competitors for jobs and other scarce resources. Future efforts to develop a comprehensive understanding of the Black condition in the urban diaspora will have to devote greater attention to these ethnic trends.

The 21st Century and Beyond

As we round out the twentieth century and prepare for the new millennium, rhetoric about new policy and planning continues to swell in international circles. What is needed is not more rhetoric and quick-fix solutions but policies and plans that will withstand the test of time. I am reminded that when warring nations put down their arms to begin peace talks, when corporations draft future growth projections, or when societies create new institutions they do so with the objective of permanence or sustainability. It is to this same objective that we must become fastened when considering policy measures to relieve the suffering of the urban poor. In other words, the idea of short-term planning to address long-term needs can no longer be tolerated.

As we have seen, the urban poor continue to demonstrate their resilience and ability to cope using a variety of creative strategies, from street hawking and vending to rapping. But presented with difficult questions about the effectiveness of these strategies and how much longer they will hold up, neither the victims nor their strongest supporters are able to respond. Where the recommendations from this volume converge is at recognizing the need for the poor to become better organized and mobilized locally, regionally, and globally in order to take charge of their destinies. While the findings report activity in some quarters, the reality is that for most diasporans, the crisis is fuelled by their inability to build and sustain popular, progressive movements for change. In the case of the "inner-city bloods," it will mean identifying progressive leaders in cities across the United States who will press for political empowerment, full employment with a creative jobs program for youth, and culturally relevant educational programs. For the "Jua Kali" of Nairobi, it will mean their mobilization and unification in order to force the Kenyan state to adopt policies that are sensitive to their day-to-day struggles. In Panama and in Venezuela, it will mean stimulating and building popular movements among the urban poor to stem the tide of narrow and destructive neoliberal state policies. For the urban sufferers of the West African city of Dakar, it will mean building voter confidence and the sense of hope.

Understandably, many of the recommendations considered here are societal specific and we must be careful not to interpret these for the diaspora as a whole. But this question redirects our attention to the matter of the global economy and the fact that nations are becoming more interconnected than ever before. The emergence of economic alliances between nations is one such indicator. We find for example, the G–7 summit, the alliance of the European community of nations, the summit of the Asian-Pacific rim states, and the North Atlantic Free Trade Agreement that links the United States, Canada, and Mexico. An alliance of Blacks from the African continent, Europe, the Caribbean, Latin America, and North America would be consistent with this trend. Such a body would provide a permanent forum to debate the ways and means of empowering persons of African descent and challenging the new global order. As well, it would offer an alternative model—independent of the United Nations General Assembly—to address the social and economic problems that they commonly experience or that are specific to states and regions. An important outgrowth of this might be proposals for a multiracial—international alliance to challenge global poverty and racism. However, this objective need not threaten the existence of smaller regional entities such as the Caribbean Community and Common Market (CARICOM), The Organization of Eastern Caribbean States (OECS), or The Economic Cooperation of West African States (ECOWAS).

Such a strategy is not unprecedented. Between 1911 and 1945, five Pan-African Congresses were convened that concerned the building of solidarity among African Americans and other oppressed Blacks, who at that time were still considered colonial peoples (Allen 1992:96–98; Adi and Sherwood 1995). Due to organizational problems, the Sixth Congress was not held until nearly thirty years later in 1974 in Dar es Salaam, Tanzania. The Seventh Congress was held in April 1994 in Uganda and by all accounts was not a very successful assembly. A complete analysis of the Pan-African Congress Movement is not possible here, however, the Congress model does offer a useful framework from which to strategize a new alliance of people in the diaspora.

At present, leaders and their constituents are left with two options: they can elect to forge a broad-based inter-hemispheric alliance for unity or perhaps alliances with states in their immediate region. On the other hand, they can choose to remain disconnected and support the status quo.

We are optimistic that as the crisis continues to unravel, the first option will be viewed as the only logical choice. It is not certain, though, who will ignite the flame and lead the charge. At various points in history, African Americans have assumed that role. What immediately comes to mind are the anti-apartheid movement in support of South Africa's oppressed Black masses,

W.E.B. DuBois's diligent work in organizing the first five Pan-African Congresses, and the Black Power Movement of the late 1960s. What prompted these activities was African Americans' history of oppression and subjugation and their unquestioned cameraderie with other oppressed people, in particular other Blacks.[2]

Given the resurgence of nationalism and resistance in urban Black America, it is possible that the spark might originate there. Much more important, though, than the source of the action is our recognition of the inevitability of change and that the dawn of a new century is a fresh opportunity to begin that process.

In sum, *Globalization and Survival in the Black Diaspora* should be viewed as a trumpeter for change. If it can inspire, arouse, and invigorate its readers to achieve a new level of awareness about the condition of those at the bottom and to take action, then it will have achieved its ultimate objective.

NOTES

1. See Samuel P. Huntington's discussion in, "The Clash of Civilizations." *Foreign Affairs* 72:3 (Summer 1993): pp.22–49. also, Andrew Bell-Fialkoff's, "A Brief History of Ethnic cleansing." *Foreign Affairs* 72:3 (Summer 1993).

2. The political force and influence of America's urban Blacks on the international scene has been captured by a number of observers. C.L.R. James, that prolific West Indian political historian, situated it best when he stated: "It is from America's urban blacks that many people all over the world have historically gained a consciousness of the problems that black people suffer and their attempts to overcome them." See, C.L.R. James, "Black People in the Urban Areas of the United States," pp. 374–379, in Anna Grimshaw (ed.), *The C.L.R. James Reader.* (London and U.S.A.: Blackwell Pub., 1992).

REFERENCES

Adi, Hakim and Marika Sherwood. 1995. *The Manchester Pan-African Congress Revisited.* London: New Beacon Books.

Allen, Robert L. 1992. *Black Awakening in Capitalist America.* Trenton, N.J.: Africa World Press.

Bell, Derrick. 1992. *Faces at the Bottom of the Well: The Permanence of Racism.* New York: Basic Books.

Hacker, Andrew. 1992. *Two Nations: Black And White, Separate, Hostile, Unequal*. New York: Ballantine.

Grimshaw, Anna (ed.). 1992. *The C.L.R. James Reader*. London and U.S.A.: Blackwell Publishers.

West, Cornel. 1993. *Race Matters*. Boston: Beacon Press.

About the Contributors

KEVIN ARLYCH studied history and sociology at New College of the University of South Florida, where he wrote his thesis on rap music. He has worked extensively with urban youth in New York and Florida and is currently teaching elementary school students in Louisiana through the Teach For America Program.

OBIKA GRAY is a Professor of political science at the University of Wisconsin, Eau Claire. His publications have focused on Caribbean politics and development. He is the author of *Radicalism and Social Change in Jamaica 1960–1972*.

CHARLES GREEN is a Professor of sociology at Hunter Colllege, CUNY. He was the 1989–1990 Fulbright Scholar in sociology at the University of Dar es Salaam, Tanzania. His published works have dealt with urban politics in the United States, comparative urban development, and social policy. He is co-author (with Basil Wilson) of *The Struggle For Black Empowerment in New York City: Beyond the Politics of Pigmentation* and is preparing a book entitled *Manufacturing Powerlessness*, which compares the urban crisis in the U.S. Black Belt, the Caribbean, and East Africa.

GERALD HORNE is Professor and Director of the Institute of African-American Research at the University of North Carolina-Chapel Hill. He is the author of numerous books and articles devoted to the historical and contemporary experience of African Americans.

388 ABOUT THE CONTRIBUTORS

His articles have appeared in the major print media and scholarly journals such as *Political Affairs* and *American Historical Review*. Among his published books are *Black and Red: W.E.B. DuBois and the Afro-American Response to the Cold War 1944–1963*, *Reversing Discrimination: The Case for Affirmative Action*, and most recently, *The Fire This Time: The Watts Uprising and the 1960s*.

CARL E. JAMES is an Associate Professor in the Faculty of Education at York University, Toronto. He has published extensively on the experiences of Black urban youth in Canada. His is the author of *Making It: Black Youth, Racism And Career Aspirations in a Big City* and most recently, *Seeing Ourselves: Exploring Race, Ethnicity, and Culture*.

KWANDO M. KINSHASA is an Associate Professor of social psychology in the Department of African-American Studies at The John Jay College of Criminal Justice (CUNY). He is the author of *Emigration vs. Assimilation: Debates in the African-American Press 1827–1861* and is completing his latest book, *The Man From Scottsboro: the Life and Philosophy of Clarence Norris*.

JOE L. P. LUGALLA is an Assistant Professor of urban sociology at the Universty of New Hampshire and, formerly, Senior Lecturer of sociology at the University of Dar es Salaam, Tanzania. He is the author of *Crisis, Urbanization And Poverty In Tanzania: A Study of Urban Poverty and Survival Politics*.

KINUTHIA MACHARIA is an Assistant Professor of development and urban sociology at American University. His scholarly works have dealt with the urban condition in sub-Saharan Africa. He is the author of the forthcoming book, *The Informal Economy in African Cities*.

ESTHER I. MADRIZ is an Assistant Professor of sociology at The University of San Francisco where she teaches on gender and criminology. Her scholarly interests also include research on socio-politics in the developing world, specifically Latin America. She is the author of the forthcoming book, *Nothing Bad Happens to Good Girls: Fear of Crime on Women's Lives*.

VÂNIA PENHA-LOPES is a doctoral candidate in sociology at New York University and the (1996–1998) Fellow at the Carter G. Woodson Institute for Afro-American Studies at the University of Virginia. Her research interests center on family sociology and comparative race and ethnic relations. Her most recent journal publication is entitled, "What Next: On Race and Assimilation in the United States and Brazil."

GEORGE PRIESTLEY is an Associate Professor of political science and Director of the Latin American Studies Program at Queens College (CUNY). He is widely published on Central and Latin American politics and his articles have appeared in such journals as *Central American Politics* and *Radical History*. He is the author of *Military Government and Popular Participation in Panama*.

RAQUEL Z. RIVERA is a doctoral student in sociology at The City University of New York Graduate Center. She is also an accomplished freelance writer on Puerto Rican popular culture whose articles have appeared in various print media and journals including *Claridad*, *The San Juan Star*, and *Centro* (Centro de Estudios de Puertorriqueños, CUNY).

STEPHEN SMALL is an Assistant Professor of sociology in the Department of African-American Studies at University of California, Berkeley. He spent three years at the University of Leicester, U.K., as a Senior Lecturer of sociology. His published works have centered on comparative race and ethnic relations. He is the author of the recently released book, *Racialised Barriers*, which compares the Black condition in England and the United States.

CAROLYN SOMERVILLE is an Associate Professor of political science at Hunter College (CUNY). Her research interest covers politics and development in West Africa. She is currently working on a book-length manuscript that assesses the implications of political structural adjustment for women in Mozambique.

JOYCE TONEY is an Associate Professor of history in the Department of Black & Puerto Rican Studies at Hunter College (CUNY). She has published widely on the history of Caribbean immigrants in metropole New York City and is currently working on a book on the development of the culture of migration.

LOÏC J.D. WACQUANT is an Associate Professor of Sociology at the University of California, Berkeley, and a Research Associate of the Center for European Sociology at the Collegè de France. He has published extensively in the area of urban inequality and marginality in the U.S. and Europe. A former member of Harvard's Society of Fellows and Visiting Scholar at the Russell Sage Foundation, he has published extensively in the areas of comparative urban inequality, culture and economy, violence, race, and social theory. He is the co-author with Pierre Bourdieu, of *An Invitation to Reflexive Sociology* (translated in 14 languages) and is completing an ethnographic study of prize fighting as ghetto trade and bodily craft entitled, *The Passion of the Pugilist*.

Index